iOS Components and Frameworks

iOS Components and Frameworks

Understanding the Advanced Features of the iOS SDK

Kyle Richter
Joe Keeley

✦Addison-Wesley

Upper Saddle River, NJ • Boston • Indianapolis • San Francisco
New York • Toronto • Montreal • London • Munich • Paris • Madrid
Cape Town • Sydney • Tokyo • Singapore • Mexico City

The publisher offers excellent discounts on this book when ordered in quantity for bulk purchases or special sales, which may include electronic versions and/or custom covers and content particular to your business, training goals, marketing focus, and branding interests. For more information, please contact:

U.S. Corporate and Government Sales
(800) 382-3419
corpsales@pearsontechgroup.com

For sales outside the United States, please contact:

International Sales
international@pearsoned.com

Visit us on the Web: informit.com/aw

Library of Congress Control Number: 2013944841

ISBN-13: 978-0-321-85671-5
ISBN-10: 0-321-85671-6

Text printed in the United States on recycled paper at Edwards Brothers Malloy in Ann Arbor, Michigan.

First printing: October 2013

Editor-in-Chief
Mark Taub

Senior Acquisitions Editor
Trina MacDonald

Development Editor
Thomas Cirtin

Managing Editor
Kristy Hart

Project Editor
Elaine Wiley

Copy Editor
Cheri Clark

Indexer
Brad Herriman

Proofreader
Debbie Williams

Technical Reviewers
Collin Ruffenach
Dave Wood

Editorial Assistant
Olivia Basegio

Cover Designer
Chuti Prasertsith

Compositor
Nonie Ratcliff

❖

I would like to dedicate this book to my co-workers who continually drive me to never accept the first solution.

—Kyle Richter

I dedicate this book to my wife, Irene, and two daughters, Audrey and Scarlett. Your boundless energy and love inspire me daily.

—Joe Keeley

❖

Contents

Foreword

I have been working with the iPhone SDK (now iOS SDK) since the first beta released in 2008. At the time, I was focused on writing desktop apps for the Mac and hadn't thought much about mobile app development.

If you chose to be an early adopter, you were on your own. In typical Apple fashion, the documentation was sparse, and since access to the SDK required an NDA—and apparently, a secret decoder ring—you were on your own. You couldn't search Google or turn to StackOverflow for help, and there sure as hell weren't any books out yet on the SDK.

In the six years (yes, it really has only been six years) since Apple unleashed the original iPhone on the world, we've come a long way. The iPhone SDK is now the iOS SDK. There are dozens of books and blogs and podcasts and conferences on iOS development. And ever since 2009, WWDC has been practically impossible to get into, making it even harder for developers—old and new—to learn about the latest features coming to the platform. For iOS developers, there is so much more to learn.

One of the biggest challenges I have as an iOS developer is keeping on top of all the components and frameworks available in the kit. The iOS HIG should help us with that, but it doesn't go far enough—deep enough. Sure, now I can find some answers by searching Google or combing through StackOverflow but, more often than not, those answers only explain the how and rarely the why, and they never provide the details you really need.

And this is what Kyle and Joe have done with this book—they're providing the detail needed so you can fully understand the key frameworks that make up the iOS SDK.

I've had the pleasure of knowing Kyle and Joe for a number of years. They are two of the brightest developers I have ever met. They have each written some amazing apps over the years, and they continuously contribute to the iOS development community by sharing their knowledge—speaking at conferences and writing other books on iOS development. If you have a question about how to do something in iOS, chances are good that Kyle and Joe have the answer for you.

But what makes these guys so awesome is not just their encyclopedic knowledge of iOS, it's their willingness to share what they know with everyone they meet. Kyle and Joe don't have competitors, they have friends.

Kyle and Joe's in-depth knowledge of the iOS SDK comes through in this book. It's one of the things I like about this book. It dives into the details for each component covered at a level that you won't always find when searching online.

I also like the way the book is structured. This is not something that you'll read cover to cover. Instead, you'll pick up the book because you need to learn how to implement a collection view or sort out some aspect of running a task in a background thread that you can't quite wrangle. You'll pick up the book when you need it, find the solution, implement it in your own code, and then toss the book back on the floor until you need it again. This is what makes *iOS Components and Frameworks* an essential resource for any iOS developer—regardless of your experience level. You might think you're a master with Core Location and MapKit, but I reckon you'll find something here that you never knew before.

Kyle and Joe don't come with egos. They don't brag. And they sure don't act like they are better than any other developer in the room. They instill the very spirit that has made the Mac and iOS developer community one of the friendliest, most helpful in our industry, and this book is another example of their eagerness to share their knowledge.

This book, just like the seminal works from Marks and LaMarche or Sadun, will always be within arm's reach of my desk. This is the book I wish I had when I first started developing iOS apps in 2008. Lucky you, it's here now.

—Kirby Turner,

Chief Code Monkey at White Peak Software, author of *Learning iPad Programming, A Hands on Guide to Building Apps for the iPad, Second Edition* (Addison-Wesley Professional), and Cocoa developer community organizer and conference junkie

August 28, 2013

Preface

Welcome to *iOS Components and Frameworks: Understanding the Advanced Features of the iOS SDK*!

There are hundreds of "getting started with iOS" books available to choose from, and there are dozens of advanced books in specific topics, such as Core Data or Security. There was, however, a disturbing lack of books that would bridge the gap between beginner and advanced niche topics.

This publication aims to provide development information on the intermediate-to-advanced topics that are otherwise not worthy of standalone books. It's not that the topics are uninteresting or lackluster, it's that they are not large enough topics. From topics such as working with JSON to accessing photo libraries, these are frameworks that professional iOS developers use every day but are not typically covered elsewhere.

Additionally, several advanced topics are covered to the level that many developers need in order to just get started. Picking up a 500-page Core Data book is intimidating, whereas Chapter 13 of this book provides a very quick and easy way to get started with Core Data. Additional introductory chapters are provided for debugging and instruments, TextKit, language features, and iCloud.

Topics such as Game Center leaderboards and achievements, AirPrint, music libraries, Address Book, and Passbook are covered in their entirety. Whether you just finished your first iOS project or you are an experienced developer, this book will have something for you.

The chapters have all been updated to work with iOS 7 Beta 4. As such, there were several iOS 7 features that were still in active development that might not work the same as illustrated in the book after the final version of iOS 7 is released. Please let us know if you encounter issues and we will release updates and corrections.

If you have suggestions, bug fixes, corrections, or anything else you'd like to contribute to a future edition, please contact us at icf@dragonforged.com. We are always interested in hearing what would make this book better and are very excited to continue refining it.

—Kyle Richter and Joe Keeley

Prerequisites

Every effort has been made to keep the examples and explanations simple and easy to digest; however, this is to be considered an intermediate to advanced book. To be successful with it, you should have a basic understanding of iOS development, Objective-C, and C. Familiarity of the tools such as Xcode, Developer Portal, iTunes Connect, and Instruments is also assumed. Refer to *Programming in Objective-C,* by Stephen G. Kochan, and *Learning iOS Development,* by Maurice Sharp, Rod Strougo, and Erica Sadun, for basic Objective-C and iOS skills.

What You'll Need

Although you can develop iOS apps in the iOS simulator, it is recommended that you have at least one iOS device available for testing:

- **Apple iOS Developer Account:**The latest version of the iOS developer tools including Xcode and the iOS SDKs can be downloaded from Apple's Developer Portal (http://developer.apple.com/ios). To ship an app to the App Store or to install and test on a personal device, you will also need a paid developer account at $99 per year.

- **Macintosh Computer:**To develop for iOS and run Xcode, you will need a modern Mac computer capable of running the latest release of OS X.

- **Internet Connection:**Many features of iOS development require a constant Internet connection for your Mac as well as for the device you are building against.

How This Book Is Organized

With few exceptions (Game Center and Core Data), each chapter stands on its own. The book can be read cover to cover but any topic can be skipped to when you find a need for that technology; we wrote it with the goal of being a quick reference for many common iOS development tasks.

Here is a brief overview of the chapters you will encounter:

- **Chapter 1, "UIKit Dynamics":** iOS 7 introduced UI Kit Dynamics to add physics-like animation and behaviors to UIViews. You will learn how to add dynamic animations, physical properties, and behaviors to standard objects. Seven types of behaviors are demonstrated in increasing difficulty from gravity to item properties.

- **Chapter 2, "Core Location, MapKit, and Geofencing":** iOS 6 introduced new, Apple-provided maps and map data. This chapter covers how to interact with Core Location to determine the device's location, how to display maps in an app, and how to customize the map display with annotations, overlays, and callouts. It also covers how to set up regional monitoring (or geofencing) to notify the app when the device has entered or exited a region.

- **Chapter 3, "Leaderboards":** Game Center leaderboards provide an easy way to add social aspects to your iOS game or app. This chapter introduces a fully featured iPad game called Whack-a-Cac, which walks the reader through adding leaderboard support. Users will learn all the required steps necessary for implementing Game Center leaderboards, as well as get a head start on implementing leaderboards with a custom interface.

- **Chapter 4, "Achievements":** This chapter continues on the Whack-a-Cac game introduced in Chapter 3. You will learn how to implement Game Center achievements in a fully featured iPad game. From working with iTunes Connect to displaying achievement progress, this chapter provides all the information you need to quickly get up and running with achievements.

- **Chapter 5, "Getting Started with Address Book":** Integrating a user's contact information is a critical step for many modern projects. Address Book framework is one of the oldest available on iOS; in this chapter you'll learn how to interact with that framework. You will learn how to use the people picker, how to access the raw address book data, and how to modify and save that data.

- **Chapter 6, "Working with Music Libraries":** This chapter covers how to access the user's music collection from a custom app, including how to see informational data about the music in the collection, and how to select and play music from the collection.

- **Chapter 7, "Working with and Parsing JSON":** JSON, or JavaScript Object Notation, is a lightweight way to pass data back and forth between different computing platforms and architectures. As such, it has become the preferred way for iOS client apps to communicate complex sets of data with servers. This chapter describes how to create JSON from existing objects, and how to parse JSON into iOS objects.

- **Chapter 8, "Getting Started with iCloud":** This chapter explains how to get started using iCloud, for syncing key-value stores and documents between devices. It walks though setting up an app for iCloud, how to implement the key-value store and document approaches, and how to recognize and resolve conflicts.

- **Chapter 9, "Notifications":** Two types of notifications are supported by iOS: local notifications, which function on the device with no network required, and remote notifications, which require a server to send a push notification through Apple's Push Notification Service to the device over the network. This chapter explains the differences between the two types of notifications, and demonstrates how to set them up and get notifications working in an app.

- **Chapter 10, "Bluetooth Networking with Game Kit":** This chapter will walk you through creating a real-time Bluetooth-based chat client, enabling you to connect with a friend within Bluetooth range and send text messages back and forth. You will learn how to interact with the Bluetooth functionality of Game Kit, from finding peers to connecting and transferring data.

- **Chapter 11, "AirPrint":** An often underappreciated feature of the iOS, AirPrint enables the user to print documents and media to any wireless-enabled AirPrint-compatible printer. Learn how to quickly and effortlessly add AirPrint support to your apps. By the end of this chapter you will be fully equipped to enable users to print views, images, PDFs, and even rendered HTML.

- **Chapter 12, "Core Data Primer":** Core Data can be a vast and overwhelming topic. This chapter tries to put Core Data in context for the uninitiated, and explains when Core Data might be a good solution for an app and when it might be overkill. It also explains some of the basic concepts of Core Data in simple terminology.

- **Chapter 13, "Getting Up and Running with Core Data":** This chapter demon-strates how to set up an app to use Core Data, how to set up a Core Data data model, and how to implement many of the most commonly used Core Data tools in an app. If you want to start using Core Data without digging through a 500-page book, this chapter is for you.

- **Chapter 14, "Language Features":** Objective-C has been evolving since iOS was introduced. This chapter covers some of the language and compiler-level changes that have occurred, and explains how and why a developer would want to use them. It covers the new literal syntaxes for things like numbers, array, and dictionaries; it also covers blocks, ARC, property declarations, and some oldies but goodies including dot notation, fast enumeration, and method swizzling.

- **Chapter 15, "Integrating Twitter and Facebook Using Social Framework":** Social integration is the future of computing and it is accepted that all apps have social features built in. This chapter will walk you through adding support for Facebook and Twitter to your app using the Social Framework. You will learn how to use the built-in composer to create new Twitter and Facebook posts. You will also learn how to pull down feed information from both services and how to parse and interact with that data. Finally, using the frameworks to send messages from custom user interfaces is covered. By the end of this chapter, you will have a strong background in Social Framework as well as working with Twitter and Facebook to add social aspects to your apps.

- **Chapter 16, "Working with Background Tasks":** Being able to perform tasks when the app is not the foreground app was a big new feature introduced in iOS 4, and more capabilities have been added since. This chapter explains how to perform tasks in the background after an app has moved from the foreground, and how to perform specific background activities allowed by iOS.

- **Chapter 17, "Grand Central Dispatch for Performance":** Performing resource-intensive activities on the main thread can make an app's performance suffer with stutters and lags. This chapter explains several techniques provided by Grand Central Dispatch for doing the heavy lifting concurrently without affecting the performance of the main thread.

- **Chapter 18, "Using Keychain to Secure Data":** Securing user data is important and an often-overlooked stage of app development. Even large public companies have been called out in the news over the past few years for storing user credit card info and passwords in plain text. This chapter provides an introduction to not only using the Keychain to secure user data but developmental security as a whole. By the end of the chapter, you will be able to use Keychain to secure any type of small data on users' devices and provide them with peace of mind.

- **Chapter 19, "Working with Images and Filters":** This chapter covers some basic image-handling techniques, and then dives into some advanced Core Image techniques to apply filters to images. The sample app provides a way to explore all the options that Core Image provides and build filter chains interactively in real time.

- **Chapter 20, "Collection Views":** Collection views, a powerful new API introduced in iOS6, give the developer flexible tools for laying out scrollable, cell-based content. In addition to new content layout options, collection views provide exciting new animation capabilities, both for animating content in and out of a collection view, and for switching between collection view layouts. The sample app demonstrates setting up a basic collection view, a customized flow layout collection view, and a highly custom, nonlinear collection view layout.

- **Chapter 21, "Introduction to TextKit":** iOS 7 introduced TextKit as an easier-to-use and greatly expanded update to Core Text. TextKit enables developers to provide rich and interactive text formatting to their apps. Although TextKit is a very large subject, this chapter provides the basic groundwork to accomplish several common tasks, from adding text wrapping around an image to inline custom font attributes. By the end of this chapter, you will have a strong background in TextKit and have the groundwork laid to explore it more in depth.

- **Chapter 22, "Gesture Recognizers":** This chapter explains how to make use of gesture recognizers in an app. Rather than dealing with and interpreting touch data directly, gesture recognizers provide a simple and clean way to recognize common gestures and respond to them. In addition, custom gestures can be defined and recognized using gesture recognizers.

- **Chapter 23, "Accessing Photo Libraries":** The iPhone has actually become a very popular camera, as evidenced by the number of photos that people upload to sites such as Flickr. This chapter explains how to access the user's photo library, and handle photos and videos in a custom app. The sample app demonstrates rebuilding the iOS 6 version of Photos.app.

- **Chapter 24, "Passbook and PassKit":** With iOS6, Apple introduced Passbook, a standalone app that can store "passes," or things like plane tickets, coupons, loyalty cards, or concert tickets. This chapter explains how to set up passes, how to create and distribute them, and how to interact with them in an app.

- **Chapter 25, "Debugging and Instruments":** One of the most important aspects of development is to be able to debug and profile your software. Rarely is this topic covered even in a cursory fashion. This chapter will introduce you to debugging in Xcode and performance analysis using Instruments. Starting with a brief history of computer bugs, the chapter walks you through common debugging tips and tricks. Topics of breakpoints and debugger commands are briefly covered, and the chapter concludes with a look into profiling apps using the Time Profiler and memory analysis using Leaks. By the end of this chapter, you will have a clear foundation on how to troubleshoot and debug iOS apps on both the simulator and the device.

About the Sample Code

Each chapter of this book is designed to stand by itself; therefore, each chapter with the exception of Chapter 25, "Debugging and Instruments," Chapter 12, "Core Data Primer," and Chapter 14, "Language Features," has its own sample project. Chapter 3, "Leaderboards," and Chapter 4, "Achievements," share a base sample project, but each expands on that base project in unique ways. Each chapter provides a brief introduction to the sample project and walks the reader through any complex sections of the sample project not relating directly to the material in the chapter.

Every effort has been made to create simple-to-understand sample code, which often results in code that is otherwise not well optimized or not specifically the best way of approaching a problem. In these circumstances the chapter denotes where things are being done inappropriately for a real-world app. The sample projects are not designed to be standalone or finished apps; they are designed to demonstrate the functionality being discussed in the chapter. The sample projects are generic with intention; the reader should be able to focus on the material in the chapter and not the unrelated sample code materials. A considerable amount of work has been put into removing unnecessary components from the sample code and condensing subjects into as few lines as possible.

Many readers will be surprised to see that the sample code in the projects is not built using Automatic Reference Counting (ARC); this is by design as well. It is easier to mentally remove the memory management than to add it. The downloadable sample code is made available to suit both tastes; copies of ARC and non-ARC sample code are bundled together. The sample code is prefixed with "ICF" and most, but not all, sample projects are named after the chapter title.

When working with the Game Center chapters, the bundle ID is linked to a real app, which is in our personal Apple account; this ensures that examples continue to work. Additionally, it has the small additional benefit of populating multiple users' data as developers interact with the sample project. For chapters dealing with iCloud, Push Notifications, and Passbook, the setup required for the apps is thoroughly described in the chapter, and must be completed using a new App ID in the reader's developer account in order to work.

Getting the Sample Code

You will be able to find the most up-to-date version of the source code at any moment at https://github.com/dfsw/icf. The code is publicly available and open source. The code is separated into two folders, one for ARC and one running non-ARC. Each chapter is broken down into its own folder containing an Xcode project; there are no chapters with multiple projects. We encourage readers to provide feedback on the source code and make recommendations so that we can continue to refine and improve it long after this book has gone to print.

Installing Git and Working with GitHub

Git is a version control system that has been growing in popularity for several years. To clone and work with the code on GitHub, you will want to first install Git on your Mac. A current installer for Git can be found at http://code.google.com/p/git-osx-installer. Additionally, there are several GUI front ends for Git, even one written by GitHub, which might be more appealing to developers who avoid command-line interfaces. If you do not want to install Git, GitHub also allows for downloading the source files as a Zip.

GitHub enables users to sign up for a free account at https://github.com/signup/free. After Git has been installed, from the terminal's command line $git clone git@github.com:dfsw/icf.git will download a copy of the source code into the current working directory. You are welcome to fork and open pull requests with the sample code projects.

Contacting the Authors

If you have any comments or questions about this book, please drop us an e-mail message at icf@dragonforged.com, or on Twitter at @kylerichter and @jwkeeley.

Acknowledgments

This book could not have existed without a great deal of effort from far too many behind-the-scenes people; although there are only two authors on the cover, dozens of people were responsible for bringing this book to completion. We would like to thank Trina MacDonald first and foremost; without her leadership and her driving us to meet deadlines, we would never have been able to finish. The editors at Pearson have been exceptionally helpful; their continual efforts show on every page, from catching our typos to pointing out technical concerns. The dedicated work of Dave Wood, Olivia Basegio, Collin Ruffenach, Sheri Cain, Tom Cirtin, Elaine Wiley, and Cheri Clark made the following pages possible.

We would also like to thank Jordan Langille of Langille Design (http://jordanlangille.com) for providing the designs for the Whack-a-Cac game featured in Chapters 3 and 4. His efforts have made the Game Center sample projects much more compelling.

The considerable amount of time spent working on this book was shouldered not only by us but also by our families and co-workers. We would like to thank everyone who surrounds us in our daily lives for taking a considerable amount of work off of our plates, as well as understanding the demands that a project like this brings.

Finally, we would like to thank the community at large. All too often we consulted developer forums, blog posts, and associates to ask questions or provide feedback. Without the hard efforts of everyone involved in the iOS community, this book would not be nearly as complete.

About the Authors

Kyle Richter is the founder of Dragon Forged Software, an award-winning iOS and Mac Development Company, and co-founder of Empirical Development, a for-hire iOS shop. Kyle began writing code in the early 1990s and has always been dedicated to the Mac platform. He has written several books on iOS development, as well as articles on many popular developer blogs and websites. He manages a team of more than 20 full-time iOS developers and runs day-to-day operations at three development companies. Kyle travels the world speaking on development and entrepreneurship; currently he calls Key West his home, where he spends his time with his border collie Landis. He can be found on Twitter at @kylerichter.

Joe Keeley is the CTO of Dragon Forged Software, and Project Lead at Empirical Development. Joe works on Resolve and Slender, and has led a number of successful client projects to completion. He has liked writing code since first keying on an Apple II, and has worked on a wide variety of technology and systems projects in his career. Joe has presented several different technical topics at iOS and Mac conferences around the U.S. Joe lives in Denver, Colorado, with his wife and two daughters, and hopes to get back into competitive fencing again in his spare time. He can be reached on Twitter at @jwkeeley.

UIKit Dynamics

iOS 7 introduced UIKit Dynamics, which provides realistic physics simulations that can be applied to UIViews. For many years developers have been incorporating realistic-feeling effects to sections of their apps such as swipeable cells and pull-to-refresh animations. Apple has taken a big step in iOS 7 to bring these animations into the core OS, as well as encourage developers to implement them at an aggressive rate.

The `UIDynamicItem` *protocol, along with the dynamic items that support it, is a giant leap forward in user experience. It is now incredibly easy to add effects like gravity, collisions, springs, and snaps to interfaces to provide a polished feel to an app. The APIs introduced for dynamic items are simple and easy to implement, providing very low-hanging fruit to increase the user experience of an app.*

Sample App

The sample app (shown in Figure 1.1) is a basic table demoing the various functions of UIKit Dynamics. Seven demos are presented in the app from gravity to properties. Each demo will be covered in order with a dedicated section. Besides the table view and basic navigation, the sample app does not contain any functionality not specific to UIKit Dynamics.

Although the sample app will run and perform in the iOS Simulator running iOS 7, the best performance is seen on physical devices. It is recommended that UIKit dynamic code be thoroughly tested on devices before shipping.

Note

UIKit Dynamics does not currently work well on UIViews that have auto-layout enabled. Until these issues have been addressed, it is recommended to disable auto-layout on any views that will be animated using UIKit Dynamics.

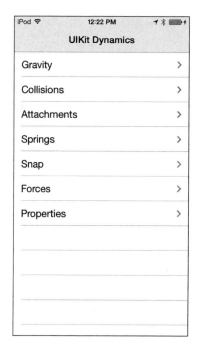

Figure 1.1   First glance at the sample app for UIKit Dynamics showing the list of demos available.

Introduction to UIKit Dynamics

UIKit Dynamics is a new set of classes and methods that was first introduced to iDevices starting with iOS 7. In short, it provides an easy-to-implement method to improve user experience of apps by incorporating real-world behaviors and characteristics attached to UIViews. UIKit Dynamics is, in the simplest terms, a basic physics engine for UIKit; however, it is not designed for game development like most traditional physics engines.

Dynamic behavior becomes active when a new `UIDynamicAnimator` is created and added to a UIView. Each animator item can be customized with various properties and behaviors, such as gravity, collision detection, density, friction, and additional items detailed in the following sections.

There are six additional classes that support the customization of a UIDynamicAnimator item: `UIAttachmentBehavior`, `UICollisionBehavior`, `UIDynamicItemBehavior`, `UIGravityBehavior`, `UIPushBehavior`, and `UISnapBehavior`. Each of these items allows for specific customization and will result in realistic behavior and animation of the UIView to which they are attached.

Implementing UIKit Dynamics

Creating a new animation and attaching it to a view is accomplished using two lines of code. In this example `self.view` is now set up to use UIKit Dynamic behavior. Each specific dynamic item must be added to the animator using the `addBehavior:` method.

```
UIDynamicAnimator *animator = [[UIDynamicAnimator alloc]
initWithReferenceView:self.view];


[animator addBehavior:aDynamicBehavior];
```

Each `UIDynamicAnimator` is independent and multiple animators can be run at the same time. For an animator to continue to run, a reference to it must be kept valid. When all items associated with an animator are at rest, the animator is not executing any calculations and will pause; however, best practices recommend removing unused animators.

Lessons from Game Developers

Physics simulations are something that game developers have been working with for many years, and some hard lessons have been learned. Now that physics is spreading into the non-game world, there are some basic truths every developer can benefit from.

When adding physics to a game or an app, do so in small increments. Writing a dozen interacting pieces and trying to figure out where the bug lies is next to impossible. The smaller steps that are taken toward the end result, the easier the process will be to polish and debug.

In the physical world there are limits and boundaries often not addressed in computer simulations. In the classic computer game Carmageddon, released in 1997, the physics were based on an uncapped frame rate. When computers became faster, the frame rates increased significantly, creating variables in formulas that produced unexpected results. When applying any type of calculation into a physics engine, ensure that both min and max values are enforced and tested.

Expect the unexpected; when dealing with collisions, shoving 30 objects into an overlapping setup, things can go awry. UIKit Dynamics has some great catches in place to ensure that you cannot push objects through boundaries with tremendous applications of force, and collisions are handled rather gracefully. However, there will most certainly be edge cases and bugs when you're dealing with many objects with complex interactions. The more that is going on with a physics engine, the more it needs to be tested and debugged; expect to see the laws of the universe toyed with in unexpected and unusual fashions.

Gravity

Gravity is arguably the easiest UIDynamicItem to implement as well as one of the most practical. Apple makes heavy use of the gravity item in iOS 7, and a user does not need to go further than the lock screen to interact with gravity. Dragging up on the camera icon from the iOS 7 lock screen and releasing it under the halfway point will drop the home screen back into place using `UIGravityBehavior`. This functionality, even prior to iOS 7, was often cloned and implemented by hand using timers and animations.

The following will set up a gravity effect on `frogImageView` that is a subview of `self.view`. First a new UIDynamicAnimator is created for the enclosing view that the animated view will appear in, in this example `self.view`. A new UIGravityBehavior object is created and initialized with an array of views that should have the gravity effect applied to them. The gravity behavior is then set; the example will apply a downward y-axis force of 0.1. When the behavior is configured, it is added to the UIDynamicAnimator using the `addBehavior:` method.

```
animator = [[UIDynamicAnimator alloc] initWithReferenceView:self.view];

UIGravityBehavior* gravityBehavior = [[[UIGravityBehavior alloc]
➥initWithItems:@[frogImageView]] autorelease];


[gravityBeahvior setXComponent:0.0f yComponent:0.1f];
[animator addBehavior:gravityBehavior];
```

> **Note**
>
> The dynamic item must be a subview of the reference view; if the item is not a subview, the animator will simply not provide any movement.

UIKit Dynamics uses their own physics system, jokingly referred to as UIKit Newtons. Although there is no direct correlation to standard formulas, they do provide a close approximation. A force of 1.0 equals roughly 9.80655 m/s^2, which is the force of gravity on earth. To apply gravity roughly 1/10th of that found on earth, 0.1 would be used. Gravity in UIKit Dynamics does not need to be specified as only a downward force; if a negative value is provided for the `yComponent`, gravity will pull up. Likewise, gravity can be specified for the x-axis in the same fashion. Items also have a density property, which is discussed in more detail in the "Item Properties" section.

Running the sample code for gravity results in the `imageView` simply falling at roughly 1/10th the rate of earth gravity (shown in Figure 1.2) and completely sliding off the screen. Because there are no boundaries or collisions set, the object isn't aware that it hit something that should cause it to stop falling, so it falls in essence forever.

Collisions

In the preceding section gravity was covered; however, the object that the gravity was applied to fell through the bottom of the screen and continued on its way into infinity. This is because no collision points were defined and the object had nothing to stop its descent.

The previous example will be modified to add collision boundaries to the enclosing view, as well as adding a secondary image object. The collision example begins the same way as gravity; however, two image views are now used.

Figure 1.2   An image view with the force of gravity applied to it falling down the screen in the gravity example from the sample app.

Creating a `UICollisionBehavior` object is very similar to creating a `UIGravityBehavior` object. The object is initialized with the UIViews that should be affected, in this case two UIImageViews. In addition to the views, collision behavior also needs to be specified with one of three possible values. `UICollisionBehaviorModeItems` will cause the items to collide with each other. `UICollisionBehaviorModeBoundaries` will cause the items not to collide with each other but to collide with boundaries. Finally, `UICollisionBehaviorModeEverything` will cause the items to collide both with each other and with the boundaries.

For objects to interact with boundaries, those boundaries first need to be defined. The easiest boundary to define is set through a Boolean property on the UICollisionBehavior object called `translatesReferenceBoundsIntoBoundary`. In the example this will use the bounds of `self.view`. Boundaries can also be set to follow an `NSBezierPath` using the method `addBoundaryWithIdentifier:forPath:` or based on two points using `addBoundaryWithIdentifier:fromPoint:toPoint:`.

```
animator = [[UIDynamicAnimator alloc] initWithReferenceView:self.view];

UIGravityBehavior* gravityBehavior = [[[UIGravityBehavior alloc]
➡initWithItems:@[frogImageView, dragonImageView]] autorelease];

[gravityBehavior setXComponent:0.0f yComponent:1.0f];
```

```
UICollisionBehavior* collisionBehavior = [[[UICollisionBehavior alloc]
➥initWithItems:@[frogImageView, dragonImageView]] autorelease];

[collisionBehavior setCollisionMode: UICollisionBehaviorModeBoundaries];

collisionBehavior.translatesReferenceBoundsIntoBoundary = YES;

[animator addBehavior:gravityBehavior];
[animator addBehavior:collisionBehavior];
```

UICollisionBehavior also provides a delegate callback that conforms to the
UICollisionBehaviorDelegate protocol.

```
collisionBehavior.collisionDelegate = self;
```

The UICollisionBehaviorDelegate has four callback methods, two for beginning collisions and two for ended collisions. Each set of callbacks has one method that will identify the boundary hit and one that will not. All methods provide a reference to the object that has caused the callback method to fire. Collision began methods also provide a CGPoint to reference the exact area of contact. The sample code will update a label after it has detected that an object has been hit.

```
-(void)collisionBehavior:(UICollisionBehavior *)behavior
➥beganContactForItem:(id<UIDynamicItem>)item
➥withBoundaryIdentifier:(id<NSCopying>)identifier atPoint:(CGPoint)p
{
    if([item isEqual:frogImageView])
        collisionOneLabel.text = @"Frog Collided";
    if([item isEqual:dragonImageView])
        collisionTwoLabel.text = @"Dragon Collided";
}


-(void)collisionBehavior:(UICollisionBehavior *)behavior
➥endedContactForItem:(id<UIDynamicItem>)item
➥withBoundaryIdentifier:(id<NSCopying>)identifier
{

    NSLog(@"Collision did end");
}
```

Attachments

An attachment specifies a dynamic connection between two objects. This allows for the behavior and movement of one object to be tied to the movement of another object. By default, UIAttachmentBehaviors are fixed to the center of an object although any point can be defined as the attachment point.

The sample app builds on the work done in the "Collisions" section. Once again, two image views are used. A boundary collision is created and applied to the `UIDynamicAnimator`. A new `CGPoint` is created and set to the reference point of the center of the frog image view. A new `UIAttachmentBehavior` object is created and initialized using `initWithItem:attachedTo Anchor:`. There are also additional initialization methods on `UICollisionBehavior` that allow specification of points or other objects. The collision and the attachment behavior are both added to the animator object.

```
animator = [[UIDynamicAnimator alloc] initWithReferenceView:self.view];

UICollisionBehavior* collisionBehavior = [[[UICollisionBehavior alloc]
➥initWithItems:@[dragonImageView, frogImageView]] autorelease];

[collisionBehavior setCollisionMode: UICollisionBehaviorModeBoundaries];

collisionBehavior.translatesReferenceBoundsIntoBoundary = YES;

CGPoint frogCenter = CGPointMake(frogImageView.center.x,
➥frogImageView.center.y);

self.attachmentBehavior = [[[UIAttachmentBehavior alloc]
➥initWithItem:dragonImageView attachedToAnchor:frogCenter] autorelease];

[animator addBehavior:collisionBehavior];
[animator addBehavior:self.attachmentBehavior];
```

These objects are now bound by an invisible connector the length equal to their initial distance. If the frog image view moves, the dragon image view will move with it holding onto the center point. However, the frog image view has no capability to move; to solve this, the sample app implements a simple pan gesture. As the frog image view is moved around the view, the center point is updated and the updated anchor point is set.

```
- (IBAction)handleAttachmentGesture:(UIPanGestureRecognizer*)gesture
{
    CGPoint gesturePoint = [gesture locationInView:self.view];

    frogImageView.center = gesturePoint;
    [self.attachmentBehavior setAnchorPoint:gesturePoint];
}
```

During the movement, the collision boundaries are still in effect and override the desired behavior of the attachment. This can be demonstrated by pushing the dragon image into the boundaries of the view.

It is also possible to update the length property of the attachment view in order to change the distance the attachment gives to the two objects. The attachment point itself does not need to be the center of the attached object and can be updated to any offset desired using the `setAnchorPoint` call.

Springs

Springs (shown in Figure 1.3) are an extension of the behavior of attachments. UIKitDynamics allows for additional properties to be set on UIAttachmentBehavior, frequency and damping.

Figure 1.3   A spring effect attaching the dragon image to the frog, which demonstrates using the effects of gravity as well as UIAttachmentBehavior damping and frequency.

The following section of the sample app adds three new properties after creating the UIAttachmentBehavior. The first, setFrequency, sets the oscillation or swing for the object. Next, setDamping evens out the animation peaks. The length is also adjusted for this example from its initial position. To better demonstrate these behaviors, gravity is added to this example.

```
animator = [[UIDynamicAnimator alloc] initWithReferenceView:self.view];

UICollisionBehavior* collisionBehavior = [[[UICollisionBehavior alloc]
➥initWithItems:@[dragonImageView, frogImageView]] autorelease];

UIGravityBehavior* gravityBeahvior = [[[UIGravityBehavior alloc]
➥initWithItems:@[dragonImageView]] autorelease];

CGPoint frogCenter = CGPointMake(frogImageView.center.x,
➥frogImageView.center.y);
```

```
self.attachmentBehavior = [[[UIAttachmentBehavior alloc]
➡initWithItem:dragonImageView attachedToAnchor:frogCenter] autorelease];

[self.attachmentBehavior setFrequency:1.0f];
[self.attachmentBehavior setDamping:0.1f];
[self.attachmentBehavior setLength: 100.0f];

[collisionBehavior setCollisionMode: UICollisionBehaviorModeBoundaries];

collisionBehavior.translatesReferenceBoundsIntoBoundary = YES;

[animator addBehavior:gravityBeahvior];
[animator addBehavior:collisionBehavior];
[animator addBehavior:self.attachmentBehavior];
```

Moving the frog around the screen now results in the dragon hanging 100 pixels from the bottom and swinging from the effect of the attachment and gravity combined.

Snap

An item can be dynamically moved to another point in a view with a snapping motion. Snapping is a very simple behavior. In the sample app the action is tied to a tap gesture, and tapping anywhere on the screen causes the image to jump to that spot. Each UISnapBehavior is linked to a single item at a time, and during initialization an end point where the item should end up is specified. A damping property can also be specified to affect the amount of bounce in the snap.

```
CGPoint point = [gesture locationInView:self.view];
animator = [[UIDynamicAnimator alloc] initWithReferenceView:self.view];

UISnapBehavior* snapBehavior = [[[UISnapBehavior alloc]
➡initWithItem:frogImageView snapToPoint:point] autorelease];

snapBehavior.damping = 0.75f;
[animator addBehavior:snapBehavior];
```

Push Forces

UIKit Dynamics also allows for the application of force, called pushing. UIPushBehavior is slightly more complex to use than the previously covered behaviors, but it is fairly easy compared to most other physics engines. The sample uses a UICollisionBehavior object as in many of the previous demos. This ensures that the image view stays on the screen while push effects are applied.

A new UIPushBehavior behavior is created and initialized with a reference to an image view. For the time being, properties for angle and magnitude are set to 0.0.

The sample app also features a reference in the form of a small black square in the center of the screen.

```
animator = [[UIDynamicAnimator alloc] initWithReferenceView:self.view];

UICollisionBehavior* collisionBehavior = [[[UICollisionBehavior alloc]
➥initWithItems:@[dragonImageView]] autorelease];

collisionBehavior.translatesReferenceBoundsIntoBoundary = YES;
[animator addBehavior:collisionBehavior];

UIPushBehavior *pushBehavior = [[[UIPushBehavior alloc]
➥initWithItems:@[dragonImageView]
➥mode:UIPushBehaviorModeInstantaneous]autorelease];

pushBehavior.angle = 0.0;
pushBehavior.magnitude = 0.0;

self.pushBehavior = pushBehavior;
[animator addBehavior:self.pushBehavior];
```

If the code were to be run now, the image view would stay fixed on the screen since the push effect has no values associated with it. A new pan gesture is created and in its associated action a new value for magnitude and angle are calculated and applied. In the example an angle is calculated to determine where the push force is coming from. This is based on the angle from the center reference point. A distance is also calculated to apply increasing force. The result is that tapping outside of the black square will apply an amount of force in that direction to the image view. The farther away from the square, the more force is applied.

```
CGPoint point = [gesture locationInView:self.view];

CGPoint origin = CGPointMake(CGRectGetMidX(self.view.bounds),
➥CGRectGetMidY(self.view.bounds));

CGFloat distance = sqrtf(powf(point.x-origin.x, 2.0)+powf(point.y-
➥origin.y, 2.0));

CGFloat angle = atan2(point.y-origin.y,point.x-origin.x);
distance = MIN(distance, 100.0);

[self.pushBehavior setMagnitude:distance / 100.0];
[self.pushBehavior setAngle:angle];

[self.pushBehavior setActive:TRUE];
```

In addition to setting an angle and a magnitude by hand, they can be calculated and applied automatically by using setTargetPoint:forItem: to specify a target point. It might also become necessary to apply force to a part of the view that is not the center, in which case `setXComponent:yComponent:` can be used to specify a `CGPoint` to which the focus of the force will be applied.

There are two types of push force that can be applied, `UIPushBehaviorModeContinuous` and `UIPushBehaviorModeInstantaneous`. When working with continuous push, the object accelerates under the force, where as with instantaneous the force is immediately applied.

Item Properties

Dynamic items have a number of default properties set on them when they are created, and these properties can be heavily configured to customize their reactions to the physics engine. The sample app (shown in Figure 1.4) demonstrates modifying these properties for one image view while leaving the defaults in place for the other image.

Figure 1.4   Modifying properties on dynamic items to create a unique physics reaction applied under identical forces.

To modify the properties on an object, create a new `UIDynamicItemBehavior` initialized with the views that the properties should be applied to. The result is that one object acts like a rubber ball and becomes much more prone to bounce when gravity and collisions are applied to it. The properties and their descriptions are presented in Table 1.1.

```
animator = [[UIDynamicAnimator alloc] initWithReferenceView:self.view];

UIGravityBehavior* gravityBeahvior = [[UIGravityBehavior alloc]
➥initWithItems:@[dragonImageView, frogImageView]];

UICollisionBehavior* collisionBehavior = [[[UICollisionBehavior alloc]
➥initWithItems:@[dragonImageView, frogImageView]] autorelease];

collisionBehavior.translatesReferenceBoundsIntoBoundary = YES;

UIDynamicItemBehavior* propertiesBehavior = [[[UIDynamicItemBehavior
➥alloc] initWithItems:@[frogImageView]] autorelease];

propertiesBehavior.elasticity = 1.0f;
propertiesBehavior.allowsRotation = NO;
propertiesBehavior.angularResistance = 0.0f;
propertiesBehavior.density = 3.0f;
propertiesBehavior.friction = 0.5f;
propertiesBehavior.resistance = 0.5f;

[animator addBehavior:propertiesBehavior];
[animator addBehavior:gravityBehavior];
[animator addBehavior:collisionBehavior];
```

Table 1.1   **UIDynamicItem Properties and Their Descriptions**

Property	Description
allowsRotation	A Boolean value that specifies whether the item will rotate as the result of forces applied; defaults to YES.
angularResistance	A CGFloat from 0.0 to CGFLOAT_MAX that indicates angular damping; the higher the number, the faster rotation will slow down.
density	A representation of density. Density is defaulted to 1.0 for a 100x100 object, or 2.0 for a 100x200 object. Adjustments to density affect the reactions of gravity and collisions.
elasticity	Valid for ranges of 0.0 to 1.0, indicating the amount of bounce an object has when colliding with other objects. 0.0 indicates no bounce, whereas 1.0 indicates that the entire force will be applied back into the bounce.
friction	The linear resistance applied when two items slide across each other. 0.0 indicates no friction and 1.0 indicates strong friction; however, values greater than 1.0 can be applied for additional friction.
resistance	A linear resistance encountered in open space. Values of 0.0 to CGFLOAT_MAX are accepted. 0.0 indicates no resistance, whereas 1.0 indicates that the item should stop as soon as no force is applied to it.

In-Depth UIDynamicAnimator and UIDynamicAnimatorDelegate

The beginning of this chapter introduced `UIDynamicAnimator`, and the samples have all used `addBehavior`; however, this class has much more power that can be leveraged. In addition to adding dynamic effects, they can also be removed either one at a time or as a group using `removeBehavior:` and `removeAllBehaviors`. To get a list of all behaviors currently attached to a UIDynamicAnimator, the behaviors property can be used to return an array of behaviors.

It is also possible not only to poll whether the animator is running using the running property but also to determine the length of time using `elapsedTime`. The `UIDynamicAnimator` also has an associated delegate `UIDynamicAnimatorDelegate`. The delegate provides two methods to handle pausing and resuming. `UIDynamicAnimator` cannot be explicitly paused by the developer. The animation effects are automatically paused when all items have come to a rest and are no longer moving. Any new effect that is applied will cause the items to begin moving and they will be moved back into the active state.

```
- (void)dynamicAnimatorDidPause:(UIDynamicAnimator *)animator
{
    NSLog(@"Animator did pause");
}

- (void)dynamicAnimatorWillResume:(UIDynamicAnimator *)animator
{
    NSLog(@"Animator will resume");
}
```

Summary

UIKit Dynamics is an interesting topic not only from a development standpoint but also as to what it means for the direction of iOS in the future. Apple is making a very strong push to bring software into the real world. Interacting with an app should feel like interacting with the physical world. Users expect to see apps respond in the same way the world around them does. This is not new for Apple; one of the main selling features of the original iPhone was momentum scrolling, and they are now giving the tools to add that type of functionality to developers.

This chapter covered the basics of UIKit Dynamics and its basic components; however, the real power of these methods will be in what developers create with them. There are endless possibilities and combinations for the effects that have been described, and what developers will create with these tools will surprise even Apple. The one definite in the redefined mobile user experience world, though, is that realistic physical reactions in software are no longer optional, and users will be expecting them.

Exercises

1. Modify the values throughout the sample app to see how changes to damping, frequency, gravity, density, friction, and resistance affect the way in which objects interact with each other and the enclosing view.

2. Replicate the pull for camera behavior of the lock screen on iOS 7; both gravity and collision will need to be used. Try to match the exact behavior using item properties.

2

Core Location, MapKit, and Geofencing

Maps and location information are some of the most useful features of iOS. They give apps the capability to help users find their way with relevant, local information. Apps exist today to help users find locations for very specific needs, find roads and directions, and use specialized transportation services, and even to bring an element of fun to visiting the same locations over and over. With the addition of Apple's new maps, some powerful new features have been added that developers can take advantage of to take their apps to the next level.

iOS offers two frameworks to assist with locations and maps. The Core Location framework provides classes that help the device determine its location and heading, and work with location-based information. The MapKit framework provides the user interface aspect of location awareness. It includes Apple Maps, which provides map views, satellite views, and hybrid views in normal 2D and a new 3D view. MapKit offers the capability to manage map annotations like pins, and map overlays for highlighting locations, routes, or other features on a map.

The Sample App

The sample app for this chapter is called FavoritePlaces. It allows users to collect favorite places and view them on a map, along with the device's current location. Users can use Core Location to geocode, or find the latitude and longitude, for an address. In addition, it can notify users when they go within a radius that they set around a favorite location. The app also provides a special location (signified with a green arrow) that can be dragged around the map to pinpoint a desired next destination; when that arrow is dropped at a location it will automatically reverse-geocode the location to display the name and address of the location.

Obtaining User Location

To use Core Location to obtain the current location, several steps need to take place. The app must obtain permission from the user to access the current location. In addition, the app needs to ensure that location services are enabled for the device before attempting to acquire a location. Once those requirements have been met, the app can start a location request and parse the result for usage once it is provided by Core Location. This section will describe all these steps in detail.

Requirements and Permissions

To use Core Location in an app, add the CoreLocation framework to the project target, and import the CoreLocation header as needed:

```
#import <CoreLocation/CoreLocation.h>
```

To use MapKit in an app, add the MapKit framework to the project target and import the MapKit header in any classes that need it:

```
#import <MapKit/MapKit.h>
```

Core Location respects the privacy of the user, and requires the user to provide permission to have access to the current location of the device. Location Services can be turned on or off for all apps on the device in the Settings app under the Privacy section, and can be turned on or off for each app individually, as shown in Figure 2.1.

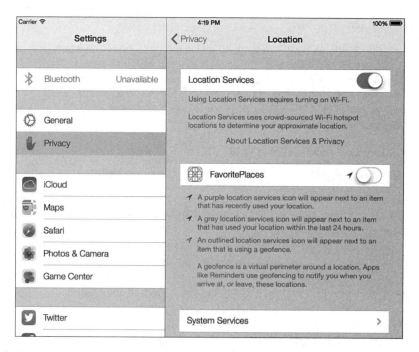

Figure 2.1   Settings.app, Location Services privacy settings.

To request permission to use Location Services, the app needs to ask `CLLocationManager` to start updating the current location, or the app needs to enable the Shows User Location setting on an instance of `MKMapView`. If Location Services are turned off for the device, Core Location will prompt the user to turn on Location Services in Settings.app to allow the app to access the current location, as shown in Figure 2.2.

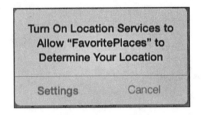

Figure 2.2   FavoritePlaces sample app location services disabled alert.

If the location manager has not requested permission previously to get the device's location, it will present an alert view to ask the user's permission, as shown in Figure 2.3.

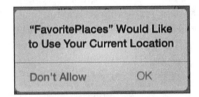

Figure 2.3   FavoritePlaces sample app location permission request alert.

If the user taps OK, permission will be granted and the location manager will acquire the current location. If the user taps Don't Allow, permission for the current location will be denied, and the `CLLocationManager`'s delegate method for authorization status changes will be called in `ICFLocationManager`.

```
- (void)locationManager:(CLLocationManager *)manager
didChangeAuthorizationStatus:(CLAuthorizationStatus)status
{
    if (status == kCLAuthorizationStatusDenied)
    {
        [self.locationManager stopUpdatingLocation];

        NSString *errorMessage =
        @"Location Services Permission Denied for this app.";
```

```
            NSDictionary *errorInfo =
            @{NSLocalizedDescriptionKey : errorMessage};

            NSError *deniedError =
            [NSError errorWithDomain:@"ICFLocationErrorDomain"
                              code:1
                          userInfo:errorInfo];

            [self setLocationError:deniedError];
            [self getLocationWithCompletionBlock:nil];
        }
        if (status == kCLAuthorizationStatusAuthorized)
        {
            [self.locationManager startUpdatingLocation];
            [self setLocationError:nil];
        }
    }
}
```

The sample app's `ICFLocationManager` class uses completion blocks for location requests from the rest of the app to be able to easily handle multiple requests for the current location. The `getLocationWithCompletionBlock:` method will process any completion blocks after a location is available or an error has occurred so that the calling logic can use the location or handle the error as appropriate in the local context. In this case, the caller will present an alert view to display the location permission-denied error, as shown in Figure 2.4.

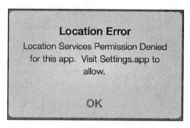

Location Error

Location Services Permission Denied for this app. Visit Settings.app to allow.

OK

Figure 2.4   FavoritePlaces sample app location permission denied alert.

If the user changes the authorization status for location services, either for the app specifically or for the device overall (as shown in Figure 2.1), a delegate method can be implemented to respond appropriately.

```
- (void)locationManager:(CLLocationManager *)manager
didChangeAuthorizationStatus:(CLAuthorizationStatus)status
{
    if (status == kCLAuthorizationStatusDenied)
    {
        [self.locationManager stopUpdatingLocation];
```

```
        NSString *errorMessage =
        @"Location Services Permission Denied for this app.
          Visit Settings.app to allow.";

        NSDictionary *errorInfo =
        @{NSLocalizedDescriptionKey : errorMessage};

        NSError *deniedError =
        [NSError errorWithDomain:@"ICFLocationErrorDomain"
                             code:1
                         userInfo:errorInfo];

        [self setLocationError:deniedError];
        [self getLocationWithCompletionBlock:nil];
    }

    if (status == kCLAuthorizationStatusAuthorized)
    {
        [self.locationManager startUpdatingLocation];
        [self setLocationError:nil];
    }
}
```

In ICFLocationManager the method is implemented to display an error alert if the permission is denied, or to restart updating the current location and clear the last error if permission is granted.

Checking for Services

To directly determine whether location services are enabled for the device, there is a class method available on the CLLocationManager called locationServicesEnabled.

```
if ([CLLocationManager locationServicesEnabled])
{
    ICFLocationManager *appLocationManager =
    [ICFLocationManager sharedLocationManager];

    [appLocationManager.locationManager startUpdatingLocation];
}
else
{
    NSLog(@"Location Services disabled.");
}
```

This can be used to customize how the app deals with having or not having the current location available. An app that deals with locations should gracefully handle when the user does not grant access to the current location, and give the user clear instructions for enabling access to the current location if desired.

Starting Location Request

When permission for location services has been granted, an instance of CLLocationManager can be used to find the current location. In the sample app, ICFLocationManager provides a central class to manage location functionality, so it manages an instance of CLLocationManager for the app. In the init method of ICFLocationManager, a CLLocationManager is created and customized for the desired location-searching approach.

```
[self setLocationManager:[[CLLocationManager alloc] init]];

[self.locationManager
setDesiredAccuracy:kCLLocationAccuracyBest];

[self.locationManager setDistanceFilter:100.0f];
[self.locationManager setDelegate:self];
```

A CLLocationManager has several parameters that can be set to dictate how it manages the current location. By specifying the desired accuracy parameter, the app can tell the CLLocationManager whether it is worthwhile to achieve the best accuracy possible at the expense of the battery, or whether a lower-level accuracy is preferred to preserve battery life. Using lower accuracy also reduces the amount of time necessary to acquire a location. Setting the distance filter indicates to the CLLocationManager how much distance must be traveled before new location events are generated; this is useful to fine-tune functionality based on changing locations. Lastly, setting the delegate for the CLLocationManager provides a place for custom functionality in response to location events and permission changes. When the app is ready to get a location, it asks the location manager to start updating the location.

```
ICFLocationManager *appLocationManager =
[ICFLocationManager sharedLocationManager];

[appLocationManager.locationManager startUpdatingLocation];
```

The CLLocationManager will engage the GPS and/or Wi-Fi as needed to determine the current location according to the parameters specified. There are two delegate methods that should be implemented to handle when the location manager has updated the current location or has failed to update the current location. When a location is acquired, the locationManager:did UpdateLocations: method will be called.

```
- (void)locationManager:(CLLocationManager *)manager
    didUpdateLocations:(NSArray *)locations
{
    //Filter out inaccurate points
    CLLocation *lastLocation = [locations lastObject];
    if(lastLocation.horizontalAccuracy < 0)
    {
        return;
    }

    [self setLocation:lastLocation];
    [self setHasLocation:YES];
    [self setLocationError:nil];

    [self getLocationWithCompletionBlock:nil];
}
```

The location manager can deliver multiple locations in the array of locations provided. The last object in the array is the most recently updated location. The location manager can also return the last location the GPS was aware of very quickly before actually starting to acquire a location; in that case, if the GPS has been off and the device has moved, the location might be very inaccurate. The method will check the accuracy of the location and ignore it if the value is negative. If a reasonably accurate location has been found, the method will store it and execute completion blocks. Note that the location manager might call this method multiple times as the location is refined, and any logic here should work with that in mind.

```
- (void)locationManager:(CLLocationManager *)manager
      didFailWithError:(NSError *)error
{
    [self.locationManager stopUpdatingLocation];
    [self setLocationError:error];
    [self getLocationWithCompletionBlock:nil];
}
```

If the location manager failed to acquire a location, it will call the `locationManager:didFail WithError:` method. The error might be due to lack of authorization, or might be due to GPS or Wi-Fi not being available (in Airplane Mode, for example). The sample app implementation will tell the location manager to stop updating the current location if an error is encountered, will capture the location error, and will execute the completion blocks so that the code requesting the current location can handle the error appropriately.

A location manager delegate can monitor for course changes. This could be useful, for example, to update a map indicator to display what direction the user is going relative to the direction of the map. To receive course or heading information, the location manager needs to start monitoring for it. A filter can optionally be set to prevent getting updates when changes are smaller than the number of degrees provided.

```
CLLocationDegrees degreesFilter = 2.0;
if ([CLLocationManager headingAvailable])
{
    [self.locationManager setHeadingFilter:degreesFilter];
    [self.locationManager startUpdatingHeading];
}
```

Heading change events are then delivered to the `locationManager:didUpdateHeading:` delegate method.

```
- (void)locationManager:(CLLocationManager *)manager
        didUpdateHeading:(CLHeading *)newHeading
{
    NSLog(@"New heading, magnetic: %f",
    newHeading.magneticHeading);

    NSLog(@"New heading, true: %f",newHeading.trueHeading);
    NSLog(@"Accuracy: %f",newHeading.headingAccuracy);
    NSLog(@"Timestamp: %@",newHeading.timestamp);
}
```

The new heading provides several pieces of useful information. It includes both a magnetic and a true heading, expressed in degrees from north. It provides an accuracy reading, expressed as the number of degrees by which the magnetic heading might be off. A lower, positive value indicates a more accurate heading, and a negative number means that the heading is invalid and there might be magnetic interference preventing a reading. The time stamp reflects when the reading was taken, and should be checked to prevent using an old heading.

Parsing and Understanding Location Data

When the location manager returns a location, it will be an instance of `CLLocation`. The `CLLocation` contains several pieces of useful information about the location. First is the latitude and longitude, expressed as a `CLLocationCoordinate2D`.

```
CLLocationCoordinate2D coord = lastLocation.coordinate;

NSLog(@"Location lat/long: %f,%f",coord.latitude, coord.longitude);
```

Latitude is represented as a number of degrees north or south of the equator, where the equator is zero degrees, the north pole is 90 degrees, and south pole is –90 degrees. Longitude is represented as a number of degrees east or west of the prime meridian, which is an imaginary line (or meridian) running from the north pole to the south pole, going through the

Royal Observatory in Greenwich, England. Going west from the prime meridian gives negative longitude values to –180 degrees, whereas going east gives positive longitude values up to 180 degrees.

Complementary to the coordinate is a horizontal accuracy. The accuracy is expressed as a CLLocationDistance, or meters. The horizontal accuracy means that the actual location is within the number of meters specified from the coordinate.

```
CLLocationAccuracy horizontalAccuracy =
lastLocation.horizontalAccuracy;

NSLog(@"Horizontal accuracy: %f meters",horizontalAccuracy);
```

The location also provides the altitude of the current location and vertical accuracy in meters, if the device has a GPS capability. If the device does not have GPS, then the altitude is returned as the value zero and the accuracy will be –1.

```
CLLocationDistance altitude = lastLocation.altitude;
NSLog(@"Location altitude: %f meters",altitude);

CLLocationAccuracy verticalAccuracy =
lastLocation.verticalAccuracy;

NSLog(@"Vertical accuracy: %f meters",verticalAccuracy);
```

The location contains a time stamp that indicates when the location was determined by the location manager. This can be useful to determine whether the location is old and should be ignored, or for comparing time stamps between location checks.

```
NSDate *timestamp = lastLocation.timestamp;
NSLog(@"Timestamp: %@",timestamp);
```

Lastly, the location provides the speed, expressed in meters per second, and course, expressed in degrees from true north.

```
CLLocationSpeed speed = lastLocation.speed;
NSLog(@"Speed: %f meters per second",speed);

CLLocationDirection direction = lastLocation.course;
NSLog(@"Course: %f degrees from true north",direction);
```

Significant Change Notifications

After a location has been acquired by the app, Apple strongly recommends stopping location updates to preserve battery life. If the app does not require a constant, accurate location, then monitoring for significant location changes can provide an efficient way of informing the app when the device has moved without consuming a lot of power to keep the GPS and Wi-Fi monitoring the current location.

```
[self.locationManager startMonitoringSignificantLocationChanges];
```

Typically, a notification is generated when the device has moved at least 500 meters, or has changed cell towers. Notifications are not sent unless at least five minutes has elapsed since the last notification. Location update events are delivered to the `locationManager:didUpdate Locations:` delegate method.

Using GPX Files to Test Specific Locations

Testing location-based apps can be daunting, especially when specific locations need to be tested that are not convenient to test from. Fortunately, there is robust support for testing locations provided by Xcode using GPX files. A GPX file is a GPS Exchange Format document, which can be used to communicate GPS information between devices using XML. In debugging mode, Xcode can use a "waypoint" defined in a GPX file to set the current location for the iOS Simulator or device.

In the sample app, the current location is set with the file `DMNS.gpx`, or the location of the Denver Museum of Nature and Science.

```
<?xml version="1.0"?>
<gpx version="1.1" creator="Xcode">

    <wpt lat="39.748039" lon="-104.94000">
        <name>Denver Museum of Nature and Science</name>
    </wpt>

</gpx>
```

To tell Xcode to use a GPX file in debugging, select Edit Scheme from the Scheme selection drop-down in the upper-left corner of a project window, select the Options tab, and check the Allow Location Simulation check box, as shown in Figure 2.5. When this is checked, a location can be selected from the drop-down next to Default Location. This drop-down includes some built-in locations, and any GPX files that have been added to the project.

When the app is run in debug mode, Core Location will return the location specified in the GPX file as the current location of the device or simulator. To change the location while debugging, select Debug, Simulate Location from the menu in Xcode and select a location (as shown in Figure 2.6). Core Location will change the location to the selected location, and will fire the `locationManager:didUpdateLocations:` delegate method.

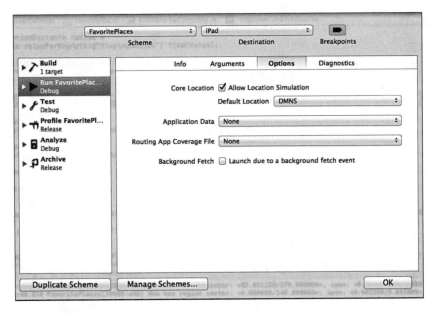

Figure 2.5   Xcode FavoritePlaces scheme.

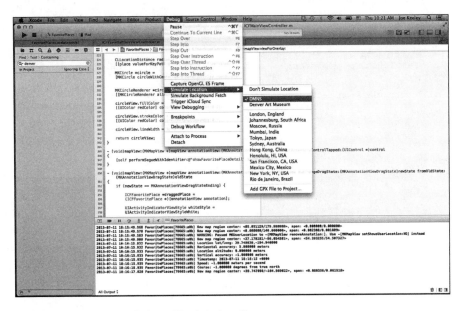

Figure 2.6   Xcode Product, Debug, Simulate Location.

Displaying Maps

MapKit provides mapping user-interface capabilities for iOS. The base class used is an `MKMapView`, which displays a map, handles user interactions with the map, and manages annotations (like pins) and overlays (like routing graphics or region highlights). To better understand how maps in iOS work, it is important to understand the coordinate systems at work.

Understanding the Coordinate Systems

There are two coordinate systems at work in MapKit: the coordinate system for the map, and the coordinate system for the view. The map uses a Mercator Projection, which takes the 3D map of the world and flattens it into a 2D coordinate system. Coordinates can be specified using latitude and longitude. The map view represents the portion of the map displayed on the screen using standard UIKit view coordinates. The map view then determines where in the view to display points determined by map coordinates.

MKMapKit Configuration and Customization

In `ICFMainViewController` in the sample app, the map view is configured in Interface Builder to default to the standard map type, to display the user location on the map, and to allow scrolling and zooming. `ICFMainViewController` has a segmented control to allow the user to adjust the type of map displayed.

```
- (IBAction)mapTypeSelectionChanged:(id)sender
{
    UISegmentedControl *mapSelection =
    (UISegmentedControl *)sender;

    switch (mapSelection.selectedSegmentIndex)
    {
        case 0:
            [self.mapView setMapType:MKMapTypeStandard];
            break;
        case 1:
            [self.mapView setMapType:MKMapTypeSatellite];
            break;
        case 2:
            [self.mapView setMapType:MKMapTypeHybrid];
            break;

        default:
            break;
    }
}
```

Beyond setting the map type, another common customization is to set the region displayed by the map. In `ICFMainViewController`, a method called `zoomMapToFitAnnotations` will examine the current favorite places, and will size and center the map to fit them all. The method starts by setting default maximum and minimum coordinates.

```
CLLocationCoordinate2D maxCoordinate =
CLLocationCoordinate2DMake(-90.0, -180.0);

CLLocationCoordinate2D minCoordinate =
CLLocationCoordinate2DMake(90.0, 180.0);
```

Looking at the existing annotations on the map (described in more detail in the next main section, "Map Annotations and Overlays"), the method calculates the maximum and minimum latitude and longitude values for all the coordinates represented in the annotations.

```
NSArray *currentPlaces = [self.mapView annotations];

maxCoordinate.latitude =
[[currentPlaces valueForKeyPath:@"@max.latitude"] doubleValue];

minCoordinate.latitude =
[[currentPlaces valueForKeyPath:@"@min.latitude"] doubleValue];

maxCoordinate.longitude =
[[currentPlaces valueForKeyPath:@"@max.longitude"] doubleValue];

minCoordinate.longitude =
[[currentPlaces valueForKeyPath:@"@min.longitude"] doubleValue];
```

The method then calculates the center coordinate from the maximum and minimum latitude and longitude coordinates.

```
CLLocationCoordinate2D centerCoordinate;

centerCoordinate.longitude =
(minCoordinate.longitude + maxCoordinate.longitude) / 2.0;

centerCoordinate.latitude =
(minCoordinate.latitude + maxCoordinate.latitude) / 2.0;
```

Next, the method calculates the span needed to display all the coordinates from the calculated center coordinate. The calculated span for each dimension is multiplied by 1.2 to create a margin between the farthest-out points and the edge of the view.

```
MKCoordinateSpan span;
```

```
span.longitudeDelta =
(maxCoordinate.longitude - minCoordinate.longitude) * 1.2;

span.latitudeDelta =
(maxCoordinate.latitude - minCoordinate.latitude) * 1.2;
```

After the center point and span have been calculated, a map region can be created and used to set the map view's displayed region.

```
MKCoordinateRegion newRegion =
MKCoordinateRegionMake(centerCoordinate, span);

[self.mapView setRegion:newRegion
               animated:YES];
```

Setting `animated:` to YES will zoom the map in as if the user had zoomed to it; setting it to NO will instantaneously change the region with no animation.

Responding to User Interactions

An `MKMapViewDelegate` can be specified to react to user interactions with the map. Typical user interactions with a map include responding to panning and zooming, handling draggable annotations, and responding when the user taps a callout.

When the map is being panned and zoomed, the `mapView:regionWillChangeAnimated:` and `mapView:regionDidChangeAnimated:` delegate methods are called. In the sample app no additional action is required for the map to resize and adjust the annotations; however, in an app with a large number of potential items to display on the map or an app that shows different information at different zoom levels, these delegate methods are useful for removing map annotations that are no longer visible and for adding annotations that are newly visible. The delegate method in the sample app demonstrates how one would get the newly displayed map region, which could be used to query items for display on the map.

```
- (void)mapView:(MKMapView *)mapView
regionDidChangeAnimated:(BOOL)animated
{
    MKCoordinateRegion newRegion = [mapView region];
    CLLocationCoordinate2D center = newRegion.center;
    MKCoordinateSpan span = newRegion.span;

    NSLog(@"New map region center: <%f/%f>, span: <%f/%f>",
    center.latitude, center.longitude, span.latitudeDelta,
    span.longitudeDelta);
}
```

Handling draggable annotations and callout taps is described in the next section.

Map Annotations and Overlays

A map view (MKMapView) is a scroll view that behaves specially; adding a subview to it in the standard way will not add the subview to the scrollable part of the map view, but rather the subview will remain static relative to the frame of the map view. Although that might be a feature for items like hovering buttons or labels, being able to identify and mark points and details on the map is a key feature. Map annotations and overlays are a way to mark items or areas of interest in a map view. Annotations and overlays maintain their position on a map as the map is scrolled and zoomed. Map annotations are defined by a single coordinate point on the map, and map overlays can be lines, polygons, or complex shapes. MapKit draws a distinction between the logical annotation or overlay and the associated view. Annotations and overlays are data that represent where on the map they should be displayed, and are added to the map view directly. The map view will then request a view for an annotation or overlay when it needs to be displayed, much like a table view will request cells for index paths as needed.

Adding Annotations

Any object can be an annotation in a map view. To become an annotation, the object needs to implement the MKAnnotation protocol. Apple recommends that the annotation objects should be lightweight, since the map view will keep a reference to all the annotations added to it, and map scrolling and zooming performance can suffer if there are too many annotations. If the requirements for the annotation are very simple and basic, an MKPointAnnotation can be used. In the sample app the ICFFavoritePlace class, which implements the MKAnnotation protocol, is a subclass of NSManagedObject so that it can be persisted using Core Data. Refer to Chapter 13, "Getting Up and Running with Core Data," for more information on using Core Data and NSManagedObject subclasses.

To implement the MKAnnotation protocol, a class must implement the coordinate property. This is used by the map view to determine where the annotation should be placed on the map. The coordinate needs to be returned as a CLLocationCoordinate2D.

```
- (CLLocationCoordinate2D)coordinate
{
    CLLocationDegrees lat =
    [[self valueForKeyPath:@"latitude"] doubleValue];

    CLLocationDegrees lon =
    [[self valueForKeyPath:@"longitude"] doubleValue];

    CLLocationCoordinate2D coord =
    CLLocationCoordinate2DMake(lat, lon);

    return coord;
}
```

Because the `ICFFavoritePlace` class stores the latitude and longitude for the place individually, the `coordinate` property method creates a `CLLocationCoordinate2D` from the latitude
and longitude using the `CLLocationCoordinate2DMake` function provided by Core Location.
`ICFFavoritePlace` will break apart a `CLLocationCoordinate2D` in the setter method for the
`coordinate` property to store the latitude and longitude.

```
- (void)setCoordinate:(CLLocationCoordinate2D)newCoordinate
{
    [self setValue:@(newCoordinate.latitude)
        forKeyPath:@"latitude"];

    [self setValue:@(newCoordinate.longitude)
        forKeyPath:@"longitude"];
}
```

Two other properties for the `MKAnnotation` protocol can optionally be implemented: `title`
and `subtitle`. These are used by the map view to display the callout when the user taps an
annotation view, as shown in Figure 2.7.

Figure 2.7   FavoritePlaces sample app: displaying map annotation view callout.

The `title` property is used for the top line of the callout, and the `subtitle` property is used
for the bottom line of the callout.

```
- (NSString *)title
{
    return [self valueForKeyPath:@"placeName"];
}

- (NSString *)subtitle
{
    NSString *subtitleString = @"";

    NSString *addressString =
    [self valueForKeyPath:@"placeStreetAddress"];

    if ([addressString length] > 0)
```

```
{
    NSString *addr =
    [self valueForKeyPath:@"placeStreetAddress"];

    NSString *city = [self valueForKeyPath:@"placeCity"];
    NSString *state = [self valueForKeyPath:@"placeState"];
    NSString *zip = [self valueForKeyPath:@"placePostal"];

    subtitleString =
    [NSString stringWithFormat:@"%@, %@, %@ %@",
     addr,city,state,zip];
}
return subtitleString;
}
```

In `ICFMainViewController`, the `updateMapAnnotations` method is called from `viewDidLoad:` to populate the map annotations initially, and again after the favorite place detail editing view is dismissed. The method starts by removing all the annotations from the map view. Although this approach works fine for a small number of annotations, with more annotations a more intelligent approach should be developed to efficiently remove unneeded annotations and add new ones.

```
[self.mapView removeAnnotations:self.mapView.annotations];
```

Next, the method performs a Core Data fetch request to get an `NSArray` of the stored favorite places, and adds that array to the map view's annotations.

```
NSFetchRequest *placesRequest =
[[NSFetchRequest alloc] initWithEntityName:@"FavoritePlace"];

NSManagedObjectContext *moc = kAppDelegate.managedObjectContext;

NSError *error = nil;

NSArray *places = [moc executeFetchRequest:placesRequest
                                     error:&error];

if (error)
{
    NSLog(@"Core Data fetch error %@, %@", error,
    [error userInfo]);
}
[self.mapView addAnnotations:places];
```

The map view will then manage displaying the added annotations on the map.

Displaying Standard and Custom Annotation Views

An annotation view is the representation of the annotation on the map. Two types of standard annotation views are provided with MapKit, the pin for searched locations and the pulsing blue dot for the current location. Annotation views can be customized with a static image, or can be completely customized with a subclass of MKAnnotationView. The sample app uses standard pins for favorite places, the standard blue dot for the current location, and a green arrow for a draggable annotation example, as shown in Figure 2.8.

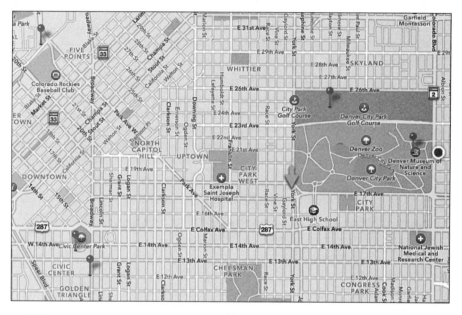

Figure 2.8   FavoritePlaces sample app: displaying map annotation views.

To allow a map view to display annotation views for annotations, the map view delegate needs to implement the mapView:viewForAnnotation method. In the sample app, the mapView:viewForAnnotation method is implemented in the ICFMainViewController. The method first checks whether the annotation is the current location.

```
if (annotation == mapView.userLocation)
{
    return nil;
}
```

For the current location, returning nil for an annotation view will tell the map view to use the standard blue dot. The method then examines the ICFFavoritePlace annotation to determine what type of annotation it is. If the annotation represents the "going next" location, then a custom annotation view will be returned; otherwise, a standard pin annotation view will be returned.

```
MKAnnotationView *view = nil;

ICFFavoritePlace *place = (ICFFavoritePlace *)annotation;

if ([[place valueForKeyPath:@"goingNext"] boolValue])
{
    ...
}
else
{
    ...
}

return view;
```

To return a standard pin annotation view, the method first attempts to dequeue an existing, but no longer used, annotation view. If one is not available, the method will create an instance of `MKPinAnnotationView`.

```
MKPinAnnotationView *pinView = (MKPinAnnotationView *)
[mapView dequeueReusableAnnotationViewWithIdentifier:@"pin"];

if (pinView == nil)
{
    pinView = [[MKPinAnnotationView alloc]
    initWithAnnotation:annotation reuseIdentifier:@"pin"];
}
```

After the pin annotation is created, it can be customized by setting the pin color (choices are red, green, and purple), indicating whether the callout can be displayed when the user taps the annotation view, and indicating whether the annotation view can be dragged.

```
[pinView setPinColor:MKPinAnnotationColorRed];
[pinView setCanShowCallout:YES];
[pinView setDraggable:NO];
```

The callout view that appears when the annotation view is tapped has left and right accessory views that can be customized. The left accessory view is set to a custom image, and the right accessory view is set to a standard detail disclosure button. If the left or right accessory views are customized with objects that descend from `UIControl`, the delegate method `mapView:a nnotationView:calloutAccessoryControlTapped:` will be called when they are tapped.

Otherwise, the objects should be configured by the developer to handle the tap as desired. Note that Apple states that the maximum height for the accessory views is 32 pixels.

```
UIImageView *leftView = [[UIImageView alloc]
initWithImage:[UIImage imageNamed:@"annotation_view_star"]];

[pinView setLeftCalloutAccessoryView:leftView];

UIButton* rightButton = [UIButton buttonWithType:
                             UIButtonTypeDetailDisclosure];

[pinView setRightCalloutAccessoryView:rightButton];
view = pinView;
```

To return a custom pin annotation view, the method will attempt to dequeue an existing but no longer used annotation view by a string identifier. If one is not available, the method will create an instance of `MKAnnotationView`.

```
view = (MKAnnotationView *)
[mapView dequeueReusableAnnotationViewWithIdentifier:@"arrow"];

if (view == nil)
{
    view = [[MKAnnotationView alloc]
    initWithAnnotation:annotation reuseIdentifier:@"arrow"];
}
```

The annotation can be customized much like a standard pin annotation, indicating whether the callout can be displayed when the user taps the annotation view, and indicating whether the annotation view can be dragged. The main difference is that the image for the annotation can be set directly using the `setImage:` method.

```
[view setCanShowCallout:YES];
[view setDraggable:YES];

[view setImage:[UIImage imageNamed:@"next_arrow"]];

UIImageView *leftView = [[UIImageView alloc]
initWithImage:[UIImage imageNamed:@"annotation_view_arrow"]];

[view setLeftCalloutAccessoryView:leftView];
[view setRightCalloutAccessoryView:nil];
```

The annotation view will display with a green arrow instead of a standard pin, as shown previously in Figure 2.8.

Draggable Annotation Views

Draggable annotation views can be useful to allow the user to mark a place on a map. In the sample app, there is one special favorite place to indicate where the user is going next, represented by a green arrow. An annotation view can be made draggable by setting the `draggable` property when the annotation view is being configured for presentation.

```
[view setDraggable:YES];
```

The user can then drag the annotation view anywhere on the map. To get more information about the dragging performed on an annotation view, the map view delegate implements the `mapView:annotationView:didChangeDragState:fromOldState:` method. That method will fire anytime the dragging state changes for a draggable annotation view, and indicates whether the dragging state is none, starting, dragging, canceling, or ending. By examining the new dragging state and old dragging state, custom logic can handle a number of different use cases presented by dragging.

When the user stops dragging the arrow in the sample app, it will reverse-geocode the new location indicated by the arrow (described in more detail in the later section "Geocoding and Reverse-Geocoding") to get the name and address of the new location. To do this, the method needs to check whether dragging is completed.

```
if (newState == MKAnnotationViewDragStateEnding)
{
    ....
}
```

If dragging is complete, the method will get the annotation associated with the annotation view to figure out the new coordinates that need to be reverse-geocoded.

```
ICFFavoritePlace *draggedPlace =
(ICFFavoritePlace *)[annotationView annotation];
```

The method adds a standard spinner to the callout view so that the user knows it is being updated, and then calls the method to reverse-geocode the new place, described later in the chapter in the geocoding section.

```
UIActivityIndicatorViewStyle whiteStyle =
UIActivityIndicatorViewStyleWhite;

UIActivityIndicatorView *activityView =
[[UIActivityIndicatorView alloc]
initWithActivityIndicatorStyle:whiteStyle];

[activityView startAnimating];
[annotationView setLeftCalloutAccessoryView:activityView];

[self reverseGeocodeDraggedAnnotation:draggedPlace
            forAnnotationView:annotationView];
```

Working with Map Overlays

Map overlays are similar to map annotations, in that any object can implement the `MKOverlay` protocol, and the map view delegate is asked to provide the associated view for a map overlay. Map overlays are different from annotations in that they can represent more than just a point. They can represent lines and shapes, so they are very useful for representing routes or areas of interest on a map. To demonstrate map overlays, the sample app provides a feature to add a geofence (described in more detail later in the section "Geofencing") with a user-defined radius for a favorite place. When a geofence is added for a favorite place, the user's selected radius will be displayed on the map with a circle around the place's coordinate, as shown in Figure 2.9.

Figure 2.9   FavoritePlaces sample app: displaying map overlay view.

As mentioned previously in the "Adding Annotations" section, the `updateMapAnnotations` method adds annotations to the map. This method also adds overlays to the map at the same time. The method starts by clearing all existing overlays from the map view.

```
[self.mapView removeOverlays:self.mapView.overlays];
```

Since overlays are displayed only for places that have the geofence feature enabled, the method iterates over the places, and adds an overlay to the map only for those places.

```
for (ICFFavoritePlace *favPlace in places)
{

    BOOL displayOverlay =
    [[favPlace valueForKeyPath:@"displayProximity"] boolValue];

    if (displayOverlay)
    {
        [self.mapView addOverlay:favPlace];
        ...
    }
}
```

When the map needs to display a map overlay, the map view will call the delegate method `mapView:viewForOverlay`. This method will create an overlay view for the map to display. There are three options provided by MapKit: circle, polygon, or polyline; custom shapes and overlays can also be created if the MapKit options are insufficient. The sample app creates a circle around the location, using the radius and map coordinate from the favorite place.

```
ICFFavoritePlace *place = (ICFFavoritePlace *)overlay;

CLLocationDistance radius =
[[place valueForKeyPath:@"displayRadius"] floatValue];

MKCircle *circle =
[MKCircle circleWithCenterCoordinate:[overlay coordinate]
                              radius:radius];
```

After the map kit circle is ready, the method creates a map kit circle view, and customizes the stroke and fill colors and the line width. This circle view is then returned, and the map will display it.

```
MKCircleRenderer *circleView =
[[MKCircleRenderer alloc] initWithCircle:circle];

circleView.fillColor =
[[UIColor redColor] colorWithAlphaComponent:0.2];

circleView.strokeColor =
[[UIColor redColor] colorWithAlphaComponent:0.7];

circleView.lineWidth = 3;

return circleView;
```

Geocoding and Reverse-Geocoding

Geocoding is the process of finding latitude and longitude coordinates from a human-readable address. Reverse-geocoding is the process of finding a human readable address from coordinates. As of iOS 5.0, Core Location supports both, with no special terms or limitations (as with MapKit in iOS 5.1 and earlier).

Geocoding an Address

The sample app enables the user to add a new favorite place by entering an address in `ICFFavoritePlaceViewController`. The user can tap Geocode Location Now to get the latitude and longitude, as shown in Figure 2.10.

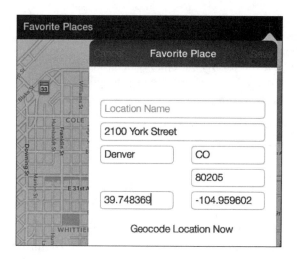

Figure 2.10   FavoritePlaces sample app: adding a new favorite place.

When the user taps the Geocode Location Now button, the `geocodeLocationTouched:` method is called. That method begins by concatenating the address information provided by the user into a single string, like "2100 York St, Denver, CO 80205," to provide to the geocoder.

```
NSString *geocodeString = @"";
if ([self.addressTextField.text length] > 0)
{
    geocodeString = self.addressTextField.text;
}
if ([self.cityTextField.text length] > 0)
{
    if ([geocodeString length] > 0)
    {

        geocodeString =
        [geocodeString stringByAppendingFormat:@", %@",
        self.cityTextField.text];

    }
    else
    {
        geocodeString = self.cityTextField.text;
    }
}
if ([self.stateTextField.text length] > 0)
    {
```

```
    if ([geocodeString length] > 0)
    {

        geocodeString =
        [geocodeString stringByAppendingFormat:@", %@",
        self.stateTextField.text];

    }
    else
    {
        geocodeString = self.stateTextField.text;
    }
}
if ([self.postalTextField.text length] > 0)
    {
    if ([geocodeString length] > 0)
    {

        geocodeString =
        [geocodeString stringByAppendingFormat:@" %@",
         self.postalTextField.text];

    }
    else
    {
        geocodeString = self.postalTextField.text;
    }
}
```

The method will then disable the Geocode Location Now button to prevent additional requests from getting started by multiple taps. Apple explicitly states that the geocoder should process only one request at a time. The method also updates the fields and button to indicate that geocoding is in process.

```
[self.latitudeTextField setText:@"Geocoding..."];
[self.longitudeTextField setText:@"Geocoding..."];

[self.geocodeNowButton setTitle:@"Geocoding now..."
                        forState:UIControlStateDisabled];

[self.geocodeNowButton setEnabled:NO];
```

The method gets a reference to an instance of CLGeocoder.

```
CLGeocoder *geocoder =
[[ICFLocationManager sharedLocationManager] geocoder];
```

The `geocoder` is then asked to geocode the address string, with a completion handler block, which is called on the main queue. The completion handler will first reenable the button so that it can be tapped again, and will then check to see whether an error was encountered with `geocoding` or whether the `geocoder` completed successfully.

```
[geocoder geocodeAddressString:geocodeString
completionHandler:^(NSArray *placemarks, NSError *error) {

    [self.geocodeNowButton setEnabled:YES];
    if (error)
    {
        ...
    }
    else
    {
        ...
    }
}];
```

If the geocoder encountered an error, the latitude and longitude fields are populated with "Not found" and an alert view is presented with the localized description of the error. The geocoder will fail without an Internet connection, or if the address is not well formed or cannot be found.

```
[self.latitudeTextField setText:@"Not found"];
[self.longitudeTextField setText:@"Not found"];

UIAlertView *alert =
[[UIAlertView alloc] initWithTitle:@"Geocoding Error"
                          message:error.localizedDescription
                          delegate:nil
                 cancelButtonTitle:@"OK"
                 otherButtonTitles: nil];

[alert show];
```

If geocoding succeeded, an array called `placemarks` will be provided to the completion handler. This array will contain instances of `CLPlacemark`, which each contain information about a potential match. A placemark has a latitude/longitude coordinate, and address information.

```
if ([placemarks count] > 0)
{
    CLPlacemark *placemark = [placemarks lastObject];

    NSString *latString =
    [NSString stringWithFormat:@"%f",
    placemark.location.coordinate.latitude];
```

```
    [self.latitudeTextField setText:latString];

    NSString *longString =
    [NSString stringWithFormat:@"%f",
     placemark.location.coordinate.longitude];

    [self.longitudeTextField setText:longString];
}
```

If more than one placemark is returned, the user interface could allow the user to select the one that most closely matches his intention (Maps.app uses this approach). For simplicity the sample app selects the last placemark in the array and updates the user interface with the coordinate information.

Reverse-Geocoding a Location

The sample app allows users to drag the green arrow to indicate where they would like to go next, as shown in Figure 2.11.

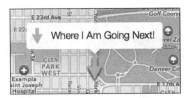

Figure 2.11   FavoritePlaces sample app: Where I Am Going Next.

When the user drags the green arrow, the map view delegate method `mapView:annotation View:didChangeDragState:fromOldState:` in ICFMainViewController gets called. That method checks the drag state as described earlier in the chapter in the "Draggable Annotation Views" section, and if the green arrow has stopped being dragged, updates the callout view with a spinner and starts the reverse-geocoding.

```
ICFFavoritePlace *draggedPlace =
(ICFFavoritePlace *)[annotationView annotation];

UIActivityIndicatorViewStyle whiteStyle =
UIActivityIndicatorViewStyleWhite;

UIActivityIndicatorView *activityView =
[[UIActivityIndicatorView alloc]
initWithActivityIndicatorStyle:whiteStyle];
```

```
[activityView startAnimating];
[annotationView setLeftCalloutAccessoryView:activityView];

[self reverseGeocodeDraggedAnnotation:draggedPlace
            forAnnotationView:annotationView];
```

The reverseGeocodeDraggedAnnotation:forAnnotationView: method gets a reference to an instance of CLGeocoder.

```
CLGeocoder *geocoder =
[[ICFLocationManager sharedLocationManager] geocoder];
```

An instance of CLLocation is created for use by the geocoder from the coordinate of the moved arrow.

```
CLLocationCoordinate2D draggedCoord = [place coordinate];

CLLocation *draggedLocation =
[[CLLocation alloc] initWithLatitude:draggedCoord.latitude
                        longitude:draggedCoord.longitude];
```

The geocoder is then asked to reverse-geocode the location from where the annotation has been dragged with a completion handler block, which is called on the main queue. The completion handler will replace the spinner in the callout with the green arrow, and will then check to see whether an error was encountered with geocoding or whether the geocoder completed successfully.

```
[geocoder reverseGeocodeLocation:draggedLocation
completionHandler:^(NSArray *placemarks, NSError *error) {

    UIImage *arrowImage =
    [UIImage imageNamed:@"annotation_view_arrow"];

    UIImageView *leftView =
    [[UIImageView alloc] initWithImage:arrowImage];

    [annotationView setLeftCalloutAccessoryView:leftView];

    if (error)
    {
        ...
    }
    else
    {
        ...
    }
}];
```

If the geocoder encountered an error, an alert view is presented with the localized description of the error. The geocoder will fail without an Internet connection.

```
UIAlertView *alert =
[[UIAlertView alloc] initWithTitle:@"Geocoding Error"
                        message:error.localizedDescription
                        delegate:nil
              cancelButtonTitle:@"OK"
              otherButtonTitles: nil];

[alert show];
```

If the reverse-geocoding process completes successfully, an array of CLPlacemark instances will be passed to the completion handler. The sample app will use the last placemark to update the name and address of the next place.

```
if ([placemarks count] > 0)
{
    CLPlacemark *placemark = [placemarks lastObject];
    [self updateFavoritePlace:place withPlacemark:placemark];
}
```

The placemark contains detailed location information with internationalized terms. For example, a street address is represented by the number (or subThoroughfare) and a street (or thoroughfare), and the city and state are subAdministrativeArea and administrativeArea.

```
[kAppDelegate.managedObjectContext performBlock:^{
    NSString *newName =
    [NSString stringWithFormat:@"Next: %@",placemark.name];

    [place setValue:newName forKey:@"placeName"];

    NSString *newStreetAddress =
    [NSString stringWithFormat:@"%@ %@",
    placemark.subThoroughfare, placemark.thoroughfare];

    [place setValue:newStreetAddress
            forKey:@"placeStreetAddress"];

    [place setValue:placemark.subAdministrativeArea
            forKey:@"placeCity"];

    [place setValue:placemark.postalCode
            forKey:@"placePostal"];

    [place setValue:placemark.administrativeArea
            forKey:@"placeState"];
```

```
    NSError *saveError = nil;
    [kAppDelegate.managedObjectContext save:&saveError];
    if (saveError) {
        NSLog(@"Save Error: %@",saveError.localizedDescription);
    }
}];
```

> **Tip**
>
> CLPlacemark instances provided by the geocoder include an addressDictionary property, which
> is formatted for easy insertion into the Address Book (see Chapter 5, "Getting Started with
> Address Book," for more information).

The place is then saved using Core Data so that it will survive app restarts. Now when the user taps the green arrow annotation view, it will reflect the name and address of the location it was dragged to, as shown in Figure 2.12.

Figure 2.12   FavoritePlaces sample app: Where I Am Going Next after reverse-geocode.

Geofencing

Geofencing, also called regional monitoring, is the capability to track when a device enters or exits a specified map region. iOS uses this to great effect with Siri to accomplish things like, "Remind me to pick up bread when I leave the office," or, "Remind me to put the roast in the oven when I get home." iOS also uses geofencing in Passbook, to help users see the passes that are relevant to them on the home screen (see Chapter 24, "Passbook and PassKit," for more details).

Checking for Regional Monitoring Capability

The Core Location location manager has a class method that indicates whether regional monitoring is available for the device. This can be used to customize whether an app performs regional monitoring tasks. For example, the sample app will conditionally display a switch to enable geofencing for a favorite location in the ICFFavoritePlaceViewController.

```
BOOL hideGeofence =
![CLLocationManager regionMonitoringAvailable];

[self.displayProximitySwitch setHidden:hideGeofence];

if (hideGeofence)
{
    [self.geofenceLabel setText:@"Geofence N/A"];
}
```

Defining Boundaries

Core Location's location manager (CLLocationManager) keeps a set of regions being monitored for an app. In ICFMainViewController, the updateMapAnnotations: method clears out the set of monitored regions when a change has been made.

```
CLLocationManager *locManager =
[[ICFLocationManager sharedLocationManager] locationManager];

NSSet *monitoredRegions = [locManager monitoredRegions];

for (CLRegion *region in monitoredRegions)
{
    [locManager stopMonitoringForRegion:region];
}
```

Next, the method iterates over the user's list of favorite places to determine which places the user has set to geofence. For each place that the user has set to geofence, the method will add the overlay view as described in the previous section, and will then tell the location manager to start monitoring that region. A region to be monitored needs a center coordinate, a radius, and an identifier so that the region can be tracked in the app. The sample app uses the Core Data universal resource ID representation as an identifier for the region, so that the same place can be quickly retrieved when a regional monitoring event is generated for the region.

```
NSString *placeObjectID =
[[[favPlace objectID] URIRepresentation] absoluteString];


CLLocationDistance monitorRadius =
[[favPlace valueForKeyPath:@"displayRadius"] floatValue];

CLRegion *region = [[CLRegion alloc]
```

```
initCircularRegionWithCenter:[favPlace coordinate]
                     radius:monitorRadius
                     identifier:placeObjectID];

[locManager startMonitoringForRegion:region];
```

Note that currently only circular regions are supported for regional monitoring.

Monitoring Changes

When the device either enters or exits a monitored region, the location manager will inform its delegate of the event by calling either the `locationManager:didEnterRegion:` or the `locationManager:didExitRegion:` method.

In `locationManager:didEnterRegion:`, the method first gets the identifier associated with the monitored region. This identifier was assigned when telling the location manager to monitor the region, and is the Core Data URI of the saved favorite place. This URI is used to get the managed object ID, which is used to retrieve the favorite place from the managed object context.

```
NSString *placeIdentifier = [region identifier];
NSURL *placeIDURL = [NSURL URLWithString:placeIdentifier];

NSManagedObjectID *placeObjectID =
[kAppDelegate.persistentStoreCoordinator
managedObjectIDForURIRepresentation:placeIDURL];
```

The method gets details from the favorite place and presents them in an alert to the user.

```
[kAppDelegate.managedObjectContext performBlock:^{

    ICFFavoritePlace *place =
    (ICFFavoritePlace *)[kAppDelegate.managedObjectContext
    objectWithID:placeObjectID];

    NSNumber *distance = [place valueForKey:@"displayRadius"];
    NSString *placeName = [place valueForKey:@"placeName"];

    NSString *baseMessage =
    @"Favorite Place %@ nearby - within %@ meters.";

    NSString *proximityMessage =
    [NSString stringWithFormat:baseMessage,placeName,distance];
```

```
        UIAlertView *alert =
        [[UIAlertView alloc] initWithTitle:@"Favorite Nearby!"
                              message:proximityMessage
                             delegate:nil
                   cancelButtonTitle:@"OK"
                   otherButtonTitles: nil];
        [alert show];
}];
```

To test this using the sample app, start the app in debug mode using the included GPX file for the Denver Museum of Nature and Science (DMNS), as described previously in the chapter in the section "Using GPX Files to Test Specific Locations." Ensure that the Denver Art Museum is set to Geofence, as shown in Figure 2.9 in the section "Working with Map Overlays." After the app is running, use Xcode to change the location using the debug location menu from DMNS (as shown in Figure 2.6) to the Denver Art Museum. This should trigger the geofence and display the alert as shown in Figure 2.13.

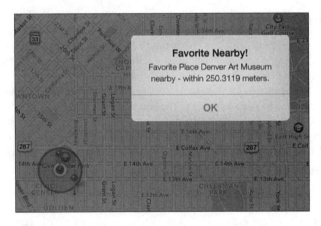

Figure 2.13   FavoritePlaces sample app: favorite place nearby alert.

The `locationManager:didExitRegion:` method also gets the Core Data identifier from the region, uses Core Data to get the managed object ID, looks up the favorite place, and presents an alert when the user exits the region. To test this using the sample app, start from the Favorite Nearby alert just shown in Figure 2.13. Tap the OK button, and then select Debug, Location, Apple from the iOS Simulator menu. After a few seconds, the simulator will change locations and present the user with an alert, as shown in Figure 2.14.

The location manager intentionally delays calling the delegate methods until a cushion distance has been crossed for at least 20 seconds to prevent spurious messages when the device is close to the boundary of a region.

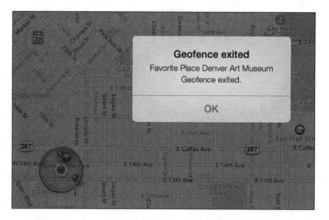

Figure 2.14   FavoritePlaces sample app: favorite place geofence exited alert.

Getting Directions

As of iOS 6, the standard Maps.app was enhanced to provide turn-by-turn navigation in addition to directions. Maps.app was also enhanced to allow other apps to open it with specific instructions on what to display. Apps can request that Maps.app display an array of map items, provide directions between two locations, or provide directions from the current location. Maps.app can be configured with a center point and span, and a type of map (standard, satellite, or hybrid). As of iOS 7, MapKit offers a directions request, which can provide directions to be used directly in an app. The directions request can return an array of polylines representing route options, with accompanying route steps that can be presented in a table view. Both approaches are demonstrated in the sample app.

To open Maps.app, the class method `openMapsWithItems:launchOptions:` on the `MKMapItem` class can be used, or the instance method `openInMapsWithlaunchOptions:`. In the sample app, there is a button on `ICFFavoritePlaceViewController` to get directions to a favorite place. When that button is tapped, the `getDirectionsButtonTouched:` method is called. In that method, an instance of `MKMapItem` is created for the favorite place.

```
CLLocationCoordinate2D destination =
[self.favoritePlace coordinate];

MKPlacemark *destinationPlacemark =
[[MKPlacemark alloc] initWithCoordinate:destination
                    addressDictionary:nil];

MKMapItem *destinationItem =
[[MKMapItem alloc] initWithPlacemark:destinationPlacemark];

destinationItem.name =
[self.favoritePlace valueForKey:@"placeName"];
```

A dictionary of launch options is set up to instruct Maps.app how to configure itself when opened.

```
NSDictionary *launchOptions = @{
    MKLaunchOptionsDirectionsModeKey :
    MKLaunchOptionsDirectionsModeDriving,
    MKLaunchOptionsMapTypeKey :
    [NSNumber numberWithInt:MKMapTypeStandard]
};
```

Then, an array of map items is created with the favorite place to pass to Maps.app with the dictionary of launch options. If two map items are passed in the array with a directions launch option, the map will provide directions from the first item to the second item.

```
NSArray *mapItems = @[destinationItem];

BOOL success = [MKMapItem openMapsWithItems:mapItems
                        launchOptions:launchOptions];

if (!success)
{
    NSLog(@"Failed to open Maps.app.");
}
```

Maps.app will be opened and will provide directions to the favorite place. If an error is encountered, the openMapsWithItems:launchOptions: will return NO.

To request directions to be displayed in the app, instantiate an MKDirections object with an MKDirectionsRequest instance, specifying a source (or starting point) and destination map item expressed as MKMapItem instances.

```
CLLocationCoordinate2D destination =
[self.favoritePlace coordinate];

MKPlacemark *destinationPlacemark =
[[MKPlacemark alloc] initWithCoordinate:destination
                        addressDictionary:nil];

MKMapItem *destinationItem =
[[MKMapItem alloc] initWithPlacemark:destinationPlacemark];

MKMapItem *currentMapItem =
[self.delegate currentLocationMapItem];

MKDirectionsRequest *directionsRequest =
[[MKDirectionsRequest alloc] init];
```

```
[directionsRequest setDestination:destinationItem];
[directionsRequest setSource:currentMapItem];

MKDirections *directions =
[[MKDirections alloc] initWithRequest:directionsRequest];
```

Then call the `calculateDirectionsWithCompletionHandler:` method, specifying
a completion block. The completion block should handle any errors, and inspect the
`MKDirectionsResponse` provided. For this example the method ensures that at least one
route (which is an instance of `MKRoute`) was returned, and then performs actions with the first
route. The method iterates over the `steps` property of the first route, which contains instances
of `MKRouteStep`, and logs strings to display the distance and instructions for each route step.
Then the method calls the delegate to add the route to the map.

```
[directions calculateDirectionsWithCompletionHandler:
^(MKDirectionsResponse *response, NSError *error){
    if (error) {

        NSString *dirMessage =
        [NSString stringWithFormat:@"Failed to get directions: %@",
         error.localizedDescription];

        UIAlertView *dirAlert =
        [[UIAlertView alloc] initWithTitle:@"Directions Error"
                                   message:dirMessage
                                   delegate:nil
                          cancelButtonTitle:@"OK"
                          otherButtonTitles: nil];

        [dirAlert show];
    }
    else
    {
        if ([response.routes count] > 0) {
            MKRoute *firstRoute = response.routes[0];
            NSLog(@"Directions received.  Steps for route 1 are: ");
            NSInteger stepNumber = 1;
            for (MKRouteStep *step in firstRoute.steps) {

                NSLog(@"Step %d, %f meters: %@",stepNumber,
                        step.distance,step.instructions);

                stepNumber++;
            }
            [self.delegate displayDirectionsForRoute:firstRoute];
        }
        else
```

```
        {
            NSString *dirMessage = @"No directions available";

            UIAlertView *dirAlert =
            [[UIAlertView alloc] initWithTitle:@"No Directions"
                                       message:dirMessage
                                      delegate:nil
                             cancelButtonTitle:@"OK"
                             otherButtonTitles: nil];

            [dirAlert show];
        }
    }
}];
```

In the delegate method, the polyline for the route is added to the map's overlays, and the dialog is dismissed.

```
- (void)displayDirectionsForRoute:(MKRoute *)route
{
    [self.mapView addOverlay:route.polyline];

    if (self.favoritePlacePopoverController)
    {
        [self.favoritePlacePopoverController
         dismissPopoverAnimated:YES];

        self.favoritePlacePopoverController = nil;
    } else
    {
        [self dismissViewControllerAnimated:YES
                                 completion:nil];
    }
}
```

Since the polyline has been added as an overlay, the map delegate method to return overlay views must now handle polylines instead of just the custom geofence radius overlays.

```
- (MKOverlayRenderer *)mapView:(MKMapView *)mapView
            viewForOverlay:(id < MKOverlay >)overlay
{
    MKOverlayRenderer *returnView = nil;

    if ([overlay isKindOfClass:[ICFFavoritePlace class]]) {
        ...
    }
    if ([overlay isKindOfClass:[MKPolyline class]]) {
        MKPolyline *line = (MKPolyline *)overlay;
```

```
        MKPolylineRenderer *polylineRenderer =
        [[MKPolylineRenderer alloc] initWithPolyline:line];

        [polylineRenderer setLineWidth:3.0];
        [polylineRenderer setFillColor:[UIColor blueColor]];
        [polylineRenderer setStrokeColor:[UIColor blueColor]];
        returnView = polylineRenderer;
    }

    return returnView;
}
```

The `mapView:viewForOverlay:` method will now check which class the overlay belongs to, and build the correct type of view for it. For the polyline, the method will create an instance of `MKPolylineRenderer` using the polyline from the overlay, and customize it with a line width and blue fill and stroke color, which will show a directions line on the map between the starting location and the destination location, as shown in Figure 2.15.

Figure 2.15   FavoritePlaces sample app: displaying a direction polyline on the map.

Summary

This chapter covered Core Location and MapKit. It described how to set up Core Location, how to check for available services, how to deal with user permissions, and how to acquire the device's current location.

Next, this chapter explained how to use MapKit to display locations on a map using standard and custom annotations. The chapter covered how to display more detail about an annotation in a callout, and how to respond to the user tapping the callout or dragging the annotation on the map. It also explained how to add overlays to a map to highlight map features.

This chapter then described how to use the geocoder to get latitude and longitude information from a street address, or to get address information from a latitude and longitude coordinate.

Geofencing, or regional monitoring, was demonstrated. The sample app showed how to specify and monitor when the user enters or exits map regions.

Lastly, this chapter demonstrated two techniques for providing directions to a favorite place: using Maps.app to provide directions and using a directions request to get information to display directly in the user interface.

Exercises

1. Geofence events can occur while the app is in the background, but the app cannot display an alert while it is in the background. Enhance the sample app to send a local notification when a geofence event is received in the background, and an alert while the app is active. Hint: Refer to Chapter 16, "Working with Background Tasks," and Chapter 9, "Notifications," for more info on those topics.

2. Currently in the sample app, when a user taps a pin for a favorite place to display the callout, and then taps the right detail disclosure button, a view to edit the details of the favorite place is presented modally. Modify this to present the detailed view in a popover, using the pin as an anchor point. While the popup is being presented, have the associated pin display green instead of red.

3

Leaderboards

Leaderboards have become an important component of nearly every mobile game, as well as having numerous applications outside of gaming. Leveraging Game Center to add leaderboards makes it easier than it has ever been in the past to include them in an iOS app. Although leaderboards have been around almost as long as video games themselves—the first high-score list appeared in 1976—they have more recently become critical parts of a social gaming experience. In this chapter you will learn how to add a full-featured leaderboard to a real-world game, from setting up the required information in iTunes Connect to displaying the leaderboard using GKLeaderboardViewController.

Whack-a-Cac

In this chapter and in Chapter 4, "Achievements," the same sample game will be used. It is important that you are familiar with the game itself so that you can remove the complexity of it from the process of integrating Game Center. Whack-a-Cac was designed to use minimal code and be simple to learn, so the game can act as a generic placeholder for whatever app you are integrating Game Center into. If you already have an app that you are ready to work with, skip this section and follow along with your existing project.

Whack-a-Cac, as shown in Figure 3.1, is a simple whack-a-mole type of game. Cacti will pop up and you must tap them before the timer fires and they go back into the sand dunes. As the game progresses it continues to get more difficult, and after you have missed five cacti the game ends and you are left with a score. The game itself is controlled through ICFGameViewController. Cacti can appear anywhere along the x-axis and on one of three possible rows on the y-axis. The player will have two seconds from the time a cactus appears to tap it before it goes back down and the player is deducted a life. Up until a score of 50, every 10 cacti that are hit will increase the maximum number shown at once by one. The game can also be paused and resumed.

Figure 3.1   A first look at Whack-a-Cac, the game that is used for the Game Center chapters of this book.

Before you can dig into the game-specific code, attention must first be paid to the home screen of the game. IFCViewController.m will not only handle launching the gameplay but also enable the user to access the leaderboards as well as the achievements. The Game Center-specific functionality of this class is discussed in detail later in this chapter, but for the time being the focus should be on the play: method. When a new game is created, IFCViewController simply allocs and inits a new copy of IFCGameViewController and pushes it onto the navigation stack. The rest of the game will be handled by that class.

Whack-a-Cac is a very simplified example of an iOS game. It is based on a state engine containing three states: playing, paused, and game over. While the game is playing, the engine will continue to spawn cacti until the user runs out of life and enters the game-over state. The user can pause the game at any time by tapping the pause button in the upper-left corner of the screen. To begin, direct your attention to the viewDidLoad: method.

```
- (void)viewDidLoad
{
    [[ICFGameCenterManager sharedManager] setDelegate: self];

    score = 0;
    life = 5;
```

```
    gameOver = NO;
    paused = NO;

    [super viewDidLoad];

    [self updateLife];

    [self spawnCactus];
    [self performSelector:@selector(spawnCactus) withObject:nil
    ➥afterDelay:1.0];
}
```

On the first line `ICFGameCenterManager` has its delegate set to `self`, which is covered in depth later in this section. During the `viewDidLoad` execution, a few state variables are set. First the score is reset to zero along with the life being set to five. The next requirement is setting two Booleans that represent the current state of the game; since the game starts with gameplay on launch, both `gameOver` and `paused` are set to `NO`. A method named `updateLife` is called. Although this is discussed later in this section, for now just note that it handles rendering the player's lives to the upper right of the screen, as shown in Figure 3.1. The final initialization step is to spawn two cacti at the start of the game. One is spawned instantly and the other is delayed by one second.

Spawning a Cactus

One of the most important functions in `IFCGameViewController` is spawning the actual cacti to the screen. In the `viewDidLoad` method `spawnCactus` was called twice; turn your attention to that method now. In a state-based game the first thing that should be done is to check to make sure you are in the correct state. The first test that is run is a `gameOver` check; if the game has ended, the cactus should stop spawning. The next check is a pause test; if the game is paused, you don't want to spawn a new cactus either, but when the game is resumed you want to start spawning again. The test performed on the paused state will retry spawning every second until the game is resumed or quit.

```
if(gameOver)
{
    return;
}

if(paused)
{
    [self performSelector:@selector(spawnCactus) withObject:nil
    ➥afterDelay:1];

    return;
}
```

If the method has passed both the state checks, it is time to spawn a new cactus. First the game must determine where to randomly place the object. To randomly place the cactus in the game, two random numbers are generated, the first for the row to be spawned in, followed by the x-axis location.

```
int rowToSpawnIn = arc4random()%3;
int horizontalLocation = (arc4random()%1024);
```

To create a more interesting gaming experience, there are three different images for the cactus. With each new cactus spawned, one image is randomly selected through the following code snippet:

```
int cactusSize = arc4random()%3;
UIImage *cactusImage = nil;

switch (cactusSize)
{
        case 0:
            cactusImage = [UIImage imageNamed:
            @"CactusLarge.png"];
            break;
        case 1:
            cactusImage = [UIImage imageNamed: @"CactusMed.png"];
            break;
        case 2:
            cactusImage = [UIImage imageNamed:
            @"CactusSmall.png"];
            break;
        default:
            break;
}
```

A simple check is performed next to make sure that the cactus is not being drawn off the right side of the view. Since the x-axis is calculated randomly and the widths of the cacti are variable, a simple if statement tests to see whether the image is being drawn too far right and if so moves it back to the edge.

```
if(horizontalLocation > 1024 - cactusImage.size.width)
        horizontalLocation = 1024 - cactusImage.size.width;
```

Whack-a-Cac is a depth- and layer-based game. There are three dunes, and a cactus should appear behind the dune for the row it is spawned in but in front of dunes that fall behind it. The first step in making this work is to determine which view the new cactus needs to fall behind. This is done using the following code snippet:

```
UIImageView *duneToSpawnBehind = nil;

switch (rowToSpawnIn)
{
```

```
    case 0:
        duneToSpawnBehind = duneOne;
        break;
    case 1:
        duneToSpawnBehind = duneTwo;
        break;
    case 2:
        duneToSpawnBehind = duneThree;
        break;
    default:
    break;
}
```

Now that the game knows where it needs to layer the new cactus, a couple of convenience variables are created to increase the readability of the code.

```
float cactusHeight = cactusImage.size.height;
float cactusWidth = cactusImage.size.width;
```

All the important groundwork has now been laid, and a new cactus can finally be placed into the game view. Since the cactus will act as a touchable item, it makes sense to create it as a UIButton. The frame variables are inserted, which cause the cactus to be inserted behind the dune and thus be invisible. An action is added to the cactus that calls the method cactusHit:, which is discussed later in this section.

```
UIButton *cactus = [[UIButton alloc]
➥initWithFrame:CGRectMake(horizontalLocation,
➥(duneToSpawnBehind.frame.origin.y), cactusWidth, cactusHeight)];

[cactus setImage:cactusImage forState: UIControlStateNormal];

[cactus addTarget:self action:@selector(cactusHit:)
➥forControlEvents:UIControlEventTouchDown];

[self.view insertSubview:cactus      belowSubview:duneToSpawnBehind];
```

Now that a cactus has been spawned, it is ready to be animated up from behind the dunes and have its timer started to inform the game when the user has failed to hit it within two seconds. The cactus will slide up from behind the dune in a 1/4th-second animation using information about the height of the cactus to make sure that it ends up in the proper spot. A two second timer is also begun that will fire cactusMissed:, which is discussed in the "Cactus Interaction" section.

```
[UIView beginAnimations: @"slideInCactus" context:nil];
[UIView setAnimationCurve: UIViewAnimationCurveEaseInOut];
[UIView setAnimationDuration: 0.25];
```

```
cactus.frame = CGRectMake(horizontalLocation,
➥(duneToSpawnBehind.frame.origin.y)-cactusHeight/2, cactusWidth,
➥cactusHeight);

[UIView commitAnimations];

[self performSelector:@selector(cactusMissed:) withObject:cactus
➥afterDelay:2.0];
```

Cactus Interaction

There are two possible outcomes of a cactus spawning: Either the user has hit the cactus within the two-second limit or the user has failed to hit it. In the first scenario cactusHit: is called in response to a UIControlEventTouchDown on the cactus button. When this happens, the cactus is quickly faded off the screen and then removed from the superView. Using the option UIViewAnimationOptionsBeginFromCurrentState will ensure that any existing animations on this cactus are cancelled. The score is incremented by one and displayNewScore: is called to update the score on the screen; more on that later in this section. After a cactus has been hit, a key step is spawning the next cactus. This is done in the same fashion as in viewDidLoad but with a randomized time to create a more engaging experience.

```
- (IBAction)cactusHit:(id)sender;
{
    [UIView animateWithDuration:0.1
                      delay:0.0
                    options: UIViewAnimationCurveLinear |
                    UIViewAnimationOptionBeginFromCurrentState
                 animations:^
    {
        [sender setAlpha: 0];
    }
        completion:^(BOOL finished)
    {
        [sender removeFromSuperview];
    }];

    score++;

    [self displayNewScore: score];

    [self performSelector:@selector(spawnCactus) withObject:nil
    ➥afterDelay:(arc4random()%3) + .5];
}
```

Two seconds after any cactus are spawned, the cactusMissed: method will be called, even on cacti that have been hit. Since this method is called regardless of whether it has been hit already, it is important to provide a state check. The cactus was removed from the `superView` when it was hit, and therefore it will no longer have a `superView`. A simple `nil` check and a quick return prevent the user from losing points for cactus that were successfully hit.

You also don't want to penalize the player for pausing the game, so while the game is in the pause state, the user should not lose any life. If the method has gotten this far without returning, you know that the user has missed a cactus and needs to be penalized. As with the `cactusHit:` method, the game still needs to remove this missed cactus from the `superView` and start a timer to spawn a replacement. In addition, instead of incrementing the score, you need to decrement the user's life, and a call to `updateLife` is performed to update the display.

> **Note**
>
> The pause-state approach here creates an interesting usability bug. If you pause the game, the cactus that would have disappeared while paused will remain on the screen forever. Although there are ways to resolve this bug, for the sake of example simplicity this weakened experience was left in the game.

```objectivec
- (void)cactusMissed:(UIButton *)sender;
{
    if([sender superview] == nil)
    {
        return;
    }

    if(paused)
    {
        return;
    }

    CGRect frame = sender.frame;
    frame.origin.y += sender.frame.size.height;


    [UIView animateWithDuration:0.1
                          delay:0.0
                        options: UIViewAnimationCurveLinear |
                        UIViewAnimationOptionBeginFromCurrentState
                     animations:^
    {
        sender.frame = frame;
    }
                     completion:^(BOOL finished)
    {
        [sender removeFromSuperview];
        [self performSelector:@selector(spawnCactus)
        withObject:nil afterDelay:(arc4random()%3) + .5];
```

```
            life--;
            [self updateLife];
    }];
}
```

Displaying Life and Score

What fun would Whack-a-Cac be with no penalties for missing and no way to keep track of how well you are doing? Displaying the user's score and life are crucial game-play elements in our sample game, and both methods have been called from methods that have been looked at earlier in this section.

Turn your focus now to `displayNewScore:` in `IFCGameViewController.m`. Anytime the score is updated, a call to `displayNewScore:` is necessary to update the score display in the game. In addition to displaying the score, every time the score reaches a multiple of 10 while less than or equal to 50, a new cactus is spawned. This new cactus spawning has the effect of increasing the difficulty of the game as the player progresses.

```
- (void)displayNewScore:(float)updatedScore;
{
    int scoreInt = score;

    if(scoreInt % 10 == 0 && score <= 50)
    {
        [self spawnCactus];
    }

    scoreLabel.text = [NSString stringWithFormat: @"%06.0f",
    updatedScore];
}
```

Displaying life is similar to displaying the user's score but with some additional complexity. Instead of a text field being used to display a score, the user's life is represented with images. After a `UIImage` is created to represent each life, the first thing that must be done is to remove the existing life icons off the view. This is done with a simple tag search among the subviews. Next, a loop is performed for the number of lives the user has left, and each life icon is drawn in a row in the upper right of the game view. Finally, the game needs to check that the user still has some life left. If the user has reached zero life, a `UIAlert` informs him that the game has ended and what his final score was.

```
- (void)updateLife
{
    UIImage *lifeImage = [UIImage imageNamed:@"heart.png"];

    for(UIView *view in [self.view subviews])
    {
        if(view.tag == kLifeImageTag)
```

```
        {
            [view removeFromSuperview];
        }
    }


    for (int x = 0; x < life; x++)
    {
        UIImageView *lifeImageView = [[UIImageView alloc]
        initWithImage: lifeImage];

        lifeImageView.tag = kLifeImageTag;

        CGRect frame = lifeImageView.frame;
        frame.origin.x = 985 - (x * 30);
        frame.origin.y = 20;
        lifeImageView.frame = frame;

        [self.view addSubview: lifeImageView];
        [lifeImageView release];
    }

    if(life == 0)
    {
        gameOver = YES;
        UIAlertView *alert = [[UIAlertView alloc]
                initWithTitle:@"Game Over!"
                    message: [NSString stringWithFormat: @"You
                    ➥scored %0.0f points!", score]
                    delegate:self
            cancelButtonTitle:@"Dismiss"
            otherButtonTitles:nil];

        alert.tag = kGameOverAlert;
        [alert show];
        [alert release];
    }
}
```

Pausing and Resuming

Whack-a-Cac enables the user to pause and resume the game using the pause button in the upper-left corner of the game view. Tapping that button calls the pause: action. This method is very simple: The state variable for paused is set to YES and an alert asking the user to exit or resume is presented.

```
- (IBAction)pause:(id)sender
{
    paused = YES;

    UIAlertView *alert = [[UIAlertView alloc] initWithTitle:@""
        message:@"Game Paused!"
        delegate:self
        cancelButtonTitle:@"Exit"
        otherButtonTitles:@"Resume", nil];

    alert.tag = kPauseAlert;
    [alert show];
    [alert release];
}
```

Game over and pause both use UIAlerts to handle user responses. In the event of game over or the exit option in pause, the navigation stack is popped back to the menu screen. If the user has resumed the game, all that needs to be done is to set the pause state back to NO.

```
- (void)alertView:(UIAlertView *)alertView
➥clickedButtonAtIndex:(NSInteger)buttonIndex
{
    if(alertView.tag == kGameOverAlert)
    {
        [self.navigationController popViewControllerAnimated: YES];
    }

    else if (alertView.tag == kPauseAlert)
    {
        if(buttonIndex == 0)
        {
            [self.navigationController popViewControllerAnimated: YES];
        }
        else
        {
            paused = NO;
        }
    }
}
```

Final Thoughts on Whack-a-Cac

You should now be very familiar and confident with the gameplay and functionality of Whack-a-Cac. Although there are some additional cleanup methods that might warrant a look in the source code, depending on your usage of ARC they might not be needed. In the following sections you will learn how to add leaderboards into Whack-a-Cac.

iTunes Connect

Leaderboard data is stored on Apple's Game Center servers. To configure your app to interact with leaderboards, you must first properly configure everything in iTunes Connect. Using the iTunes Connect Portal (http://itunesconnect.apple.com), create a new app as you would when submitting an app for sale. If you already have an existing app, you can use that as well. After you have populated the basic information, your app page should look similar to the one shown in Figure 3.2.

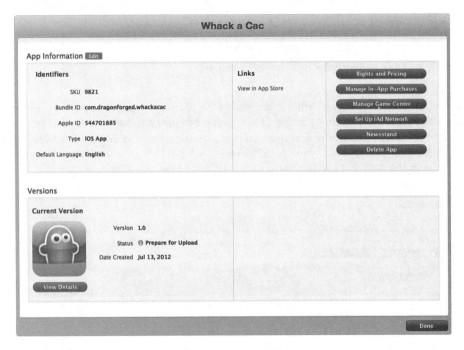

Figure 3.2   A basic app page as seen through iTunes Connect.

Warning

From the time that you create a new app in iTunes Connect, you have 90 days to submit it for approval. This policy was enacted to prevent people from name squatting app names. Although you can work around this by creating fake test apps to hook the Game Center to for testing, it is an important limitation to keep in mind.

Direct your attention to the upper-right corner of the app page, where you will find a button called Manage Game Center. This is where you will configure all the Game Center behavior for your app. Inside the Game Center configuration page the first thing you will notice is a slider to enable Game Center, as shown in Figure 3.3. Additionally, with iOS 6 and newer there is now the option of using shared leaderboards across multiple apps, such as a free and paid version. To set up shared group leaderboards, you will need to create a reference name that then can be shared across multiple apps associated with your iTunes Connect account. This configuration is done under the Move to Group option after a leaderboard has been created.

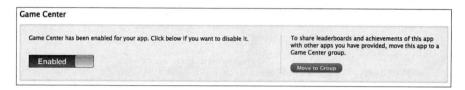

Figure 3.3   Enabling Game Center behavior in your app.

After you have enabled Game Center functionality for your app, you will need to set up the first leaderboard as shown in Figure 3.4. It is important to note that after an app has been approved and made live on the App Store, you cannot delete that leaderboard anymore. Apple has also recently provided an option to delete test data for your leaderboard. It is recommended to wipe your test data that was generated during testing before shipping your app.

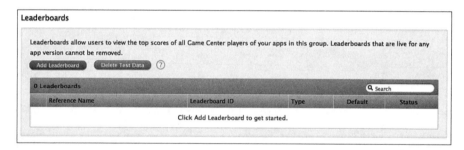

Figure 3.4   Setting up a new leaderboard.

After you have selected Add Leaderboard, you will be presented with two options. The first, Single Leaderboard, is for a standalone leaderboard, like the type used in Whack-a-Cac. The Single Leaderboard will store a set of scores for your app or a game mode within your app. The second option is for a Combined Leaderboard; this option enables you to combine two or more Single Leaderboards to create an ultimate high-score list. For example, if you have a leaderboard for each level of your game, you can create a combined leaderboard to see the top score across all levels at once. For the purpose of this chapter, you will be working only with a Single Leaderboard.

> **Note**
> Apple currently limits the number of leaderboards allowed per app to 25.

When setting up a leaderboard, you will be required to enter several fields of information, as shown in Figure 3.5. The first entry is the Leaderboard Reference Name. This field is entirely used by you within iTunes Connect to be able to quickly locate and identify the leaderboard. Leaderboard ID is the attribute that will be used to query the leaderboard within the actual project. Apple recommends using a reverse DNS system. The Leaderboard ID used for Whack-a-Cac was `com.dragonforged.whackacac.leaderboard`; if you are working with your own app, be sure to substitute whatever entry you have here in all following code examples as well.

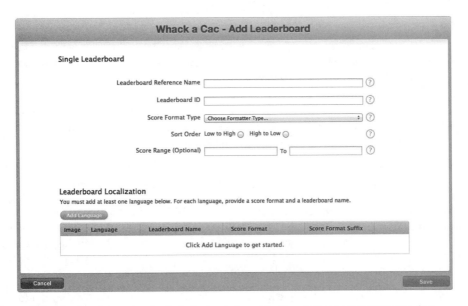

Figure 3.5   Configuring a standard single leaderboard in iTunes Connect for Whack-a-Cac.

Apple has provided several preset options for formatting the score data in the leaderboard list. In Table 3.1 examples for each type of formatting are provided.

Table 3.1   **A Detailed Breakdown of Available Score Formatting Options and Associated Sample Output**

Score Format Type	Output
Integer	123456789
Fixed Point—1 decimal	123456789.0
Fixed Point—2 decimals	123456789.01

Score Format Type	Output
Fixed Point—3 decimals	123456789.012
Elapsed Time—minutes	3:20
Elapsed Time—seconds	3:20:59
Elapsed Time—1/100th seconds	3:20:58.99
Money—whole numbers	$497,776
Money—2 decimals	$497,766.98

> **Note**
>
> If your score doesn't conform to one of the formats shown in Table 3.1, all is not lost; however, you will be required to work with custom leaderboard presentation. Retrieving raw score values is discussed in the section "Going Further with Leaderboards."

The sort-order option controls whether Game Center shows the highest score at the top of the chart or the lowest score. Additionally, you can specify a score range that will automatically drop scores that are too high or too low from being accepted by Game Center.

The final step when creating a new leaderboard is to add localization information. This is required information and you will want to provide at a minimum localized data for the app's primary language; however, you can also provide information for additional languages that you would like to support. In addition to the localized name, you have the option to fine-tune the score format, associate an image with this leaderboard, and enter the suffix to be used. When you're entering the score suffix, it is important to note that you might need a space before the entry because Game Center will print whatever is here directly after the score. For example, if you enter "Points" your score output will look like "123Points" instead of "123 Points."

After you've finished entering all the required data, you will need to hit the Save button for the changes to take effect. Even after you save, it might take several hours for the leaderboard information to become available for use on Apple's servers. Now that you have a properly configured Game Center leaderboard, you can return to your Xcode project and begin to set up the required code to interact with it.

Game Center Manager

When you are working with Game Center, it is very likely that you will have multiple classes that need to directly interact with a single shared manager. In addition to the benefits of isolating Game Center into its own manager class, it makes it very easy to drop all the required Game Center support into new projects to quickly get up and running. In the Whack-a-Cac project turn your attention to the IFCGameCenterManager class. The first thing you might notice in this class is that it is created around a singleton, which means that you will have only one instance of it in your app at any given time. The first thing that needs to be done is to create the foundation of the Game Center manager that you will be building on top of. The Game Center manager will handle all the direct Game Center interaction and will use a protocol to send a delegate information regarding the successes and failures of these calls. Since Game Center calls are not background thread safe, the manager will need to direct all delegate callbacks onto the main thread. To accomplish this, you have two new methods. The first will ensure that it is using the main thread to create callbacks with.

```
- (void)callDelegateOnMainThread: (SEL)selector withArg:(id)arg
⮡error:(NSError*)error
{
    dispatch_async(dispatch_get_main_queue(), ^(void)
    {
        [self callDelegate: selector withArg: arg error: error];
    });
}
```

The `callDelegateOnMainThread:` method will pass along all arguments and errors into the `callDelegate:` method. The first thing the `callDelegate` method does is ensure that it is being called from the main thread, which it will be if it is never called directly. Since the `callDelegate` method does not function correctly without a delegate being set, this is the next check that is performed. At this point it is clear that we are on the main thread and have a delegate. Using `respondsToSelector:` you can test whether the proper delegate method has been implemented; if it has not, some helpful information is logged as shown in this example.

```
2012-07-28 17:12:41.816 WhackACac[10121:c07] Unable to find delegate
⮡method 'gameCenterLoggedIn:' in class ICFViewController
```

When all the safety and sanity tests have been performed, the delegate method is called with the required arguments and error information. Now that a basic delegate callback system is in place, you can begin working with actual Game Center functionality.

```
- (void)callDelegate: (SEL)selector withArg: (id)arg
⮡error:(NSError*)error
{
    assert([NSThread isMainThread]);

    if(delegate == nil)
    {
        NSLog(@"Game Center Manager Delegate has not been set");
        return;
    }

    if([delegate respondsToSelector: selector])
    {
        if(arg != NULL)
        {
            [delegate performSelector: selector withObject:
```

```
            arg withObject: error];
        }

        else
        {
            [delegate performSelector: selector withObject:
            error];
        }
    }

    else
    {
        NSLog(@"Unable to find delegate method '%s' in class
        ➥%@", sel_getName(selector), [delegate class]);
    }
}
```

Authenticating

Game Center is an authenticated service, which means that you cannot do anything but authenticate when you are not logged in. With this in mind you must first authenticate before being able to proceed with any of the leaderboard relevant code. Authenticating with Game Center is handled mostly by iOS for you. The following code will present a UIAlert allowing the user to log in to Game Center or create a new Game Center account.

> **Note**
>
> Do not forget to include the GameKit.framework and import GameKit/GameKit.h whenever you are working with Game Center.

```
- (void) authenticateLocalUser
{
    if([GKLocalPlayer localPlayer].authenticated == NO)
    {
        [[GKLocalPlayer localPlayer]
        ➥authenticateWithCompletionHandler: ^(NSError *error)
        {
            if(error != nil)
            {
                NSLog(@"An error occurred: %@", [error
                ➥localizedDescription]);

                return;
            }
```

```
        [self callDelegateOnMainThread:
        ➡@selector(gameCenterLoggedIn:) withArg: NULL
        ➡error: error];
    }];
  }
}
```

In the event that an error occurs it is logged to the console. If the login completes without error, a delegate method is called. You can see how these delegate methods are set up in the `ICFGameCenterManager.h` file.

Common Authentication Errors

There are several common cases that can be helpful to catch when dealing with authentication errors. The following method is a modified version of `authenticateLocalUser` with additional error handling built in.

> **Note**
>
> If you are receiving an alert that says your game is not recognized by Game Center, check to make sure that the bundle ID of your app matches the one configured in iTunes Connect. A new app might take a few hours to have Game Center fully enabled, and a lot of Game Center problems can be resolved by waiting a little while and retrying.

```
- (void) authenticateLocalUser
{
    if([GKLocalPlayer localPlayer].authenticated == NO)
    {
        [[GKLocalPlayer localPlayer]
        ➡authenticateWithCompletionHandler:^(NSError *error)
        {
            if(error != nil)
            {
                if([error code] == GKErrorNotSupported)
                {
                    UIAlertView *alert = [[UIAlertView
                    ➡alloc] initWithTitle:@"Error"
                    ➡message:@"This device does not support
                    ➡Game Center" delegate:nil
                    ➡cancelButtonTitle:@"Dismiss"
                    ➡otherButtonTitles:nil];

                    [alert show];
                    [alert release];
                }
```

```
            else if([error code] == GKErrorCancelled)
            {
                UIAlertView *alert = [[UIAlertView
                ➥alloc] initWithTitle:@"Error"
                ➥message:@"This device has failed login
                ➥too many times from the app; you will
                ➥need to log in from the Game
                ➥Center.app" delegate:nil
                ➥cancelButtonTitle:@"Dismiss"
                ➥otherButtonTitles:nil];

                [alert show];
                [alert release];
            }

            else
            {
                UIAlertView *alert = [[UIAlertView
                ➥alloc] initWithTitle:@"Error" message:
                 ➥[error localizedDescription]
                ➥delegate:nil
                ➥cancelButtonTitle:@"Dismiss"
                ➥otherButtonTitles:nil];

                [alert show];
                [alert release];
            }

            return;
        }

    [self callDelegateOnMainThread:
    ➥@selector(gameCenterLoggedIn:) withArg: NULL
    ➥error: error];
    }];
    }
}
```

In the preceding example three additional error cases are handled. The first error that is caught is when a device does not support Game Center for any reason. In this event a UIAlert is presented to the user informing her that she is unable to access Game Center. The second error rarely appears in shipping apps but can be a real headache when debugging; if your app has failed to log in to Game Center three times in a row, Apple disables its capability to log in. In this case you must log in from the Game Center.app. The third error case is a catchall for any additional errors to provide information to the user.

Upon successful login, your user is shown a login message from Game Center. This message will also inform you of whether you are currently in a Sandbox environment, as shown in Figure 3.6.

Figure 3.6   A successful login to Game Center from the Whack-a-Cac sample game.

> **Note**
>
> Any nonshipping app will be in the Sandbox environment. After your app is downloaded from the App Store, it will be in a normal production environment.

iOS 6 Authentication

Although the preceding method of authentication continues to work on iOS 6, Apple has introduced a new streamlined approach to handling authentication on apps that do not need to support iOS 5 or older.

With the new approach, an `authenticateHandler` block is now used. Errors are captured in the same manner as in the previous examples, but now a `viewController` can be passed back to your application by Game Center. In the case in which the `viewController` parameter of the `authenticateHandler` block is not `nil`, you are expected to display the `viewController` to the user.

The first time a new `authenticateHandler` is set, the app will automatically authenticate. Additionally, the app will automatically reauthenticate on return to the foreground. If you do need to call `authenticate` manually, you can use the `authenticate` method.

```
-(void)authenticateLocalUseriOSSix
{
    if([GKLocalPlayer localPlayer].authenticateHandler == nil)
    {
        [[GKLocalPlayer localPlayer]
        ➥setAuthenticateHandler:^(UIViewController
        ➥*viewController, NSError *error)
        {
            if(error != nil)
            {
                if([error code] == GKErrorNotSupported)
                {
                    UIAlertView *alert = [[UIAlertView alloc]
                    ➥initWithTitle:@"Error" message:@"This
                    ➥device does not support Game Center"
                    ➥delegate:nil cancelButtonTitle:@"Dismiss"
                    ➥otherButtonTitles:nil];

                    [alert show];
                    [alert release];
                }

                else if([error code] == GKErrorCancelled)
                {
                    UIAlertView *alert = [[UIAlertView alloc]
                    ➥initWithTitle:@"Error" message:@"This
                    ➥device has failed login too many times from
                    ➥the app; you will need to log in from the
                    ➥Game Center.app" delegate:nil
                    ➥cancelButtonTitle:@"Dismiss"
                    ➥otherButtonTitles:nil];

                    [alert show];
                    [alert release];
                }

                else
```

```
        {
                UIAlertView *alert = [[UIAlertView alloc]
                ➥initWithTitle:@"Error" message:[error
                ➥localizedDescription] delegate:nil
                ➥cancelButtonTitle:@"Dismiss"
                ➥otherButtonTitles:nil];

                [alert show];
                [alert release];
        }
    }

    else
    {
        if(viewController != nil)
        {
                [(UIViewController *)delegate
                ➥presentViewController:viewController
                ➥animated:YES completion: nil];
        }
    }
    }];
    }

    else
    {
        [[GKLocalPlayer localPlayer] authenticate];
    }
}
```

Submitting Scores

When authenticated with Game Center, you are ready to begin submitting scores. In the
IFCGameCenterManager class there is a method called reportScore:forCategory. This
allows you to post a new score for the Leaderboard ID that was configured in iTunes Connect.
All new scores are submitted by creating a new GKScore object; this object holds onto several
values such as the score value, playerID, date, rank, formattedValue, category, and context.

When a new score is submitted, most of this data is automatically populated. The value and
category are the only two required fields. An optional context can be provided which is an
arbitrary 64-bit unsigned integer. A context can be used to store additional information about
the score, such as game settings or flags that were on when the score was achieved; it can be set
and retrieved using the context property. The date, playerID, formattedValue, and rank are
read-only and are populated automatically when the GKScore object is created or retrieved.

> **Note**
>
> Leaderboards support default categories when being set in iTunes Connect. If a score is being submitted to a default leaderboard, the `category` parameter can be left blank. It is best practice to always include a `category` argument to prevent hard-to-track-down bugs.

After a new `GKScore` object has been created using the proper category for the leaderboard, you can assign a raw score value. When dealing with integers or floats, the score is simply the number of the score. When dealing with elapsed time, however, the value should be submitted in seconds or seconds with decimal places if tracking that level of accuracy.

When a score has been successfully submitted, it will call `gameCenterScoreReported:` on the `GameCenterManager` delegate. This is discussed in more detail in the next section, "Adding Scores to Whack-a-Cac."

```
- (void) reportScore: (int64_t) score forCategory: (NSString*) category
{
    GKScore *scoreReporter = [[[GKScore alloc]
    initWithCategory:category] autorelease];

    scoreReporter.value = score;

    [scoreReporter reportScoreWithCompletionHandler: ^(NSError *error)
    {
        if (error != nil)
        {
            NSData* savedScoreData = [NSKeyedArchiver
            ➥archivedDataWithRootObject:scoreReporter];

            [self storeScoreForLater: savedScoreData];
        }

        [self callDelegateOnMainThread:@selector
        ➥(gameCenterScoreReported:) withArg: NULL error:
        ➥error];
    }];
}
```

It is important to look at the failure block of `reportScoreWithCompletionHandler`. If a score fails to successfully transmit to Game Center, it is your responsibility as the developer to attempt to resubmit this score later. There are few things more frustrating to a user than losing a high score due to a bug or network failure. In the preceding code example, when a score has failed, `NSKeyedArchiver` is used to create a copy of the object as `NSData` and passed to `storeScoreForLater:`. It is critical that the `GKScore` object itself is used, and not just the score value. Game Center ranks scores by date if the scores match; since the date is populated automatically when creating a new `GKScore`, the only way to not lose the player's info is to archive the entire `GKScore` object.

When saving the score data, the sample app uses the NSUserDefaults; this data could also be easily stored into Core Data or any other storage system. After the score is saved, it is important to retry sending that data when possible. A good time to do this is when Game Center successfully authenticates.

```
- (void)storeScoreForLater:(NSData *)scoreData;
{
    NSMutableArray *savedScoresArray = [[NSMutableArray alloc]
    ➥initWithArray: [[NSUserDefaults standardUserDefaults]
    objectForKey:@"savedScores"]];

    [savedScoresArray addObject: scoreData];

    [[NSUserDefaults standardUserDefaults]
    ➥setObject:savedScoresArray forKey:@"savedScores"];

    [savedScoresArray release];
}
```

The attempt to resubmit the saved scores is no different than submitting a score initially. First the scores need to be retrieved from the NSUserDefaults, and since the object was stored in NSData, that data needs to be converted back into a GKScore object. Once again, it is important to catch failed submissions and try them again later.

```
-(void)submitAllSavedScores
{
    NSMutableArray *savedScoreArray = [[NSMutableArray alloc]
    ➥initWithArray: [[NSUserDefaults standardUserDefaults]
    ➥objectForKey:@"savedScores"]];

    [[NSUserDefaults standardUserDefaults] removeObjectForKey:
    ➥@"savedScores"];

    for(NSData *scoreData in savedScoreArray)
    {
        GKScore *scoreReporter = [NSKeyedUnarchiver
        ➥unarchiveObjectWithData: scoreData];

        [scoreReporter reportScoreWithCompletionHandler:
        ➥^(NSError *error)
        {
            if (error != nil)
            {
                NSData* savedScoreData = [NSKeyedArchiver
                ➥archivedDataWithRootObject: scoreReporter];
```

```
                    [self storeScoreForLater: savedScoreData];
            }

        else
        {
            NSLog(@"Successfully submitted scores that
            ➥were pending submission");

            [self callDelegateOnMainThread:
            ➥@selector(gameCenterScroreReported:)
            ➥withArg:NULL error:error];
        }
    }];
    }
}
```

> **Tip**
>
> If a score does fail to submit, it is always a good idea to inform the user that the app will try to
> submit again later; otherwise, it might seem as though the app has failed to submit the score
> and lost the data for the user.

Adding Scores to Whack-a-Cac

In the preceding section the Game Center Manager component of adding scores to an app was
explored. In this section you will learn how to put these additions into practice in Whack-
a-Cac. Before proceeding, Game Center must first authenticate a user and specify a delegate.
Modify the `viewDidLoad` method of `IFCViewController.m` to complete this process.

```
- (void)viewDidLoad
{
    [super viewDidLoad];

    [[ICFGameCenterManager sharedManager] setDelegate: self];
    [[ICFGameCenterManager sharedManager] authenticateLocalUser];
}
```

`IFCViewController` will also need to respond to the `GameCenterManagerDelegate`.
The first delegate method that needs to be handled is `gameCenterLoggedIn:`. Since the
`GameCenterManager` is handling all the `UIAlerts` associated with informing the user of failures, any errors here are simply logged for debugging purposes.

```
- (void)gameCenterLoggedIn:(NSError*)error
{
    if(error != nil)
    {
        NSLog(@"An error occurred trying to log into Game
```

```
   ➥Center: %@", [error localizedDescription]);
   }

   else
   {
       NSLog(@"Successfully logged into Game Center!");
   }
}
```

After the user has decided to begin a new game of Whack-a-Cac, it is important to update the `GameCenterManager`'s delegate to the `IFCGameViewController` class. In Whack-a-Cavc the delegate will always be set to the front-most view to simplify providing user feedback and errors. This is done by adding the following line of code to the `viewDidLoad:` method of `IFCGameViewController`. Don't forget to declare this class as conforming to `GameCenterManagerDelegate`.

```
[[ICFGameCenterManager sharedManager] setDelegate: self];
```

The game will need to submit a score under two scenarios: when the user loses a game, and when the user quits from the pause menu. Using the `IFCGameCenterManager`, submitting a score is very easy. Add the following line of code to both the test for zero life in the `updateLife` method and the exit button action on the pause `UIAlert`:

```
[[ICFGameCenterManager sharedManager] reportScore:
➥(int64_t) scoreforCategory:
➥@"com.dragonforged.whackacac.leaderboard"];
```

> **Note**
>
> The category ID you set for your leaderboard might differ from the one used in these examples. Be sure that the one used matches the ID that appears in iTunes Connect.

While the `GameCenterManager` `reportScore:` method will handle submitting the scores and all error recovery, it is important to add the delegate method `gameCenterScoreReported:` to watch for potential errors and successes.

```
- (void) gameCenterScoreReported: (NSError *) error;
{
    if(error != nil)
    {
        NSLog(@"An error occurred trying to report a score to
        ➥Game Center: %@", [error localizedDescription]);
    }

    else
    {
        NSLog(@"Successfully submitted score");
    }
}
```

> **Note**
>
> Scores should be submitted only when finalized; sending scores to Game Center at every incre-
> ment can create a poor user experience.

When a user is exiting the game, the delegate for `GameCenterManager` will disappear while
the network operations for submitting the score are still taking place. It is important to have
`IFCViewController` reset the `GameCenterManagerDelegate` to `SELF` and implement the
`gameCenterScoreReported:` delegate as well.

Presenting Leaderboards

A new high score is not of much use to your users if they are unable to view their high scores.
In this section you will learn how to use Apple's built-in view controllers to present the leaderboards. The leaderboard view controllers saw significant improvements with the introduction
of iOS 6, as shown in Figure 3.7. In previous versions of iOS, leaderboards and achievements
were handled by two separate view controllers; these have now been combined. In addition, a
new section for Game Center challenges and Facebook liking have been added.

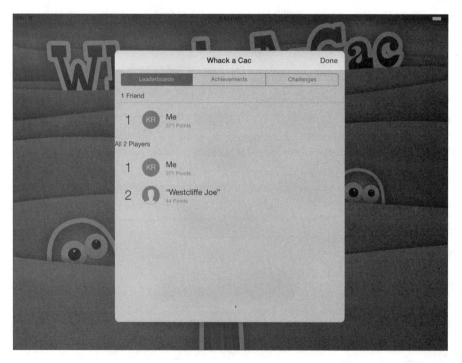

Figure 3.7   The `GKLeaderboardViewController` saw major improvements and changes in
iOS 6.

In `ICFViewController` there is a method called `leaderboards:` that handles presenting the leaderboard view controllers. When a new `GKLeaderboardViewController` is being created, there are a couple of properties that need to be addressed. First set the category. This is the same category that is used for submitting scores and refers to which leaderboard should be presented to the user. A `timeScope` can also be provided, which will default the user onto the correct tab as shown in Figure 3.7. In the following example the time scope for all time is supplied. Additionally, a required `leaderboardDelegate` must be provided; this delegate will handle dismissing the leaderboard modal.

```
- (IBAction)leaderboards:(id)sender
{
    GKLeaderboardViewController *leaderboardViewController =
    [[GKLeaderboardViewController alloc] init];

    if(leaderboardViewController == nil)
    {
        NSLog(@"Unable to create leaderboard view controller");
        return;
    }

    leaderboardViewController.category =
    ➥@"com.dragonforged.whackacac.leaderboard";

    leaderboardViewController.timeScope =
    ➥GKLeaderboardTimeScopeAllTime;

    leaderboardViewController.leaderboardDelegate = self;

    [self presentViewController:leaderboardViewController
    ➥animated:YES completion: nil];

    [leaderboardViewController release];
}
```

For a `GKLeaderboardViewController` to be fully functional, a delegate method must also be provided. When this method is invoked, it is required that the view controller be dismissed as shown in this code snippet:

```
- (void)leaderboardViewControllerDidFinish:(GKLeaderboardViewController
➥*) viewController
{
    [self dismissModalViewControllerAnimated: YES completion: nil];
}
```

> **Note**
>
> In iOS 6 the `GKLeaderboardViewController` will bring up a combined view controller for challenges, leaderboards, and achievements. In iOS 4 and 5 it will present just the leaderboard view controller.

The preceding example works on iOS 4.1 and up; however, in iOS 6 a new class was provided to streamline the process of presenting leaderboards and achievements. The following example will function only on iOS 6 and newer:

```
- (IBAction)leaderboards:(id)sender
{
    [[GKGameCenterViewController sharedController] setDelegate:
    self];

    [[GKGameCenterViewController sharedController]
    setLeaderboardCategory:
    @"com.dragonforged.whackacac.leaderboard"];

    [[GKGameCenterViewController sharedController]
    setLeaderboardTimeScope:GKLeaderboardTimeScopeAllTime];

    [self presentViewController:[GKGameCenterViewController
    sharedController] animated:YES completion: nil];
}
```

There is also a new delegate method to be used with this view controller. It is implemented in the following fashion:

```
- (void)gameCenterViewControllerDidFinish:(GKGameCenterViewController
*)gameCenterViewController
{
    [self dismissModalViewControllerAnimated: YES completion: nil];
}
```

It is also possible to work with the raw leaderboard data and create customized leaderboards. For more information on this, see the later section "Going Further with Leaderboards."

Score Challenges

iOS 6 introduced Challenges into the Game Center functionality. Challenges enable your users to dare their Game Center friends to beat their high scores or achievements. They provide a great avenue for your users to socially spread your game to their friends. All the work with Challenges are handled for you by Game Center using the new `GameCenterViewController`, as shown in the previous example and in Figure 3.8. However, it is also possible to create challenges in code. Calling `issueChallengeToPlayers:withMessage:` on a `GKScore` object will initiate the challenge. When a player beats a challenge, it automatically rechallenges the person who initiated the original challenge.

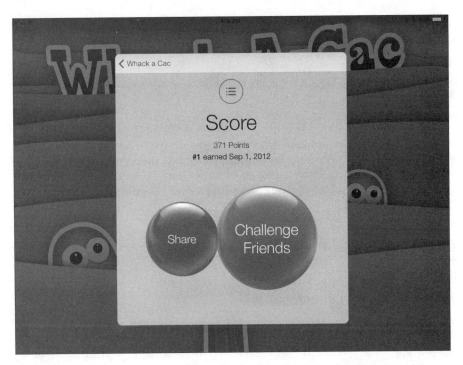

Figure 3.8   Challenging a friend to beat a score using iOS 6's built-in Game Center challenges.

```
[(GKScore *)score issueChallengeToPlayers: (NSArray *)players
➥message:@"Can you beat me?"];
```

It is also possible to retrieve an array of all pending GKChallenges for the authenticated user by implementing the following code:

```
[GKChallenge loadReceivedChallengesWithCompletionHandler:^(NSArray
➥*challenges, NSError *error)
{
    if (error != nil)
    {
        NSLog(@"An error occurred: %@", [error localizedDescription]);
    }

    else
    {
        NSLog(@"Challenges: %@", challenges);
    }
}];
```

A challenge exists in one of four states: invalid, pending, completed, and declined.

```
if(challenge.state == GKChallengeStateCompleted)
    NSLog(@"Challenge Completed");
```

Finally, it is possible to decline an incoming challenge by simply calling `decline` on it as shown here:

```
[challenge decline];
```

Challenges create a great opportunity to have your users do your marketing for you. If a user challenges someone who has not yet downloaded your game, that person will be prompted to buy it. Challenges are provided for you for no effort by Game Center using the default GUI, and using the earlier examples, it is fairly easy to implement your own challenge system.

> **Note**
>
> Whack-a-Cac does not implement code-based challenges.

Going Further with Leaderboards

The focus of this chapter has been implementing leaderboards using Apple's standard Game Center GUI; however, it is entirely possible to implement a customized leaderboard system within your app. In this section, a brief introduction will be given to working with raw `GKScore` values, as well as retrieving specific information from the Game Center servers.

The following method can be added to the `ICFGameCenterManager`. This method accepts four different arguments. The first, `category`, is the leaderboard ID set in iTunes Connect for the leaderboard that this request will pertain to. This is followed by `withPlayerScore:`, which accepts `GKLeaderboarPlayerScopeGlobal` or `GKLeaderboarPlayerScopeFriendsOnly`. `TimeScope` will retrieve scores for today, this week, or all time. The last argument required is for range. Here you can specify receiving scores that match a certain range. For example, `NSMakeRange(1, 50)` will retrieve the top 50 scores.

```
- (void)retrieveScoresForCategory:(NSString *)category
➥withPlayerScope:(GKLeaderboardPlayerScope)playerScope
➥timeScope:(GKLeaderboardTimeScope)timeScope
➥withRange:(NSRange)range
{
    GKLeaderboard *leaderboardRequest = [[GKLeaderboard alloc] init];

    leaderboardRequest.playerScope = playerScope;
    leaderboardRequest.timeScope = timeScope;
    leaderboardRequest.range = range;
    leaderboardRequest.category = category;
```

```
[leaderboardRequest loadScoresWithCompletionHandler: ^(NSArray
➥*scores,NSError *error)
{
    [self callDelegateOnMainThread:@selector
    (scoreDataUpdated:error:) withArg:scores error: error];
}];
}
```

There will also be a newly associated delegate callback for this request called scoreDataUpdated:error:.

```
-(void)scoreDataUpdated:(NSArray *)scores error:(NSError *)error
{
    if(error != nil)
    {
        NSLog(@"An error occurred: %@", [error localizedDescription]);
    }
    else
    {
        NSLog(@"The following scores were retrieved: %@", scores);
    }
}
```

If this example were to be introduced into Whack-a-Cac, it could look like the following:

```
-(void)fetchScore
{
    [[ICFGameCenterManager sharedManager]
    ➥retrieveScoresForCategory:
    ➥@"com.dragonforged.whackacac.leaderboard"
    ➥withPlayerScope:GKLeaderboardPlayerScopeGlobal
    ➥timeScope:GKLeaderboardTimeScopeAllTime
    ➥withRange:NSMakeRange(1, 50)];
}
```

The delegate method will print something similar to the following:

```
2012-07-29 14:38:03.874 WhackACac[14437:c07] The following scores were
➥retrieved: (

"<GKScore: 0x83c5010>player:G:94768768 rank:1 date:2012-07-28 23:54:19
➥+0000 value:201 formattedValue:201 Points context:0x0"
)
```

> **Tip**
>
> To find the displayName for the GKPlayer associated with a GKScore, use [(GKPlayer *) player displayName]. Don't forget to cache this data because it requires a network call.

Summary

Game Center leaderboards are an easy and fun way to increase the social factor of your game or app. Users love to compete and with iOS 6's Game Center Challenge system it is easier than ever for users to share apps that they love. In this chapter you learned how to fully integrate Game Center's leaderboards into your game or app. You should now have a strong understanding of not only Game Center authenticating but also submitting scores and error recovery. Chapter 4 will continue to expand on the capabilities of Game Center by adding social achievements to the Whack-a-Cac game.

Exercises

1. Modify Whack-a-Cac to use a custom table view for retrieving and presenting scores.

2. Modify Whack-a-Cac to use a timer-based score system instead of an integer-based system; the longer the player stays alive, the higher the score the player will earn.

Achievements

Like leaderboards, achievements are quickly becoming a vital component of modern gaming. Although the history of achievements isn't as well cemented into gaming history as that of leaderboards, today it could be argued that they are even more important to the social success of a game.

An achievement is, in short, an unlockable accomplishment that, although not necessary to the completion of a game, tracks the user's competition of additional aspects of the game. Commonly, achievements are issued for additional side tasks or extended play, such as beating a game on hard difficulty, exploring areas, or collecting items. One of the primary features of Game Center is the achievement system, which makes adding your own achievements to your game much simpler than it was previously.

Unlike most other chapters, this chapter shares the sample app, Whack-a-Cac, with Chapter 3, "Leaderboards." Although it is not necessary to complete that chapter before beginning this one, there are several instances of overlap. For the sake of the environment and trees, that information will not be reprinted here; it is recommended that you read the "Whack-a-Cac," "iTunes Connect," "Game Center Manager," and "Authenticating" sections of Chapter 3 before proceeding with this chapter. These sections provide the background required to interact with the sample app as well as the basic task of setting up Game Center and authenticating the local user. This chapter continues to expand on the already existing Game Center Manager sample code provided to you in Chapter 3.

iTunes Connect

Before beginning to write code within Xcode for achievements, first visit iTunes Connect (http://itunesconnect.apple.com) to set up the achievements. For an introduction to working with Game Center in iTunes Connect, see the "iTunes Connect" section of Chapter 3.

When entering the Manage Game Center section of iTunes Connect, there are two configuration options: one to set up leaderboards, and the other to set up achievements. In the sample app, Whack-a-Cac, there will be six achievements.

To create a new achievement, click the Add Achievement button, as shown in Figure 4.1.

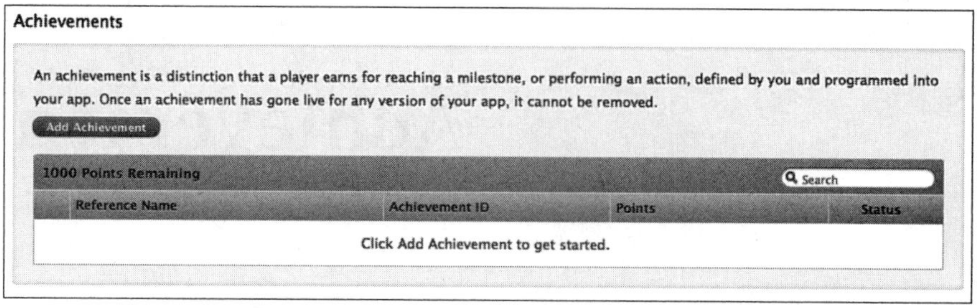

Figure 4.1   A view of the Achievements section before any achievements have been added in iTunes Connect.

Similar to the leaderboards from Chapter 3, several fields are required in order to set up a new achievement, as shown in Figure 4.2. The Achievement Reference Name is simply a reference to your achievement in iTunes Connect; it is not seen anywhere outside of the Web portal. Achievement ID, on the other hand, is what will be referenced from the code in order to interact with the achievement. Apple recommends the use of a reverse DNS type of system for the Achievement ID, such as com.dragonforged.whackacac.100whacks.

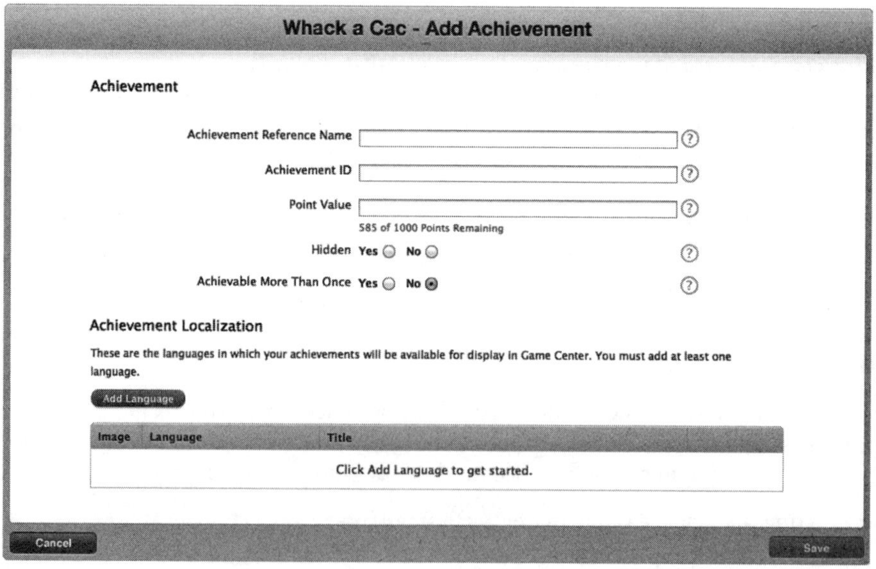

Figure 4.2   Adding a new achievement in iTunes Connect.

The Point Value attribute is unique to achievements in Game Center. Achievements can have an assigned point value from 1 to 100. Each app can have a maximum of 1,000 achievement points. Points can be used to denote difficulty or value of an achievement. The achievement points are not required, nor are they required to add up to exactly 1,000.

Also unique to achievements is the Hidden property, which keeps the achievement hidden from the user until it has been achieved or the user has made any progress toward achieving it. The Achievable More Than Once setting is new to iOS 6; it allows the user to accept Game Center challenges based on achievements that they have previously earned.

As with leaderboards, at least one localized description needs to be set up for each achievement. This information consists of four attributes. The title will appear above the achievement description. Each achievement will have two descriptions, one that will be displayed before the user unlocks it and one that is displayed after it has been completed. Additionally, an image will need to be supplied for each achievement; the image must be at least 512×512 in size. To see how this information is laid out, see Figure 4.3.

> **Note**
>
> As with leaderboards, after an achievement has gone live in a shipping app, it cannot be removed.

See the section "Adding Achievements into Whack-a-Cac" for a walk-through of adding several achievements into the sample game.

Displaying Achievement Progress

Without being able to display the current progress of achievements to the user, they are next to useless. If required to present a custom interface for achievements, refer to the section "Going Further with Achievements." The following method launches the combined Game Center View Controller that is new in iOS 6, as shown in Figure 4.3:

```
- (void)showAchievements
{
    [[GKGameCenterViewController sharedController] setDelegate:self];

    [[GKGameCenterViewController sharedController]
    ➡setViewState:GKGameCenterViewControllerStateAchievements];

    [self presentViewController:[GKGameCenterViewController
    ➡sharedController] animated:YES completion: nil];
}
```

Figure 4.3   The new combined Game Center View Controller, launching to the Achievement section.

In the preceding method, used to launch the new iOS 6 Game Center View Controller, you will notice that a delegate was set. There is also a new required delegate method to be used with this view controller, and it is implemented in the following fashion:

```
- (void)gameCenterViewControllerDidFinish:(GKGameCenterViewController
➥*)gameCenterViewController
{
    [self dismissModalViewControllerAnimated: YES completion: nil];
}
```

It might be necessary to support devices that are not yet running iOS 6. In that instance, you need to implement a different method of displaying achievements. When you use the older version of displaying achievements on devices running iOS 6, it will present a view controller identical to the iOS 6 version, as shown in Figure 4.3. The sample game uses the pre-iOS 6 type of implementation.

A new instance of GKAchievementViewController is allocated and initialized, followed by a delegate being set. The view is presented the same as any modal view controller and the memory is then cleaned up.

```
- (IBAction)achievements:(id)sender
{
    GKAchievementViewController *achievementViewController =
    ➥[[GKAchievementViewController alloc] init];

    if(achievementViewController == nil)
    {
        NSLog(@"Unable to create achievement view controller");
        return;
    }

    achievementViewController.achievementDelegate = self;

    [self presentViewController:achievementViewController
    ➥animated:YES completion: nil];

    [achievementViewController release];
}
```

There is also a required delegate method that is attached to using this approach. The following method must be implemented. Don't forget to declare that the class conforms to the GKAchievementViewControllerDelegate protocol.

```
- (void)achievementViewControllerDidFinish:(GKAchievementViewController
➥*)viewController
{
    [self dismissModalViewControllerAnimated: YES completion: nil];
}
```

Game Center Manager and Authentication

In Chapter 3, a new reusable class called Game Center Manager was introduced. This class provides the groundwork for quickly implementing Game Center into your apps. That information will not be reprinted in this chapter. Reference the sections "Game Center Manager" and "Authenticating" in Chapter 3 before continuing with the material in this chapter.

The Achievement Cache

When a score is being submitted to Game Center, it's simply a matter of sending the score in and having Game Center determine its value compared to previously submitted scores. However, achievements are a bit tricky; all achievements have a percentage complete value, and users can work toward completing an achievement over many days or even months. It is important to make sure that users don't lose the progress they have already earned and that they continue to make steady progress toward their goals. This is solved by using an achievement cache to store all of the cloud achievement data locally and refresh it with each new session.

A new convenience method will need to be added to the ICFGameCenterManager class, as well as a new classwide NSMutableDictionary, which will be called achievementDictionary. The first thing that is done in this method is to post an alert if it is being run after an achievement cache has already been established. Although you should not attempt to populate the cache more than once, it will not cause anything to stop functioning as expected. If the achievementDictionary does not yet exist, a new NSMutableDictionary will need to be allocated and initialized.

After the achievementDictionary is created, it can be populated with the data from the Game Center servers. This is accomplished by calling the loadAchievementsWithCompletionHandler class method on GKAchievement. The resulting block will return the user's progress for all achievements. If no errors are returned an array of GKAchievements will be returned. These are then inserted into the achievementDictionary using the achievement identifier as the key.

> **Note**
>
> The loadAchievementsWithCompletionHandler method does not return GKAchievement objects for achievements that do not have progress stored on them yet.

```
-(void)populateAchievementCache
{
    if(achievementDictionary != nil)
    {
        NSLog(@"Repopulating achievement cache: %@",
        achievementDictionary);
    }

    else
    {
        achievementDictionary = [[NSMutableDictionary alloc] init];
    }


    [GKAchievement loadAchievementsWithCompletionHandler:^(NSArray
    ➥*achievements, NSError *error)
    {

        if(error != nil)
        {
            NSLog(@"An error occurred while populating the
            ➥achievement cache: %@", [error localizedDescription]);
        }

        else
        {
```

```
        for(GKAchievement *achievement in achievements)
        {
            [achievementDictionary setObject:achievement
            ➥forKey:[achievement identifier]];
        }
    }
}];
}
```

> **Note**
>
> You cannot make any Game Center calls until a local user has been successfully authenticated.

Reporting Achievements

After an achievement cache has been implemented, it is safe to submit progress on an achievement. A new method `reportAchievement:withPercentageComplete:` will need to be added to the `ICFGameManager` class to accomplish this task. When this method is called, the achievement ID and percentage complete are used as arguments. For information on how to determine the current percentage of an achievement, see the section "Adding Achievement Hooks."

When submitting achievement progress, the first thing that needs to be done is make sure that the `achievementDictionary` has already been populated. Making sure to check Game Center for the current progress of any achievements prevents users from losing progress when switching devices or reinstalling the app. In this example we fail out with a log message if `achievementDictionary` is nil; however, a more complex system of initializing and populating the achievement cache and retrying can be implemented as well.

After it has been determined that the `achievementDictionary` is initialized, a new `GKAchievement` object is created. When created, the `GKAchievement` object is stored in the `achievementDictionary` using the achievement identifier. If this achievement has not yet been progressed, it will not appear in the `achievementDictionary` and the achievement object will be `nil`. In this case a new instance of `GKAchievement` is allocated and initialized using the achievement identifier.

If the achievement object is non-`nil`, it can be assumed that the achievement has previously had some sort of progress made. A safety check is performed to make sure that the percentage complete that is being submitted isn't lower than the percentage complete that was found on Game Center. Additionally, a check is performed to make sure that the achievement isn't already fully completed. In either case an `NSLog` is printed to the console and the method returns.

At this point, a valid `GKAchievement` object has been created or retrieved and the percentage complete is greater than the one that is in the cache. A call on the achievement object with `setPercentComplete:` is used to update the percentage-complete value. At this point the achievement object is also stored back into the `achievementDictionary` so that the local achievement cache is up-to-date.

To report the actual achievement value to Game Center, `reportAchievementWith CompletionHandler:` is called on the achievement object. When it is finished checking for errors, a new delegate callback is used to inform the `GameCenterManager` Delegate of the success or failure.

```
-(void)reportAchievement:(NSString *)identifier
 withPercentageComplete:(double)percentComplete
{
    if(achievementDictionary == nil)
    {
            NSLog(@"An achievement cache must be populated before
            ➡submitting achievement progress");

            return;
    }

    GKAchievement *achievement = [achievementDictionary objectForKey: identifier];

    if(achievement == nil)
    {
        achievement = [[[GKAchievement alloc]
        ➡initWithIdentifier: identifier] autorelease];

        [achievement setPercentComplete: percentComplete];

        [achievementDictionary setObject: achievement forKey:identifier];
    }

    else
    {
        if([achievement percentComplete] >= 100.0 || [achievement
        ➡percentComplete] >= percentComplete)
        {
            NSLog(@"Attempting to update achievement %@ which is either
            ➡already completed or is decreasing percentage complete
            ➡(%f)", identifier, percentComplete);

            return;
        }

            [achievement setPercentComplete: percentComplete];
```

```
            [achievementDictionary setObject: achievement forKey:identifier];
    }

    [achievement reportAchievementWithCompletionHandler:^(NSError *error)
    {
            if(error != nil)
            {
                NSLog(@"There was an error submitting achievement
                ➥%@:%@", identifier, [error localizedDescription]);
            }

            [self callDelegateOnMainThread:
            ➥@selector (gameCenterAchievementReported:)
            ➥withArg: NULL error:error];
    }];
}
```

> **Note**
>
> Achievements like leaderboards in Chapter 3 will not attempt to resubmit if they fail to success-
> fully reach the Game Center servers. The developer is solely responsible for catching errors and
> resubmitting achievements later. However, unlike with leaderboards, there is no stored date
> property so it isn't necessary to store the actual GKAchievement object.

Adding Achievement Hooks

Arguably the most difficult aspect of incorporating achievements into your iOS app is hooking
them into the workflow. For example, the player might earn an achievement after collecting
100 coins in a role-playing game. Every time a coin is collected, the app will need to update the
achievement value.

A more difficult example is an achievement such as play one match a week for six months. This
requires a number of hooks and checks to make sure that the user is meeting the requirements
of the achievement. Although attempting to document every single possible hook is a bit ambi-
tious, the section "Adding Achievements into Whack-a-Cac" has several types of hooks that
will be demonstrated.

Before an achievement can be progressed, first your app must determine its current progress. Since Game Center achievements don't take progressive arguments (for example, add
1% completion to existing completion), this legwork is left up to the developer. Following
is a convenience for quickly getting back a GKAchievement object for any identifier. After a

GKAchievement object has been returned, a query to percentageComplete can be made to determine the current progress.

```
-(GKAchievement *)achievementForIdentifier:(NSString *)identifier
{
    GKAchievement *achievement = nil;

    achievement = [achievementDictionary objectForKey:identifier];

    if(achievement == nil)
    {
        achievement = [[[GKAchievement alloc]
        ➥initWithIdentifier:identifier] autorelease];

        [achievementDictionary setObject: achievement forKey:identifier];
    }

    return achievement;
}
```

If the achievement requires more precision than 1%, the true completion value cannot be retrieved from Game Center. Game Center will return and accept only whole numbers for percentage complete. In this case you have two possible options. The easy path is to round off to the nearest percentage. A slightly more difficult approach would be to store the true value locally and use that to calculate the percentage. Keep in mind that a player might be using more than one device, and storing a true achievement progress locally can be problematic in these cases; refer to Chapter 8, "Getting Started with iCloud," for additional solutions.

Completion Banners

In iOS 5.0, Apple added the capability to use an automatic message to let the user know that an achievement has been successfully earned. If supporting an iOS version that predates iOS 5, you will need to implement a custom system. There is no functional requirement to inform users that they have completed an achievement beyond providing a good user experience.

To automatically show achievement completion, set the showsCompletionBanner property to YES before submitting the achievement to Game Center, as shown in Figure 4.4. A good place to add this line of code is in the reportAchievement: withPercentageComplete: method.

```
achievement.showsCompletionBanner = YES;
```

Figure 4.4   A Game Center automatic achievement completion banner shown on an iPad with the achievement title and earned description.

Achievement Challenges

iOS 6 brought a new feature to Game Center called Challenges, in which a user can challenge a Game Center friend to beat her score or match her achievements, as shown in Figure 4.5.

> **Note**
>
> Game Center allows the user to challenge a friend to beat an unearned achievement as long as it is visible to the user.

```
- (void) showChallenges
{
    [[GKGameCenterViewController sharedController]setDelegate:self];

    [[GKGameCenterViewController sharedController] setViewState:
    ➥GKGameCenterViewControllerStateAchievements];
```

```
    [self presentViewController:[GKGameCenterViewController
↵sharedController] animated:YES completion: nil];
}
```

The `gameCenterViewControllerDidFinish` delegate method will also need to be implemented if that was not already done for the previous examples in this chapter.

```
- (void)gameCenterViewControllerDidFinish:(GKGameCenterViewController
↵*)gameCenterViewController
{
    [self dismissModalViewControllerAnimated: YES completion: nil];
}
```

Figure 4.5   Challenging a friend to complete an achievement that is still being progressed.

> **Note**
>
> If users need to be able to accept achievement challenges for achievements that they have
> already earned, you will need to select the Achievable More Than Once option when creating
> the achievement in iTunes Connect.

A challenge can also be created pragmatically using the following approach:

```
[(GKAchievement *)achievement issueChallengeToPlayers: (NSArray
➥*)players message:@"I earned this achievement, can you?"];
```

If it is required to get a list of users that can receive an achievement challenge for a particular achievement (if you do not have the Achievable More Than Once property set to on), use the following snippet to get a list of those users:

```
[achievement selectChallengeablePlayerIDs:arrayOfPlayersToCheck
➥withCompletionHandler:^(NSArray *challengeablePlayerIDs, NSError
➥*error)
{
      if(error != nil)
      {
            NSLog(@"An error occurred while retrieving a list of
            ➥challengeable players: %@", [error localizedDescription]);
      }

      NSLog(@"The following players can be challenged: %@",
      ➥challengeablePlayerIDs);
}];
```

It is also possible to retrieve an array of all pending GKChallenges for the authenticated user by implementing the following code:

```
[GKChallenge loadReceivedChallengesWithCompletionHandler:^(NSArray
➥*challenges, NSError *error)
{
      if (error != nil)
      {
            NSLog(@"An error occurred: %@", [error
            ➥localizedDescription]);
      }

      else
      {
            NSLog(@"Challenges: %@", challenges);
      }

}];
```

Challenges have states associated with them that can be queried on the current state of the challenge. The SDK provides the states invalid, pending, completed, and declined.

```
if(challenge.state == GKChallengeStateCompleted)
      NSLog(@"Challenge Completed");
```

Finally, it is possible to decline an incoming challenge by simply calling `decline` on it, as shown here:

```
[challenge decline];
```

Challenges are an exciting new feature of iOS 6. By leveraging them and encouraging users to challenge their friends, you will increase the retention rates and play times of the game. If using the built-in GUI for Game Center, you don't even have to write any additional code to support challenges.

> **Note**
>
> Whack-a-Cac does not contain sample code for creating programmatic achievement challenges.

Adding Achievements into Whack-a-Cac

Whack-a-Cac will be using six different achievements using various hook methods. The achievements that will be implemented are listed and described in Table 4.1.

Table 4.1   **Achievements Used in Whack-a-Cac with Details on Required Objectives to Earn**

Achievement ID	Description
`com.dragonforged.whackacac.killone`	Achieved after whacking your first cactus. This is also a hidden achievement and it will not be visible to the user until it is earned.
`com.dragonforged.whackacac.score100`	Achieved after reaching a score of 100 in a single game. This achievement is hidden and is not visible until the user has begun to progress it.
`com.dragonforged.whackacac.100whacks`	Achieved after hitting 100 whacks; can be across multiple games.
`com.dragonforged.whackacac.1000whacks`	Achieved after hitting 1,000 whacks; can be across multiple games.
`com.dragonforged.whackacac.play5`	Achieved after playing five games.
`com.dragonforged.whackacac.play5Mins`	Achieved after spending five combined minutes in game play.

Assuming that all the `ICFGameCenterManager` changes detailed earlier in this chapter have been implemented already, you can begin adding in the hooks for the achievements. You will need to add the delegate callback method for achievements into `ICFGameViewController`.

This will allow the delegate to receive success messages as well as any errors that are encountered.

```
-(void)gameCenterAchievementReported:(NSError *)error;
{
    if(error != nil)
    {
        NSLog(@"An error occurred trying to report an achievement to
        ➥Game Center: %@", [error localizedDescription]);
    }

    else
    {
        NSLog(@"Achievement successfully updated");
    }
}
```

> **Note**
>
> In Whack-a-Cac the `populateAchievementCache` method is called as soon as the local user is successfully authenticated.

Earned or Unearned Achievements

The easiest achievement from Table 4.1 to implement is the `com.dragonforged.whackacac.killone` achievement. Whenever you're working with adding a hook for an achievement, the first step is to retrieve a copy of the `GKAchievement` that will be incremented. Use the method discussed in the section "Adding Achievement Hooks" to grab an up-to-date copy of the achievement.

```
GKAchievement *killOneAchievement = [[ICFGameCenterManager
➥sharedManager] achievementForIdentifier:
➥@"com.dragonforged.whackacac.killone"];
```

Next a query is performed to see whether this achievement has already been completed. If it has, there is no need to update it again.

```
if(![killOneAchievement isCompleted])
```

Since the Kill One achievement cannot be partially achieved because it is impossible to kill fewer than one cactus, it is incremented to 100% at once. This is done using the `reportAchievement:withPercentageComplete:` method that was added to the `ICFGameCenterManager` class earlier in the chapter.

```
[[ICFGameCenterManager sharedManager]
➥reportAchievement:@"com.dragonforged.whackacac.killone"
➥withPercentageComplete:100.00];
```

Since this achievement is tested and submitted when a cactus is whacked, an appropriate place for it is within the `cactusHit:` method. The updated `cactusHit:` method is presented for clarity.

```
- (IBAction)cactusHit:(id)sender;
{
    [UIView animateWithDuration:0.1
                    delay:0.0
                  options: UIViewAnimationCurveLinear |
                  ➥UIViewAnimationOptionBeginFromCurrentState
                animations:^
                {
                    [sender setAlpha: 0];
                }
                completion:^(BOOL finished)
                {
                    [sender removeFromSuperview];
                }];

    score++;

    [self displayNewScore: score];

    GKAchievement *killOneAchievement = [[ICFGameCenterManager
    ➥sharedManager] achievementForIdentifier:
    ➥@"com.dragonforged.whackacac.killone"];

    if(![killOneAchievement isCompleted])
    {
        [[ICFGameCenterManager sharedManager]reportAchievement:
        ➥@"com.dragonforged.whackacac.killone"
        ➥withPercentageComplete:100.00];
    }

    [self performSelector:@selector(spawnCactus) withObject:nil
    ➥afterDelay:(arc4random()%3) + .5];
}
```

Partially Earned Achievements

In the previous example, the achievement was either fully earned or not earned at all. The next achievement that will be implemented into Whack-a-Cac is `com.dragonforged.whackacac.score100`. Unlike the Kill One achievement, this one can be partially progressed, although it is nonstackable between games. The user is required to score 100 points in a single game. The process begins the same way as the preceding example, in that a reference to the `GKAchievement` object is created.

```
GKAchievement *score100Achievement = [[ICFGameCenterManager
sharedManager] achievementForIdentifier:
@"com.dragonforged.whackacac.score100"];
```

A quick test is performed to ensure that the achievement is not already completed.

```
if(![score100Achievement isCompleted])
```

After the achievement has been verified as not yet completed, it can be incremented by the appropriate amount. Since this achievement is completed at 100% and is for 100 points tied to the score, there is a 1%-to-one point ratio. The score can be used to substitute for a percentage complete when populating this achievement.

```
[[ICFGameCenterManager sharedManager]
reportAchievement:@"com.dragonforged.whackacac.score100"
withPercentageComplete:score];
```

Although this hook could be placed into the `cactusHit:` method again it makes more sense to place it into the `displayNewScore:` method since it is dealing with the score. The entire updated `displayNewScore:` method with the new achievement hook follows for clarity.

```
- (void)displayNewScore:(float)updatedScore;
{
    int scoreInt = score;

    if(scoreInt % 10 == 0 && score <= 50)
    {
        [self spawnCactus];
    }

    scoreLabel.text = [NSString stringWithFormat: @"%06.0f",
    ↪updatedScore];

    GKAchievement *score100Achievement = [[ICFGameCenterManager
    ↪sharedManager] achievementForIdentifier:
    ↪@"com.dragonforged.whackacac.score100"];

    if(![score100Achievement isCompleted])
    {
        [[ICFGameCenterManager sharedManager] reportAchievement:
        ↪@"com.dragonforged.whackacac.score100"
        ↪withPercentageComplete:score];
    }
}
```

Since the Score 100 achievement is hidden, it will not appear to the user until the user has completed progress toward it (at least one point). At any time after beginning working on this achievement, the user can see the progress in the Game Center View Controllers, as shown in Figure 4.6.

Figure 4.6   Viewing the partially progressed Score 100 achievement after scoring 43 points in a game; note the completion of the Kill One achievement.

Multiple Session Achievements

In the previous example, the Score 100 achievement required the player to earn the entire 100 points while in a single match. However, there often will be times when it will be required to track a user across multiple matches and even app launches as they progress toward an achievement. The first of the multiple session achievements that will be implemented is the com.dragonforged.whackacac.play5 achievement.

Each time the player completes a round of game play, the com.dragonforged.whackacac. play5 achievement will be progressed. Since the achievement is completed at five games played, each game increments the progress by 20%. This hook will be added to the viewWillDisappear method of ICFGameViewController. As with the previous examples, first a reference to the GKAchievement object is created. After making sure that the achievement isn't already completed, it can be incremented. A new variable is created to determine the number of matches played, which is the percentage complete divided by 20. The matchesPlayed is then incremented by one, and submitted using reportAchievement: withPercentageComplete: by multiplying matchesPlayed by 20.

```
- (void) viewWillDisappear: (BOOL) animated
{
    GKAchievement *play5MatchesAchievement = [[ICFGameCenterManager
    ➥sharedManager] achievementForIdentifier:
    ➥@"com.dragonforged.whackacac.play5"];

    if(![play5MatchesAchievement isCompleted])
    {
        double matchesPlayed = [play5MatchesAchievement
        ➥percentComplete]/20.0f;

        matchesPlayed++;

        [[ICFGameCenterManager sharedManager]
        ➥reportAchievement: @"com.dragonforged.whackacac.play5"
        ➥withPercentageComplete: matchesPlayed*20.0f];
    }

    [super viewWillDisappear: animated];
}
```

Piggybacked Achievements and Storing Achievement Precision

Sometimes, it is possible to piggyback two achievements off of each other, such as the next case when dealing with the Whack 100 and Whack 1000 achievements. Since both of these achievements are tracking the same type of objective (whacks) a more streamlined approach can be taken.

As with the other achievement hooks that have been implemented in this chapter, the first thing that is done is to create a reference to a GKAchievement. In the following example a reference to the larger of the two achievements is used. Since the largest achievement has more objectives to complete than it does percentage, it will be rounded down to the nearest multiple of 10. To help combat this problem, a localKills variable is populated from NSUserDefaults. This system falls apart when the achievement exists on two different devices, but can be further polished using iCloud to store the data (see Chapter 8).

A calculation is also made to determine how many kills Game Center reports (with loss of accuracy). If remoteKills is greater than the localKills, we know that the player either has reinstalled the game or has progressed it on another device. In this event the system will default to the Game Center's values as to not progress the user backward; otherwise, the local information is used.

This code example can be placed inside the cactusHit: method following the Kill One achievement from earlier in this section. After each hit, the localKill value is increased by one. Two checks are performed to make sure that each achievement is not already completed. Since references to both GKAchievements are not available here, a check of the kills number can be used to substitute the standard isComplete check. After the achievements are submitted, the new local value is stored into the NSUserDefaults for future reference.

```
GKAchievement *killOneThousandAchievement = [[ICFGameCenterManager
➥sharedManager] achievementForIdentifier:
➥@"com.dragonforged.whackacac.1000whacks"];

double localKills = [[[NSUserDefaults standardUserDefaults]
➥objectForKey:@"kills"] doubleValue];

double remoteKills = [killOneThousandAchievement percentComplete] *
➥10.0;

if(remoteKills > localKills)
{
    localKills = remoteKills;
}

localKills++;

if(localKills <= 1000)
{
    if(localKills <= 100)
    {
        [[ICFGameCenterManager sharedManager]
        ➥reportAchievement: @"com.dragonforged.whackacac.100whacks"
        ➥withPercentageComplete:localKills];
    }

    [[ICFGameCenterManager sharedManager]
    ➥reportAchievement:@"com.dragonforged.whackacac.1000whacks"
    ➥withPercentageComplete:(localKills/10.0)];
}

[[NSUserDefaults standardUserDefaults] setObject:[NSNumber
➥numberWithDouble: localKills] forKey:@"kills"];
```

Timer-Based Achievements

One of the most popular achievements in iOS gaming is to play for a certain amount of time. In Whack-a-Cac com.dragonforged.whackacac.play5Mins is used to track the user's progress towards five minutes of total gameplay. This particular example exists for the loss-of-accuracy problem that was faced in the Whack 1000 example from earlier in this section, and it can be overcome in the same manner.

To track time, a NSTimer will be created. To determine how often the timer should fire, you will need to determine what 1% of five minutes is.

```
play5MinTimer = [NSTimer scheduledTimerWithTimeInterval:3.0 target:self
➥selector:@selector(play5MinTick) userInfo:nil repeats:YES];
```

When the timer fires a new call to a new `play5MinTick` method is called. If the game is
paused or in a `gameOver` state, the achievement progress is ignored and the method returns.
As with the other examples, a reference to the `GKAchievement` object is created, and a check
is performed to see whether it has completed. If this achievement is completed, the timer is
invalidated to prevent wasted CPU time. Otherwise, since the timer is firing every three seconds
(1% of five minutes), the achievement is progressed by 1%.

```
- (void)play5MinTick;
{
    if(paused || gameOver)
    {
        return;
    }

    GKAchievement *play5MinAchievement = [[ICFGameCenterManager
    ➥sharedManager] achievementForIdentifier:
    ➥@"com.dragonforged.whackacac.play5Mins"];

    if([play5MinAchievement isCompleted])
    {
        [play5MinTimer invalidate];
        play5MinTimer = nil;
        return;
    }

    double percentageComplete =    play5MinAchievement.percentComplete
    ➥+ 1.0;

    [[ICFGameCenterManager sharedManager] reportAchievement:
    ➥@"com.dragonforged.whackacac.play5Mins" withPercentageComplete:
    ➥percentageComplete];
}
```

Resetting Achievements

There is often a need to reset all achievement progress for a user, more so in development than
in production. Sometimes it is helpful to provide users with a chance to take a fresh run at a
game or even some sort of prestige mode that starts everything over, but at a harder difficulty.
Resetting achievement progress is simple; the following code snippet can be added into the
`IFCGameCenterManager` class to completely reset all achievements to the unearned state. If
you are providing this functionality to users, it is a good idea to have several steps of confirmation to prevent accidental resetting.

```
- (void) resetAchievements
{
    [achievementDictionary removeAllObjects];

    [GKAchievement resetAchievementsWithCompletionHandler:
    ^(NSError *error)
    {
        if(error == nil)
        {
            NSLog(@"All achievements have been successfully
            ➥reset");
        }

        else
        {
            NSLog(@"Unable to reset achievements: %@",
            ➥[error localizedDescription]);
        }
    }];
}
```

> **Tip**
> While in development and during debugging it can be helpful to keep a call to reset achieve-
> ments in the authentication successfully completed block of the `ICFGameCenterManager`
> class that can easily be commented out to assist with testing and implementing achievements.

Going Further with Achievements

Apple provides a lot for free in regard to displaying and progressing achievements. However, Apple does not allow the customization of the provided interface for viewing achievements. The look and feel of Apple's achievement view controllers might simply not fit into the app's design. In cases like this, the raw achievement information can be accessed for display in a customized interface. Although fully setting up custom achievements is beyond the scope of this chapter, this section contains information that will assist you.

Earlier, you learned about creating a local cache of GKAchievements. However, GKAchievement objects are missing critical data that will be needed in order to display achievement data to the user, such as the description, title, name, and number of points it is worth. Additionally, when the achievement cache is used, if an achievement has not been progressed, it will not appear in the cache. To retrieve all achievements and the required information needed to present them to the user, a new class is required.

Using the GKAchievementDescription class and the class method loadAchieve-mentDescriptionsWithCompletionHandler:, you can gain access to an array of

GKAchievementDescriptions. A GKAchievementDescription object contains properties for the titles, descriptions, images, and other critical information. However, the
GKAchievementDescription does not contain any information about the current progress of
the achievement for the local user; in order to determine progress, the identifier will need to be
compared to the local achievement cache.

```
[GKAchievementDescription
➥loadAchievementDescriptionsWithCompletionHandler:^(NSArray
➥*descriptions, NSError *error)
{
    if(error != nil)
    {
        NSLog(@"An error occurred loading achievement
        ➥descriptions: %@", [error localizedDescription]);
    }

    for(GKAchievementDescription *achievementDescription in
    ➥descriptions)
    {
        NSLog(@"%@\n", achievementDescription);
    }

}];
```

When the preceding code is executed on Whack-a-Cac, the console will display the following
information:

```
2012-09-01 16:38:07.754 WhackACac[48552:c07] <GKAchievementDescription:
0x1185f810>id: com.dragonforged.whackacac.100whacks Whack 100 Cacti
visible Good job! You whacked 100 of them!

2012-09-01 16:38:07.755 WhackACac[48552:c07] <GKAchievementDescription:
0x1185f980>id: com.dragonforged.whackacac.1000whacks Whack 1000!
visible You are a master at killing those cacti.

2012-09-01 16:38:07.755 WhackACac[48552:c07] <GKAchievementDescription:
0x1185f820>id: com.dragonforged.whackacac.play5 Play 5 Matches visible
Your dedication to cactus whacking is unmatched.

2012-09-01 16:38:07.755 WhackACac[48552:c07] <GKAchievementDescription:
0x1185eae0>id: com.dragonforged.whackacac.score100 Score 100 hidden
Good work on getting 100 cacti in one match!

2012-09-01 16:38:07.755 WhackACac[48552:c07] <GKAchievementDescription:
0x1185eaf0>id: com.dragonforged.whackacac.killone Kill One  hidden You
have started on your cactus killing path, there is no turning back now.
```

```
2012-09-01 16:38:07.756 WhackACac[48552:c07] <GKAchievementDescription:
0x1185eb30>id: com.dragonforged.whackacac.play5Mins Play for 5 Minutes
visible Good work! Your dedication continues to impress your peers.

2012-09-01 16:38:07.756 WhackACac[48552:c07] <GKAchievementDescription:
0x1185eb40>id: com.dragonforged.whackacac.hit5Fast Hit 5 Quick hidden
You are truly a quick gun.
```

A list of all the achievements has now been retrieved and can be compared to the local achievement cache to determine percentages completed. You have everything that is needed to create a customized GUI for presenting the achievement data to the user.

Summary

In this chapter, you learned about integrating Game Center Achievements into an iOS project. You continued to build up the sample game Whack-a-Cac that was introduced in Chapter 3. This chapter also continued to expand on the reusable Game Center Manager class.

You should now have a firm understanding of how to create achievements, set up your app to interact with them, post and show progress, and reset all achievement progress. Additionally, a brief look at going beyond the standard behavior was provided. With the knowledge gained in this chapter, you now have the ability to fully integrate achievements into any app.

Exercises

1. Implement a system of storing and resubmitting achievements if the Game Center servers are unreachable. Look at the approach used for leaderboards in Chapter 3 for guidance. Be sure to keep only the highest percentages complete in the offline cache.

2. Add a new achievement for hitting five cacti within one second. You will need to create some timers that track sequential hits. You can use the existing achievement identifier com.dragonforged.whackacac.hit5Fast.

3. Implement a custom display for your achievement progress using the information from the section "Going Further with Achievements" as a guide.

5

Getting Started with Address Book

The iOS Address Book frameworks have existed largely unchanged from their introduction in iOS 2.0 (then called iPhone OS 2.0). These frameworks were largely ported unchanged from their OSX counterparts, which have existed since OSX 10.2, making Address Book one of the oldest frameworks available on iOS. This legacy will become evident as you begin working with Address Book technology. It is largely seated on Core Foundation framework, which might seem unfamiliar to developers who have come over to Objective-C and Cocoa development after the introduction of the iPhone SDKs.

Why Address Book Support Is Important

When developing iOS software, you are running in an environment alongside your user's mobile life. Users carry their mobile devices everywhere, and with these devices a considerable amount of their personal lives is intertwined with each device, from their daily calendar to personal photo albums. Paramount to this mobile life is the user's contact information. This data has been collected over long periods, often on several devices, by a user and contains information about the user's family, business, and social life.

An app can use a contact database to determine whether the user already has friends signed up for a service by parsing through a list of their email addresses or phone numbers to automatically add them as friends. Your app can also use a contact list for autopopulating emails or phone numbers or allow users to share their contact info with friends over Bluetooth (see Chapter 10, "Bluetooth Networking with Game Kit"). The reasons an app might need access to the user's contacts are virtually endless.

> **Note**
>
> It is important to access the contact database only if your app has a legitimate reason to do so; nothing will turn a user off from your app more quickly than a breach of privacy.

Limitations of Address Book Programming

Although the Address Book frameworks remain fairly open, there are some important limitations to consider. The most notable, especially for those coming from the Mac development world, is that there's no "me" card. Essentially, there is no way to identify your user in the list of contacts. Although there are some hacks that attempt to do this, nothing developed so far has proven to be reliable or is sanctioned by Apple.

A newer and welcome limitation—especially by privacy-concerned users—is the addition of Core Location–type authorization to access the contact database. This means that a user will be prompted to allow an app to access his contacts before being able to do so. When writing Address Book software, make an effort to ensure that your software continues to function even if a user has declined to let the app access his contact information.

Starting with iOS 6, a new privacy section exists in the Settings.app. From here, users are able to toggle on and off permissions to access Contacts, Locations, Calendars, Reminders, Photos, and Bluetooth.

Introduction to the Sample App

The sample app for this chapter is a simple address book viewer and editor. When launched, it will retrieve and display a list of all the contacts on your device. There is a plus button in the navigation bar for adding a new contact via the built-in interface, as well as a toggle button to change between showing either phone numbers or street addresses in the list. Additionally, the app has the capability to add a new contact programmatically and an example of using the built-in people picker.

Since the sample app, shown in Figure 5.1, is merely a base navigation controller project and does not have any overhead that is unrelated to Address Book programming, it is prudent to dive right into the functional code in the next section.

Getting Address Book Up and Running

The first thing you need to do before working with the Address Book frameworks is to link both frameworks in your project. You need to be concerned with two frameworks: `AddressBookUI.framework` and `AddressBook.framework`. The first of these frameworks handles the graphical user interface for picking, editing, or displaying contacts, and the second handles all the interaction layers to work with that data. You need to import two headers, as shown here:

```
#import <AddressBook/AddressBook.h>
#import <AddressBookUI/AddressBookUI.h>
```

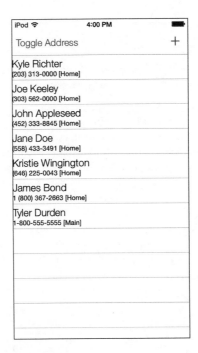

Figure 5.1   A first look at the sample app.

In the sample app, the headers are imported in `RootViewController.h` since the class will need to conform to several delegates, which is discussed later. You will also want to create a classwide instance of `ABAddressBookRef`, which in the sample app is called `addressBook`. The sample app also has an `NSArray` that will be used to store an array of the contact entries. It is a fairly expensive operation to copy the address book into memory, so you will want to minimize the number of times you will need to run that operation.

```
ABAddressBookRef addressBook;
NSArray *addressBookEntryArray;
```

To populate this new `NSArray`, you need to call `ABAddressBookCreate`. This will create a new instance of the address book data based on the current global address book database. In the sample app, this is done as part of the `viewDidLoad` method.

```
if(addressBook == NULL)
{
    NSLog(@"Error loading address book: %@",  CFErrorCopyDescription(creationError));
}


ABAddressBookRequestAccessWithCompletion(addressBook, ^(bool granted,
➥CFErrorRef error)
```

```
{
    if(!granted)
    {
        NSLog(@"No permission!");
    }
});
```

You will also want to catch the event if our address book has no contacts, which will be default behavior on the iOS Simulator. The sample app displays a UIAlert in this situation to let the user know that the app isn't broken, but that it has no data available to it. You can query the size of an ABAddressBookRef with the function ABAddressBookGetPersonCount.

```
if(ABAddressBookGetPersonCount(addressBook) == 0)
{
    UIAlertView *alertView = [[UIAlertView alloc]initWithTitle:@""
    message:@"Address book is empty!"
    delegate:nil
    cancelButtonTitle:@"Dismiss"
    otherButtonTitles: nil];

    [alertView show];
    [alertView release];
}
```

Now you have a reference to the address book but you will want to translate that into a more manageable dataset. The sample app copies these objects into an NSArray since it will be using the data to populate a table view.

You have access to three functions for copying the address book data that will return a CFArrayRef. ABAddressBookCopyArrayOfAllPeople will return an array of all people in the referenced address book (this method is shown in the next code snippet). ABAddressBookCopyArrayOfAllPeopleInSource will return all the address book items that are found in a particular source. Lastly, ABAddressBookCopyArrayOfAllPeopleInSource WithSortOrdering will allow you to sort the list of address book entries while retrieving it.

The sample app does not need to worry about sorting right now, so it simply retrieves the contacts with a call to ABAddressBookCopyArrayOfAllPeople. Since a CFArrayRef is a toll-free bridge to NSArray, it can be typecast and left with an NSArray. Now that you have an array of all the address book entries, it is just a simple task to get them displayed in a table.

```
addressBookEntryArray = (NSArray *) ABAddressBookCopyArrayOfAllPeople(addressBook);
```

> **Note**
>
> Sources in this context amount to where the contact was retrieved from; possible values can be kABSourceTypeLocal, kABSourceTypeExchange, kABSourceTypeMobileMe, and kABSourceTypeCardDAV. To get a list of all the sources found within the referenced address book, use ABAddressBookCopyArrayOfAllSources(addressBook). From there, you can query the sources that are of interest to your app.

Reading Data from the Address Book

In the preceding section, it was demonstrated how to populate an NSArray with entries from the user's address book—each of these objects is an ABRecordRef. In this section, pulling information back out of an ABRecordRef is covered.

The sample app will be displaying the user data through a UITableView. There will be two types of values contained within the ABRecordRef: The first type is a single value used for objects for which there can be only one, such as a first and last name, and the second type is a multivalue used when dealing with values that a user might have more than one of, such as a phone number or a street address.

The following code snippet pulls an ABRecordRef from the address book array that was created in the preceding section and then retrieves the contact's first and last name and sets NSString values accordingly. A full listing of available properties is shown in Table 5.1.

```
ABRecordRef record = [addressBookEntryArrayobjectAtIndex:indexPath.row];
NSString *firstName = (NSString *)ABRecordCopyValue(record,
➡kABPersonFirstNameProperty);


NSString *lastName = (NSString *)ABRecordCopyValue(record,
➡kABPersonLastNameProperty);

//...

    if(firstName)
        CFRelease(firstName);
    if(lastName)
        CFRelease(lastName);
```

Table 5.1 **Complete Listing of All Available Single-Value Constants in an** ABRecordRef

Property Name	Description
kABPersonFirstNameProperty	First name
kABPersonLastNameProperty	Last name
kABPersonMiddleNameProperty	Middle name or initial
kABPersonPrefixProperty	Name prefix (Mr., Ms., Dr.)
kABPersonSuffixProperty	Name suffix (MD, Jr., Sr.)
kABPersonNicknameProperty	Nickname
kABPersonFirstNamePhoneticProperty	Phonetically spelled first name
kABPersonLastNamePhoneticProperty	Phonetically spelled last name
kABPersonMiddleNamePhoneticProperty	Phonetically spelled middle name

Property Name	Description
kABPersonOrganizationProperty	Company or organization
kABPersonJobTitleProperty	Job title
kABPersonDepartmentProperty	Department title
kABPersonBirthdayProperty	Birthday CFDate format, which is a toll-free bridge to NSDate
kABPersonNoteProperty	Personal notes
kABPersonCreationDateProperty	Creation CFDate
kABPersonModificationDateProperty	Last modified CFDate

> **Note**
>
> NARC (New, Alloc, Retain, Copy) is how I was taught memory management in the early days of Mac OS X programming, and the same holds true today for manual memory management. New advancements to memory management such as ARC are forever changing the way we handle manual memory management. However, we will not be using ARC in the sample app for this chapter. When you perform operations on Address Book with "copy" in the name, you must release that memory using a CFRelease() call. ARC enabled versions of the source code are available online.

Reading Multivalues from the Address Book

Often, you will encounter Address Book objects that can store multiple values, such as phone numbers, email addresses, or street addresses. These are all accessed using ABMultiValueRefs. The process is similar to that for single values with one additional level of complexity.

The first thing you need to do when working with multivalues, such as phone numbers, is copy the value of the multivalue property. In the following code example, use kABPersonPhone Property from the record that was set in the previous section. This provides you with an ABMultiValueRef called phoneNumbers.

A check is then needed to make sure that the contact has at least one phone number using the ABMultiValueGetCount function. Here, you can either loop through all the phone numbers or pull the first one you find (as in the example). Additionally, you will want to handle the "no phone number found" case. From here, you need to create a new string and store the value of the phone number into it. This is done using the ABMultiValueCopyValueAtIndex call, the first parameter of the ABMultiValueRef followed by the index number.

```
ABMultiValueRef phoneNumbers = ABRecordCopyValue(record,
➥kABPersonPhoneProperty);
```

```
if (ABMultiValueGetCount(phoneNumbers) > 0)
{
    CFStringRef phoneNumber =
    ➡ABMultiValueCopyValueAtIndex(phoneNumbers, 0);

    NSLog(@"Phone Number: %@", phoneNumber);

    CFRelease(phoneNumber);
}

CFRelease(phoneNumbers);
```

Understanding Address Book Labels

In the preceding section, you retrieved a phone number from the contact database; however, you know it only by its index number. Although this is helpful to developers, it is next to useless for users. You will want to retrieve the label that was used in the contact database. In the next code snippet, the example from the preceding section will be expanded on.

The first step to attaining a label for a multivalue reference is to call ABMultiValueCopyLabel AtIndex. Call this function with the same parameters you used to get the value of the multi-value object. This function will return a nonlocalized string, such as "_$!<Mobile>!$_". Although this is much more helpful than a raw index number, it is still not ready for user presentation.

You will need to run the returned label through a localizer to get a human-readable string. Do so using the ABAddressBookCopyLocalizedLabel using the raw value CFStringRef that was just set. In the example this will now return Mobile.

```
ABMultiValueRef phoneNumbers = ABRecordCopyValue(record,
➡kABPersonPhoneProperty);

if (ABMultiValueGetCount(phoneNumbers) > 0)
{
    CFStringRef phoneNumber =
    ➡ABMultiValueCopyValueAtIndex(phoneNumbers, 0);

    CFStringRef phoneTypeRawString =
    ➡ABMultiValueCopyLabelAtIndex(phoneNumbers, 0);

    NSString *localizedPhoneTypeString = (NSString
    ➡*)ABAddressBookCopyLocalizedLabel(phoneTypeRawString);

    NSLog(@"Phone %@ [%@]", phoneNumber, localizedPhoneTypeString);
```

```
    CFRelease(phoneNumber);
    CFRelease(phoneTypeRawString);
    CFRelease(localizedPhoneTypeString);
}
```

Look back at the example in Figure 5.1—you now have the skill set to fully implement this functionality.

Working with Addresses

In the preceding two sections, you saw how to access single-value information and then how to access multivalue data. In this section, you will work with a bit of both as you learn how to handle street addresses that you encounter in the contact database. If you launch the sample app and tap the toggle button in the navigation bar, you will see that the addresses are now shown instead of phone numbers in the table cells (see Figure 5.2).

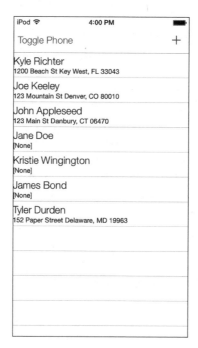

Figure 5.2   The sample app showing addresses pulled from the contact database.

You will begin working with addresses in the same manner as you did for the phone multi-values. First attain an `ABMultiValueRef` for the `kABPersonAddressProperty`. Then you will need to make sure that at least one valid address was found. When you query the multivalue object with an index value, instead of getting back a single `CFStringRef`, you are returned a dictionary containing the address components. After you have the dictionary, you can pull out specific information using the address constants shown in Table 5.2.

```
ABMultiValueRef streetAddresses = ABRecordCopyValue(record,
kABPersonAddressProperty);

if (ABMultiValueGetCount(streetAddresses) > 0)
{
    NSDictionary *streetAddressDictionary = (NSDictionary
    ➥*)ABMultiValueCopyValueAtIndex(streetAddresses, 0);

    NSString *street = [streetAddressDictionary objectForKey:
    ➥(NSString *)kABPersonAddressStreetKey];

    NSString *city = [streetAddressDictionary objectForKey:
    ➥NSString *)kABPersonAddressCityKey];

    NSString *state = [streetAddressDictionary objectForKey:
    ➥(NSString *)kABPersonAddressStateKey];

    NSString *zip = [streetAddressDictionary objectForKey:
    ➥(NSString *)kABPersonAddressZIPKey];

    NSLog(@"Address: %@ %@, %@ %@", street, city, state, zip);

    CFRelease(streetAddressDictionary);
}
```

Table 5.2   **Address Components**

Property	Description
kABPersonAddressStreetKey	Street name and number including any apartment numbers
kABPersonAddressCityKey	City name
kABPersonAddressStateKey	Two-character or full state name
kABPersonAddressZIPKey	ZIP Code, five or nine digits
kABPersonAddressCountryKey	Full country name
kABPersonAddressCountryCodeKey	Two-character country code

Address Book Graphical User Interface

As mentioned in the beginning of this chapter, user interfaces are provided as part of the Address Book framework. In this section, a look is taken at those interfaces and how they can save an incredible amount of implementation time. Whether it is editing an existing contact, creating a new contact, or allowing your user to pick a contact from a list, Apple has you covered.

People Picker

You will undoubtedly want your user to be able to simply select a contact from a list. For example, let's say you are writing an app that allows you to send a vCard over Bluetooth to another user; you will need to let your user select which contact card she wants to send. This task is easily accomplished using `ABPeoplePickerNavigationController`. You can turn on this functionality in the sample app by uncommenting line 63 (`[self showPicker: nil];`) in the `RootViewController.m` class.

Your class will first need to implement `ABPeoplePickerNavigationControllerDelegate`. You can then create a new picker controller using the following code snippet:

```
ABPeoplePickerNavigationController *picker =
➡[[ABPeoplePickerNavigationController alloc] init];

picker.peoplePickerDelegate = self;
[self presentViewController:picker animated:YES completion:nil];
[picker release];
```

This displays a people picker to the user (see Figure 5.3).

You will also need to implement three delegate methods to handle callbacks from the user interacting with the people picker. The first method you need handles the Cancel button being tapped by a user; if you do not dismiss the modal in this method, the user has no way to dismiss the view.

```
- (void)peoplePickerNavigationControllerDidCancel:(ABPeoplePickerNavigationController
➡*)peoplePicker
{
    [self dismissViewControllerAnimated:YES completion:nil];
}
```

When picking people, there are two sets of data you might be concerned with. The first is the contact itself, and by extension all the contact information. The second is a specific property, such as a specific phone number or email address from a contact. You can handle both of these cases. The first step will look at selecting an entire person's contact information.

```
- (BOOL)peoplePickerNavigationController:
➡(ABPeoplePickerNavigationController *)peoplePicker
➡shouldContinueAfterSelectingPerson: (ABRecordRef)person
{
```

```
    NSLog(@"You have selected: %@", person);

    [self dismissViewControllerAnimated:YES completion:nil];

    return NO;
}
```

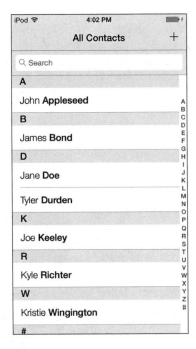

Figure 5.3   The built-in people picker.

In this code snippet, NO is returned for peoplePickerNavigationController:should
ContinueAfterSelectingPerson:. This informs the picker that you do not intend to drill
deeper into the contact and you only want to select an ABRecordRef for a person. As with the
previous example, you must dismiss the modal view controller when you are done with it. If
you do want to dive deeper, you will need to return YES here and implement the following
delegate method. Do not forget to remove the dismissModalViewControllerAnimated:
completion call from the previous method if you intend to drill deeper.

```
- (BOOL)peoplePickerNavigationController:
➥(ABPeoplePickerNavigationController *)peoplePicker
➥shouldContinueAfterSelectingPerson:(ABRecordRef)person
➥property:(ABPropertyID)property
➥identifier:(ABMultiValueIdentifier)identifier
{
```

```
    NSLog(@"Person: %@\nProperty:%i\nIdentifier:%i", person,property,
➥identifier);

    [self dismissViewControllerAnimated:YES completion:nil];

    return NO;
}
```

Customizing the People Picker

There might be times when you want to allow the picker to choose only from phone numbers or street addresses and ignore the other information. You can do so by modifying the previous method of creating the people picker to match the following example, which will show only phone numbers.

```
ABPeoplePickerNavigationController *picker =
➥[[ABPeoplePickerNavigationController alloc] init];

picker.displayedProperties = [NSArray arrayWithObject:[NSNumber
➥numberWithInt:kABPersonPhoneProperty]];

picker.peoplePickerDelegate = self;
[self presentViewController:picker animated:YES completion:nil];
```

You also can specify a specific address book for the picker using the `addressBook` property. If you do not set this, a new address book is created for you when the people picker is presented.

Editing and Viewing Existing Contacts Using ABPersonViewController

Most of the time, you will want to simply display or edit an existing contact using the built-in Address Book user interfaces. In the sample app, this is the default action when a table cell is selected. You first create a new instance of `ABPersonViewController` and set the delegate and the person to be displayed, which is an instance of `ABRecordRef`. This approach will display the contact, as shown in Figure 5.4.

```
ABPersonViewController *personViewController = [[ABPersonViewController
➥alloc] init];

personViewController.personViewDelegate = self;

personViewController.displayedPerson = personToDisplay;

[self.navigationController pushViewController:personViewController
➥animated:YES];

[personViewController release];
```

Figure 5.4   The built-in contact viewer.

If you want to allow editing of the contact, you simply add another property to the code snippet.

```
personViewController.allowsEditing = YES;
```

If you want to allow actions in the contact, such as Send Text Message or FaceTime buttons, you can add an additional `allowsActions` property.

```
personViewController.allowsActions = YES;
```

In addition to the steps you have already implemented, you need to be aware of one required delegate method, `personViewController:shouldPerformDefaultActionForPerson: property:identifier`. This is called when the user taps on a row such as a street address or a phone number. If you would like the app to perform the default action, such as call or open `Maps.app`, return `YES`; if you would like to override these behaviors, return `NO`.

```
- (BOOL)personViewController:(ABPersonViewController
➥*)personViewController
➥shouldPerformDefaultActionForPerson:(ABRecordRef)person
➥property:(ABPropertyID)property
```

```
➥identifier:(ABMultiValueIdentifier)identifierForValue
{

    return YES;
}
```

Creating New Contacts Using `ABNewPersonViewController`

When you want to create a new contact, the sample app has a plus button in the navigation bar that allows you to create a new contact using the built-in user interfaces, shown in Figure 5.5. The next code snippet is straightforward with one caveat: The `ABNewPersonViewController` must be wrapped inside of a `UINavigationController` to function properly.

```
ABNewPersonViewController *newPersonViewController =
➥[[ABNewPersonViewController alloc] init];

UINavigationController *newPersonNavigationController =
➥[[UINavigationController alloc]
➥initWithRootViewController:newPersonViewController];

[newPersonViewController setNewPersonViewDelegate: self];

[self presentViewController:newPersonNavigationController animated:YES
➥completion:nil];

[newPersonNavigationController release];
[newPersonViewController release];
```

There is also a single delegate method that is called when the user saves the contact. After you verify that you have a valid person object being returned, you need to call `ABAddressBookAddRecord` with the address book you want to add the person into, followed by `ABAddressBookSave`. If you have an array populated with the address book entries like the sample app, you will need to repopulate that array to see the changes.

```
- (void)newPersonViewController:(ABNewPersonViewController
➥*)newPersonViewController didCompleteWithNewPerson:(ABRecordRef)person
{
    if(person)
    {
        CFErrorRef error = NULL;

        ABAddressBookAddRecord(addressBook, person, &error);
        ABAddressBookSave(addressBook, &error);
        if (error != NULL)
        {
            NSLog(@"An error occurred");
```

```
        }
    }

    [self dismissViewControllerAnimated:YES completion:nil];

}
```

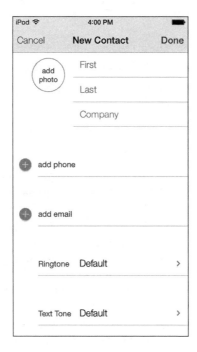

Figure 5.5   The built-in new person view controller.

Programmatically Creating Contacts

What if you want to programmatically create a new contact instead of using the built-in graphical interface? Think about a contact-sharing app again. You don't want to have to put the user through an interface when you can have the contact information entered programmatically.

In the sample project, uncomment line 66 ([self programmaticallyCreatePerson];) of the RootViewController.m and run it; you will notice that a new person appears in the contact list. The first step you will need to take in creating a new person is to generate a new empty ABRecordRef. You do this with the ABPersonCreate() method. You will also want to create a new NULL pointed CFErrorRef.

```
ABRecordRef newPersonRecord = ABPersonCreate();

CFErrorRef error = NULL;
```

Setting single-value properties is very straightforward, achieved by calling `ABRecordSetValue` with the new `ABRecordRef` as the first parameter, followed by the property constant, then the value, followed by the address of the `CFErrorRef`.

```
ABRecordSetValue(newPersonRecord, kABPersonFirstNameProperty, @"Tyler",
➥&error);

ABRecordSetValue(newPersonRecord, kABPersonLastNameProperty, @"Durden",
➥&error);

ABRecordSetValue(newPersonRecord, kABPersonOrganizationProperty,
➥@"Paperstreet Soap Company", &error);

ABRecordSetValue(newPersonRecord, kABPersonJobTitleProperty,
➥@"Salesman", &error);
```

Setting the phone number multivalue is slightly more complex than with a single-value object. You first need to create a new `ABMutableMultiValueRef` using the `ABMultiValueCreateMutable()` method with the type of multivalue property you are creating; in this instance, the phone property.

In the sample app, three different phone numbers are created, each with a different label property. After you finish adding new phone number values, you will need to call `ABRecordSetValue` with the new person record, the multivalue constant you are setting, and the mutable multivalue reference you just populated. Don't forget to release the memory when you are done.

```
ABMutableMultiValueRef multiPhoneRef =
➥ABMultiValueCreateMutable(kABMultiStringPropertyType);

ABMultiValueAddValueAndLabel(multiPhoneRef, @"1-800-555-5555",
➥kABPersonPhoneMainLabel, NULL);

ABMultiValueAddValueAndLabel(multiPhoneRef, @"1-203-426-1234",
➥kABPersonPhoneMobileLabel, NULL);

ABMultiValueAddValueAndLabel(multiPhoneRef, @"1-555-555-0123",
➥kABPersonPhoneIPhoneLabel, NULL);

ABRecordSetValue(newPersonRecord, kABPersonPhoneProperty,
➥multiPhoneRef, nil);

CFRelease(multiPhoneRef);
```

Email addresses are handled in the same manner as phone numbers. An example of an email entry is shown in the sample app. Street addresses are handled slightly differently, however.

You will still create a new mutable multivalue reference, but in this step, you also create a new mutable NSDictionary. Set an object for each key of the address that you want to set (refer to Table 5.2 for a complete list of values). Next, you need to add a label for this street address. In the code sample that follows, kABWorkLabel is used. When done, save the data in the same fashion as the phone or email entry.

```
ABMutableMultiValueRef multiAddressRef =
➥ABMultiValueCreateMutable(kABMultiDictionaryPropertyType);

NSMutableDictionary *addressDictionary = [[NSMutableDictionary alloc]
➥init];

[addressDictionary setObject:@"152 Paper Street" forKey:(NSString *)
➥kABPersonAddressStreetKey];

[addressDictionary setObject:@"Delaware" forKey:(NSString
➥*)kABPersonAddressCityKey];

[addressDictionary setObject:@"MD" forKey:(NSString
➥*)kABPersonAddressStateKey];

[addressDictionary setObject:@"19963" forKey:(NSString
➥*)kABPersonAddressZIPKey];

ABMultiValueAddValueAndLabel(multiAddressRef, addressDictionary,
➥kABWorkLabel, NULL);

ABRecordSetValue(newPersonRecord, kABPersonAddressProperty,
➥multiAddressRef, &error);

CFRelease(multiAddressRef);
➥[addressDictionary release];
```

After you set up the new contact with all the information you want to enter, you need to save it and check for any errors that occurred during the process. In the sample app, the array and the table are reloaded to display the new entry.

```
ABAddressBookAddRecord(addressBook, newPersonRecord, &error);
ABAddressBookSave(addressBook, &error);

if(error != NULL)
{
    NSLog(@"An error occurred");
}
```

Summary

This chapter covered the Address Book frameworks and how to leverage them into your iOS apps. You learned about the limitations and privacy concerns of the Address Book, as well as the importance of implementing it into appropriate apps.

Exploring the included sample app, you gained insightful and practical knowledge on how to get the Address Book frameworks quickly up and running. Additionally, you learned how to work with both retrieving and inserting new data into an address book both using Apple's provided graphical user interface and programmatically. You should now have a strong understanding of the Address Book frameworks and be comfortable adding them into your iOS apps.

Exercises

1. Sort the address book by first or last name using the `ABAddressBookCopyArrayOfAll PeopleInSourceWithSortOrdering` method. Experiment with different sorting options.

2. Create a new person view controller, which allows the user to enter fields of his or her own. When the user is done entering information programmatically, save the new contact into the address book.

6

Working with Music Libraries

When Steve Jobs first introduced the iPhone onstage at Macworld in 2007, it was touted as a phone, an iPod, and revolutionary Internet communicator. Several years later, and partially due to a lot of hard work by third-party developers, the iPhone has grown into something so much more than those three core concepts. That original marketing message has not changed, however; the iPhone itself remains primarily a phone, an iPod, and an Internet communication device. Users did not add an iPhone to their collection of devices they already carried every day; they replaced their existing phones and iPods with a single device.

Music is what gave the iPhone its humble start when Apple begun planning the device in 2004; the iPhone was always an extension of an iPod. Music inspired the iPod, which, it could be argued, brought the company back from the brink. Music is universally loved by people. It brings them together and it allows them to express themselves. Although day-to-day iPhone users might not even think of their iPhone as a music playback device, most of them will use it almost absent-mindedly to listen to their favorite songs.

This chapter discusses how to add access to the user's music library inside of an iOS app. Whether building a full-featured music player or allowing users to play their music as the soundtrack to a game, this chapter demonstrates how to provide music playback from the user's own library.

Introduction to the Sample App

The sample app for this chapter is simply called Player (see Figure 6.1). The sample app is a full-featured music player for the iPhone. It will allow the user to pick songs to be played via the Media Picker, play random songs, or play artist-specific songs. In addition, it features functionality for pause, resume, previous, next, volume, playback counter, and plus or minus 30 seconds to the playhead. In addition, the app will display the album art for the current track being played if it is available.

Figure 6.1   A first look at the sample app, Player, a fully functional music player running on
an iPod.

Since the iOS Simulator that comes bundled with Xcode does not include a copy of the Music.
app, nor does it have an easy method of transferring music into its file system, the app can be
run only on actual devices. When the app is launched on a simulator, a number of errors will
appear.

```
2013-03-02 16:04:13.392 player[80633:c07] MPMusicPlayer: Unable
➥to launch iPod music player server: application not found
2013-03-02 16:04:13.893 player[80633:c07] MPMusicPlayer: Unable to
➥launch iPod music player server: application not found
2013-03-02 16:04:14.395 player[80633:c07] MPMusicPlayer: Unable to
➥launch iPod music player server: application not found
```

Any attempt to access the media library will result in a crash on the simulator with the following error:

```
*** Terminating app due to uncaught exception
➥'NSInternalInconsistencyException', reason: 'Unable to load
➥iPodUI.framework'
```

Building a Playback Engine

Before it makes sense to pull in any audio data, an in-depth understanding of the playback controls is required. To play music from within an app, a new instance of `MPMusicPlayerController` needs to be created. This is done in the header file `ICFViewController.h`, and the new object is called `player`. The `MPMusicPlayerController` will be referenced throughout this chapter to control the playback as well as retrieve information about the items being played.

```
@interface ICFViewController : UIViewController
{
    MPMusicPlayerController *player;
}

@property (nonatomic, retain) MPMusicPlayerController *player;
```

Inside the `viewDidLoad` method, the `MPMusicPlayerController` player can be initialized using a `MPMusicPlayerController` class method. There are two possible options when creating a new `MPMusicPlayerController`. In the first option, an `applicationMusicPlayer` will play music within an app; it will not affect the iPod state and will end playback when the app is exited. The second option, `iPodMusicPlayer`, will control the iPod app itself. It will pick up where the user has left the iPod playhead and track selection, and will continue to play after the app has entered the background. The sample app uses `applicationMusicPlayer`; however, this can easily be changed without the need to change any other code or behavior.

```
- (void)viewDidLoad
{
    [super viewDidLoad];

    player = [MPMusicPlayerController applicationMusicPlayer];
}
```

Registering for Playback Notifications

To efficiently work with music playback, it is important to be aware of the state of the music player. When you are dealing with the music player, there are three notifications to watch. The "now playing" item has changed, the volume has changed, and the playback state has changed. These states can be monitored by using `NSNotificationCenter` to subscribe to the aforementioned events. The sample app uses a new convenience method, `registerMediaPlayer Notifications`, to keep the sample app's code clean and readable. After the new observers have been added to `NSNotificationCenter`, the `beginGeneratingPlaybackNotifications` needs to be invoked on the player object.

```
- (void)registerMediaPlayerNotifications
{
    NSNotificationCenter *notificationCenter =  [NSNotificationCenter
    ➥defaultCenter];
```

```
    [notificationCenter addObserver: self
                        selector: @selector
                            (nowPlayingItemChanged:)
                        name:
➥MPMusicPlayerControllerNowPlayingItemDidChangeNotification
                        object: player];

    [notificationCenter addObserver: self
                        selector: @selector
                            (playbackStateChanged:)
                        name:
➥MPMusicPlayerControllerPlaybackStateDidChangeNotification
                        object: player];

    [notificationCenter addObserver: self
                        selector: @selector (volumeChanged:)
                        name:
➥MPMusicPlayerControllerVolumeDidChangeNotification
                        object: player];

    [player beginGeneratingPlaybackNotifications];
}
```

When registering for notifications, it is important to make sure that they are properly dereg-istered during memory and view cleanup; failing to do so can cause crashes and other unex-pected behavior. A call to endGeneratingPlaybackNotifications is also performed during the viewDidUnload routine.

```
- (void)viewWillDisappear:(BOOL)animated
{
    [[NSNotificationCenter defaultCenter] removeObserver: self
                                          name:
➥MPMusicPlayerControllerNowPlayingItemDidChangeNotification
                                          object: player];

    [[NSNotificationCenter defaultCenter] removeObserver: self
                                          name:
➥MPMusicPlayerControllerPlaybackStateDidChangeNotification
                                          object: player];

    [[NSNotificationCenter defaultCenter] removeObserver: self
                                          name:
➥MPMusicPlayerControllerVolumeDidChangeNotification
                                          object: player];
```

```
[player endGeneratingPlaybackNotifications];



    [super viewWillDisappear: animated];
}
```

In addition to registering for callbacks from the music player, a new `NSTimer` will be created to handle updating the playback progress and playhead time label. In the sample app, the `NSTimer` is simply called `playbackTimer`. For the time being, the notification callback selectors and the `NSTimer` behavior will be left uncompleted. These are discussed later, in the section "Handling State Changes."

User Controls

The sample app provides the user with several buttons designed to allow them to interact with the music, such as play, pause, skip, and previous, as well as jumping forward and backward by 30 seconds. The first action that needs to be implemented is the play and pause method. The button functions as a simple toggle: If the music is already playing, it is paused; if it is paused or stopped, it resumes playing. The code to update the text of the button from play to pause and vice versa is discussed as part of the state change notification callback in the section "Handling State Changes."

```
- (IBAction)playButtonAction:(id)sender
{
    if ([player playbackState] == MPMusicPlaybackStatePlaying)
    {
        [player pause];
    }

    else
    {
        [player play];
    }
}
```

The user should also have the ability to skip to the previous or next track while listening to music. This is done through two additional calls on the `player` object.

```
- (IBAction)previousButtonAction:(id)sender
{
    [player skipToPreviousItem];
}
```

```
- (IBAction)nextButtonAction:(id)sender
{
    [player skipToNextItem];
}
```

Users can also be provided with actions that allow them to skip 30 seconds forward or backward in a song. If the user hits the end of the track, the following code will skip to the next track; likewise, if they hit further than the start of a song, the audio track will start over. Both of these methods make use of the currentPlaybackTime property of the player object. This property can be used to change the current playhead, as well as determine what the current playback time is.

```
- (IBAction)skipBack30Seconds:(id)sender
{
    int newPlayHead = player.currentPlaybackTime - 30;

    if(newPlayHead < 0)
    {
        newPlayHead = 0;
    }

    player.currentPlaybackTime = newPlayHead;
}


- (IBAction)skipForward30Seconds:(id)sender
{
    int newPlayHead = player.currentPlaybackTime + 30;

    if(newPlayHead > currentSongDuration)
    {
        [player skipToNextItem];
    }

    else
    {
        player.currentPlaybackTime = newPlayHead;
    }
}
```

In addition to these standard controls to give the user control over the item playing, the sample app enables the user to change the volume of the audio. The player object takes a float value of 0.0 for muted to 1.0 for full volume. Since the sample uses a UISlider, the value can directly be passed into the player.

```
- (IBAction)volumeSliderChanged:(id)sender
{
    [player setVolume:[volumeSlider value]];
}
```

Handling State Changes

Earlier in this section, three notifications were registered to receive callbacks. These notifications allow the app to determine the current state and behavior of the `MPMusicPlayerController`. The first method that is being watched will be called whenever the currently playing item changes. This method contains two parts. The first part updates the album artwork, and the second updates the labels that indicate the artist, song title, and album being played.

Every audio or video item being played through the `MPMusicPlayerController` is represented by an `MPMediaItem` object. This object can be retrieved by invoking the method `nowPlaying-Item` on an instance of `MPMusicPlayerController`.

A new `UIImage` is created to represent the album artwork and is initially set to a placeholder that will be used in the event that the user does not have album artwork for the `MPMediaItem`. `MPMediaItem` uses key value properties for stored data; a full list is shown in Table 6.1. A new `MPMediaItemArtwork` is created and set with the artwork data. Although the documentation specifies that if no artwork is available this will return `nil`, in practice this is not the case. A workaround is to load the artwork into a `UIImage` and check the resulting value. If it is `nil`, the assumption is that there is no album artwork and the placeholder is loaded. The code used in the sample app will continue to function in the event that `MPMediaItemArtwork` begins returning `nil` when no album artwork is available.

Table 6.1 **Available Keys When Working with `MPMediaItem`**

Keys for `MPMediaItem` Properties	Available for Predicate Searching
MPMediaItemPropertyPersistentID	YES
MPMediaItemPropertyAlbumPersistentID	YES
MPMediaItemPropertyArtistPersistentID	YES
MPMediaItemPropertyAlbumArtistPersistentID	YES
MPMediaItemPropertyGenrePersistentID	YES
MPMediaItemPropertyComposerPersistentID	YES
MPMediaItemPropertyPodcastPersistentID	YES
MPMediaItemPropertyMediaType	YES
MPMediaItemPropertyTitle	YES
MPMediaItemPropertyAlbumTitle	YES
MPMediaItemPropertyArtist	YES
MPMediaItemPropertyAlbumArtist	YES
MPMediaItemPropertyGenre	YES
MPMediaItemPropertyComposer	YES
MPMediaItemPropertyPlaybackDuration	NO

Keys for `MPMediaItem` Properties	Available for Predicate Searching
`MPMediaItemPropertyAlbumTrackNumber`	NO
`MPMediaItemPropertyAlbumTrackCount`	NO
`MPMediaItemPropertyDiscNumber`	NO
`MPMediaItemPropertyDiscCount`	NO
`MPMediaItemPropertyArtwork`	NO
`MPMediaItemPropertyLyrics`	NO
`MPMediaItemPropertyIsCompilation`	YES
`MPMediaItemPropertyReleaseDate`	NO
`MPMediaItemPropertyBeatsPerMinute`	NO
`MPMediaItemPropertyComments`	NO
`MPMediaItemPropertyAssetURL`	NO
`MPMediaItemPropertyIsCloudItem`	YES

The second part of the `nowPlayingItemChanged:` method handles updating the song title, artist info, and album name, as shown earlier in Figure 6.1. In the event that any of these properties returns `nil`, a placeholder string is set. A complete list of accessible properties on a `MPMediaItem` can be found in Table 6.1. When referencing the table, note that if the media item is a podcast, additional keys will be available, which are available in Apple's documentation for `MPMediaItem`. Also indicated is whether the key can be used for predicate searching when programmatically finding `MPMediaItems`.

```
- (void) nowPlayingItemChanged: (id) notification
{
    MPMediaItem *currentItem = [player nowPlayingItem];

    UIImage *artworkImage = [UIImage imageNamed:@"noArt.png"];

    MPMediaItemArtwork *artwork = [currentItem valueForProperty:
    ➥MPMediaItemPropertyArtwork];

    if (artwork)
    {
        artworkImage = [artwork imageWithSize: CGSizeMake (120,120)];

        if(artworkImage == nil)
        {
            artworkImage = [UIImage imageNamed:@"noArt.png"];
        }
    }
```

```objc
[albumImageView setImage:artworkImage];

NSString *titleString = [currentItem
➥valueForProperty:MPMediaItemPropertyTitle];

if (titleString)
{
    songLabel.text = titleString;
}

else
{
    songLabel.text = @"Unknown Song";
}

NSString *artistString = [currentItem
➥valueForProperty:MPMediaItemPropertyArtist];

if (artistString)
{
        artistLabel.text = artistString;

}

else
{
    artistLabel.text = @"Unknown artist";
}

NSString *albumString = [currentItem
➥valueForProperty:MPMediaItemPropertyAlbumTitle];

if (albumString)
{
        recordLabel.text = albumString;
}

else
{
    recordLabel.text = @"Unknown Record";
    }
}
```

Monitoring the state of the music player is a crucial step, especially since this value can be affected by input outside the control of the app. In the event that the state is updated, the playbackStateChanged: method is fired. A new variable playbackState is created to hold onto the current state of the player. This method performs several important tasks, the first of which is updating the text on the play/pause button to reflect the current state. In addition, the NSTimer that was mentioned in the "Registering for Playback Notifications" section is both created and torn down. While the app is playing audio, the timer is set to fire every 0.3 seconds; this is used to update the playback duration labels as well as the UIProgressIndicator that informs the user of the placement of the playhead. The method that the timer fires, updateCurrentPlaybackTimer, is discussed in the next subsection.

In addition to the states that are shown in the sample app, there are three additional states. The first, MPMusicPlaybackStateInterrupted, is used whenever the audio is being interrupted, such as by an incoming phone call. The other two states, MPMusicPlaybackStateSeekingForward and MPMusicPlaybackStateSeekingBackward, are used to indicate that the music player is seeking either forward or backward.

```
- (void) playbackStateChanged: (id) notification
{
    MPMusicPlaybackState playbackState = [player playbackState];

    if (playbackState == MPMusicPlaybackStatePaused)
    {
            [playButton setTitle:@"Play"
            ➥forState:UIControlStateNormal];

        if([playbackTimer isValid])
        {
            [playbackTimer invalidate];
        }
    }

    else if (playbackState == MPMusicPlaybackStatePlaying)
    {
            [playButton setTitle:@"Pause" forState:
            ➥UIControlStateNormal];

        playbackTimer = [NSTimer
        scheduledTimerWithTimeInterval:0.3
        target:self
        selector:@selector(updateCurrentPlaybackTime)
        userInfo:nil
        repeats:YES];
    }
```

```
    else if (playbackState == MPMusicPlaybackStateStopped)
    {
            [playButton setTitle:@"Play"
            ➥forState:UIControlStateNormal];

            [player stop];

            if([playbackTimer isValid])
            {
                    [playbackTimer invalidate];
            }
    }
}
```

In the event that the volume has changed, it is also important to reflect that change on the volume slider found in the app. This is done by watching for the `volumeChanged:` notification callback. From inside this method the current volume of the player can be polled and the `volumeSlider` can be set accordingly.

```
- (void) volumeChanged: (id) notification
{
    [volumeSlider setValue:[player volume]];
}
```

Duration and Timers

Under most circumstances, users will want to have information available to them about the current status of their song, such as how much time has been played and how much time is left in the track. The sample app features two methods for generating this data. The first `updateSongDuration` is called whenever the song changes or when the app is launched. A reference to the current track being played is created, and the song duration expressed in seconds is retrieved through the key `playbackDuration`. The total hours, minutes, and seconds are derived from this data, and the song duration is displayed in a label next to the `UIProgressIndicator`.

```
-(void)updateSongDuration;
{
    currentSongPlaybackTime = 0;

    currentSongDuration = [[[player nowPlayingItem] valueForProperty:
    ➥@"playbackDuration"] floatValue];

    int tHours = (currentSongDuration / 3600);
    int tMins = ((currentSongDuration / 60) - tHours*60);
    int tSecs = (currentSongDuration) - (tMins*60) - (tHours *3600);
```

```
    songDurationLabel.text = [NSString stringWithFormat:@"%i:
➡%02d:%02d", tHours, tMins, tSecs ];

    currentTimeLabel.text = @"0:00:00";
}
```

The second method, updateCurrentPlaybackTime, is called every 0.3 seconds via an NSTimer that is controlled from the playbackStateChanged: method discussed in the "Handling State Changes" section. The same math is used to derive the hours, minutes, and seconds as in the updateSongDuration method. A percentagePlayed is also calculated based on the previously determined song duration and is used to update the playbackProgressIndicator. Since the currentPlaybackTime is accurate only to one second, this method does not need to be called more often. However, the more regularly it is called, the better precision to the actual second it will be.

```
- (void)updateCurrentPlaybackTime;
{
    currentSongPlaybackTime = player.currentPlaybackTime;

    int tHours = (currentSongPlaybackTime / 3600);
    int tMins = ((currentSongPlaybackTime / 60) - tHours*60);
    int tSecs = (currentSongPlaybackTime) - (tMins*60) - (tHours*3600);

    currentTimeLabel.text = [NSString stringWithFormat:@"%i:
➡%02d:%02d", tHours, tMins, tSecs ];

    float percentagePlayed = currentSongPlaybackTime/
    currentSongDuration;

    [playbackProgressIndicator setProgress:percentagePlayed];
}
```

Shuffle and Repeat

In addition to the properties and controls mentioned previously, an MPMusicPlayer Controller also allows the user to specify the repeat and shuffle properties. Although the sample app does not implement functionality for these two properties, they are fairly easy to implement.

```
player.repeatMode = MPMusicRepeatModeAll;
player.shuffleMode = MPMusicShuffleModeSongs;
```

The available repeat modes are MPMusicRepeatModeDefault, which is the user's predefined preference, MPMusicRepeatModeNone, MPMusicRepeatModeOne, and MPMusicRepeatModeAll.

The available modes for shuffle are `MPMusicShuffleModeDefault`, `MPMusicShuffleModeOff`, `MPMusicShuffleModeSongs`, and `MPMusicShuffleModeAlbums`, where the `MPMusicShuffleModeDefault` mode represents the user's predefined preference.

Media Picker

The simplest way to allow a user to specify which song he wants to hear is to provide him access to an `MPMediaPickerController`, as shown in Figure 6.2. The `MPMediaPickerController` allows the user to browse his artists, songs, playlists, and albums to specify one or more songs that should be considered for playback. To use an `MPMediaPickerController`, the class first needs to specify that it handles the delegate `MPMediaPickerControllerDelegate`, which has two required methods. The first `media Picker:didPickMediaItems:` is called when the user has completed selecting the songs she would like to hear. Those songs are returned as an `MPMediaItemCollection` object, and the `MPMusicPlayerController` can directly take this object as a parameter of `setQueueWith ItemCollection:`. After a new queue has been set for the `MPMusicPlayerController`, it can begin to play the new items. The `MPMediaPickerController` does not dismiss itself after completing a selection and requires explicit use of `dismissViewControllerAnimated: completion:`.

```
- (void) mediaPicker: (MPMediaPickerController *) mediaPicker
➥didPickMediaItems: (MPMediaItemCollection *) mediaItemCollection
{
    if (mediaItemCollection)
    {
        [player setQueueWithItemCollection: mediaItemCollection];
        [player play];
    }

    [self dismissViewControllerAnimated:YES completion:nil];
}
```

In the event that the user cancels or dismisses the `MPMediaPickerController` without making a selection, the delegate method `mediaPickerDidCancel:` is called. The developer is required to dismiss the `MPMediaPickerController` as part of this method.

```
- (void) mediaPickerDidCancel: (MPMediaPickerController *) mediaPicker
{
    [self dismissViewControllerAnimated:YES completion:nil];
}
```

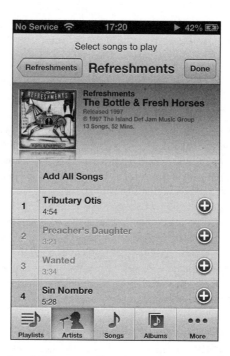

Figure 6.2   Selecting songs using the `MPMediaPickerController`. Two songs are selected by the user, indicated by the titles and info changing to light gray.

After the delegate methods have been implemented, an instance of `MPMediaPickerController` can be created. During allocation and initialization of a `MPMediaPickerController`, a parameter for supported media types is required. A full list of the available options is shown in Table 6.2. Note that each media item can be associated with multiple media types. Additional optional parameters for the `MPMediaPickerController` include specifying the selection of multiple items, and a prompt to be shown during selection, shown in Figure 6.2. An additional Boolean property also exists for setting whether iCloud items are shown; this is defaulted to `YES`.

```
- (IBAction)mediaPickerButtonAction:(id)sender
{
    MPMediaPickerController *mediaPicker =
    ➥[[MPMediaPickerController alloc] initWithMediaTypes:
    ➥MPMediaTypeAny];

    mediaPicker.delegate = self;
    mediaPicker.allowsPickingMultipleItems = YES;
    mediaPicker.prompt = @"Select songs to play";
```

```
[self presentViewController:mediaPicker animated:YES completion:
➥nil];

    [mediaPicker release];
}
```

Table 6.2 **Available Constant Accepted During the Specification of Media Types When Creating a New `MPMediaPickerController`**

Constant	Definition
MPMediaTypeMusic	Any type of music media item
MPMediaTypePodcast	An audio podcast media item
MPMediaTypeAudioBook	An audiobook media item
MPMediaTypeAudioITunesU	Audio media type associated with iTunes U
MPMediaTypeAnyAudio	Any audio media type
MPMediaTypeMovie	A media item that contains a movie
MPMediaTypeTVShow	A media item that contains a TV show
MPMediaTypeVideoPodcast	A video podcast, not to be confused with audio podcast (MPMediaTypePodcast)
MPMediaTypeMusicVideo	A music video media item
MPMediaTypeVideoITunesU	Video media from iTunes U, not to be confused with an audio iTunes U item (MPMediaTypeAudioITunesU)
MPMediaTypeAnyVideo	Any video media item
MPMediaTypeAny	Any media item both video and audio

These are all the steps required to allow a user to pick songs for playback using the `MPMediaPickerController`; however in many circumstances it might be necessary to provide a custom user interface or select songs with no interface at all. The next section, "Programmatic Picker," covers these topics.

Programmatic Picker

Often, it might be required to provide a more customized music selection option to a user. This might include creating a custom music selection interface or automatically searching for an artist or album. In this section the steps necessary to provide programmatic music selection are discussed.

To retrieve songs without using the `MPMediaPickerController`, a new instance of `MPMediaQuery` needs to be allocated and initialized. The `MPMediaQuery` functions as a store that references a number of `MPMediaItems`, each of which represents a single song or audio track to be played.

The sample app provides two methods that implement an `MPMediaQuery`. The first method, `playRandomSongAction:`, will find a single random track from the user's music library and play it using the existing `MPMusicPlayerController`. Finding music programmatically begins by allocating and initializing a new instance of `MPMediaQuery`.

Playing a Random Song

Without providing any predicate parameters, the `MPMediaQuery` will contain all the items found within the music library. A new `NSArray` is created to hold onto these items, which are retrieved using the item's method on the `MPMediaQuery`. Each item is represented by an `MPMediaItem`. The random song functionality of the sample app will play a single song at a time. If no songs were found in the query a `UIAlert` is presented to the user; however if multiple songs are found a single one is randomly selected.

After a single (or multiple) `MPMediaItem` has been found, a new `MPMediaItemCollection` is created by passing an array of `MPMediaItems` into it. This collection will serve as a playlist for the `MPMusicPlayerController`. After the collection has been created, it is passed to the player object using `setQueueWithItemCollection`. At this point the player now knows which songs the user intends to listen to, and a call of play on the player object will begin playing the `MPMediaItemCollection` in the order of the array that was used to create the `MPMediaItemCollection`.

```
- (IBAction)playRandomSongAction:(id)sender
{
    MPMediaItem *itemToPlay = nil;
    MPMediaQuery *allSongQuery = [MPMediaQuery songsQuery];
    NSArray *allTracks = [allSongQuery items];

    if([allTracks count] == 0)
    {
        UIAlertView *alert = [[UIAlertView alloc]
            initWithTitle:@"Error"
                message:@"No music found!"
                delegate:nil
        cancelButtonTitle:@"Dismiss"
        otherButtonTitles:nil];

        [alert show];
        [alert release];
```

```
        return;
    }

    if ([allTracks count] < 2)
    {
        itemToPlay = [allTracks lastObject];
    }

    int trackNumber = arc4random() % [allTracks count];
    itemToPlay = [allTracks objectAtIndex:trackNumber];

    MPMediaItemCollection * collection = [[MPMediaItemCollection
    alloc] initWithItems:[NSArray arrayWithObject:itemToPlay]];

    [player setQueueWithItemCollection:collection];
    [collection release];

    [player play];

    [self updateSongDuration];
    [self updateCurrentPlaybackTime];
}
```

Note

`arc4random()` is a member of the standard C library and can be used to generate a random number in Objective-C projects. Unlike most random-number-generation functions, `arc4random` is automatically seeded the first time it is called.

Predicate Song Matching

Often, an app won't just want to play random tracks and will want to perform a more advanced search. This is done using predicates. The following example uses a predicate to find music library items that have an artist property equal to `"Bob Dylan"`, as shown in Figure 6.3. This method functions very similarly to the previous random song example, except that `addFilterPredicate` is used to add the filter to the `MPMediaQuery`. In addition, the results are not filtered down to a single item, and the player is passed an array of all the matching songs. For a complete list of available predicate constants, see the second column of Table 6.1 in the "Handling State Changes" section. Multiple predicates can be used with supplemental calls to `addFilterPredicate` on the `MPMediaQuery`.

```objc
- (IBAction)playDylan:(id)sender
{
    MPMediaPropertyPredicate *artistNamePredicate =
    [MPMediaPropertyPredicate predicateWithValue: @"Bob Dylan"
                                   forProperty:
                MPMediaItemPropertyArtist];

    MPMediaQuery *artistQuery = [[MPMediaQuery alloc] init];

    [artistQuery addFilterPredicate: artistNamePredicate];

    NSArray *tracks = [artistQuery items];

    if([tracks count] == 0)
    {
        UIAlertView *alert = [[UIAlertView alloc]
        initWithTitle:@"Error"
        message:@"No music found!"
        delegate:nil
        cancelButtonTitle:@"Dismiss"
        otherButtonTitles:nil];

        [alert show];
        [alert release];

        return;
    }

    MPMediaItemCollection * collection = [[MPMediaItemCollection
    ➥alloc] initWithItems:tracks];

    [player setQueueWithItemCollection:collection];
    [collection release];

    [player play];

    [self updateSongDuration];
    [self updateCurrentPlaybackTime];
}
```

Figure 6.3   Using a predicate search to play tracks by the artist Bob Dylan.

Summary

This chapter covered accessing and working with a user's music library. The first topic covered was building a playback engine to allow a user to interact with the song playback, such as pausing, resuming, controlling the volume, and skipping. The next two sections covered accessing and selecting songs from the library. The media picker demonstrated using the built-in GUI to allow the user to select a song or group of songs, and the "Programmatic Picker" section dealt with finding and searching for songs using predicates.

The sample app demonstrated how to build a fully functional albeit simplified music player for iOS. The knowledge demonstrated in this chapter can be applied to creating a fully featured music player or adding a user's music library as background audio into any app.

Exercises

1. Add a scrubber to the playback indicator in the sample app to allow the user to drag the playhead back and forth, allowing for real-time seeking.

2. Add functionality to the sample app to allow the user to enter an artist or a song name and return a list of all matching results, which can then be played.

7

Working with and Parsing JSON

JSON is a great way to send data back and forth between servers, websites, and iOS apps. It is lighter and easier to handle than XML, and with iOS's built-in support for JSON, it is easy to integrate into an iOS project. Many popular websites, including Flickr, Twitter, and Google, offer APIs that provide results in JSON format, and many languages offer JSON support. This chapter demonstrates how to parse and present JSON from a sample message-board server in an app, and encode a new message entry in JSON to send to the server.

JSON

JavaScript Object Notation (JSON) is a lightweight format for sharing data. It is technically a part of the language JavaScript and provides a way to serialize JavaScript objects; however, practically, it is supported in a wide variety of programming languages, making it a great candidate for sharing data between different platforms. JSON also has the benefit of being human-readable.

JSON has a simple and intuitive syntax. At its most basic level, a JSON document can contain "objects," which are essentially key-value dictionaries like Objective-C programmers are familiar with, or arrays. JSON can contain arrays of objects and arrays of values, and can nest arrays and objects. Values stored in JSON, either in arrays or associated with a key, can be other JSON objects, strings, numbers, or arrays, or true, false, or null.

Benefits of Using JSON

There are many reasons to use JSON in an iOS app:

- **Server Support:** Communicating information to and from a remote server is a common use case for iOS apps. Since so many server languages have built-in support for JSON, it is a natural choice as a data format.

- **Lightweight:** JSON has little formatting overhead when compared to XML and can present a significant savings in the amount of bandwidth needed to transmit data between a server and a device.

- **iOS Support:** JSON is now fully supported as of iOS 5 with the addition of the NSJSONSerialization class. This class can conveniently provide an NSDictionary or NSArray (or even mutable varieties) from JSON data or can encode an NSDictionary or NSArray into JSON.

- **Presentation and Native Handling:** The simplest method to get data from a server to an iOS device is just to use a UIWebView and display a web page; however, this approach has drawbacks in terms of performance and presentation. In many cases it is much better to just pull the data from the server, and present it on the device using native tools like UITableView. Performance can be much better, and presentation can be optimized to work on iOS screen sizes and take advantage of available retina displays.

JSON Resources

For more information on JSON, visit http://json.org. That site has a formal definition of JSON, with specific information on format and syntax.

Sample App Overview

The sample app for this chapter is Message Board, including a Ruby on Rails server and an iOS app.

The Ruby on Rails server consists of just one object: the message. It has been set up to support sending a list of messages in JSON, and to accept new messages in JSON format. The server also supports Web-based interactions.

The iOS app will pull messages from the server and display them in a standard table view and will be able to post new messages to the server in JSON format.

Accessing the Server

To view the Message Board Ruby on Rails server, visit http://freezing-cloud-6077.herokuapp. com/. The Messages home screen will be visible, as shown in Figure 7.1.

The messages server has been set up to handle creating and displaying messages on the Web and with JSON.

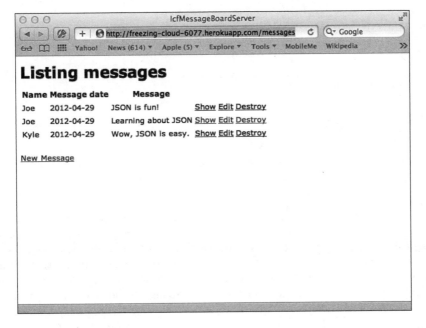

Figure 7.1   Messages home screen.

Getting JSON from the Server

To update the sample iOS app to handle JSON, the first thing to address is pulling the message list from the server and displaying it.

Building the Request

First set up the URL (in the `MessageBoard-Prefix.pch` file) so that the app can make calls to the right location:

```
#define kMessageBoardServerURLString

@"http://freezing-cloud-6077.herokuapp.com/messages.json"
```

In the `ICFViewController.m` implementation, look at the `viewWillAppear:` method. This code will initiate the request to the server:

```
NSURL *msgURL = [NSURL URLWithString:kMessageBoardURLString];
NSURLRequest *msgRequest =
[NSURLRequest requestWithURL:msgURL
                cachePolicy:NSURLRequestUseProtocolCachePolicy
            timeoutInterval:60.0];
```

```
NSURLConnection *theConnection =
[[NSURLConnection alloc] initWithRequest:msgRequest
                                  delegate:self];

if (theConnection) {
    NSMutableData *connData = [[NSMutableData alloc] init];
    [self setConnectionData:connData];
} else {
    NSLog(@"Connection failed...");
    [self.activityView setHidden:YES];
    [self.activityIndicator stopAnimating];

}
```

This creates and initiates a network request to the `messages.json` resource at the server URL. If the connection works, it sets up an `NSData ivar` to store the response data; otherwise, it just logs a failure. The network request will run asynchronously, and when data comes back it will hit the delegate methods set up in the class. The important thing to note is that nothing special is required here for JSON; this is a standard network call. The only difference is that the `.json` extension used in the URL tells the server the response should be in JSON format.

> **Note**
>
> Using the `.json` extension is not required for servers to return JSON format data; that is just how the sample server was set up. It is a common approach but is not required.

Inspecting the Response

To receive data from the network connection, implement two delegate methods:

```
- (void)connection:(NSURLConnection *)connection
didReceiveResponse:(NSURLResponse *)response
{
    [self.connectionData setLength:0];
}


- (void)connection:(NSURLConnection *)connection
    didReceiveData:(NSData *)data
{
    [self.connectionData appendData:data];
}
```

The first method just sets the data length to zero when the response from the server is initiated. Note that, in some cases, this can happen more than once (if the server initiates a redirect, for example). The second method just appends any received data to a local data object.

When the network connection is complete, it will call this delegate method:

```
- (void)connectionDidFinishLoading:(NSURLConnection *)connection
{
    NSString *retString =
    [NSString stringWithUTF8String:[connectionData bytes]];

    NSLog(@"json returned: %@", retString);

    ...

}
```

The log message will display on the console the data received:

```
json returned: [{"message":{"created_at":"2012-04-29T21:59:28Z",
"id":3, "message":"JSON is fun!", "message_date":"2012-04-29",
"name":"Joe","updated_at":"2012-04-29T21:59:28Z"}},
{"message":{"created_at":"2012-04-29T21:58:50Z","id":2,
"message":"Learning about JSON", "message_date":"2012-04-
29","name":"Joe", "updated_at":"2012-04-29T21:59:38Z"}},
{"message":{"created_at":"2012-04-29T22:00:00Z","id":4,
"message":"Wow, JSON is easy.", "message_date":"2012-04-
29","name":"Kyle", "updated_at":"2012-04-29T22:00:00Z"}},
{"message":{"created_at":"2012-04-29T22:46:18Z","id":5,
"message":"Trying a new message.", "message_date":"2012-04-
29","name":"Joe", "updated_at":"2012-04-29T22:46:18Z"}}]
```

Parsing JSON

Now that JSON has been received from the server, it is just a simple step to parse it. In the case of the sample app, an array of messages is expected, so parse the JSON into an NSArray:

```
- (void)connectionDidFinishLoading:(NSURLConnection *)connection
{
    ...

    NSError *parseError = nil;
    NSArray *jsonArray =
    [NSJSONSerialization JSONObjectWithData:connectionData
                               options:0
                                  error:&parseError];

    if (!parseError) {
        [self setMessageArray:jsonArray];
        NSLog(@"json array is %@", jsonArray);
        [messageTable reloadData];
    } else {
        NSString *err = [parseError localizedDescription];
```

```
        NSLog(@"Encountered error parsing: %@", err);
    }

    [connection release], connection = nil;
    [connectionData release], connectionData = nil;

    [self.activityView setHidden:YES];
    [self.activityIndicator stopAnimating];
}
```

NSJSONSerialization's method JSONObjectWithData:options:error: expects as parameters the data to be serialized, any desired options (for example, returning a mutable array
instead of a regular array), and a reference to an NSError in case there are any parsing errors.

In this example, a local instance variable has been updated to the just-parsed array, and the
table view has been told to reload data now that there is data to display.

Displaying the Data

Now that the JSON has been parsed into an NSArray, it can be displayed in a UITableView.
The magic here is that there is no magic; the JSON received from the server is now just an array
of NSDictionary instances. Each NSDictionary contains information for a message from the
server, with attribute names and values. To display this in a table, just access the array and
dictionaries as if they had been created locally.

```
- (UITableViewCell *)tableView:(UITableView *)tableView
        cellForRowAtIndexPath:(NSIndexPath *)indexPath
{
    UITableViewCell *cell =
    [tableView dequeueReusableCellWithIdentifier:@"MsgCell"];

    if (cell == nil) {
        cell = [[[UITableViewCell alloc]
                initWithStyle:UITableViewCellStyleSubtitle
                reuseIdentifier:@"MsgCell"] autorelease];

        cell.selectionStyle = UITableViewCellSelectionStyleNone;
    }
    NSDictionary *message =
    (NSDictionary *)[[self.messageArray
                    objectAtIndex:indexPath.row]
                    objectForKey:@"message"];

    NSString *byLabel =
    [NSString stringWithFormat:@"by %@ on %@",
     [message objectForKey:@"name"],
     [message objectForKey:@"message_date"]];
```

```
    cell.textLabel.text = [message objectForKey:@"message"];
    cell.detailTextLabel.text = byLabel;
    return cell;
}

- (NSInteger)tableView:(UITableView *)tableView
 numberOfRowsInSection:(NSInteger)section
{
    return [[self messageArray] count];
}
```

The parsed JSON data will be visible in a standard table view, as shown in Figure 7.2.

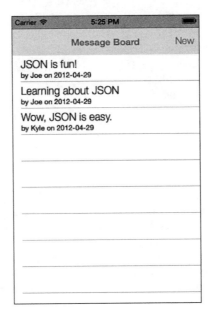

Figure 7.2   Sample app message table view.

Posting a Message

The sample app includes ICFNewMessageViewController to post new messages to the server. There are two fields on that controller: one for a name and one for a message (see Figure 7.3). After the user enters that information and hits Save, it will be encoded in JSON and sent to the server.

Figure 7.3   Sample app new message view.

Encoding JSON

An important detail for sending JSON to a Ruby on Rails server is to encode the data so that it mirrors what the Rails server provides. When sending a new message to the server, it should have the same structure as an individual message received in the message list. To do this, a dictionary with the attribute names and values for the message is needed, and then a wrapper dictionary with the key "message" pointing to the attribute dictionary. This will exactly mirror what the server sends for a message. In the `saveButtonTouched:` method set up this dictionary, like so:

```
NSMutableDictionary *messageDictionary =
[NSMutableDictionary dictionaryWithCapacity:1];

[messageDictionary setObject:[nameTextField text]
                   forKey:@"name"];

[messageDictionary setObject:[messageTextView text]
                   forKey:@"message"];

NSDate *today = [NSDate date];

NSDateFormatter *dateFormatter =
[[NSDateFormatter alloc] init];
```

```
NSString *dateFmt = @"yyyy'-'MM'-'dd'T'HH':'mm':'ss'Z'";
[dateFormatter setDateFormat:dateFmt];
[messageDictionary setObject:[dateFormatter stringFromDate:today]
                      forKey:@"message_date"];

[dateFormatter release];

NSDictionary *postDictionary =
[NSDictionary dictionaryWithObject:messageDictionary
                           forKey:@"message"];
```

Note that NSJSONSerialization accepts only instances of NSDictionary, NSArray, NSString, NSNumber, or NSNull. For dates or other data types not directly supported by NSJSONSerialization, they will need to be converted to a supported format. For example, in this example the date was converted to a string in a format expected by the server. Now that there is a dictionary, it is a simple step to encode it in JSON:

```
NSError *jsonSerializationError = nil;
NSData *jsonData = [NSJSONSerialization
                   dataWithJSONObject:postDictionary
                   options:NSJSONWritingPrettyPrinted
                   error:&jsonSerializationError];

if (!jsonSerializationError)
{
    NSString *serJSON =
    [[NSString alloc] initWithData:jsonData
                          encoding:NSUTF8StringEncoding];

    NSLog(@"serialized json: %@", serJSON);
        ...
} else
{
    NSLog(@"JSON Encoding failed: %@",
         [jsonSerializationError localizedDescription]);
}
```

NSJSONSerialization expects three parameters:

1. An NSDictionary or NSArray with the data to be encoded.

2. Serialization options (in our case, we specified NSJSONWritingPrettyPrinted so that it's easy to read; otherwise, the JSON is produced with no whitespace for compactness).

3. A reference to an NSError.

If there are no errors encoding the JSON, it will look like this:

```
serialized json: {
  "message" : {
    "message" : "Six Test Messages",
    "name" : "Joe",
    "message_date" : "2012-04-01T14:31:11Z"
  }
}
```

Sending JSON to the Server

After the JSON is encoded, there are a few important additional steps to send it to the server:

```
NSURL *messageBoardURL =
[NSURL URLWithString:kMessageBoardURLString];

NSMutableURLRequest *request = [NSMutableURLRequest
                          requestWithURL:messageBoardURL
                    cachePolicy:NSURLRequestUseProtocolCachePolicy
                    timeoutInterval:30.0];

[request setHTTPMethod:@"POST"]; // 1

[request setValue:@"application/json"
forHTTPHeaderField:@"Accept"]; //2

[request setValue:@"application/json"
forHTTPHeaderField:@"Content-Type"]; //2

[request setValue:[NSString stringWithFormat:@"%d",
[jsonData length]] forHTTPHeaderField:@"Content-Length"]; //3

[request setHTTPBody: jsonData]; //4

NSURLConnection *jsonConnection =
        [[NSURLConnection alloc] initWithRequest:request
                                    delegate:self];

if (jsonConnection)
{
    NSMutableData *connData = [[NSMutableData alloc] init];
    [self setConnectionData:connData];
    [connData release];
} else
{
    NSLog(@"Connection failed...");
}
```

The first step is to make sure that the request method is set to POST. This will ensure that the correct method on the server (create) gets called.

The second step is to set the "Accept" and "Content-Type" headers on the request to "application/json". This will inform the server that the app is sending JSON and it should treat the body of the request as JSON data.

The third step is to set the content length of the post. This is simple to determine; it is just the length of the JSON data being attached as the body of the request.

The fourth step (and arguably the most important) is to set the body of the request to be the encoded JSON data.

After all that is complete, the connection can be initiated, which will send the new message to the server asynchronously. When the connection finishes, dismiss the create view and refresh the message list.

Summary

This chapter introduced JSON (or JavaScript Object Notation). It explained how to request JSON data from a server in an iOS app, parse it, and display it in a table. The chapter described how to encode an NSDictionary or NSArray into JSON, and send it over the network to a server.

Exercise

1. Add logic to the message list network call and the message post network call to check the HTTP response code. Handle the error if it is not 200 OK.

Getting Started with iCloud

iCloud is a set of cloud-based services provided by Apple. It was introduced with iOS 5 as a replacement for MobileMe, and generally provides cloud storage and automatic syncing between iOS devices, OS X devices, and the Web. iCloud includes email, address book, and calendar syncing; automated iOS device backup and restore; a "Find My iPhone" feature to locate and/or disable a lost device; a "Find My Friends" feature to share locations with family or friends; "Photo Stream," which automatically syncs photos to other devices; "Back to My Mac," which allows configurationless access to a user's Mac over the Internet; and "iTunes Match," which provides access to a user's music library without uploading and syncing. In addition, iCloud provides the ability for apps to store app-specific data in the cloud and automatically sync between devices. At the time of this writing, iCloud provides 5GB of storage free, and offers paid plans for additional storage.

For app-specific storage and syncing, iCloud supports three approaches: document-based storage and syncing (based on NSDocument *or* UIDocument*), key-value storage and syncing (similar to* NSUserDefaults*), and Core Data syncing. This chapter explains how to set up an app to sync via iCloud using* UIDocument *and key-value store syncing. Using Core Data with iCloud is not covered; although the setup and initial implementation are relatively straightforward, there are some challenging implementation issues that make using iCloud with Core Data risky. Specifically, there are complexities associated with initial data syncing when migrating from an existing dataset, problems with users shutting off iCloud or deleting iCloud data, and several other detailed issues. Refer to Marcus Zarra's second edition of* Core Data *from The Pragmatic Programmers for a thorough explanation of these issues and some recommended approaches to handle them.*

The Sample App

The sample app for this chapter is called MyNotes, which is a simple note editor. Notes are constructed using a custom subclass of UIDocument, and are synced between devices using iCloud. The sample app also uses the iCloud-based key-value store to keep track of which note has most recently been edited, and syncs that information between devices.

In a shipping app, support for iCloud would typically be optional, because not all users have or use iCloud accounts. The sample app assumes that iCloud is available for simplicity, and does not support "local only" usage without an iCloud account. The major difference is the URL where files are stored; for local-only storage, user-generated files should be in the `Documents` directory inside the app sandbox. For iCloud, documents are stored in a special directory with a URL provided by the system (as seen in the next section, "Setting Up the App for iCloud Support," and in the later section "Initializing iCloud").

Setting Up the App for iCloud Support

To set up an app to use iCloud, it used to be that several steps were required. Entitlements for the app needed to be set up, and the app needed to be configured in the iOS Provisioning Portal for iCloud support. iCloud usage can be tested only on the device, so the provisioning profile work needed to be completed in order for an iCloud app to work. With the introduction of Xcode 5, this process has been significantly streamlined and can be done entirely within Xcode 5.

Account Setup

Xcode 5 needs iOS developer account information in order to connect to the Member Center and perform all the setup necessary for iCloud on the developer's behalf. Select Xcode, Preferences from the Xcode 5 menu, and then select the Accounts tab, as shown in Figure 8.1.

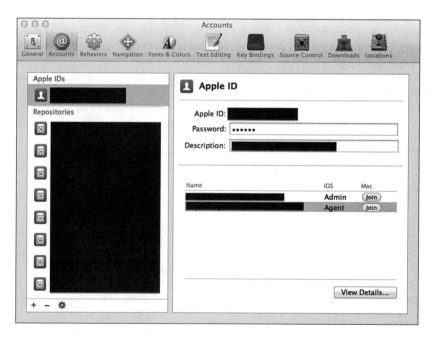

Figure 8.1   Xcode 5 Accounts tab.

To add a new account, click the plus sign in the lower left of the Accounts tab, and select Apple ID. Enter the account credentials and click the Add button. Xcode will validate the credentials and gather account information if valid. Click the View Details button to see what certificates and provisioning profiles are currently configured for an account, as shown in Figure 8.2.

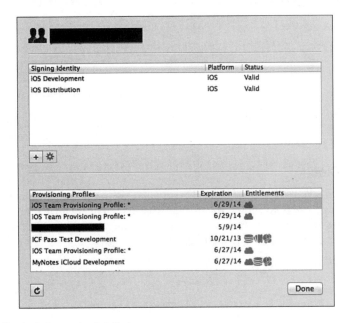

Figure 8.2   Xcode 5 Accounts detail view.

Enabling iCloud Capabilities

After Xcode 5 has account credentials, it can configure apps with capabilities on behalf of the account. It can set up App IDs, entitlements, and provisioning profiles as needed. To set up the iCloud capability, view the MyNotes Target in Xcode, click the Capabilities tab, and find the iCloud section. Change the iCloud switch to On and Xcode will automatically create an entitlements file for the project. Check the Use Key-Value Store checkbox to enable the key-value store for the app. Xcode will automatically populate an entry with the project's bundle ID in the Ubiquity Containers table. For the sample app, this is all that is needed; for a more complex app that shares with a Mac OS X application and that would need to support more than one ubiquity container name, additional ubiquity container names can be added here. Xcode will check with the developer portal to see whether the App ID is configured correctly for iCloud. If not, Xcode will display the issue as shown in Figure 8.3. Tap the Fix Issue button and Xcode will communicate with the developer portal and fix any issues with the app setup.

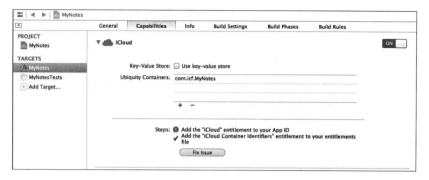

Figure 8.3   Xcode 5 Accounts detail view.

Initializing iCloud

Each time the app is run, a call must be made to the `URLForUbiquityContainerIdentifier`
method of `NSFileManager` to get the URL for the iCloud container where files can be stored
and synced. The `setupiCloud` method is called from the app delegate's `application:`
`didFinishLaunchingWithOptions:` method.

```objc
- (void)setupiCloud
{
    dispatch_queue_t background_queue =
    dispatch_get_global_queue(DISPATCH_QUEUE_PRIORITY_DEFAULT,
                              0);

    dispatch_async(background_queue, ^{

        NSFileManager *fileManager =
        [NSFileManagerdefaultManager];

        NSURL *iCloudURL =
        [fileManager URLForUbiquityContainerIdentifier:nil];

        if (iCloudURL != nil)
        {
            NSLog(@"iCloud URL is available");
        }
        else
        {
            NSLog(@"iCloud URL is NOT available");
        }
    });
}
```

The first time this call is made, it will set up the directory for the app. Subsequent calls will confirm that the URL still exists. If iCloud support is enabled for the app, a valid URL will be returned. If iCloud is not available, `nil` is returned. It is entirely possible that the user might disable iCloud for an app (or altogether on a device) and iCloud might no longer be available. A shipping app would need a sensible strategy to notify the user when iCloud support has been lost, and to redirect any file activity to the local `Documents` directory in that case.

An important detail to note is that the call to `URLForUbiquityContainer:` is made on a background queue. This is done because the call might take an indeterminate amount of time to return. If this is the first instance of the app and there is no data, it will complete and return quickly. However, if this is a second instance of the app on another device and there are several documents to download, it might take some time for the system to set up the directory and begin populating the files from the cloud. The user interface will need to take this timing issue into consideration.

Introducing `UIDocument`

When an app's functionality works around user-centric, document-style data, subclassing `UIDocument` is appropriate. `UIDocument` is designed to automate many of the typical functions needed when interacting with documents. For example, `UIDocument` supports automatic saving, and background loading and saving of documents to avoid affecting the main queue and slowing down the user interface. In addition, `UIDocument` abstracts away the loading and saving logic into simple calls, so the developer just needs to write simple logic to translate the document data to and from `NSData`. Most important for this chapter, `UIDocument` automates interactions with iCloud as well.

Subclassing `UIDocument`

In the sample app, each note that a user creates is an instance of a custom `UIDocument` subclass called `ICFMyNoteDocument`. Subclasses of `UIDocument` should implement the `contentsForType:error:` method and the `loadFromContents:ofType:error:` method, and then implement change tracking to enable `UIDocument`'s autosaving feature. Because the notes in the sample app are only storing the note text in a string, these methods are simple to implement.

```
- (id)contentsForType:(NSString *)typeName
               error:(NSError *__autoreleasing *)outError
{
    if (!self.myNoteText)
    {
        [self setMyNoteText:@""];
    }
}
```

```
    NSData *myNoteData =
    [self.myNoteText dataUsingEncoding:NSUTF8StringEncoding];

    return myNoteData;
}
```

In the `contentsForType:error:`, the method first checks whether there is a value in `myNoteText`; if not, it provides a default to prevent a crash. Next, `myNoteText` is translated to `NSData` and returned. The `NSData` is what the `UIDocument` will save. The `loadFromContents:ofType:error:` method reverses the process.

```
- (BOOL)loadFromContents:(id)contents
                  ofType:(NSString *)typeName
                   error:(NSError *__autoreleasing *)outError
{
    if ([contents length] >0)
    {
        NSString *textFromData =
        [[NSStringalloc] initWithData:contents
                             encoding:NSUTF8StringEncoding];

        [self setMyNoteText:textFromData];
    }

    else
    {
        [self setMyNoteText:@""];
    }

    if (self.delegate && [self.delegaterespondsToSelector:
                         @selector(documentContentsDidChange:)])
    {
        [self.delegate documentContentsDidChange:self];
    }

    return YES;
}
```

The `UIDocument` returns the saved contents in `NSData` format, and it is up to the method to translate it into the properties in the subclass. The method checks the length of the content. If there does not appear to be any content, the method defaults `myNoteText` to an empty string; otherwise, it converts the `NSData` to `NSString` and populates `myNoteText` with the results. Lastly, the method informs the delegate of the change to the document so that it can take the appropriate action, such as update the user interface with the newly loaded data.

To enable the automatic save feature that `UIDocument` provides, the subclass needs to implement change tracking. Change tracking is enabled with the `undoManager` provided by `UIDocument`.

```
- (void)setMyNoteText:(NSString *)newMyNoteText
{
    NSString *oldNoteText = _myNoteText;
    _myNoteText = [newMyNoteText copy];

    SEL setNoteText = @selector(setMyNoteText:);

    [self.undoManager setActionName:@"Text Change"];
    [self.undoManager registerUndoWithTarget:self
                                    selector:setNoteText
                                      object:oldNoteText];
}
```

Note that no additional action is required to get autosaving; the app does not need to actually implement undo functionality. After the `undoManager` has an action, registered autosaving is enabled.

Interacting with `UIDocument`

To create a new instance of a `UIDocument` subclass, first determine the URL where the file needs to be saved. When the user taps the plus button in the sample app, the master view controller has a method to determine a filename for a new note called `newMyNoteName`. That method starts with "MyNote" as a base, and adds a number at the end. It checks for the existence of a note with that filename, and then increments the number if one already exists, until an unused filename is created. That filename is added to the end of the iCloud directory URL path to get the full path for the file. That URL is then passed to the detail view controller, where the `configureView` method determines whether the file already exists using `NSFileManager`, and then creates or loads it as necessary.

```
[self.myNoteTextView setText:@""];

myNoteDocument =
[[ICFMyNoteDocument alloc] initWithFileURL:[self myNoteURL]];

[myNoteDocument setDelegate:self];

NSFileManager *fileManager = [NSFileManager defaultManager];

if ([fileManager fileExistsAtPath:[self.myNoteURL path]])
{

    [myNoteDocument openWithCompletionHandler:^(BOOL success)
    {

        [self.myNoteTextView
         setText:[myNoteDocument myNoteText]];
```

```
        UIDocumentState state = myNoteDocument.documentState;

        if (state == UIDocumentStateNormal)
        {
            [self.myNoteTextView becomeFirstResponder];
        }
    }];
}
else
{
    [myNoteDocument saveToURL:[self myNoteURL]
            forSaveOperation:UIDocumentSaveForCreating
            completionHandler:nil];
    [self.myNoteTextView becomeFirstResponder];
}
```

To create a document, the `saveToURL:forSaveOperation:completionHandler:` method on `UIDocument` is used, specifying the `UIDocumentSaveForCreating` save operation. To open an existing document, the `openWithCompletionHandler` method is used, specifying a completion block. In this case the completion block will update the user interface and make the text view the first responder to begin editing the note. Note that the logic checks the `documentState` for the document. This indicates whether the document can be edited, or whether it is in a conflict state that needs to be resolved (covered later in the chapter). See the later section "Detecting Conflicts in iCloud" for more detail.

Interacting with iCloud

The introduction of iCloud to an app adds some additional complexity that the app needs to handle. Listing available documents in a non-iCloud-enabled app is simple; however, with iCloud the list of available documents can change at any time, even when the list is being generated and displayed. In addition, since documents can potentially be edited on multiple devices at the same time, conflicts can occur that otherwise wouldn't in a non-iCloud app. This section describes how to handle these situations correctly.

Listing Documents in iCloud

To show the list of notes created and available, the app needs to query the iCloud directory to find out what files are there. This is done with an `NSMetadataQuery`.

```
- (NSMetadataQuery*)noteListQuery
{
    NSMetadataQuery *setupQuery = [[NSMetadataQuery alloc] init];
    [setupQuery setSearchScopes:
    @[NSMetadataQueryUbiquitousDocumentsScope]];
```

```
    NSString *filePattern = [NSStringstringWithFormat:
    @"*.%@",kICFMyNoteDocumentExtension];

    [setupQuery setPredicate:[NSPredicate predicateWithFormat:
    @"%K LIKE %@",NSMetadataItemFSNameKey,filePattern]];

    return setupQuery;
}
```

The `NSMetadataQuery` is set up with the `NSMetadataQueryUbiquitousDocumentsScope` search scope, which is the iCloud directory for the app. Then a predicate is set up using a file pattern string that will match all documents with the file extension `.icfnote`. The metadata query is set up in the `ICFMasterViewController`'s `viewDidLoad` method, and the view controller is set up to receive notifications from the `NSMetadataQuery`.

```
if (!noteQuery)
{
    noteQuery = [self noteListQuery];
}

NSNotificationCenter *notifCenter =
[NSNotificationCenter defaultCenter];

NSString *metadataFinished =
NSMetadataQueryDidFinishGatheringNotification;

[notifCenter addObserver:self
              selector:@selector(processFiles:)
                  name:metadataFinished
                object:nil];

NSString *metadataUpdated =
NSMetadataQueryDidUpdateNotification;

[notifCenter addObserver:self
              selector:@selector(processFiles:)
                  name:metadataUpdated
                object:nil];
```

The two notifications will call the `processFiles:` method when the `NSMetadataQuery` has finished gathering information that matches the predicate, and when external changes from iCloud have occurred. The directory will be updated when iCloud syncs a new file from another device.

```
- (void)processFiles:(NSNotification*)notification
{
    NSMutableArray *foundFiles = [[NSMutableArrayalloc] init];
    [noteQuery disableUpdates];
```

```
NSArray *queryResults = [noteQuery results];
for (NSMetadataItem *result in queryResults)
{

    NSURL *fileURL =
    [result valueForAttribute:NSMetadataItemURLKey];

    NSNumber *isHidden = nil;

    [fileURL getResourceValue:&isHidden
                       forKey:NSURLIsHiddenKey
                        error:nil];

    if (isHidden && ![isHidden boolValue])
    {
        [foundFiles addObject:fileURL];
    }
}

[noteList removeAllObjects];
[noteList addObjectsFromArray:foundFiles];
[self.tableViewreloadData];

[noteQuery enableUpdates];
}
```

When `processFiles:` is called, it is important to have the `NSMetadataQuery` stop getting updates while the results are being processed. This will prevent it from getting called again in the middle of an update and potentially crashing or getting spurious results. Then the results from the query can be iterated, and an updated list of notes can be created. After the list is created, the table view will be updated, as shown in Figure 8.4. Then the `NSMetadataQuery` is instructed to resume getting file-system updates.

The list of files produced by `NSMetadataQuery` is an array of `NSURL`s. In the `tableView:cell ForRowAtIndexPath:`, the `NSURL` is trimmed to be just the filename without the extension for display in the table cell.

```
NSURL *myNoteURL =
[noteList objectAtIndex:[indexPath row]];

NSString *noteName =
[[myNoteURL lastPathComponent] stringByDeletingPathExtension];

if ([self.lastUpdatedNote isEqualToString:noteName])
{
```

```
        NSString *lastUpdatedCellTitle =
        [NSString stringWithFormat:@"★ %@",noteName];

        [cell.textLabel setText:lastUpdatedCellTitle];
}
else
{
        [cell.textLabelsetText:noteName];
}
```

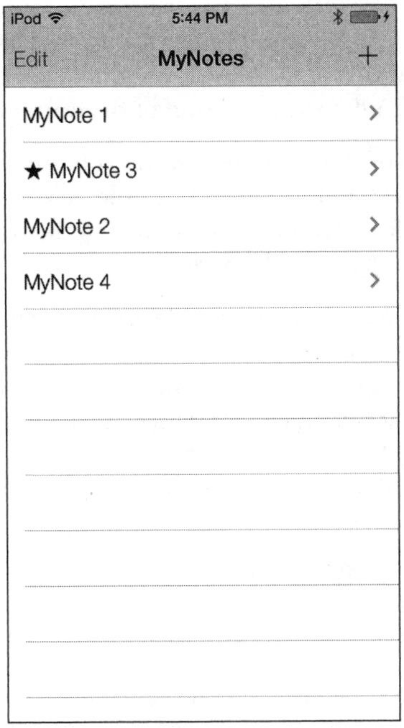

Figure 8.4   MyNotes sample app—note list.

The if logic checks to see whether the note for a row is the last updated note, which is maintained using iCloud's key value store, described later (see the section "Key-Value Store Syncing" for more detail). If so, it adds a star to the filename.

Opening a document or creating a new document has already been covered, in the "Interacting with UIDocument" section. When a row in the table is selected or the Add button is tapped, the URL for the new or existing document will be passed to the detail view controller, which will open or create the document, set up the text view with the text from the document, and make the text view the first responder so that editing can begin immediately.

Closing the document is simple. In the detail view controller's `viewWillDisappear:` method, the document is updated with the current text from the text view, and is then closed. Saving is automatic since autosave is turned on.

```
NSString *newText = [self.myNoteTextView text];
[myNoteDocument setMyNoteText:newText];

[myNoteDocument closeWithCompletionHandler:nil];
```

Detecting Conflicts in iCloud

With all syncing technologies it is possible, even probable, to have conflicts. A conflict occurs when a document has been edited simultaneously on more than one device, and iCloud is unable to decide based on sync rules which version of the document should be current.

To get a conflict, test with two devices simultaneously. Turn on airplane mode on the first device, edit a note, and save. Edit and save the same note on the second device. Turn off airplane mode on the first device, and then attempt to edit the note again on the second device. A conflict will occur on the second device.

The `UIDocument` class has a document state that will indicate whether the document is in conflict or is able to be edited normally. An instance of `UIDocument` will also post a notification when the document state changes, which is useful since a conflict might occur while the document is being edited, and it is a much better user experience to be notified of the conflict and resolve it immediately. To detect conflicts, the detail view controller needs to register to receive document state change notifications from the document; this can be done in the `viewWillAppear:` method.

```
[[NSNotificationCenter defaultCenter] addObserver:self
selector:@selector(documentStateChanged)
name:UIDocumentStateChangedNotification object:myNoteDocument];
```

A method called `documentStateChanged` is set up to handle the document state changes. That method will check the new document state, and adjust the user interface as necessary depending on the state of the document.

```
- (void)documentStateChanged
{
    UIDocumentState state = myNoteDocument.documentState;
    if (state & UIDocumentStateEditingDisabled)
    {
        [self.myNoteTextView resignFirstResponder];
        return;
    }
    if (state &UIDocumentStateInConflict)
    {
        [self showConflictButton];
        return;
```

```
    }
    else
    {
        [self hideConflictButton];
        [self.myNoteTextView becomeFirstResponder];
    }
}
```

If the document state is `UIDocumentStateEditingDisabled`, the method will resign first-responder status for the text view, which will end editing right away. If the document status is `UIDocumentStateInConflict`, the user interface will be updated to display a button that the user can tap to resolve the conflict (see Figure 8.5); otherwise, the user interface will return to normal editing status.

Figure 8.5   MyNotes sample app—document in conflict.

Conflict Resolution

Information about different versions of a document in conflict is available through the `NSFileVersion` class. When the user taps the Resolve Conflict button, the `resolveConflict-Tapped:` method is called. This method gathers information about versions of the document in conflict, and instantiates a custom page view controller to allow the user to browse through the versions in conflict and select a winner.

```
- (IBAction)resolveConflictTapped:(id)sender
{
    NSArray *versions = [NSFileVersion
    unresolvedConflictVersionsOfItemAtURL:self.myNoteURL];

    NSFileVersion *currentVersion =
    [NSFileVersion currentVersionOfItemAtURL:self.myNoteURL];

    NSMutableArray *conflictVersions =
    [NSMutableArray arrayWithObject:currentVersion];

    [conflictVersions addObjectsFromArray:versions];

    ICFConflictResolutionViewController *conflictResolver =
    [self.storyboard instantiateViewControllerWithIdentifier:
    @"ICFConflictResolutionViewController"];

    [conflictResolver setVersionList:conflictVersions];
    [conflictResolver setCurrentVersion:currentVersion];
    [conflictResolver setConflictNoteURL:self.myNoteURL];
    [conflictResolver setDelegate:self];
    [selfpresentViewController:conflictResolver
                       animated:YES
                     completion:nil];
}
```

First the method grabs the conflict versions, or the remote versions that cannot be merged with the local version, of the document in an array because there might be more than one. Then the method grabs the current version of the document, where the current version is the locally edited version, and adds it to a mutable array with the conflict versions. This mutable array represents all the version choices the user needs to evaluate to select the correct version. The method then creates an instance of ICFConflictResolutionViewController, a custom page view controller for navigating and selecting from the available conflict versions. It then sets properties so that the controller knows about the conflict versions, what the current version is (which is important in resolving the conflict later), the URL of the note in conflict, and the delegate to be called when the user has selected a version.

> **Note**
>
> The page view controller is a convenient way to browse through conflict versions, but it is by no means the only way. Any method that can display information about the conflict versions and allow the user to select one will work just fine.

The conflict resolution view controller is then presented to the user, as shown in Figure 8.6.

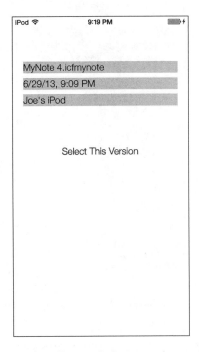

Figure 8.6   MyNotes sample app—conflict resolution page view controller.

For each conflict version of the note, the conflict resolution page view controller creates an instance of ICFConflictVersionViewController, which presents the information specific to a single conflict version of the note. The page view controller instantiates each version control-ler as needed in the viewControllerAtIndex:storyboard: method, and tells the controller which NSFileVersion it represents.

```
NSString *viewIdentifier = @"ICFConflictVersionViewController";

ICFConflictVersionViewController *versionViewController =
[storyboard instantiateViewControllerWithIdentifier:viewIdentifier];

[versionViewController setFileVersion:self.versionList[index]];
[versionViewController setDelegate:self];
return versionViewController;
```

The user can page between the conflict versions, as shown in Figure 8.7.

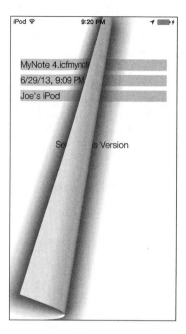

Figure 8.7   MyNotes sample app—conflict resolution view controller, paging between versions.

To display information about each version, the version view controller gets information from its NSFileVersion and updates the user interface in the viewDidLoad method.

```
NSDateFormatter *dateFormatter = [[NSDateFormatter alloc] init];
[dateFormatter setDateStyle:NSDateFormatterShortStyle];
[dateFormatter setTimeStyle:NSDateFormatterShortStyle];

NSString *dateString =
[dateFormatter stringFromDate:
[self.fileVersion modificationDate]];

[self.versionLabel setText:[self.fileVersion localizedName]];
[self.versionDate setText:dateString];

[self.versionComputer setText:
[self.fileVersion localizedNameOfSavingComputer]];
```

When the user selects a version, the version view controller tells its delegate, the page view controller, which version was selected.

```
- (IBAction)selectVersionTouched:(id)sender
{
    [self.delegate conflictVersionSelected:self.fileVersion];
}
```

The page view controller in turn tells the detail view controller which version was selected, and whether the selected version is the current, local version.

```
- (void)conflictVersionSelected:(NSFileVersion *)selectedVersion
{
    BOOL isCurrentVersion =
    (selectedVersion == self.currentVersion);

    [self.delegate noteConflictResolved:selectedVersion
                     forCurrentVersion:isCurrentVersion];
}
```

The detail view controller will then take the appropriate actions to resolve the conflict, depending on whether the selected version is the current version, in the noteConflictResolve:forCurrentVersion: method. The method checks the isCurrentVersion parameter passed in; if the value is YES, the method removes the other versions of the file for the note URL, and then tells the remaining version that the conflict is resolved.

```
if (isCurrentVersion)
{
    [NSFileVersion
    removeOtherVersionsOfItemAtURL:myNoteDocument.fileURL
    error:nil];

    NSArray* conflictVersions =
    [NSFileVersionunresolved ConflictVersionsOfItemAtURL:
    myNoteDocument.fileURL];

    for (NSFileVersion* fileVersion in conflictVersions)
    {
        fileVersion.resolved = YES;
    }
}
```

If the selected version is not the current version, the method handles resolution slightly differently. It replaces the current version with the selected version, removes the other versions, and then indicates that the conflict has been resolved for the remaining version.

```
else
{
    [selectedVersion replaceItemAtURL:myNoteDocument.fileURL
                              options:0
                                error:nil];

    [NSFileVersion
    removeOtherVersionsOfItemAtURL:myNoteDocument.fileURL
    error:nil];
```

```
    NSArray* conflictVersions =
    [NSFileVersion unresolvedConflictVersionsOfItemAtURL:
    myNoteDocument.fileURL];

    for (NSFileVersion* fileVersion in conflictVersions)
    {
        fileVersion.resolved = YES;
    }
}
```

After that is completed, the document will issue a notification that it has returned to a normal state, and editing will recommence when the `documentStateChanged` method receives and handles the notification (described earlier in the chapter, in "Detecting Conflicts in iCloud").

Key-Value Store Syncing

iCloud also supports key-value store syncing. This is similar to storing information in an `NSMutableDictionary` or `NSUserDefaults`, where a key is associated with an object value for storage and retrieval. The difference with the iCloud key-value store is that the keys and values are synced automatically between devices. At the time of this writing, iCloud supports a total of 1MB of usage for the key-value store for an app, and up to 1,024 key-value pairs, so the key-value storage mechanism is appropriate only for small amounts of information.

The sample app utilizes the iCloud key-value store to keep track of the last edited note. The detail view controller will store the name of the last updated note when the `configureView` method is called.

```
NSUbiquitousKeyValueStore *iCloudKeyValueStore =
[NSUbiquitousKeyValueStore defaultStore];

NSString *noteName = [[[selfmyNoteURL] lastPathComponent]
                        stringByDeletingPathExtension];

[iCloudKeyValueStore setString:noteName
                        forKey:kICFLastUpdatedNoteKey];

[iCloudKeyValueStore synchronize];
```

The method gets a reference to the iCloud key-value store, which is an instance of `NSUbiquitousKeyValueStore`. It sets the note name for key `kICFLastUpdatedNoteKey`, and then calls `synchronize` to ensure that the data is synced immediately.

The master view controller registers for the `NSUbiquitousKeyValueStoreDidChangeExternallyNotification` notification in the `viewDidLoad` method.

```
NSNotificationCenter *notifCenter =
[NSNotificationCenter defaultCenter];
...
NSString *keyValueStoreUpdated =
NSUbiquitousKeyValueStoreDidChangeExternallyNotification;

[notifCenter addObserver:self
                selector:@selector(updateLastUpdatedNote:)
                    name: keyValueStoreUpdated
                  object:nil];
```

When a notification is received that the key-value store was updated, the `updateLast UpdatedNote:` method is called.

```
- (void)updateLastUpdatedNote:(NSNotification *)notification
{
    NSUbiquitousKeyValueStore *iCloudKeyValueStore =
    [NSUbiquitousKeyValueStore defaultStore];

    self.lastUpdatedNote =
    [iCloudKeyValueStore stringForKey:kICFLastUpdatedNoteKey];

    [self.tableView reloadData];
}
```

The method gets a reference to the iCloud key-value store, updates a property with the last updated note from the store, and reloads the table view. When the table cells are displayed in the `tableView:cellForRowAtIndexPath:` method, logic there adds a star next to the last updated note.

```
if ([self.lastUpdatedNote isEqualToString:noteName])
{

    NSString *lastUpdatedCellTitle =
    [NSString stringWithFormat:@"[ss] %@",noteName];

    [cell.textLabel setText:lastUpdatedCellTitle];
}
else
{
    [cell.textLabel setText:noteName];
}
```

Try updating a note on one device, with the list of notes displayed on a second device. Notice that the star appears next to the edited note in a few seconds on the second device.

Summary

This chapter explained how to sync application data between devices running the same app using iCloud. It demonstrated how to set up an app to be able to use iCloud, including establishing entitlements, setup required in the Provisioning Portal, and setup required in the app. The chapter described how to create a subclass of `UIDocument`, and how to set up autosaving for a document. Next, this chapter explained how to list and display documents stored in iCloud and how to detect conflicts. Examining conflict information and resolving document conflicts was demonstrated as well. Lastly, the chapter showed how to use the iCloud key-value store to sync application data.

Exercises

1. The note document stores only a single string of information. Enhance the note to include and display a created date and time, a last updated date and time, and an image.

2. Currently, the conflict resolution approach only uses file metadata to help the user decide which version should be kept. Extend the solution to download and display the actual text for each version.

9

Notifications

Notifications are Apple's method of keeping the user informed of important iOS app-related events when you are not actively using an app. Because only one iOS app can be active and in the foreground at a time, notifications provide a mechanism to have inactive apps receive important and time-sensitive information and notify the user. This chapter will guide you through how to set up your app to receive local and remote push notifications, and how to customize what happens when the user receives a notification with an app badge, a sound, and a message. This chapter will also guide you through how to set up your own Ruby on Rails server to respond to events and push out notifications.

Differences Between Local and Push Notifications

Two types of notifications are supported by iOS: local notifications and remote, or push, notifications. Local notifications do not use or require any external infrastructure; they happen entirely on the device. That means that the device does not require any connectivity—besides being "on"—to present a local notification. Push notifications, however, require connectivity and a server infrastructure of some kind to send the notification through the Apple Push Notification service (APNs) to the intended device. It is important to note that push notification delivery is not guaranteed, so it is not appropriate to assume that every notification gets to its intended target. Do not make your application depend on push notifications.

To understand why push notification delivery is not guaranteed, you need to understand how push notifications get to a device. The APNs first will try to use the cellular network to communicate with an iOS device if it is available, then will attempt over Wi-Fi. Some devices need to be in an active state (on fourth-generation iPod touches, for example, the screen actually has to be visible) in order to receive Wi-Fi communication. Other devices, like iPads, can be asleep and maintain a connection to a Wi-Fi network.

The process that each type of notification goes through is also different. For local notifications these are the steps:

1. Create a local notification object, and specify options like schedule time and date, message, sound, and badge update.

2. Schedule the local notification.

3. iOS presents the notification, plays a sound, and updates the badge.

4. Receive the local notification in the application delegate.

For push notifications this is the process:

1. Register the application for push notifications and receive a token.

2. Notify your server that the device (identified by a token) would like to receive push notifications.

3. Create a push notification on your server and communicate to APNs.

4. APNs delivers the notification to the device.

5. iOS presents the notification, plays a sound, and updates the badge.

6. Receive the notification in the application's delegate.

With these differences, it's clear that there are different use cases in which local and push notifications make sense. If no information from outside the device is required, use a local notification. If information not available to the device is required, use a push notification.

Sample App

The sample app for this chapter is called ShoutOut. It allows the user to Shout Out a message to all the other users of the app via a push notification and to add reminders to Shout Out. The sample app will illustrate setting up reminders as local notifications, as well as all the steps necessary to set up an app to receive push notifications, to communicate with a server, and to have the server send push notifications via the APNs.

App Setup

There are several steps to prepare the app for push notifications. To begin, set up an App ID in the iOS Provisioning Portal. Visit the iOS Dev Center (https://developer.apple.com/devcenter/ios/index.action), log in, and choose Certificates, Identifiers & Profiles in the menu titled iOS Developer Program on the right side of the screen (you must be logged in to see this menu). Choose Identifiers from the menu on the left side of the screen. Then, click the button with a plus sign in the upper-right corner to create a new App ID, as shown in Figure 9.1.

Specify a Description for the App ID. The Description will be used to display the app throughout the iOS Provisioning Portal. Select an App ID Prefix (previously called the Bundle Seed ID). Scroll down to specify the App ID Suffix, as shown in Figure 9.2.

Certificates, Identifiers & Profiles
Joe Keeley
iOS Apps
Register iOS App ID
Certificates
All
Pending
Development
Production
Identifiers
App IDs
Pass Type IDs
Website Push IDs
Devices
All
Provisioning Profiles
All
Development
Distribution
ID
Registering an App ID
The App ID string contains two parts separated by a period (.)—an App ID Prefix that is defined as your Team ID by default and an App ID Suffix that is defined as a Bundle ID search string. Each part of an App ID has different and important uses for your app. Learn More
App ID Description
Name: ICF Shout Out
You cannot use special characters such as @, &, *, ', "
App ID Prefix
Value: 59QS4EHA9F (Team ID)

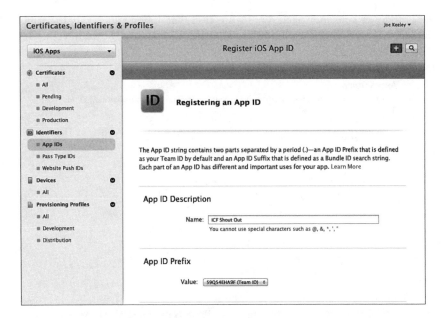

Figure 9.1 iOS Provisioning Portal: Registering an App ID, App ID Description and Prefix.

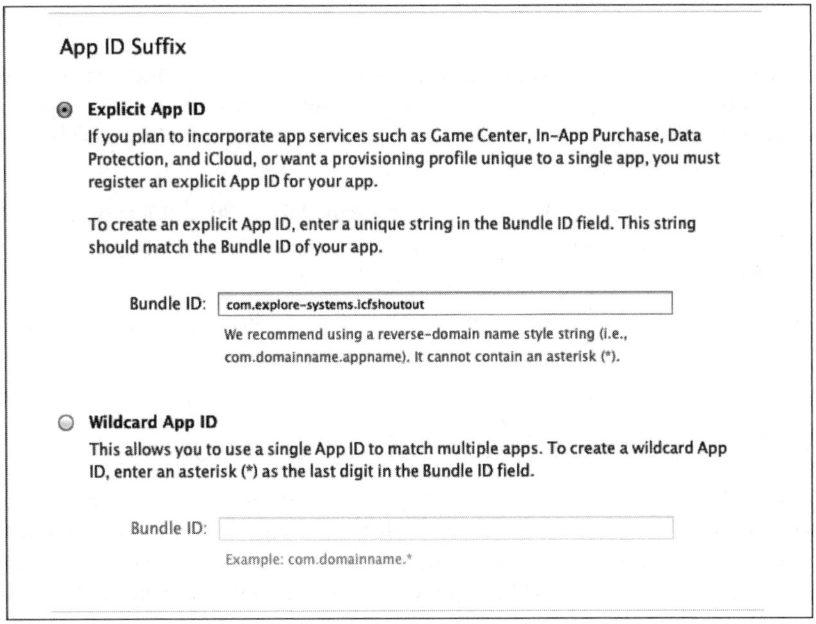

App ID Suffix
Explicit App ID
If you plan to incorporate app services such as Game Center, In-App Purchase, Data Protection, and iCloud, or want a provisioning profile unique to a single app, you must register an explicit App ID for your app.
To create an explicit App ID, enter a unique string in the Bundle ID field. This string should match the Bundle ID of your app.
Bundle ID: com.explore-systems.icfshoutout
We recommend using a reverse-domain name style string (i.e., com.domainname.appname). It cannot contain an asterisk (*).
Wildcard App ID
This allows you to use a single App ID to match multiple apps. To create a wildcard App ID, enter an asterisk (*) as the last digit in the Bundle ID field.
Bundle ID:
Example: com.domainname.*

Figure 9.2 iOS Provisioning Portal: Registering an App ID, App ID Suffix.

Push notifications require an explicit App ID, so select that option and specify the same string as the Bundle ID for your app. Scroll down to select App Services, as shown in Figure 9.3.

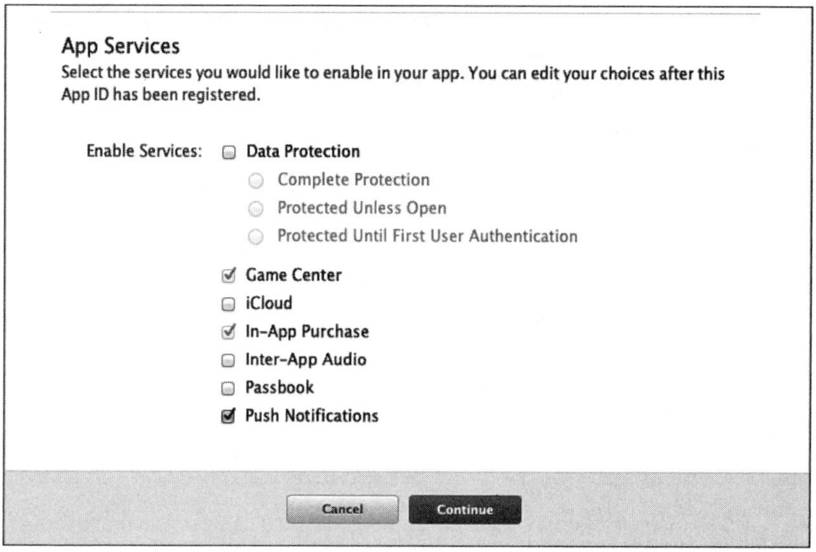

Figure 9.3   iOS Provisioning Portal: Registering an App ID, App Services.

Select the check box for Push Notifications in the list of App Services to indicate that push notifications should be enabled for the App ID. Click Continue to save the new App ID, and it will be visible in the list of App IDs. Click on the App ID to expand it and view the status of services for the App ID, as shown in Figure 9.4.

Now that the App ID is prepared, it needs to be configured for push notifications. Click Settings at the bottom of the App ID detail list, and scroll to the bottom to view the push notifications, as shown in Figure 9.5.

Make sure that Enabled for Apple Push Notification service is checked. If so, the App ID is ready and push certificates can be created.

Create Development Push SSL Certificate

A Development Push SSL Certificate is what the push server uses to identify and authorize a specific account to APNs when connecting to APNs to send push notifications. To start the process of creating a certificate, click the Create Certificate button on the Development line (refer to Figure 9.5). Instructions will be presented to help generate a certificate signing request, as shown in Figure 9.6.

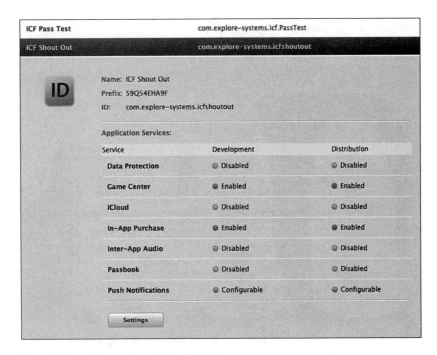

Figure 9.4   iOS Provisioning Portal: App ID in list.

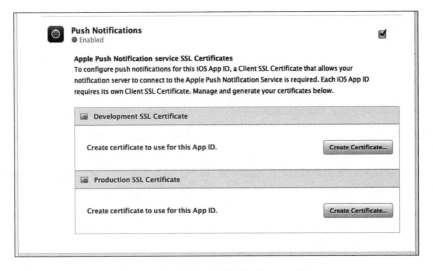

Figure 9.5   iOS Provisioning Portal: App ID Push Notifications settings.

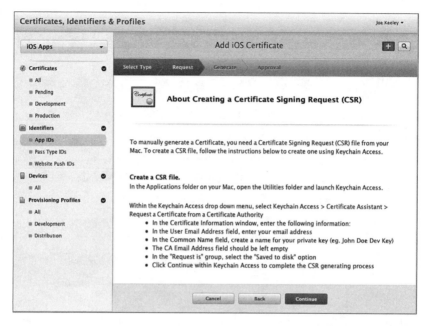

Figure 9.6   iOS Provisioning Portal: About Creating a Certificate Signing Request (CSR).

Leave the Add iOS Certificate page open in the browser, and open Keychain Access (in Applications, Utilities). Select Keychain Access, Certificate Assistant, Request a Certificate from a Certificate Authority from the application menu. A certificate request form will be presented, as shown in Figure 9.7.

Enter an email address, a common name (typically a company name or an entity name—it is safe to use your Apple Developer account name), and then select Saved to Disk. Click Continue, and specify where to save the request. When that step is complete, return to the iOS Provisioning Portal and click Continue. Select the saved request, as shown in Figure 9.8.

After selecting it, click Generate. The development SSL certificate will be generated, as shown in Figure 9.9.

After your certificate has been created, click the Download button to download the certificate so that the certificate can be installed on the notification server.

Double-click the downloaded certificate file, and it will automatically be installed in Keychain Access. It should be visible in the list of certificates, as shown in Figure 9.10. Click on the triangle to confirm that the private key was delivered with the certificate.

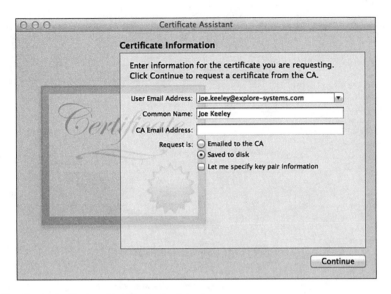

Figure 9.7   Keychain Access Certificate Assistant.

Figure 9.8   iOS Provisioning Portal: Add iOS Certificate—Generate Your Certificate.

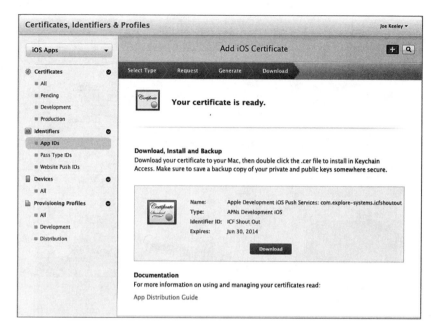

Figure 9.9   iOS Provisioning Portal: Add iOS Certificate—Your Certificate Is Ready.

Figure 9.10   Keychain Access: Apple Development iOS Push Services SSL Certificate and private key.

Because you have not yet set up the notifications server, you will not yet take the next step to install the certificate on the server; you will come back to that after we complete the server setup steps later in this chapter. Also note that this procedure needs to be repeated for your Production SSL Certificate when you are ready to distribute your application.

Development Provisioning Profile

For most apps, it is sufficient to use the development provisioning profile automatically generated by Xcode. If you are testing push notifications, however, you need to create and use a development provisioning profile specific to your app to allow it to receive push notifications. To do this, stay in the iOS Provisioning Portal where you created the App ID and SSL Certificate, and click Provisioning Profiles in the left menu.

> **Note**
>
> This presumes that you have already created a development certificate (under Certificates, Development); if not, you should create one first. The procedure is well documented in the portal and similar to creating the SSL Certificate. This also presumes that you have set up at least one device for development in the portal; if not, you will need to do that as well (under Devices).

You will be presented with a list of development provisioning profiles. To create a new one, click the button with the plus sign just above and to the right of the list. Select which type of provisioning profile to create (in this case, iOS App Development) and click Continue, as shown in Figure 9.11.

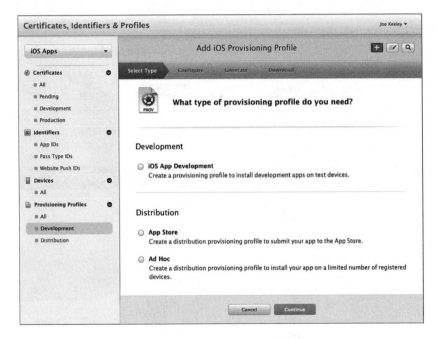

Figure 9.11   iOS Provisioning Profile: Add iOS Provisioning Profile.

Select the App ID just created, as shown in Figure 9.12, and click Continue.

Next select the Development Certificate(s) to be used when signing the app with this provisioning profile, as shown in Figure 9.13, and click Continue.

Figure 9.12   iOS Provisioning Profile: Add iOS Provisioning Profile—Select App ID.

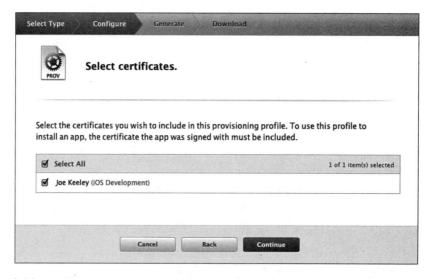

Figure 9.13   iOS Provisioning Profile: Add iOS Provisioning Profile—Select Certificates.

Select the devices that can be used to run the app using this provisioning profile, as shown in Figure 9.14. It is generally a good practice to select all available devices to prevent having to regenerate the provisioning profile when it is discovered that a team member was not added the first time around.

Figure 9.14   iOS Provisioning Profile: Add iOS Provisioning Profile—Select Devices.

Finally, provide a name for the provisioning profile, and review the summary presented for the provisioning profile, as shown in Figure 9.15. If the profile looks correct, click Generate to create it.

Note
Be descriptive with your provisioning profile name; these names tend to get confusing in Xcode when you have a lot of them. One approach is to use the app name and environment in the name, such as "ICF Shout Out Development."

Figure 9.15   iOS Provisioning Profile: Add iOS Provisioning Profile—Name This Profile and Generate.

When the provisioning profile has been created, a download page will be presented, as shown in Figure 9.16.

Click Download to get a copy of the provisioning profile. Double-click the profile after it is downloaded and it will be automatically installed and available in Xcode. One last step remains to make sure that the app is using the new provisioning profile. In Xcode, edit the Build Settings for your project (not the target). Find the section titled Code Signing, specifically Code Signing Identity. For Debug, choose the provisioning profile just created and downloaded, as shown in Figure 9.17.

When that step is complete, you have completed all the configuration steps necessary on the app side to receive push notifications. Now you are ready to write some code.

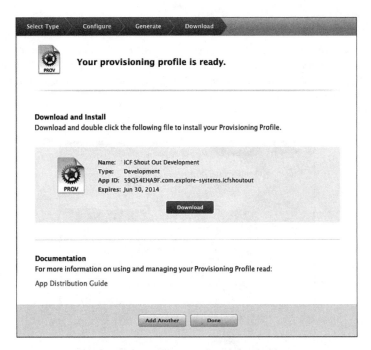

Figure 9.16   iOS Provisioning Profile: Your Provisioning Profile Is Ready.

Figure 9.17   Xcode Project Build Settings: Code Signing Identity.

Custom Sound Preparation

One detail that can really distinguish receipt of your push notification is a custom sound. iOS will play any sound less than 30 seconds in length that you specify if it is available in your app bundle. You can create a custom sound in GarageBand and export the sound. It is worth exporting under each of the compression options to see what sounds good while meeting your size requirements (see Figure 9.18).

Figure 9.18   GarageBand: export song settings.

Now that you have a sound file, it will need to be converted to Core Audio format in order for your app to use it. Apple provides a command-line tool called afconvert that is up to the job. Open a Terminal session, navigate to the directory where the audio file is, and issue this command to convert your audio file to Core Audio format:

```
$ afconvert -f -caff -d ima4 shout_out.m4a shout_out.caf
```

This command will convert the shout_out.m4a file to ima4 format (which is a compressed format that works well on the device) and package it in a Core Audio–formatted sound file. When that process is complete, copy your new Core Audio format sound file into your Xcode project, and when it is specified in a notification, it will play.

Registering for Remote Notifications

To enable the ShoutOut app to receive push notifications, the app needs to register with the APNs to receive push notifications. The app can be customized to register for push notifications at any point that makes sense, when the user has a good idea what value push notifications will provide from the app. For this example, however, the sample app will register with the APNs right away in the app delegate, the `applicationDidFinishLaunchingWithOptions` method:

```
- (BOOL)application:(UIApplication *)application
didFinishLaunchingWithOptions:(NSDictionary *)launchOptions
{
    [[UIApplication sharedApplication]
     registerForRemoteNotificationTypes:
     (UIRemoteNotificationTypeBadge |
      UIRemoteNotificationTypeAlert |
      UIRemoteNotificationTypeSound)];

}
```

Notice that you can specify how the user should be alerted when a push notification is received, including updating the application badge, presenting an alert, and playing a sound. The `registerForRemoteNotificationTypes:` method will actually call the APNs and get a token to identify the device. Two delegate methods need to be implemented to handle receipt of that token, or an error in registering with APNs:

```
- (void)application:(UIApplication *)app

didRegisterForRemoteNotificationsWithDeviceToken:(NSData *)devToken
{
    [self setPushToken:devToken];
}

 (void)application:(UIApplication *)app
didFailToRegisterForRemoteNotificationsWithError:(NSError *)err
{
    NSLog(@"Error in registration. Error: %@", err);
}
```

If the registration is successful, the token will be returned to the app in NSData format. For ShoutOut, we will just temporarily store the token until we are ready to send it to our server. One approach would be to just perform this registration one time and store the token, and then skip the registration if it has already been completed. Apple recommends that you perform the registration every time, however, since the user might have switched devices and might need a new token. If there are specific failure actions that need to take place, they can be specified in the `didFailToRegisterForRemoteNotificationsWithError:` method. For the purposes of the sample app, just log the failure.

At this point, ShoutOut is ready to receive remote push notifications.

Scheduling Local Notifications

For local notifications, no additional setup is required for the app. In ShoutOut, you will use a local notification to be able to schedule a reminder. In `ICFMainViewController`, there is a method that gets called when the user hits the Set Reminder button:

```
- (IBAction)setReminder:(id)sender
{
    NSDate *now = [NSDate date];
    UILocalNotification *reminderNotification = [[UILocalNotification alloc] init];
    [reminderNotification setFireDate:[now dateByAddingTimeInterval:60]];
    [reminderNotification setTimeZone:[NSTimeZone defaultTimeZone]];
    [reminderNotification setAlertBody:@"Don't forget to Shout Out!"];
    [reminderNotification setAlertAction:@"Shout Now"];
    [reminderNotification setSoundName:UILocalNotificationDefaultSoundName];
    [reminderNotification setApplicationIconBadgeNumber:1];
    [[UIApplication sharedApplication]
     scheduleLocalNotification:reminderNotification];
    [reminderNotification release];

    UIAlertView *successAlert = [[UIAlertView alloc]
        initWithTitle:@"Reminder"
        message:@"Your Reminder has been Scheduled"
        delegate:nil
        cancelButtonTitle:@"OK Thanks!"
        otherButtonTitles:nil];
    [successAlert show];
    [successAlert release];
}
```

To create a local notification, create an instance of `UILocalNotification`. Specify the fire date for the notification. It also is generally a good idea to specify a time zone so that if the user is traveling, he will receive the reminder at the correct time. To make it easy to see, just set the fire date to 60 seconds from now. Then set how the user will receive the notification, including specifying alert text, setting whether a sound (or a specific sound) should be played, and updating the application badge. Finally schedule the local notification. Do not forget to release it when complete. To see it in action, run the app, hit Set Reminder, and then close the app. In a minute, you will see an alert with your custom text, sound, and alert badge.

> **Note**
>
> Local notifications can be tested in the simulator, but remote push notifications cannot.

Receiving Notifications

When your device receives a notification, either local or remote, the device will check whether your app is currently active and in the foreground. If not, the parameters included guide the device to play a sound, display an alert, or update the badge on your app icon. If an alert is displayed, the user will have the opportunity to dismiss the alert or to follow the alert into the app.

If the user chooses to go into the app, then either the app delegate's `appDidFinishLaunching WithOptions:` method is called if the app is in a terminated state and is launching, or a delegate method will be called when the app is brought to the foreground. The same delegate method will be called if the app happens to be in the foreground when the notification is received.

If the app was launched as a result of tapping on a notification, the notification payload will be present in the launch options passed to the `appDidFinishLaunchingWithOptions:` method, and can be used to drive any desired custom functionality, like navigating to a view specific to the navigation or displaying a message.

```
NSDictionary *notif = [launchOptions
objectForKey:UIApplicationLaunchOptionsRemoteNotificationKey];

if (notif) {
    //custom logic here using notification info dictionary
}
```

There are two delegate methods for receiving notifications, one for local and one for remote:

```
- (void)application:(UIApplication *)application
didReceiveLocalNotification:(UILocalNotification *)notif
{
    application.applicationIconBadgeNumber = 0;
    if ([application applicationState] == UIApplicationStateActive) {
        NSLog(@"Received local notification - app active");
    } else {
        NSLog(@"Received local notification - from background");
    }
}

- (void)application:(UIApplication *)application
didReceiveRemoteNotification:(NSDictionary *)userInfo
{
    application.applicationIconBadgeNumber = 0;
    if ([application applicationState] == UIApplicationStateActive) {
        NSLog(@"Received remote notification - app active");
    } else {
        NSLog(@"Received remote notification - from background");
    }
}
```

The local notification delegate method receives the local notification, and the remote notification delegate receives a dictionary with the notification information. In both cases the `application` parameter can be inspected to determine the state of the app when the notification was received. Then the response to the notification can be customized depending on whether the app is currently active or whether the app was awakened from the background.

Push Notification Server

Because the app is prepared to receive notifications, you can set up the server to send push notifications. You can send push notifications via the APNs from any type of server that can communicate over a secure TCP socket connection (an SSL stack is required). Apple requires that your server maintain a persistent connection while sending push notification requests to APNs to avoid the overhead of establishing connections. For our sample app, we will use a Ruby on Rails server since it is quick to set up, and there is a `gem` (or prebuilt module) available to automate communication with APNs.

> **Note**
>
> If you want more detail on communication with APNs, look at Apple's documentation at https://developer.apple.com/library/mac/#documentation/NetworkingInternet/Conceptual/RemoteNotificationsPG/CommunicatingWIthAPS/CommunicatingWIthAPS.html#//apple_ref/doc/uid/TP40008194-CH101-SW1.

Basic Rails Setup

To set up your Ruby on Rails server, you will need the following components on your system:

- Ruby version 1.9.2 or higher
- Rails 3.0 or higher
- SQLite 3.0 or higher

There are plenty of resources on the Web to help install those components. You will need access to a wireless network so that your iOS device can communicate with your server system. This example assumes that your server system is running Mac OS X 10.7 with Bonjour networking for the server URL; if that is not the case, you can use an IP address or another technique for your server URL.

To start the server project, just issue the new project command:

```
$ rails new icf_message_board_server
```

That will create the project in a new directory called `icf_message_board_server`. Switch to the new directory, and run the following:

```
$ rails server
```

Then in your Web browser, visit http://0.0.0.0:3000. You will see the standard Rails welcome page (see Figure 9.19). Note that any additional commands or path references in this section are relative to this project directory, unless otherwise noted.

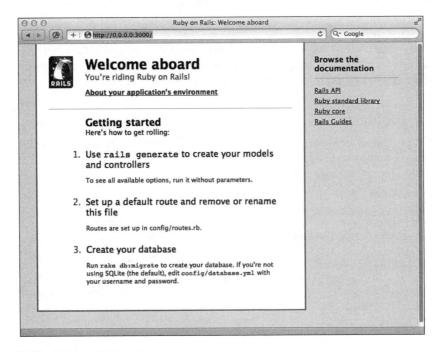

Figure 9.19   Ruby on Rails welcome screen.

Add Support for Devices and Shouts

Now that you have the basic project set up, you need to set up objects and controllers that can handle the two basic functions: capturing device tokens and receiving shouts. Rails has a function called a "scaffold" that will build out a model object, a controller, and basic views; you just need to specify the name of your object, and what attributes and data types you want. Rails automatically supports the following data types:

:binary	:decimal	:string
:boolean	:float	:text
:date	:integer	:time
:datetime	:primary_key	:timestamp

First, set up your `Shout` object:

```
$ rails generate scaffold Shout name:string shout_date:date shout_message:string
```

The `Shout` object will have a name, a date, and a message. Now set up your `Device` object:

```
$ rails generate scaffold Device name:string token:string
```

The `Device` object will be able to capture a username and a device token. Each time you create a new object or make changes to attributes for an object, Rails creates a database migration, allowing you to apply and roll back changes. Run the `migrate` command to update the database:

```
$ rake db:migrate
```

Now that the objects are set up, you need to change the project's routing so that the list of shouts will be displayed instead of the default Rails welcome screen. In the `config / routes. rb` file, add a line at the beginning:

```
root :to => "shouts#index"
```

Then delete the `index.html` file in the public directory. Reload http://0.0.0.0:3000 in your browser, and you will see the Shouts home screen (see Figure 9.20).

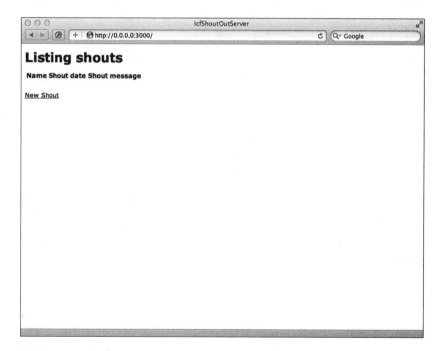

Figure 9.20   Shouts home screen.

The default index screen for a Rails model object includes links to add new instances of that object, and to edit and delete instances that are displayed. Since you will be displaying this view on the device and do not want the user modifying the shout information, you need to remove these capabilities from the view. In `app/views/shouts`, edit the `index.html.erb` file to match the following code example:

```erb
<h1>Shout Outs</h1>
<table>
  <tr>
    <th>Name</th>
    <th>Shout date</th>
    <th>Shout message</th>
  </tr>
<% @shouts.each do |shout| %>
  <tr>
    <td><%= shout.name %></td>
    <td><%= shout.shout_date %></td>
    <td><%= shout.shout_message %></td>
  </tr>
<% end %>
</table>
```

The basic infrastructure is in place to handle receiving device information and shouts, and to display shouts in a Web view. Next you need to install support to send push notifications to APNs. To do that, you will install the `apn_on_rails` gem. First, add this line to the Gemfile:

```
gem 'apn_on_rails', :git =>
➥'https://github.com/natescherer/apn_on_rails.git', :branch => 'rails3'
```

Install the `gem`:

```
$ bundle install
```

Build and run the database migrations needed by the `gem`:

```
$ rails g apn_migrations
$ rake db:migrate
```

The application needs to be aware of the `gem`; add a `require` statement in the `config/environment.rb` file:

```
require 'apn_on_rails'
```

To handle the rake tasks needed by the `gem`, add this to the `rakefile`:

```
begin
  require 'apn_on_rails_tasks'
rescue MissingSourceFile => e
  puts e.message
end
```

One last thing and then the server is ready: You need to add the SSL certificate to the project that you created earlier in the chapter. Open Keychain Access, and locate the certificate and key illustrated in Figure 9.10. Select them both, and choose File, Export Items. Save them as ShoutOutSSLCert.p12 (you can use any name with your own p12 files). For communication with APNs, the certificate and key need to be in PEM format, so issue the following openssl command to convert them (note that it is wrapped, it is not two separate commands):

```
$ openssl pkcs12 -in ShoutOutSSLCert.p12 -out
➥apple_push_notification_development.pem -nodes -clcerts
```

Move the apple_push_notification_development.pem file to the project config directory, and the project will be ready to send push notifications. Note that the filename must be apple_push_notification_development.pem for the gem to find it, unless you modify the gem's configuration.

Device Controller

You have to make a few small modifications to the default controller for devices to make sure that it will work for our purposes. In app/controllers/devices_controller.rb, you need to update the create method. First, you need to reformat the token data sent to us from the device, because it will contain chevron brackets ("<" and ">"). This approach will just remove the brackets from the data.

```
deviceInfo = params[:device]
deviceInfo[:token] = deviceInfo[:token].sub("<","")
deviceInfo[:token] = deviceInfo[:token].sub(">","")
```

Next, the create method built by Rails assumes that you will create a new record only when a POST is received. The logic needs to be able to handle new devices, and updates to existing devices.

```
@device = Device.find_by_token(deviceInfo[:token])
if @device
  @device.update_attributes(deviceInfo)
else
  @device = Device.new(params[:device])
end
```

This logic either will create a new record if there is not already one for the token, or will update an existing record.

Shout Controller

The app should display the most recent shouts at the top of the list. To do this, you need to change the sort order of shouts in the default index method in app/controllers/shouts_controller.rb:

```
@shouts = Shout.all.sort_by(&:shout_date).reverse
```

Next, you need to modify the `create` method to send a push notification when a new shout has been created. Add this line after you have created the new shout object:

```
sendPush (@shout.name + ' just shouted ' + @shout.shout_message)
```

This implies a new method in the controller class called `sendPush`. This method looks like the following:

```
def sendPush (message)
  deviceList = Device.all

  deviceList.each do |sendItem|
    device = APN::Device.find_or_create_by_token(sendItem.token)
    notification = APN::Notification.new
    notification.device = device
    notification.badge = 1
    notification.sound = "shout_out.caf"
    notification.alert = message
    notification.save
  end
end
```

There are a couple of items to take note of here. The first is that you are creating a list of devices to be recipients of the push notifications:

```
deviceList = Device.all
```

Then, you are iterating over that list of devices, and creating a push notification for each one. To create a push notification, you first need to create a `Device` object for the APN:

```
device = APN::Device.find_or_create_by_token(sendItem.token)
```

This creates a device record for the APN gem to use. Next, you can create the notification:

```
notification = APN::Notification.new
notification.device = device
notification.badge = 1
notification.sound = "shout_out.caf"
notification.sound = "default"
notification.alert = message
notification.save
```

You assign the APN device we just created to the new notification object, set the `badge`, `sound`, and `alert` parameters, and save the notification. After you have completed iterating over the list of devices, you will have a stack of notifications ready to send.

Now that the server is ready, you can modify the iOS project so that it can talk to the server.

Tying It All Together

Return to the iOS project. The first thing you need to do is update the URL for the server, so your device knows where to make the network calls. There is an NSString constant called kShoutOutServerURLString in the ShoutOut-Prefix.pch file to identify the server on the local network:

```
#define kShoutOutServerURLString    @"http://twiki.local:3000"
```

Replace twiki in that address with the name of your computer that is running the Rails server—if it has Bonjour networking that address will work.

> **Note**
>
> Check to be sure your computer and wireless network are not set up to block port 3000.

You need to add logic to tell the server about the user's device. In the ICFMainView Controller, there is a method called showInfo: that is called when the View and Shout! button is pressed. In this method, you will first check to see whether the user has entered a name—if not, an alert view asking for a name will be displayed.

```
if ([[userNameTextField text] length] > 0)
{
    ...
} else
{
    UIAlertView *successAlert = [[UIAlertView alloc]
        initWithTitle:@"Shout Out"
        message:@"Please enter your name"
        delegate:nil
        cancelButtonTitle:@"OK Will Do!"
        otherButtonTitles:nil];
    [successAlert show];
    [successAlert release];
}
```

If the user provides a name, you will perform an HTTP POST operation on the server with the name and the token you received when you completed the push notification registration. The first step is to create a dictionary with the post parameters (name and token. token is stored in the app delegate after registering the device for push notifications):

```
ICFAppDelegate *appDelegate =
(ICFAppDelegate *)[[UIApplication sharedApplication] delegate];
NSDictionary *postDictionary =
@{@"device[token]":[appDelegate pushToken],
  @"device[name]":[userNameTextField text]};
```

After you have the dictionary set up, you can call the `post` method, specifying the path, `post` parameters, and blocks of code for success and failure of the post.

> **Note**
>
> To make our network calls simple and easy to read, we are using the AFNetworking open source library, written by the folks at Gowalla. It is available at https://github.com/ AFNetworking/AFNetworking.

```
AFHTTPClient *httpClient = [AFHTTPClient clientWithBaseURL:
[NSURL URLWithString:kShoutOutServerURLString]];
[httpClient postPath:@"/devices" parameters:postDictionary
    success:^(AFHTTPRequestOperation *operation, id responseObject)
{
    ICFFlipsideViewController *controller =
        [[[ICFFlipsideViewController alloc]
        initWithNibName:@"ICFFlipsideViewController" bundle:nil]
        autorelease];
    [controller setDelegate:self];
    [controller setModalTransitionStyle:UIModalTransitionStyleFlipHorizontal];
    [controller setShoutName:[self.userNameTextField text]];

    [self presentViewController:controller
                    animated:YES
                  completion:nil];

    NSLog(@"Device has been successfully logged on server");
    [activityView setHidden:YES];
    [activityIndicator stopAnimating];
}
    failure:^(AFHTTPRequestOperation *operation, NSError *error)
{
    NSLog(@"Device setup on server failed: %@",error);
    [activityView setHidden:YES];
    [activityIndicator stopAnimating];
}];
```

If the POST operation fails, log an error and turn off the activity view. If the POST completes, display the `ICFFlipsideViewController`, which will show shouts already posted, and allow the user to post a shout.

When you display the `ICFFlipsideViewController`, the first thing you need to do is pull down existing shouts and display them in the Web view. In the `viewWillAppear` method for that controller, add the following:

```
NSURLRequest *shoutListURLRequest = [NSURLRequest requestWithURL:
[NSURL URLWithString:kShoutOutServerURLString]];
[self.shoutsWebView loadRequest:shoutListURLRequest];
```

Now, add support for posting a shout. There is a simple text field to enter the shout. In the `textFieldShouldReturn:` method, first check whether there is any text, and do nothing if not. If there is some text, display the activity indicator, and then build the post dictionary like so:

```
NSMutableDictionary *postDictionary = [NSMutableDictionary
    dictionaryWithCapacity:5];
[postDictionary setObject:[textField text]
    forKey:@"shout[shout_message]"];
[postDictionary setObject:[self shoutName]
    forKey:@"shout[name]"];
NSDate *today = [NSDate date];
NSDateFormatter *dateFormatter = [[NSDateFormatter alloc] init];
[dateFormatter setDateFormat:@"yyyy"];
[postDictionary setObject:[dateFormatter stringFromDate:today]
forKey:@"shout[shout_date(1i)]"];
[dateFormatter setDateFormat:@"MM"];
[postDictionary setObject:[dateFormatter stringFromDate:today]
forKey:@"shout[shout_date(2i)]"];
[dateFormatter setDateFormat:@"d"];
[postDictionary setObject:[dateFormatter stringFromDate:today]
forKey:@"shout[shout_date(3i)]"];
[dateFormatter release];
```

After the post dictionary is ready, you can post the shout to the server, specifying the path, post dictionary, and success and failure blocks.

```
//set up post request
AFHTTPClient *httpClient = [AFHTTPClient clientWithBaseURL:
[NSURL URLWithString:kShoutOutServerURLString]];
[httpClient postPath:@"/shouts" parameters:postDictionary
    success:^(AFHTTPRequestOperation *operation, id responseObject)
{
    [self.activityView setHidden:YES];
    [self.activityIndicator stopAnimating];
    UIAlertView *successAlert = [[UIAlertView alloc]
        initWithTitle:@"Shout Out"
        message:@"Your Shout Out has been posted!"
        delegate:nil
        cancelButtonTitle:@"OK Thanks!"
        otherButtonTitles:nil];
    [successAlert show];
    [successAlert release];
    NSURLRequest *shoutListURLRequest = [NSURLRequest
    requestWithURL:[NSURL URLWithString:kShoutOutServerURLString]];
    [self.shoutsWebView loadRequest:shoutListURLRequest];
}
    failure:^(AFHTTPRequestOperation *operation, NSError *error)
```

```
{
    [self.activityView setHidden:YES];
    [self.activityIndicator stopAnimating];
    UIAlertView *failureAlert = [[UIAlertView alloc]
        initWithTitle:@"Shout Out"
        message:@"Your Shout Out has NOT been posted - ran into an error!"
        delegate:nil
        cancelButtonTitle:@"Ah Bummer!"
        otherButtonTitles:nil];
    [failureAlert show];
    [failureAlert release];
}];
```

If the request is successful, we will reload the Web view so that the new shout will be displayed. Now that all of this is in place, run the app on your device (and make sure that your Rails server is running on your computer) and post a shout.

Sending the Push Notifications

Because Apple prefers push notifications to be sent to APNs with a minimum of socket connections (in other words, they will shut you off if you open and close a connection for every notification), you need to be able to send notifications in batches. The `apn_on_rails` gem handles this task. When you created notifications in the `Shout` controller, you just saved them. To actually send them, we need to execute a rake task on our server. First, exit the app on your device so that it is not in the foreground, and then issue this command in the root directory of the server project:

```
$ rake apn:notifications:deliver
```

The `rake` command will create a socket connection to APNs, iterate over any unsent notifications, send them to APNs, and then update the "sent date" for each successfully sent notification. You would not want to execute a command-line function manually each time you need to send notifications, so this is a good candidate for a cron job or another automated approach.

After you have run this command, your notification(s) will appear quickly on your device!

Handling APNs Feedback

APNs can provide feedback to each server that connects to it and sends notifications. If any of the device tokens specified in the messages have errors (for example, if the user has deleted the app from her device), then the server should prevent sending future notifications to the disabled devices. Many APNs libraries (including `apn_on_rails`) have facilities built in to communicate with the feedback endpoint, which can be scheduled to run periodically. After the feedback has been obtained, stored device tokens on the server should be updated or removed to prevent sending additional notifications to them.

Summary

This chapter introduced you to Apple's method of communicating with apps that are not active and in the foreground: notifications. You learned about the differences between local and remote push notifications. You saw how to set up an app to receive remote push notifications, and how to schedule local notifications. The chapter guided you through how to set up a Ruby on Rails server to communicate with your app and send push notifications to your app via the Apple Push Notification service.

Exercise

1. The sample app will currently send notifications to all devices registered, even the device that has posted the shout. If your device posted the shout, you probably do not need a notification that you posted a shout. Modify the server to prevent sending a notification to the sending device.

Bluetooth Networking with Game Kit

One of the greatest injustices orchestrated by the iOS SDK has been the naming and accompanying reputation of Game Kit. When new developers begin to scour the depths of the iOS SDK and come across Game Kit, it is all too often dismissed as a framework specifically for games, and ignored by application developers. Game Kit contains a diverse set of features that can be beneficial in everything from productivity tools to social apps. In this chapter the focus will be on the Bluetooth networking components of Game Kit.

Currently, the only way to interact with the Bluetooth hardware of an iOS device is through Game Kit. Although some developers might yearn for the ability to interact directly with hardware, most have been grateful for the high-level wrapper that Apple has provided. Game Kit is one of the easiest frameworks to get up and running, whereas low-level networking is one of the most difficult disciplines for a new developer to become proficient with.

Game Kit was first introduced as part of iOS 3.0, adding support for Bluetooth and LAN networking as well as voice-chat services through these protocols. With iOS 4.0, Apple added Game Center functionality on top of Game Kit; for more information on Game Center, refer to Chapter 3, "Leaderboards," and Chapter 4, "Achievements."

Limitations of Game Kit's Bluetooth Networking

Game Kit provides an easy-to-interact-with wrapper for communicating with other devices over Bluetooth; however, it does carry with it several important restrictions and limitations.

The most notable restriction is that the developer will have no access to the underlying functionality of Bluetooth, meaning you cannot directly request data from the hardware nor can you connect to devices that do not support Game Kit. If direct Bluetooth access is needed, Core Bluetooth should be used. From a developer standpoint you will also not be able to toggle Bluetooth on and off, although if you attempt to connect through Game Kit with Bluetooth off, the OS will prompt the user to turn it on, and provide a one-touch approach to do so.

When using the Peer Picker, which we will discuss at length in this chapter, you will not be able to connect more than one peer at a time. You can support multiple peers using your own interface, as covered in the "Advanced Features" section of this chapter. The Bluetooth standard itself also has several limitations to keep in mind during development, such as high battery drainage and limited range.

Benefits of Game Kit's Bluetooth Networking

In the preceding section you saw some of the limitations of using Game Kit for Bluetooth networking. Although there are some serious limitations, the benefits that are gained from leveraging this technology far outweigh those limitations in most circumstances.

One of the most beneficial features of Bluetooth is that it works where there is no available Internet connection or other closed Wi-Fi networks. Bluetooth networking allows users to communicate with each other in the absence of these networks. There are hundreds of scenarios where users are not able to access outside networks such as while in flight or during road trips. Both of these environments offer a captive audience of users who might have plenty of spare time to interact with your app if they are able to do so.

The limited range of Bluetooth can also be a great benefit. By design, you can connect only to users who are physically close to you. For instance, if you have an app that transmits your business card to another user, it is much easier to find that user using Bluetooth than through an Internet connection. Bluetooth can also offer significantly lower latency than cellular or even Wi-Fi networks.

Sample App

The sample app for this chapter is a very basic copy of the iPhone's Messages App reimplemented with Bluetooth. When it's launched, you will be prompted to connect to another peer who has launched the app and is also searching for a peer. Upon connecting, you will be placed into a two-way chat room using Bluetooth for all communication.

The sample app has a significant amount of overhead code not related to Game Kit; most of this is to handle setting up the tableView and chat bubbles. It is important that you understand this nonrelevant code so that you can focus entirely on the functional parts of the app. As shown in Figure 10.1, the sample app uses a fairly complex tableView with variable-sized chat bubbles to display data.

The sample app will store all the chat information in a mutable array of dictionaries. This makes it easy to determine how many table cells need to be returned.

```
- (NSInteger)tableView:(UITableView *)tableView
numberOfRowsInSection:(NSInteger)section
{
    return [chatObjectArray count];
}
```

Figure 10.1   A first look at the sample app.

You will also need to return a customized cell for each row. Take a look at the first part of the cellForRowAtIndexPath: method. You will be working with two primary objects here. The first is a UIImageView, which will be used to display the chat bubble background, and the second is a UILabel, which will display the text contents of the message.

```
UIImageView *msgBackground = nil;
UILabel *msgText = nil;

static NSString *CellIdentifier = @"Cell";

UITableViewCell *cell = [tableView
dequeueReusableCellWithIdentifier:CellIdentifier];

if (cell == nil)
{

    cell = [[[UITableViewCell alloc]
    ➥initWithStyle:UITableViewCellStyleDefault
    ➥reuseIdentifier:CellIdentifier] autorelease];
```

```
    msgBackground = [[UIImageView alloc] init];
    msgBackground.backgroundColor = [UIColor clearColor];
    msgBackground.tag = kMessageTag;

    [cell.contentView addSubview:msgBackground];
    [msgBackground release];

    msgText = [[UILabel alloc] init];
    msgText.backgroundColor = [UIColor clearColor];
    msgText.tag = kBackgroundTag;
    msgText.numberOfLines = 0;
    msgText.lineBreakMode = NSLineBreakByWordWrapping;
    msgText.font = [UIFont systemFontOfSize:14];

    [cell.contentView addSubview:msgText];
    [msgText release];
}
```

When creating the table cell for the first time, you will need to set up some basic defaults for each of these objects. In regard to the `UIImageView`, you will need to set the background color to clear as well as set a tag for referencing the object later in the method.

Creating the `UILabel` is only slightly more difficult; you need to set its tag and background color, and you also need to set the `numberOfLines`, `lineBreakMode`, and font. In the next snippet you will populate the pointers for the background and label with already-existing objects when the cell is being reused.

```
else
{
    msgBackground = (UIImageView *)[cell.contentView
    ➥viewWithTag:kMessageTag];

    msgText = (UILabel *)[cell.contentView
    ➥viewWithTag:kBackgroundTag];
}
```

You will need a reference to the message that will be used to populate the cell, as well as the size that displaying that message will require. In the following sections the `chatObjectArray` is covered in detail, but for the time being, you just need to know that a message string is being retrieved. The size variable is used to calculate the height of the table row to ensure that it accommodates the entirety of the message.

```
NSString *message = [[chatObjectArray objectAtIndex:
➥indexPath.row] objectForKey:@"message"];

CGSize size = [message sizeWithFont:[UIFont systemFontOfSize:14]
constrainedToSize:CGSizeMake(180, CGFLOAT_MAX)
➥lineBreakMode: NSLineBreakByWordWrapping];
```

The next step gets a bit tricky. You will need to set the backgrounds for the chat bubbles and message labels. The first thing you need to do is determine whether the message is from "myself" or from the "peer". If the message is from "myself" we want to display it on the right side of the screen using a green chat bubble; otherwise, it will be displayed on the left of the screen with the grey chat bubble.

The first line of code in each of these conditional statements sets the frame for the chat bubble. The next step is setting the bubble background with the stretchable artwork. After you have the bubble, we need to set the label inside of it and configure the resizing mask for both objects. In the second conditional block the same steps are applied but with different numbers and art to display the chat bubble on the opposite side.

```
UIImage *bubbleImage;

if([[[chatObjectArray objectAtIndex: indexPath.row]
➥objectForKey:@"sender"] isEqualToString: @"myself"])
{
    msgBackground.frame = CGRectMake(tableView.frame.size.width-size.width-
    ➥34.0f,1.0f, size.width+34.0f, size.height+12.0f);

    bubbleImage = [[UIImage imageNamed:@"ChatBubbleGreen.png"]
    ➥stretchableImageWithLeftCapWidth:15 topCapHeight:13];

    msgText.frame = CGRectMake(tableView.frame.size.width-
    ➥size.width-22.0f, 5.0f, size.width+5.0f, size.height);

    msgBackground.autoresizingMask =
    ➥UIViewAutoresizingFlexibleLeftMargin;

    msgText.autoresizingMask =
    ➥UIViewAutoresizingFlexibleLeftMargin;
}

else
{
    msgBackground.frame = CGRectMake(0.0f, 1.0f,
    ➥size.width! +34.0f, size.height+12.0f);

    bubbleImage = [[UIImage imageNamed:@"ChatBubbleGray.png"]
    ➥stretchableImageWithLeftCapWidth:23 topCapHeight:15];

    msgText.frame = CGRectMake(22.0f, 5.0f, size.width+5.0f,
    ➥size.height);

    msgBackground.autoresizingMask =
    ➥UIViewAutoresizingFlexibleRightMargin;
```

```
msgText.autoresizingMask =
➥UIViewAutoresizingFlexibleRightMargin;
}
```

The very last thing that will need to be done is setting the bubble image and message values
into the two objects for display and returning the cell as required by the `cellForRowAt`
`IndexPath`: method.

```
msgBackground.image = bubbleImage;
msgText.text = message;

return cell;
```

Since each row will have a different height depending on the size of the message that needs to
be displayed, you will also need to override `heightForRowAtIndexPath`:. The details of this
method are similar to those in the previous code snippet. You will first need to get a copy of
the message string and determine the height required for it to be properly displayed. Then you
will return that height, in addition to 17 pixels required to fit in the chat bubble's border.

```
- (CGFloat)tableView:(UITableView *)tableView
➥heightForRowAtIndexPath:(NSIndexPath *)indexPath
{
    NSString *message = [[chatObjectArray objectAtIndex:
    ➥indexPath.row] objectForKey:@"message"];

    CGSize size = [message sizeWithFont:[UIFont
    ➥systemFontOfSize:14]

    constrainedToSize:CGSizeMake(180, CGFLOAT_MAX)
    ➥lineBreakMode: NSLineBreakByWordWrapping];

    return size.height + 17.0f;
}
```

> **Note**
>
> The preceding example uses variable-height table rows but doesn't make any use of caching.
> Although this is acceptable for a demo on Bluetooth, it is not considered best practice when
> doing production development.

The Send button in the sample app also automatically enables and disables depending on
whether there is text inside the text view. The following method handles that functionality:

```
- (BOOL)textField:(UITextField *)textField
➥shouldChangeCharactersInRange:(NSRange)range replacementString:
➥(NSString *)string
{
```

```
NSUInteger textLength = [textField.text length] + [string
➥length] - range.length;

[sendButton setEnabled:(textLength > 0)];

return YES;
}
```

There is some additional minor overhead that needs to be done, such as setting the text view to be the first responder and setting delegates for the table view and text fields. For a complete look at the sample app, spend some time looking over the sample code. The information that was provided in this section is more than enough to get you comfortable with the parts of the app that don't relate to Game Kit so that you can focus on new information in the following sections.

The Peer Picker

Apple provides a built-in interface for finding other devices to connect to called the Peer Picker (Figure 10.2). The Peer Picker makes it extremely easy for your users to find peers and automates most of the functionality of connecting so that you don't need to get your hands dirty.

Figure 10.2   The Peer Picker searching for available devices.

In the sample app, when it is launched, there is a single button in the center of the screen titled Connect to New Peer. This action will trigger the Peer Picker using the `connect:` method.

The `connect:` method starts off by allocating and initializing a new instance of `GKPeerPickerController`. A delegate for `GKPeerPickerController` also needs to be defined; in the sample project, this is done in the `RootViewController`. The Peer Picker can also take an argument for a `connectTypeMask`. The sample app specifies `GKPeerPickerConnectionTypeNearby`, which is used for Bluetooth connections. You can also specify `GKPeerPickerConnectionTypeOnline` for LAN networking or for both types together using `GKPeerPickerConnectionTypeOnline | GKPeerPickerConnectionTypeNearby`.

> **Warning**
>
> There is a known bug in iOS 3.x that requires that you supply `GKPeerPickerConnection TypeNearby` as at least one of the parameters for `connectionTypeMask` or you will trigger an exception. This bug has been resolved in newer versions.

```
- (IBAction)connect:(id)sender
{
    peerPicker = [[GKPeerPickerController alloc] init];
    peerPicker.delegate = self;

    peerPicker.connectionTypesMask =
    ➥GKPeerPickerConnectionTypeNearby;

    [peerPicker show];
}
```

Two delegate methods need to be implemented in order for the Peer Picker to be fully functional. One is called when the Peer Picker is cancelled; you are required to set the delegate to `nil` here and release the picker.

```
- (void)peerPickerControllerDidCancel:(GKPeerPickerController
➥*)picker
{
    picker.delegate = nil;
    [picker release];
}
```

There is also a delegate callback when the user selects a peer from the Peer Picker. The `peerPicketController:didConnectPeer:toSession:` method provides three important arguments. The first one is the `GKPeerPickerController`. Here, you are required to dismiss the picker and release its memory as part of this callback.

```
- (void)peerPickerController:(GKPeerPickerController *)picker
➥didConnectPeer:(NSString *)peerID toSession:(GKSession *)session
{
    NSLog(@"Peer Selected");
```

```
    [picker dismiss];
    [picker release];
}
```

The remaining two arguments are important for the app to begin the communication process between the devices. Look at the method in the sample app in the following example. The picker is still dismissed and released as in the earlier example; however, there are also a few new lines of code.

In the sample project, we have a new view controller that handles the chat functionality. The Peer Picker needs to pass the session and peerID information to this class. ICFChatViewController has two synthesized properties to hold onto this information that are set after new instances of ICFChatViewController named chatViewController are created. After that information is set, the new view is pushed onto the navigation stack, seen in Figure 10.3.

```
- (void)peerPickerController:(GKPeerPickerController *)picker
➥didConnectPeer:(NSString *)peerID toSession:(GKSession *)session
{
    NSLog(@"Peer Selected");

    [picker dismiss];
    [picker release];

    ICFChatViewController *chatViewController =
    ➥[[ICFChatViewController alloc] init];

    chatViewController.currentSession = session;
    chatViewController.peerID = peerID;

    [[self navigationController]
    pushViewController:chatViewController animated:YES];

    [chatViewController release];
}
```

These are the bare minimum steps required when using the Peer Picker to connect to a new device. In the next section you will expand on this knowledge to begin sending data between devices.

Warning

The Peer Picker is based on the bundle ID; the app will find peers only searching from apps with the same bundle ID.

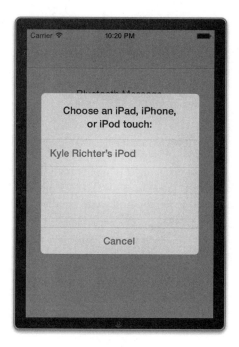

Figure 10.3   Automatic peer detection using the built-in Peer Picker.

Sending Data

Connecting to a new peer is only the first step in implementing a functional peer-to-peer networking app. After connecting to a new peer, you will want to send that peer some data. Sending data using Game Kit is extremely easy. Take a look at the following code snippet:

```
[mySession sendDataToAllPeers:messageData
➥withDataMode:GKSendDataReliable error:&error];
```

The first part of this method is a pointer to the session that was returned as part of connecting to a new peer. In the preceding example the data is being sent to all connected peers. There is an alternative method, `sendData:toPeers:withDataMode:error:`, if you wanted to send data to only a specific peer. The next part of the code snippet is an argument called `messageData`. This needs to be of the `NSData` type. You also have to specify a data mode, which is covered later in this section. (The example uses `GKSendDataReliable`.) Finally, there is a reference to an error to catch anything that goes wrong.

Data Modes

When data is sent using Game Kit, there are two possible valuables for the `dataMode` argument: `GKSendDataReliable` and `GKSendDataUnreliable`. It is important to understand the distinction between these methods:

- `GKSendDataReliable` tells Game Kit that this data is required to be received by the peer; if it is not received, it will be resent until it is received. In addition to continually retrying to send the data, `GKSendDataReliable` ensures that data packets are received in the same order in which they are sent. This method is used in the sample app since we want text messages to never get lost in the network and we want them to appear in the order in which they are sent.

- `GKSendDataUnreliable`, on the other hand, means that the data is not resent if it is not received; each packet is sent only once. This means that the networking is faster since the originating peer does not have to wait for confirmation that the packet has arrived. In addition, packets might not arrive in the order in which they were sent. `GKSendDataUnreliable` is very useful for fast networking and keeping two clients in sync when the data isn't entirely crucial to the app. For example, if you have a racing game, you will want to send the position of your car to the other player. However, if a packet doesn't reach its destination, it is better to skip it and sync up with the next packet; otherwise, the data you receive will be old and out-of-date. Each client would slowly fall further out of sync with the other.

There is a general rule of thumb for helping you decide which data mode you should use for your app. Use `GKSendDataReliable` when the data and order are more important than the time it takes to arrive. Use `GKSendDataUnreliable` when the speed at which the data is received is more important than the order and the data itself.

Sending Data in the Sample App

Take a look at how sending data is implemented in the sample app; everything is handled directly in the `sendMessage:` method. Because the app will need to send more data than just the message string, a new dictionary is created to also store information about who the message came from. For the purposes of the sample app, there is a mutable array that will hold onto all the incoming and outgoing data called `chatObjectArray`. Because we are sending a message, a local copy is inserted into that array.

Earlier, you learned that you can send only `NSData`. However, you do not want to send the dictionary since the sender key is set to `"myself"`; when the other peer receives a message, the sender should not be set to `"myself"`. A new `NSData` object is created with just the message string, and a dictionary object can be created after the message has been received.

Now that the message has been translated into an `NSData` object and a new `NSError` has been created, the session that was created when the app connected to a peer can call `sendDataToAll Peers:withDataMode:error:` with the newly created information. You will want to make sure that no errors were returned; if an error is returned, it is logged to the console in the sample app.

```
- (IBAction) sendMessage: (id) sender
{
    NSDictionary *messageDictionary = [[NSDictionary alloc]
    ➥initWithObjectsAndKeys:[inputTextField text], @"message",
    ➥@"myself", @"sender", nil];

    [chatObjectArray addObject: messageDictionary];
    [messageDictionary release];

    NSData *messageData = [inputTextField.text
    ➥ dataUsingEncoding:NSUTF8StringEncoding];

    NSError *error = nil;

    [self.currentSession sendDataToAllPeers:messageData
    ➥withDataMode:GKSendDataReliable error:&error];

    if(error != nil)
    {
        NSLog(@"An error occurred: %@", [error
        ➥localizedDescription]);
    }


    [inputTextField setText: @""];

    [sendButton setEnabled: NO];

    [chatTableView reloadData];

    //scroll to the last row
    NSIndexPath* indexPathForLastRow = [NSIndexPath
    ➥indexPathForRow:[chatObjectArray count]-1 inSection:0];

    [chatTableView scrollToRowAtIndexPath:indexPathForLastRow
    ➥atScrollPosition:UITableViewScrollPositionTop animated:YES];
}
```

The sample app has some additional cleanup that needs to be performed whenever a message is sent, such as clearing the text field and setting the Send button back to disabled. In addition, the chatTableView is reloaded and scrolled to the bottom to reflect the new outgoing message. In the next section you will learn how to receive the data that was just sent.

Receiving Data

Sending data is pointless if the receiving peer is not set up to handle that data. The first thing that needs to be done when preparing your app to receive data is letting the GKSession know which class will handle the incoming messages by setting the dataReceiveHandler. An example is shown in the following code snippet:

```
[self.currentSession setDataReceiveHandler:self withContext:nil];
```

A data handler needs to be set for each session and is session-specific. You can define a context as part of the setDataReceiveHandler: and this context will be passed along as part of any incoming data calls.

Every time your session receives data, your data handler will call receiveData:fromPeer:inS ession:context. The following example prints the received NSData to the log:

```
- (void) receiveData:(NSData *)data fromPeer:(NSString *)peer
➥inSession: (GKSession *)session context:(void *)context
{
    NSLog(@"Data Received: %@", data);
}
```

Receiving Data in the Sample App

The previous examples are really the simplest form of receiving data. Most of the time, you need to convert the NSData back into whatever format you want to work with, such as an NSString or a UIImage. In addition, you will probably want to do something with that newly received data beyond logging it. Take a look at the receiveData:fromPeer:inSession: context: method in the sample app, shown in the following code snippet. Because the sample app is working with a string, the first thing that needs to be done is retrieve the value back out of the NSData. After you have the NSString, you need to store it into the expected data format of an NSDictionary. This is the same approach taken in the sending data methods, except that the "sender" key "peer" is set instead of "myself". This allows it to be displayed correctly in the table view. After the new dictionary is inserted into the chatObjectArray, the chatTableView is refreshed and scrolled to the bottom to make the newest message visible.

```
- (void) receiveData:(NSData *)data fromPeer:(NSString *)peer
➥inSession: (GKSession *)session context:(void *)context
{
    NSString *messageString = [[NSString alloc] initWithData:data
    ➥encoding:NSUTF8StringEncoding];

    NSDictionary *messageDictionary = [[NSDictionary alloc]
    ➥initWithObjectsAndKeys:messageString, @"message", @"peer",
    ➥@"sender", nil];

    [chatObjectArray addObject: messageDictionary];
```

```
[messageString release];
[messageDictionary release];

[chatTableView reloadData];

//scroll to the last row
NSIndexPath* indexPathForLastRow = [NSIndexPath
➥indexPathForRow:[chatObjectArray count]-1 inSection:0];

[chatTableView scrollToRowAtIndexPath:indexPathForLastRow
➥atScrollPosition:UITableViewScrollPositionTop animated:YES];
}
```

State Changes

When working with remote peers, it is important to know the state of the remote device
because networks and connectivity can unexpectedly drop. You will want to inform your
user and perform appropriate error-recovery behavior in these events. To monitor state
changes, you must first declare a class as the delegate, make sure that your class conforms
to GKSessionDelegate, and then set the delegate for the session in a manner similar to the
following example. Note that this is different from the dataReceiveHandler, which can be set
to a different class.

```
[self.currentSession setDelegate: self];
```

Your newly set delegate will now receive calls to session:peer:didChangeState:. This code
snippet is from the sample app, in which a disconnected peer is caught and we present the user
with an alert informing them of such. See Table 10.1 for a complete list of possible states.

```
- (void)session:(GKSession *)session peer:(NSString *)peerID
➥didChangeState:(GKPeerConnectionState)state
{
    if(state == GKPeerStateDisconnected)
    {
        UIAlertView *alert = [[UIAlertView alloc]
        ➥initWithTitle:@"Alert!" message:@"The peer has
        ➥disconnected" delegate:nil
        ➥cancelButtonTitle: @"Dismiss"
        ➥otherButtonTitles: nil];

        [alert show];
        [alert release];

        [self.currentSession disconnectFromAllPeers];
```

```
        [[self navigationController] popViewControllerAnimated: YES];
    }
}
```

Table 10.1 **Possible State Changes and Their Definitions**

State Constant	Definition
GKPeerStateAvailable	A peer is available for a new connection.
GKPeerStateUnavailable	A peer is not interested in new connections.
GKPeerStateConnected	A peer has connected.
GKPeerStateDisconnected	A peer has disconnected.
GKPeerStateConnecting	A peer is in the process of connecting.

Advanced Features

In previous sections, you learned how to create a new basic connection using the Peer Picker and sending and receiving data from that peer. Game Kit's Bluetooth networking has several advanced features, some of which are covered in this section.

Peer Display Name

It is often useful to display the name of the peer you are connected to. Referring to Figure 10.1, the navigation bar contains a title that references the connected user; this is done using the following code snippet:

```
NSString *peerDisplayName = [self.currentSession
➥displayNameForPeer: self.peerID];

[[self navigationItem] setTitle: [NSString
➥stringWithFormat:@"Chat with %@", peerDisplayName]];
```

Connecting Without the Peer Picker

There are times when you might want to connect using Game Kit but without displaying the Peer Picker. Although this is a slightly more difficult approach, it is still entirely possible. First, you need to create a new session, as shown in the following example:

```
currentSession = [[GKSession alloc] initWithSessionID:nil
➥displayName:nil sessionMode:GKSessionModePeer];
```

```
currentSession.delegate = self;
currentSession.available = YES;
currentSession.disconnectTimeout = 15;

[currentSession setDataReceiveHandler:self withContext:nil];
```

There are some key differences in the preceding example from implementing a connection using the Peer Picker. First, you need to create the GKSession instead of the Peer Picker returning one during the connection callback. The sessionID argument can be used to define matching peers to connect to. If the session IDs do not match, the devices will not see each other. In the following section you will learn more about the sessionMode argument. You will also need to set the available property to YES, which is an important step for other devices to see the device as ready for a connection. A disconnectTimeout is also set for 15 seconds.

When you set a device to available, it will inform any other devices looking for peers that it has become available for connections. Because there is a state change from unavailable to available, the GKSession delegate will receive a callback to session:peer:didChangeState:. In the following example, when the app detects that a new device has become available, it immediately tries to connect. In real-world implementations, you might want to present your user a list of IDs before they pick one to connect to.

```
- (void)session:(GKSession *)session peer:(NSString *)peerID
➥didChangeState:(GKPeerConnectionState)state
{
    if(state == GKPeerStateAvailable)
    {
        [session connectToPeer:peerID withTimeout:15];
    }
}
```

When a device attempts to connect to your device, you receive a call to didReceive ConnectionRequestFromPeer:, which must be handled similarly to the next code snippet:

```
- (void)session:(GKSession*) session
➥didReceiveConnectionRequestFromPeer:(NSString*) peerID
{
    [session acceptConnectionFromPeer:peerID error:nil];
}
```

After you have called acceptConnectionFromPeer:, your delegate will receive another call to session:peerID:didChangeState: with a GKPeerStateConnected state. From here, you can continue with your app as if you had connected using the Peer Picker.

> **Note**
>
> Whereas the Peer Picker has a two-person limit on connections, connecting without the Peer Picker allows up to four total devices.

Session Modes

In the preceding section, you learned how to connect to a peer without using the Peer Picker. Part of creating a new `GKSession` was specifying a `sessionMode`; in the previous example, the mode supplied was `GKSessionModePeer`. There are three types of `sessionModes` that can be supplied.

`GKSessionModePeer` acts like the Peer Picker. It looks for a peer at the same time as it allows other peers to find it. Either side can initiate the connection when working with a `GKSessionModePeer`.

`GKSessionModeServer` acts differently than `GKSessionModePeer`. In this mode the `GKSession` will not look for other peers but will make itself available to be connected to by peers that are searching.

`GKSessionModeClient` is the reverse of `GKSessionModeServer`. It searches for peers to connect to but does not allow other peers to search for it.

Summary

In this chapter, you learned how to fully implement a peer-to-peer Bluetooth network using two iOS devices. The limitations and capabilities of Game Kit's Bluetooth networking were discussed, as well as some of the benefits that can be leveraged by including Bluetooth networking. The sample app for this chapter walked you through adding networking to a simple two-way chat app.

You worked with sending data and the different options available to you when transmitting, as well as how to receive and process data. In addition, you learned how to handle disconnects and other important state changes from the connected peer. There was also a short section on some of the more advanced features of Game Kit's Bluetooth networking. You should now have all the knowledge and confidence to be able to successfully add Bluetooth networking into your iOS app in minimal time.

Exercises

1. Add the capability to send and receive images into the sample app. Remember that you will need to add a way to identify the message as either an image or a string.

2. Implement a custom Peer Picker to find and establish a connection with another device.

11

AirPrint

Without a doubt, printing is going the way of the Dodo Bird and the Tasmanian Tiger, but it will not happen overnight. There are plenty of solid autumn years left for physical printing. With iOS 4.2, Apple introduced a new SDK feature called AirPrint, which as the name implies allows an iOS device to print to a wireless printer.

AirPrint Printers

There is a limited selection of AirPrint-enabled printers, even three years after the release of AirPrint. Most major printer manufacturers now have at least a few models that support AirPrint. Apple also maintains a list of compatible printers through a tech note (http://support.apple.com/kb/HT4356). In addition, some third-party Mac applications enable AirPrint for any existing printer, such as Printopia ($19.95 at www.ecamm.com/mac/printopia).

Since the release of AirPrint, there have been numerous blogs, articles, and how-tos written on testing AirPrint. Apple seems to have taken notice of the need and has started to bundle an app with the developer tools called Printer Simulator (`Developer/Platforms/iPhoneOS.platform/Developer/Applications`), as shown in Figure 11.1. Printer Simulator allows your Mac to host several printer configurations for the iOS Simulator to print to; using this tool, you can test a wide range of compatibility.

The sample app for this chapter is a simple iPhone app that provides the user with two views, as shown in Figure 11.2. The first view is a simple text editor, which will demo how to lay out pages and text. The second view is a Web browser, which will demo how to print rendered HTML as well as PDF screen grabs.

The Print app is simple and does not contain a significant amount of overhead code. It is based on the Apple TabBarController default project, containing two tabs. The text editor contains a `UITextView` as well as two buttons: one to hide the keyboard, the other to begin the print process. The Web browser view contains a Print button but also needs a URL entry text field.

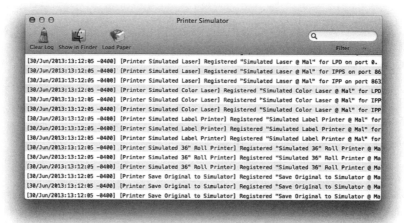

Figure 11.1   The Printer Simulator tool.

Figure 11.2   Print, the sample app for AirPrinting.

Testing for AirPrint

It is important to test for AirPrint support in your software before enabling the functionality to users, because some of your users might be running an iOS version that does not support AirPrint. In the sample app this is performed as part of the `application:didFinish` `LaunchingWithOptions:` method using the following code snippet:

```
if (![UIPrintInteractionController isPrintingAvailable])
{
    UIAlertView *alert = [[UIAlertView alloc]
    initWithTitle:@"Error"
    message:@"This device does not support printing!"
    delegate:nil
    cancelButtonTitle:@"Dismiss"
    otherButtonTitles:nil];

    [alert show];
    [alert release];
}
```

Note

AirPrint is defined as part of `UIKit` so there are no additional headers or frameworks that need to be imported.

Printing Text

Printing text is probably the most common use case for not just AirPrint but any kind of print job. Using AirPrint to print text can be complex if you aren't familiar with printing terminology. The following code is from the `ICFFirstViewController.m` class of the sample app. Look at it as a whole first; later in this section, it will be broken down by each line and discussed.

```
- (IBAction)print:(id)sender
{
    UIPrintInteractionController *print =
    ➥[UIPrintInteractionController sharedPrintController];

    print.delegate = self;

    UIPrintInfo *printInfo = [UIPrintInfo printInfo];
    printInfo.outputType = UIPrintInfoOutputGeneral;
    printInfo.jobName = @"Print for iOS";
    printInfo.duplex = UIPrintInfoDuplexLongEdge;
    print.printInfo = printInfo;
```

```
    print.showsPageRange = YES;

    UISimpleTextPrintFormatter *textFormatter =
➡[[UISimpleTextPrintFormatter alloc] initWithText:[theTextView
➡text]];

    textFormatter.startPage = 0;

    textFormatter.contentInsets = UIEdgeInsetsMake(36.0, 36.0,36.0,
➡36.0);

    textFormatter.maximumContentWidth = 540;

    print.printFormatter = textFormatter;
}
```

The preceding code takes the contents of a text view and prints it formatted for 8 1/2- by 11-inch paper with 1/2-inch margins on all sides. The first thing you need to do whenever you want to prepare for a print operation is create a reference to the sharedPrintController using the following code snippet:

```
UIPrintInteractionController *print = [UIPrintInteractionController
➡ sharedPrintController];
```

In the next line of the sample app, a delegate is set. The delegate methods for printing are defined in the upcoming section "UIPrintInteractionControllerDelegate."

Print Info

The next step is to configure the print info. This specifies a number of controls and modifiers for how the print job is set up. You can obtain a new default UIPrintInfo object using the UIPrintInfo singleton.

The first property that is set on the print info in the sample app is outputType. In the example, the output is set as UIPrintInfoOutputGeneral. This specifies that the print job can be a mix of text, graphics, and images, as well as setting the default paper size to letter. Other options for outputType include UIPrintInfoOutputPhoto and UIPrintInfoOutputGrayscale.

The next property that is set is the jobName. This is an optional field that is used to identify the print job in the print center app. If you do not set a jobName, it is defaulted to the app's name.

Duplexing in the printer world refers to how the printer handles double-sided printing. If the printer does not support double-sided printing, these properties are ignored. You can supply UIPrintInfoDuplexNone if you would like to prevent double-sided printing. To use double-sided printing you have two options: UIPrintInfoDuplexLongEdge, which will flip the back page along the long edge of the paper, and `UIPrintInfoDuplexShortEdge`, which, as the name implies, flips the back page along the short side of the paper.

In addition to the `printInfo` properties that are used in the sample code, there are two additional properties. The first, `orientation`, allows you to specify printing in either landscape or portrait. The second is `printerID`, which allows you to specify a hint on which printer to use. `PrinterID` is often used to automatically select the last used printer, which can be obtained using the `UIPrintInteractionControllerDelegate`.

After you configure the `printInfo` for the print job, you need to set the associated property on the `UIPrintInteractionController`. An example is shown in the next code snippet:

```
print.printInfo = printInfo;
```

Setting Page Range

In many cases, a print job will consist of multiple pages, and occasionally you will want to provide the user with the option of selecting which of those pages is printed. You can do this through the `showsPageRange` property. When set to `YES`, it will allow the user to select pages during the printer selection stage.

```
print.showsPageRange = YES;
```

UISimpleTextPrintFormatter

After configuring the `printInfo`, the `UIPrintInteractionController` has a good idea of what type of print job is coming but doesn't yet have any information on what to print. This data is set using a print formatter; this section discusses the print formatter for text. In following sections, additional print formatters are discussed in depth.

```
UISimpleTextPrintFormatter *textFormatter =
➥ [[UISimpleTextPrintFormatter alloc] initWithText:[theTextView
➥text]];

textFormatter.startPage = 0;

textFormatter.contentInsets = UIEdgeInsetsMake(36.0, 36.0, 36.0, 36.0);

textFormatter.maximumContentWidth = 540;

print.printFormatter = textFormatter;
[textFormatter release];
```

When you create a new instance of the `UISimpleTextPrintFormatter`, it is allocated and initialized with the text you will be printing. The sample app will print any text that appears in the `UITextView`.

The first property that is set in the sample app is for the `startPage`. This is a zero-based index of the first page to be printed. The sample app will begin printing from page one (index 0).

On the following line `contentInserts` are set. A value of `72.0` equals one inch on printed paper. The sample app will be providing half-inch values on all sides; this will print the text with half-inch margins on the top, bottom, left, and right. Additionally, the maximum width is set to 504, which specifies a 7 1/2-inch printing width (72.0×7.0).

There are two additional properties that were not used in the sample app. The `font` property allows you to specify a `UIFont` that the text is to be printed in. `font` is an optional property; if you do not specify a font, the system font at 12-point is used. You can also specify a text color using the `color` property. If you do not provide a color, `[UIColor blackColor]` is used.

When you finish configuring the `textFormatter`, you will need to set it to the `printFormatter` property of the `UIPrintInteractionController` object.

Error Handling

It is always important to gracefully handle errors, even more so while printing. With printing, there are any number of things that can go wrong outside of the developer's control, from out-of -paper issues to the printer not even being on.

The sample app defines a new block called `completionHandler`. This is used to handle any errors that are returned from the print job. In the next section, you will begin a new print job with the `completionHandler` block as one of the arguments.

```
void (^completionHandler)(UIPrintInteractionController *,BOOL, NSError
*) = ^(UIPrintInteractionController *print,BOOL completed, NSError
*error)
{
    if (!completed && error)
    {
        NSLog(@"Error!");
    }
};
```

Starting the Print Job

After you have created a new `UIPrintInteractionController`, specified the `printInfo` and the `printFormatter`, and created a block to handle any errors that are returned, you can finally print something. Call the method `presentAnimated:completionHandler:` on the `UIPrintInteractionController` object using the completion block that was created in the preceding section. This will present the user with the Printer Options view, as shown in Figure 11.3.

```
[print presentAnimated:YES completionHandler:completionHandler];
```

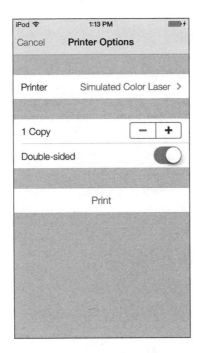

Figure 11.3   Print options while printing text with multiple pages on a printer that supports
double-sided printing.

Depending on the selected printer and the amount of text being printed, the options will
vary. For example, if the print job is only one page, the user will not be presented with a range
option; likewise, if the printer does not support double-sided printing, this option will be
disabled.

Print Simulator Feedback

If you printed to the Printer Simulator app as discussed in the "AirPrint Printers" section, after
the print job is finished, a new page will be opened in preview (or your default PDF viewing
application) showing how the final page will look. An example using the print info and print
formatter information from this section is shown in Figure 11.4.

Figure 11.4   A print preview shown when using the Printer Simulator; notice the highlighted margins.

Print Center

Just as on desktop computers, iOS provides users a way to interact with the current print queue. While any print job is active on an iOS device, a new app appears in the active app area. The Print Center app icon is shown in the Springboard in Figure 11.5. The Print Center app itself is shown in Figure 11.6. The Print Center was removed in iOS 7 and printing feedback is now handled during the print process.

UIPrintInteractionControllerDelegate

As shown earlier in the "Printing Text" section, you can optionally provide a delegate for a `UIPrintInteractionController` object. The possible delegate callbacks are used in both views of the sample app. Table 11.1 describes these delegate methods.

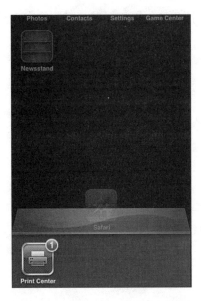

Figure 11.5   While printing is occurring, a new app will appear on an iOS 6.0 device called Print Center.app. Print Center.app is badged with the current number of print jobs. This behavior no longer exists on iOS 7.

Figure 11.6   Print Center.app provides information about the current print job as well as a way to cancel printing.

Table 11.1   **Listing of the Available** `UIPrintInteractionControllerDelegate` **Methods**

Method Name	Description
`printInteractionControllerWill PresentPrinterOptions:`	The API will present the options for the user to configure the print job.
`printInteractionControllerDid PresentPrinterOptions:`	The API did present the options for the user to configure the print job.
`printInteractionControllerWill DismissPrinterOptions:`	The API will dismiss the print options view.
`printInteractionControllerDid DismissPrinterOptions:`	The API did dismiss the print options view.
`printInteractionControllerWill StartJob:`	The method is called right before the print job is started.
`printInteractionControllerDid FinishJob:`	This method is called when the print job has been completed or has failed.

Printing Rendered HTML

Printing rendered HTML is handled automatically through a print formatter in an almost identical manner as printing plain text. The following method handles printing an HTML string, which is retrieved from the `UIWebView` in the sample app. You might notice that this is similar to how text was printed in the previous example. Take a look at the method as a whole; it is discussed in detail later in this section.

```
- (IBAction)print:(id)sender
{
    UIPrintInteractionController *print =
    ➥[UIPrintInteractionController sharedPrintController];

    print.delegate = self;

    UIPrintInfo *printInfo = [UIPrintInfo printInfo];
    printInfo.outputType = UIPrintInfoOutputGeneral;
    printInfo.jobName = @"Print for iOS";
    printInfo.duplex = UIPrintInfoDuplexLongEdge;
    print.printInfo = printInfo;

    print.showsPageRange = YES;

    NSURL *requestURL = [[theWebView request] URL];
    NSError *error;
```

```
NSString *contentHTML = [NSString
stringWithContentsOfURL:requestURL
encoding:NSASCIIStringEncoding
error:&error];

UIMarkupTextPrintFormatter *textFormatter =
➥[[UIMarkupTextPrintFormatter alloc]
➥initWithMarkupText:contentHTML];

textFormatter.startPage = 0;

textFormatter.contentInsets = UIEdgeInsetsMake(36.0, 36.0, 36.0,
➥36.0);

textFormatter.maximumContentWidth = 540;
print.printFormatter = textFormatter;
[textFormatter release];

void (^completionHandler)(UIPrintInteractionController *,BOOL,
➥NSError *) = ^(UIPrintInteractionController *print,BOOL
➥completed, NSError *error)
{
    if (!completed && error)
    {
        NSLog(@"Error!");
    }
};

[print presentAnimated:YES completionHandler:completionHandler];
}
```

The first thing that needs to be done as it was in the text printing is to create a new reference to a UIPrintInteractionController. The next step is to set the printInfo for the upcoming print job. Nothing in this code block dealing with printing differs from the printing text example; refer to that section for details on these properties.

Printing PDFs

AirPrint has built-in support for printing PDF files. PDF is arguably the easiest type of file to print when you have the PDF data. Before a PDF file can be printed, first the UIPrintInteractionController and associated UIPrintInfo need to be set up. This setup is done exactly the same as in the previous example in the section "Printing Rendered HTML." In the sample app, the PDF is generated from the UIWebView from the preceding section; however, you can specify any source for the PDF data. After the data has been created using the renderInContext method, you can assign that image value to printingItem. This method can also be used to print any UIImage data.

> **Note**
>
> The sample app does not currently have an action hooked up to the print PDF method. You will have to assign a button to that method in order to use it.

```objc
- (IBAction)printPDF:(id)sender
{
    UIPrintInteractionController *print =
    [UIPrintInteractionController sharedPrintController];

    print.delegate = self;
    UIPrintInfo *printInfo = [UIPrintInfo printInfo];
    printInfo.outputType = UIPrintInfoOutputGeneral;
    printInfo.jobName = @"Print for iOS";
    printInfo.duplex = UIPrintInfoDuplexLongEdge;
    print.printInfo = printInfo;

    print.showsPageRange = YES;

    UIGraphicsBeginImageContext(theWebView.bounds.size);

    [theWebView.layer
    renderInContext:UIGraphicsGetCurrentContext()];

    UIImage *image = UIGraphicsGetImageFromCurrentImageContext();
    UIGraphicsEndImageContext();

    print.printingItem = image;

    void (^completionHandler)(UIPrintInteractionController *,BOOL,
    ➥NSError *) = ^(UIPrintInteractionController *print,BOOL
    ➥completed,NSError *error)
    {
        if (!completed && error)
        {
            NSLog(@"Error!");
        }
    };

    [print presentAnimated:YES completionHandler:completionHandler];
}
```

Summary

In this chapter, you learned how to print documents, images, and HTML from an iOS device using AirPrint. You should have a firm grasp of the knowledge required to create new print jobs, provide the materials to be printed, format the output, handle errors, and interact with various printers. The sample app provided for this chapter walked you through the process of printing plain text, HTML, and PDF data. You should feel confident adding AirPrint support into any of your existing or future iOS projects.

Exercises

1. Set up a print operation that prints assets from the photo library. Refer to Chapter 23, "Accessing Photo Libraries," for information on how to retrieve the photo objects. Be sure to update the output type to get better photo quality.

2. Update the app to print the contents of the device screen so that you can quickly take snapshots of your app and have them printed.

12

Core Data Primer

For many apps, being able to locally store and retrieve data that persists beyond a single session is a requirement. Since iOS 3.0, Core Data has been available to address this need. Core Data is a powerful object database; it provides robust data storage and management capabilities.

Core Data has its roots in NeXT's Enterprise Object Framework (EOF), which was capable of mapping objects to relational databases. There are great advantages to writing business logic to objects, and not having to build database or persistence-specific logic. Mainly, there is a lot less code to write, and that code tends to be focused on the needs of the app rather than the needs of the database. EOF could support several brands of relational databases. Since Core Data was built to support single-user applications in Mac OS X, Core Data supports storing data in an embedded relational database called SQLite, which provides the benefits of an SQL database without the hassle and overhead of maintaining a database server.

Some features of Core Data include the following:

- *Modeling data objects with a visual model editor.*

- *Automatic and manual migration tools to handle when object schema changes.*

- *Establishing relationships between objects (one-to-one, one-to-many, many-to-many).*

- *Storing data in separate files and different file formats.*

- *Validation of object attributes.*

- *Querying and sorting data.*

- *Lazy loading data.*

- *Interacting closely with iOS table views.*

- *Managing related object changes with commit and undo capabilities.*

Many books have been written solely about Core Data; this chapter provides a brief primer on the pieces needed to integrate and utilize Core Data in an app, and some of the basic capabilities of Core Data to assist in deciding whether it is the right fit for an app. Since this chapter does not explain how to use Core Data, there is no sample app. Refer to Chapter 13, "Getting Up and Running with Core Data," for a sample app and information on how to get started with Core Data.

Deciding on Core Data

There are a few options available to iOS developers who would like to use persistent data:

- **NSUserDefaults:** This method is typically used to save app preferences. NSUserDefaults functions very much like an NSDictionary with key-value storage, and supports storing values that can be expressed as NSNumber, NSString, NSDate, NSData, NSDictionary, NSArray, or any object that conforms to the NSCoding protocol. If an app's persistence needs can be satisfied using key-value pairs, dictionaries, and arrays, then NSUserDefaults is a viable option.

- **Property List (plist):** NSDictionary and NSArray each support reading from and saving to a user-specified property list file, which is an XML file format supporting NSNumber, NSString, NSDate, NSData, NSDictionary, and NSArray. If an app's persistence needs can be satisfied using a dictionary or an array, then a property list file is a viable option.

- **Coders and Keyed Archives:** NSCoder and NSKeyedArchiver support saving an arbitrary object graph into a binary file. These options require implementing NSCoder methods in each custom object to be saved, and require the developer to manage saving and loading. If an app's persistence needs can be satisfied with a handful of custom objects, the coder/archiver approach is a viable option.

- **Direct SQLite:** Using the C library libsqlite, apps can interact with SQLite databases directly. SQLite is an embedded relational database that does not need a server; it supports most of the standard SQL language as described by SQL92. Any data persistence logic that can be built using SQL can likely be built into an iOS app utilizing SQLite, including defining database tables and relationships, inserting data, querying data, and updating and deleting data. The drawback of this approach is that the app needs to map data between application objects and SQL files, requires writing SQL queries to retrieve and save data, and requires code to track which objects need to be saved.

- **Core Data:** Provides most of the flexibility of working with SQLite directly, while insulating the app from the mechanics of working with the database. If the app requires more than a handful of data, needs to maintain relationships between different objects, or needs to be able to access specific objects or groups of objects quickly and easily, Core Data might be a good candidate.

To provide details on how Core Data is used in a typical app, this chapter first walks through using the classes that an app will typically interact with. Managed objects, or instances of NSManagedObject, are things that get stored. The managed object context (NSManagedObjectContext) is the working area that an app uses to create, query, and save managed objects. After describing these, this chapter explains the environment setup that allows Core Data to work.

Core Data Managed Objects

This section provides an overview of core data managed objects, including what managed objects are, how they are defined in a managed object model, how an app can interact with managed objects, and how changes to the definitions of the managed objects can be handled between app versions.

Managed Objects

Managed objects, or instances of NSManagedObject, are what an app will interact with the most. A managed object can be thought of as a dictionary with a known set of keys, and with known types of objects (like string or number) by key. Attributes for managed objects can always be accessed with this technique:

```
NSString *movieName = [myMovie valueForKey:@"movieName"];
```

And attributes can always be updated using setValue:forKey:

```
[myMovie setValue:@"Casablanca" forKey:@"movieName"];
```

Managed objects can be defined as subclasses of NSManagedObject, which will allow accessing the attributes as properties:

```
[myMovie setMovieName:@"Casablanca"];

NSString *movieName = [myMovie movieName];
```

Subclasses of NSManagedObject can have custom methods. For example, if there is a managed object to keep information about a movie, a custom method could be added to help keep track of how many times a movie has been watched. The method might increment the "times watched" attribute on the movie, and set the "last watched date" to today.

Managed objects can have relationships set up between them. For example, if an app tracks a movie collection, it might be useful to track if a movie has been lent to a friend. That can be modeled in the app by creating a Movie object and a Friend object, and then setting a relationship between the Movie and Friend objects.

Relationships between objects can be one-to-one. If the movie app were to store one poster image for each movie in a separate object, the movie and poster image could be related to each other:

```
[myMovie setValue:posterImageObject forKey:@"posterImage"];

NSManagedObject *movie =
[posterImageObject valueForKey:@"relatedMovie"];
```

Or a relationship can be one-to-many; for example, a movie can be lent to only one friend at a time, but a friend might be borrowing many movies at a time:

```
[myMovie setValue:myFriend forKey:@"lentToFriend"];

[myOtherMovie setValue:myFriend forKey:@"lentToFriend"];

NSSet *borrowedMovies =
[myFriend valueForKey:@"borrowedMovies"];
```

Managed Object Model

Managed objects are defined in a managed object model (NSManagedObjectModel). The managed object model includes the list of entities, the attributes associated with each entity, validations associated with attributes and entities, and the relationships established between the entities. Managed object models are typically created using Xcode's visual modeling editor (see Figure 12.1).

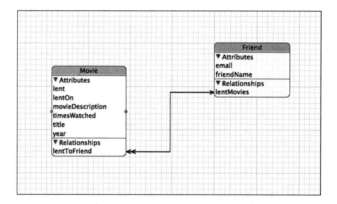

Figure 12.1   Xcode Data Model Editor: Graph style.

In Figure 12.1, two entities are represented. Each entity has attributes associated with it, and there is a one-to-many relationship set up between the two entities. To see more detail about the attributes for each entity, switch to the Table editing style using the Editor Style switch in the lower-right corner (see Figure 12.2).

Figure 12.2 shows all the attributes for the Movie entity, and the type of each attribute. The data types that Core Data supports are displayed in Table 12.1.

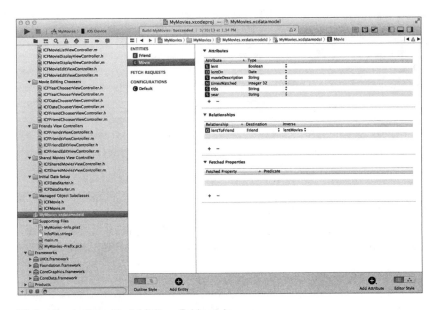

Figure 12.2 Xcode Data Model Editor: Table style.

Table 12.1 **Core Data Supported Data Types**

Data Types	Objective-C Storage
Integer 16	NSNumber
Integer 32	NSNumber
Integer 64	NSNumber
Decimal	NSNumber
Double	NSNumber
Float	NSNumber
String	NSString
Boolean	NSNumber
Date	NSDate
Binary Data	NSData
Transformable	Uses value transformer

Core Data supports entity inheritance. Any entity can have one parent entity specified (see Figure 12.3). The child entity will inherit all the characteristics of the parent entity, including attributes, validations, and indexes.

Figure 12.3   Xcode Data Model Editor: Parent Entity selection.

Managed Object Model Migrations

If an object model ever needs to change (even just adding one attribute to an entity is considered a change to the model), model versioning will need to be handled. When loading an existing persistent store, Core Data will check it against the object model to make sure it matches, using a hash calculated on the entities and attributes to determine what constitutes a unique object model. If it does not match, data from the persistent store will need to be migrated to a new persistent store based on the new object model. Core Data can handle many simple migrations automatically with options set in the persistent store coordinator (described later in the chapter), but if any logic is required, a migration might need to be written. Handling migrations is a complex topic; for more information on migrations, refer to the book *Core Data for iOS: Developing Data-Driven Applications for the iPad, iPhone, and iPod Touch*, by Tim Isted and Tom Harrington (Addison-Wesley Professional).

Creating Managed Objects

Managed objects can exist only in a managed object context (NSManagedObjectContext), which is Core Data's working area. A managed object must be either created in or fetched from the managed object context. To create a new managed object, a reference to the managed object context is needed. The managed object context is available as a property on the application delegate for projects that have been set up using Xcode's Master Detail project template. In addition, Core Data needs to know what entity the new managed object is for. Core Data has a class called NSEntityDescription that provides information about entities. Create a new instance using NSEntityDescription's class method:

```
NSManagedObjectContext *moc = kAppDelegate.managedObjectContext;

NSManagedObject *newObject =
[NSEntityDescription insertNewObjectForEntityForName:@"MyEntity"
                             inManagedObjectContext:moc];
```

After the new instance is available, the attributes can be updated. When complete, the managed object context needs to be saved to make the object persistent.

```
NSError *mocSaveError = nil;

if (![moc save:&mocSaveError])
{
    NSLog(@"Save did not complete successfully. Error: %@",
        [mocSaveError localizedDescription]);
}
```

The managed object context can be rolled back to throw away unwanted changes. This means that all the changes in the managed object context will be undone, will not be saved, and will not affect any other objects or managed object contexts.

```
if ([moc hasChanges])
{
    [moc rollback];
    NSLog(@"Rolled back changes.");
}
```

Fetching and Sorting Objects

To work with existing managed objects, they need to be fetched from the managed object context. There are two methods to fetch managed objects: directly using the `objectID`, or by constructing a fetch request.

Core Data gives each managed object a unique ID, which is an instance of `NSManagedObjectID`, called `objectID`. If that `objectID` has been stored for an object, it can be used to fetch the object:

```
NSManagedObject *myObject = [kAppDelegate.managedObjectContext
                        objectWithID:myObjectID];
```

The `objectWithID` method will return `nil` if an object with `myObjectID` is not found, or will return one `NSManagedObject` if it is found.

To fetch managed objects by specifying attribute criteria, a fetch request (instance of `NSFetchRequest`) is needed. The fetch request needs to know what entity is being fetched, which can be specified with an `NSEntityDescription`:

```
NSFetchRequest *fetchRequest = [[NSFetchRequest alloc] init];

NSEntityDescription *entity =
[NSEntityDescription entityForName:@"MyEntity"
            inManagedObjectContext:moc];

[fetchRequest setEntity:entity];
```

A fetch request can optionally have sort descriptors (`NSSortDescriptor`) to define the sort order for the returned results. Create a sort descriptor for each attribute that the search results should be sorted by, specifying the attribute name and sorting direction (ascending or descending). The sort descriptors are then added to an array in the order in which they should be applied to the results.

```
NSSortDescriptor *sortDescriptor =
[[NSSortDescriptor alloc] initWithKey:@"sortAttributeName"
                               ascending:YES];


NSArray *sortDescriptors =
[NSArray arrayWithObject:sortDescriptor];


[fetchRequest setSortDescriptors:sortDescriptors];
```

A fetch request can optionally use a predicate (`NSPredicate`) to define criteria that the returned results must match. Predicates for fetch requests are described in more detail in Chapter 13, in the "Using Predicates" subsection of the "Displaying Your Managed Objects" section.

```
NSPredicate *predicate =
[NSPredicate predicateWithFormat:@"attribute == %@",@"value"];


[fetchRequest setPredicate:predicate];
```

A fetch request will return zero, one, or multiple result objects in an `NSArray`. In cases where you would prefer to have the results attributes instead of objects, the fetch request can be set up to return just the attribute values instead of managed objects; it can even be set up to return aggregate functions like `sum` and `count`.

Fetched Results Controller

A fetched results controller is a powerful way to tie a fetch request to a `UITableView`. The fetched results controller sets up a fetch request so that the results are returned in sections and rows, accessible by index paths, and then exposes methods that make it convenient to get the information needed to implement a table view. In addition, the fetched results controller can listen to changes in Core Data and update the table accordingly using delegate methods, and can even animate changes to the table view. For a detailed explanation of setting up a fetched results controller–backed table view, refer to the section "Introducing the Fetched Results Controller" in Chapter 13.

The Core Data Environment

Core Data is able to hide the mechanics of persistence so that app code is able to work directly with model objects with no worries about how they are stored or saved. To do this, Core Data utilizes four major classes to define the environment: `NSManagedObjectModel`, `NSPersistentStoreCoordinator`, `NSPersistentStore`, and `NSManagedObjectContext`. When a Core Data–enabled project is set up in Xcode, the template provides logic to set up instances of these four classes. Adding Core Data to a new project is a fairly quick exercise, because all that is needed is to set up a managed object model, do any customizations needed to the rest of the environment, and begin writing app logic to use it.

The pattern that the Core Data template uses is to set up properties on the app delegate that are lazy loaded. When you instantiate the Core Data environment, each piece of the environment will be instantiated when it is needed. To instantiate a managed object model, load it from the model file. After the managed object model is instantiated, you can attach it to the persistent store coordinator.

Persistent Store Coordinator

The persistent store coordinator (`NSPersistentStoreCoordinator`) is the intermediary between the actual files that object data is stored in and the object model that the app interacts with. An app typically does not interact with a persistent store coordinator beyond just instantiating it when setting up the Core Data environment. The persistent store coordinator can manage communication with more than one persistent store so that the details of how the data are stored is hidden. After the persistent store coordinator is set up, a persistent store needs to be added to it to be able to access data.

Persistent Store

The persistent store (`NSPersistentStore`) represents a file where data is stored. When setting up an app to use Core Data, all that is needed is to specify the name, location, and type of the persistent store. Core Data can use SQLite and binary storage file types on iOS, and can use XML in Mac OS X (Core Data can also use an in-memory store, which does not save any data in a file). Most iOS apps use the SQLite option, since Core Data can leverage query capabilities for great performance. An important item to note is that Core Data manages the SQLite file directly. Core Data cannot use an existing SQLite file; it must create the file and schema itself, which it does when it first attempts to use the file if it is not present.

After a persistent store has been added successfully to the persistent store coordinator, it is time to set up the managed object context and interact with model objects.

Managed Object Context

The managed object context (`NSManagedObjectContext`) is a working area for managed objects. To create a new object, delete an object, or query existing objects, the app interacts with the managed object context. In addition, the managed object context can manage related changes. For example, the app could insert a few objects, update some objects, delete an object, and then save all those changes together or even roll them back if they are not needed.

More than one managed object context can be used at the same time to separate or confine work. Imagine that an app needs to display a set of data while it is importing some new data from a Web service. In that case, one managed object context would be used in the main thread to query and display existing data. Another managed object context would then be used in a background thread to import the data from the Web service. When the app is done importing data, it can merge the two managed object contexts together and dispose of the background context. Core Data is powerful enough to handle cases in which the same object is updated in both contexts, and can merge the changes together. The managed object context will also send a notification when a merge has been completed so that the app knows it is time to update the user interface. The notification contains detailed information about what changed so that the app can be very precise about updating what is on the screen.

Summary

This chapter introduced Core Data concepts, including the Core Data managed object, the managed object model, and Xcode's visual managed object model editor. It showed how to create and fetch managed objects and interact with them in your app. The chapter explained how the Core Data environment is established in an iOS app, and how the persistent store coordinator, persistent stores, managed object contexts, and managed objects all work together to give you robust access to your application data. These are all the basic concepts needed to use Core Data; if it looks as though Core Data is right for your app, you can get up and running quickly with Chapter 13.

> ### Note
>
> There are no exercises for this chapter, since it's really just an intro and the actual instruction takes place in Chapter 13.

Getting Up and Running with Core Data

At first glance, Core Data can look difficult and overwhelming. There are several books devoted solely to Core Data, and the official Apple documentation is lengthy and challenging to get through since it covers the entire breadth and depth of the topic. Most apps do not require all the features that Core Data has to offer. The goal of this chapter is to get you up and running with the most common Core Data features that apps need.

This chapter describes how to set up a project to use Core Data, and illustrates how to implement several common use cases with the sample app. It covers how to set up your data model, how to populate some starting data, and how to display data in a table using a fetched results controller. This chapter also demonstrates how to add, edit, and delete data, how to fetch data, and how to use predicates to fetch specific data. With this knowledge, you will have a good foundation for implementing Core Data quickly in your apps.

Sample App

The sample app for this chapter is called MyMovies. It is a Core Data–based app that will keep track of all your physical media movies and, if you have loaned a movie to someone, who you loaned it to and when (as shown in Figure 13.1).

The sample app has three tabs: Movies, Friends, and Shared Movies. The Movies tab shows the whole list of movies that the user has added and tracked in a table view. There are two sections in the table view demonstrating how data can be segregated with a fetched results controller. Users can add new movies from this tab, and can edit existing movies. The Friends tab lists the friends set up to share movies with, shows which friends have borrowed movies, and allows the user to add and edit friends. The Shared Movies tab displays which movies have currently been shared with friends.

Figure 13.1   Sample App: Movies tab.

Starting a Core Data Project

To start a new Core Data project, open Xcode and select File from the menu, New, and then Project. Xcode will present some project template options to get you started (see Figure 13.2).

The quickest method to start a Core Data project is to select the Master-Detail template. Click Next to specify options for your new project, and then make sure that Use Core Data is selected (see Figure 13.3). This ensures that your project has the Core Data plumbing built in.

When Next is clicked, Xcode creates the project template. The project template includes a "master" view controller, which includes a table view populated by an `NSFetchedResultsController`, a specialized controller that makes pairing Core Data with a table view a snap. The project template includes a "detail" view to display a single data record. In the sample app, the master and detail views have been renamed to fit the project.

> **Note**
>
> To add Core Data to an existing project quickly, create an empty template project with Core Data support as described, and then copy the elements described in the following section, "Core Data Environment," into the existing project. Add a new managed object model file to the project, and be sure to add the Core Data framework to the existing project as well.

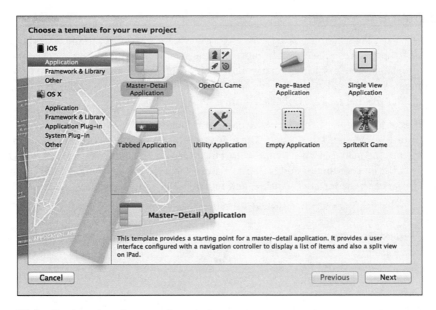

Figure 13.2   Xcode new project template choices.

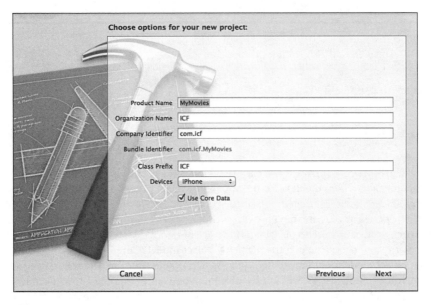

Figure 13.3   Xcode new project options.

Core Data Environment

The project template sets up the Core Data environment for the project in the class that implements the UIApplicationDelegate protocol; in the sample app this is ICFAppDelegate. The project template uses a lazy-loading pattern for each of the properties needed in the Core Data environment, so each is loaded when needed. For more information about the Core Data environment, refer to Chapter 12, "Core Data Primer."

The process of loading the Core Data environment is kicked off the first time the managed object context is referenced in the app. The managed object context accessor method will check to see whether the managed object context instance variable has a reference. If not, it will get the persistent store coordinator and instantiate a new managed object context with it, assign the new instance to the instance variable, and return the instance variable.

```
- (NSManagedObjectContext *)managedObjectContext
{
  if (__managedObjectContext != nil)
  {
    return __managedObjectContext;
  }

  NSPersistentStoreCoordinator *coordinator =
   [self persistentStoreCoordinator];

  if (coordinator != nil)
  {
    __managedObjectContext =
     [[NSManagedObjectContext alloc] init];

    [__managedObjectContext
     setPersistentStoreCoordinator:coordinator];
  }
  return __managedObjectContext;
}
```

The persistent store coordinator is the class that Core Data uses to manage the persistent stores (or files) where the data for the app is stored. To instantiate it, an instance of NSManagedObjectModel is needed so that the persistent store coordinator knows what object model the persistent stores are implementing. The persistent store coordinator also needs a URL for each persistent store to be added; if the file does not exist, Core Data will create it. If the persistent store doesn't match the managed object model (Core Data uses a hash of the managed object model to uniquely identify it, which is kept for comparison in the persistent store), then the template logic will log an error and abort. In a shipping application, logic would be added to properly handle errors with a migration from the old data model to the new one; in development having the app abort can be a useful reminder when the model changes to retest with a clean installation of the app.

```objc
- (NSPersistentStoreCoordinator *)persistentStoreCoordinator
{
  if (__persistentStoreCoordinator != nil)
  {
    return __persistentStoreCoordinator;
  }

  NSURL *storeURL =
  [[self applicationDocumentsDirectory]
   URLByAppendingPathComponent:@"MyMovies.sqlite"];

  NSError *error = nil;
  __persistentStoreCoordinator =
  [[NSPersistentStoreCoordinator alloc]
   initWithManagedObjectModel:[self managedObjectModel]];

  if (![__persistentStoreCoordinator
     addPersistentStoreWithType:NSSQLiteStoreType
     configuration:nil URL:storeURL options:nil
     error:&error])
  {
    NSLog(@"Unresolved error %@, %@", error,
        [error userInfo]);

    abort();
  }

  return __persistentStoreCoordinator;
}
```

The managed object model is loaded from the app's main bundle. Xcode will give the managed object model the same name as your project.

```objc
- (NSManagedObjectModel *)managedObjectModel
{
  if (__managedObjectModel != nil)
  {
    return __managedObjectModel;
  }

  NSURL *modelURL =
  [[NSBundle mainBundle] URLForResource:@"MyMovies"
            withExtension:@"momd"];

  __managedObjectModel =
  [[NSManagedObjectModel alloc]
   initWithContentsOfURL:modelURL];

  return __managedObjectModel;
}
```

Building Your Managed Object Model

With the project template, Xcode will create a data model file with the same name as your project. In the sample project this file is called `MyMovies.xdatamodeld`. To edit your data model, click the data model file, and Xcode will present the data model editor (see Figure 13.4).

Figure 13.4   Xcode data model editor, Table style.

Xcode has two styles for the data model editor: Table and Graph. The Table style presents the entities in your data model in a list on the left. Selecting an entity will display and allow you to edit the attributes, relationships, and fetched properties for that entity.

To change to Graph style, click the Editor Style Graph button in the lower-right corner of the data model editor (see Figure 13.5). There will still be a list of entities on the left of the data model editor, but the main portion of the editor will present an entity relationship diagram of your data model. Each box presented in the diagram represents an entity, with the name of the entity at the top, the attributes listed in the middle, and any relationships listed in the bottom. The graph will have arrows connecting entities that have relationships established, with arrows indicating the cardinality of the relationship.

When working with your data model, it is often convenient to have more working space available and to have access to additional detail for selected items. Use Xcode's View options in the upper-right corner of the window to hide the Navigator panel and display the Utilities panel (see Figure 13.5).

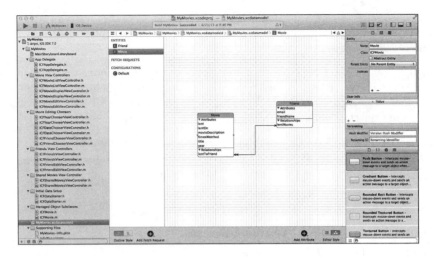

Figure 13.5   Xcode data model editor, Graph style.

Creating an Entity

To create an entity, click the Add Entity button. A new entity will be added to the list of entities, and if the editor is in Graph style, a new entity box will be added to the view. Xcode will
highlight the name of the entity and allow you to type in the desired name for the entity. The
name of the entity can be changed at any time by just clicking twice on the entity name in
the list of entities, or by selecting the desired entity and editing the entity name in the Utilities
panel.

Core Data supports entity inheritance. For any entity, you can specify a parent entity from
which your entity will inherit attributes, relationships, validations, and custom methods. To
do that, ensure that the entity to be inherited from has been created, and then select the child
entity and choose the desired parent entity in the Utilities panel.

> ### Note
>
> If you are using SQLite as your persistent store, Core Data implements entity inheritance by
> creating one table for the parent entity and all child entities, with a superset of all their attri-
> butes. This can obviously have unintended performance consequences if you have a lot of data
> in the entities, so use this feature wisely.

Adding Attributes

To add attributes to an entity, first select the entity in either the graph or the list of entities.
Then click the Add Attribute button in the lower part of the editor, just to the left of the Editor
Style buttons. Xcode will add an attribute called `attribute` to the entity. Select a Type for the

attribute. (See Table 13.1 for supported data types.) Note that Core Data treats all attributes as Objective-C objects, so if Integer 32 is the selected data type, for example, Core Data will treat the attribute as an `NSNumber`.

One thing to note is that Core Data will automatically give each instance a unique object ID, called `objectID`, which it uses internally to manage storage and relationships. You can also add a unique ID or another candidate key to the entity and add an index to it for quick access, but note that Core Data will manage relationships with the generated object ID.

`NSManagedObjects` also have a method called `description`; if you want to have a `description` attribute, modify the name slightly to avoid conflicts. In the sample app, for example, the Movie entity has a `movieDescription` attribute.

Table 13.1   **Core Data Supported Data Types**

Data Types	Objective-C Storage
Integer 16	NSNumber
Integer 32	NSNumber
Integer 64	NSNumber
Decimal	NSNumber
Double	NSNumber
Float	NSNumber
String	NSString
Boolean	NSNumber
Date	NSDate
Binary Data	NSData
Transformable	Uses value transformer

Establishing Relationships

Having relationships between objects can be a very powerful technique to model the real world in an app. Core Data supports one-to-one and one-to-many relationships. In the sample app, a one-to-many relationship between friends and movies is established. Since a friend might borrow more than one movie at a time, that side of the relationship is "many," but a movie can be lent to only one friend at a time, so that side of the relationship is "one."

To add a relationship between entities, select one of the entities, and then Ctrl-click and drag to the destination entity. Alternatively, click and hold the Add Attribute button, and select Add Relationship from the menu that appears. Xcode will create a relationship to the destination entity and will call it "relationship." In the Utilities panel, select the Data Model inspector, and change the name of the relationship. In the Data Model inspector, you can do the following:

- Indicate whether the relationship is transient.

- Specify whether the relationship is optional or required with the Optional check box.

- Specify whether the relationship is ordered.

- Establish an inverse relationship. To do this, create and name the inverse relationship first, and then select it from the drop-down.

- Specify the cardinality of the relationship by checking or unchecking the Plural check box. If checked, it indicates a to-many relationship.

- Specify minimum and maximum counts for a relationship.

- Set up the rule for Core Data to follow for the relationship when the object is deleted. Choices are No Action (no additional action taken on delete), Nullify (relationship set to nil), Cascade (objects on the other side of the relationship are deleted too), and Deny (error issued if relationships exist).

Custom Managed Object Subclasses

A custom NSManagedObject subclass can be useful if you have custom logic for your model object, or if you would like to be able to use dot syntax for your model object properties and have the compiler validate them.

Xcode has a menu option to automatically create a subclass for you. To use it, ensure that you have completed setup of your entity in the data model editor. Select your entity (or multiple entities) in the data model editor, select Editor from the Xcode menu, and then select Create NSManagedObject Subclass. Xcode will ask where you want to save the generated class files. Specify a location and click Create, and Xcode will generate the header and implementation files for each entity you specified. Xcode will name each class with the class prefix specified for your project concatenated with the name of the entity.

In the generated header file, Xcode will create a property for each attribute in the entity. Note that Xcode will also create a property for each relationship specified for the entity. If the relationship is to-one, Xcode will create an NSManagedObject property (or NSManagedObject subclass if the destination entity is a custom subclass). If the relationship is to-many, Xcode will create an NSSet property.

In the generated implementation file, Xcode will create @dynamic instructions for each entity, rather than @synthesize. This is because Core Data dynamically handles accessors for Core Data managed attributes, and does not need the compiler to build the accessor methods.

Note

There is a project called mogenerator that will generate two classes per entity: one for the attribute accessors and one for custom logic. That way, you can regenerate classes easily when making model changes without overwriting your custom logic. Mogenerator is available at http://rentzsch.github.com/mogenerator/.

Setting Up Default Data

When a Core Data project is first set up, there is no data in it. Although this might work for some use cases, frequently it is a requirement to have some data prepopulated in the app for the first run. In the sample app there is a custom data setup class called ICFDataStarter, which illustrates how to populate Core Data with some initial data. A #define variable is set up in MyMovies-Prefix.pch called FIRSTRUN, which can be uncommented to have the app run the logic in ICFDataStarter.

Inserting New Managed Objects

To create a new instance of a managed object for data that does not yet exist in your model, a reference to the managed object context is needed. The sample app uses a constant to refer to the ICFAppDelegate instance, which has a property defined for the managed object context:

```
NSManagedObjectContext *moc =
 [kAppDelegate managedObjectContext];
```

To insert data, Core Data needs to know what entity the new data is for. Core Data has a class called NSEntityDescription that provides information about entities. Create a new instance using NSEntityDescription's class method:

```
NSManagedObject *newMovie1 =
 [NSEntityDescription insertNewObjectForEntityForName:@"Movie"
               inManagedObjectContext:moc];
```

After an instance is available, populate the attributes with data:

```
[newMovie1 setValue:@"The Matrix" forKey:@"title"];
[newMovie1 setValue:@"1999" forKey:@"year"];

[newMovie1 setValue:@"Take the blue pill."
      forKey:@"movieDescription"];

[newMovie1 setValue:@NO forKey:@"lent"];
[newMovie1 setValue:nil forKey:@"lentOn"];
[newMovie1 setValue:@20 forKey:@"timesWatched"];
```

Core Data uses key-value coding to handle setting attributes. If an attribute name is incorrect, it will fail at runtime. To get compile-time checking of attribute assignments, create a custom NSManagedObject subclass and use the property accessors for each attribute directly.

The managed object context acts as a working area for changes, so the sample app sets up more initial data:

```
NSManagedObject *newFriend1 =
 [NSEntityDescription insertNewObjectForEntityForName:@"Friend"
               inManagedObjectContext:moc];
```

```
[newFriend1 setValue:@"Joe" forKey:@"friendName"];
[newFriend1 setValue:@"joe@dragonforged.com" forKey:@"email"];
```

The last step after setting up all the initial data is to save the managed object context.

```
NSError *mocSaveError = nil;

if ([moc save:&mocSaveError])
{
  NSLog(@"Save completed successfully.");
} else
{
  NSLog(@"Save did not complete successfully. Error: %@",
      [mocSaveError localizedDescription]);
}
```

After the managed object context is saved, Core Data will persist the data in the data store. For this instance of the app, the data will continue to be available through shutdowns and restarts. If the app is removed from the simulator or device, the data will no longer be available. One technique to populate data for first run is to copy the data store from the app's storage directory back into the app bundle. This will ensure that the default set of data is copied into the app's directory on first launch and is available to the app.

Other Default Data Setup Techniques

There are two other default data setup techniques that are commonly used: data model version migrations and loading data from a Web service or an API.

Core Data managed object models are versioned. Core Data understands the relationship between the managed object model and the current data store. If the managed object model changes and is no longer compatible with the data store (for example, if an attribute is added to an entity), Core Data will not be able to initiate the persistent store object using the existing data store and new managed object model. In that case, a migration is required to update the existing data store to match the updated managed object model. In many cases Core Data can perform the migration automatically by passing a dictionary of options when instantiating the persistent store; in some cases, additional steps need to be taken to perform the migration. Migrations are beyond the scope of this chapter, but be aware that migrations can be used and are recommended by Apple to do data setup.

The other approach is to pull data from a Web service or an API. This approach is most applicable when an app needs to maintain a local copy of a subset of data on a Web server, and Web calls need to be written for the app to pull data from the API in the course of normal operation. To set up the app's initial data, the Web calls can be run in a special state to pull all needed initial data and save it in Core Data.

Displaying Your Managed Objects

To display or use existing entity data in an app, managed objects need to be fetched from the managed object context. Fetching is analogous to running a query in a relational database, in that you can specify what entity you want to fetch, what criteria you want your results to match, and how you want your results sorted.

Creating Your Fetch Request

The object used to fetch managed objects in Core Data is called `NSFetchRequest`. Refer to `ICFFriendChooserViewController` in the sample app. This view controller displays the friends set up in Core Data and allows the user to select a friend to lend a movie to (see Figure 13.6).

Figure 13.6   Sample App: Friend Chooser.

To get the list of friends to display, the view controller performs a standard fetch request when the view controller has loaded. The first step is to create an instance of `NSFetchRequest` and associate the entity to be fetched with the fetch request:

```
NSManagedObjectContext *moc = kAppDelegate.managedObjectContext;

NSFetchRequest *fetchReq = [[NSFetchRequest alloc] init];

NSEntityDescription *entity =
```

```
[NSEntityDescription entityForName:@"Friend"
       inManagedObjectContext:moc];

[fetchReq setEntity:entity];
```

The next step is to tell the fetch request how to sort the resulting managed objects. To do this, we associate a sort descriptor with the fetch request, specifying the attribute name to sort by:

```
NSSortDescriptor *sortDescriptor =
  [[NSSortDescriptor alloc] initWithKey:@"friendName"
                ascending:YES];

NSArray *sortDescriptors =
  [NSArray arrayWithObjects:sortDescriptor, nil];

[fetchReq setSortDescriptors:sortDescriptors];
```

Since the friend chooser should show all the available friends to choose from, it is not necessary to specify any matching criteria. All that remains is to execute the fetch:

```
NSError *error = nil;

self.friendList = [moc executeFetchRequest:fetchReq
                                    error:&error];

  if (error)
{
  NSString *errorDesc =
    [error localizedDescription];

  UIAlertView *alert =
    [[UIAlertView alloc] initWithTitle:@"Error fetching friends"
                message:errorDesc
                delegate:nil
           cancelButtonTitle:@"Dismiss"
           otherButtonTitles:nil];
  [alert show];
}
```

To execute a fetch, create an instance of NSError and set it to nil. Then have the managed object context execute the fetch request that has just been constructed. If an error is encountered, the managed object context will return the error to the instance you just created. The sample app will display the error in an instance of UIAlertView. If no error is encountered, the results will be returned as an NSArray of NSManagedObjects. The view controller will store those results in an instance variable to be displayed in a table view.

Fetching by Object ID

When only one specific managed object needs to be fetched, Core Data provides a way to quickly retrieve that managed object without constructing a fetch request. To use this method, you must have the NSManagedObjectID for the managed object.

To get the NSManagedObjectID for a managed object, you must already have fetched or created the managed object. Refer to ICFMovieListViewController in the sample app, in the prepareForSegue:sender: method. In this case, the user has selected a movie from the list, and the view controller is about to segue from the list to the detail view for the selected movie. To inform the detail view controller which movie to display, the objectID for the selected movie is set as a property on the ICFMovieDisplayViewController:

```
if ([[segue identifier] isEqualToString:@"showDetail"])
{

  NSIndexPath *indexPath =
   [self.tableView indexPathForSelectedRow];

  ICFMovie *movie =
   [[self fetchedResultsController]
    objectAtIndexPath:indexPath];

  ICFMovieDisplayViewController *movieDispVC =
   (ICFMovieDisplayViewController *)
   [segue destinationViewController];

  [movieDispVC setMovieDetailID:[movie objectID]];
}
```

When the ICFMovieDisplayViewController is loaded, it uses a method on the managed object context to load a managed object using the objectID:

```
ICFMovie *movie = (ICFMovie *)[kAppDelegate.managedObjectContext
            objectWithID:self.movieDetailID];

[self configureViewForMovie:movie];
```

When this is loaded, the movie is available to the view controller to configure the view using the movie data (see Figure 13.7).

It is certainly possible to just pass the managed object from one view controller to the next with no problems, instead of passing the objectID and loading the managed object in the destination view controller. However, there are cases when using the objectID is highly preferable to using the managed object:

- If the managed object has been fetched or created on a different thread than the destination view controller will use to process and display the managed object—this approach must be used since managed objects are not thread safe!

- If a background thread might update the managed object in another managed object context between fetching and displaying—this will avoid possible issues with displaying the most up-to-date changes.

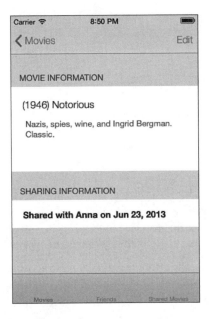

Figure 13.7   Sample App: Movie Display view.

Displaying Your Object Data

After managed objects have been fetched, accessing and displaying data from them is straightforward. For any managed object, using the key-value approach will work to retrieve attribute values. As an example, refer to the `configureCell:atIndexPath` method in `ICFFriendsViewController` in the sample app. This code will populate the table cell's text label and detail text label.

```
NSManagedObject *object =
 [self.fetchedResultsController objectAtIndexPath:indexPath];

cell.textLabel.text = [object valueForKey:@"friendName"];

NSInteger numShares = [[object valueForKey:@"lentMovies"] count];

NSString *subtitle = @"";

switch (numShares)
```

```
{
  case 0:
    subtitle = @"Not borrowing any movies.";
    break;

  case 1:
    subtitle = @"Borrowing 1 movie.";
    break;

  default:
    subtitle =
      [NSString stringWithFormat:@"Borrowing %d movies.",
      numShares];

    break;
}
```

```
cell.detailTextLabel.text = subtitle;
```

To get the attribute values from the managed object, call valueForKey: and specify the attribute name. If the attribute name is specified incorrectly, the app will fail at runtime.

For managed object subclasses, the attribute values are also accessible by calling the property on the managed object subclass with the attribute name. Refer to the configureViewForMovie: method in ICFMovieDisplayViewController in the sample app.

```
- (void)configureViewForMovie:(ICFMovie *)movie

{
  NSString *movieTitleYear = [movie yearAndTitle];

  [self.movieTitleAndYearLabel
    setText:movieTitleYear];

  [self.movieDescription setText:[movie movieDescription]];

  BOOL movieLent = [[movie lent] boolValue];

  NSString *movieShared = @"Not Shared";
  if (movieLent)
  {
    NSManagedObject *friend =
    [movie valueForKey:@"lentToFriend"];

    NSDateFormatter *dateFormatter =
      [[NSDateFormatter alloc] init];

    [dateFormatter setDateStyle:NSDateFormatterMediumStyle];
```

```
    NSString *sharedDateTxt =
    [dateFormatter stringFromDate:[movie lentOn]];

    movieShared =
      [NSString stringWithFormat:@"Shared with %@ on %@",
      [friend valueForKey:@"friendName"],sharedDateTxt];
  }

  [self.movieSharedInfoLabel setText:msh];
}
```

If the property-based approach to get attribute values from managed object subclasses is used, errors will be caught at compile time.

Using Predicates

Predicates can be used to narrow down your fetch results to data that match your specific criteria. They are analogous to a `where` clause in an SQL statement, but they can be used to filter elements from a collection (like an `NSArray`) as well as a fetch request from Core Data. To see how a predicate is applied to a fetch request, refer to method `fetchedResults Controller` in `ICFSharedMoviesViewController`. This method lazy loads and sets up an `NSFetchedResultsController`, which helps a table view interact with the results of a fetch request (this is described in detail in the next section). Setting up a predicate is simple, for example:

```
NSPredicate *predicate =
  [NSPredicate predicateWithFormat:@"lent == %@",@YES];
```

In the format string, predicates can be constructed with attribute names, comparison operators, Boolean operators, aggregate operators, and substitution expressions. A comma-separated list of expressions will be substituted in the order of the substitution expressions in the format string. Dot notation can be used to specify relationships in the predicate format string. Predicates support a large variety of operators and arguments, as shown in Table 13.2.

Table 13.2 **Core Data Predicate Supported Operators and Arguments**

Type	Operators and Arguments
Basic Comparisons	=, ==, >=, =>, <=, =<, >, <, !=, <>, BETWEEN {low,high}
Boolean	AND, && OR, || NOT, !
String	BEGINSWITH, CONTAINS, ENDSWITH, LIKE, MATCHES
Aggregate	ANY, SOME, ALL, NONE, IN
Literals	FALSE, NO, TRUE, YES, NULL, NIL, SELF. Core Data also supports string and numeric literals.

Tell the fetch request to use the predicate:

```
[fetchRequest setPredicate:predicate];
```

Now the fetch request will narrow the returned result set of managed objects to match the criteria specified in the predicate (see Figure 13.8).

Figure 13.8   Sample App: Shared Movies tab.

Introducing the Fetched Results Controller

A fetched results controller (`NSFetchedResultsController`) is a very effective liaison between Core Data and a `UITableView`. The fetched results controller provides a way to set up a fetch request so that the results are returned in sections and rows, accessible by index paths. In addition, the fetched results controller can listen to changes in Core Data and update the table accordingly using delegate methods.

In the sample app, refer to `ICFMovieListViewController` for a detailed example of a fetched results controller in action (see Figure 13.9).

Preparing the Fetched Results Controller

When the "master" view controller is set up using Xcode's Master Detail template, Xcode creates a property for the fetched results controller, and overrides the accessor method (`fetchedResultsController`) to lazy load or initialize the fetched results controller the first time it is requested. First the method checks to see whether the fetched results controller has already been initialized:

```
if (__fetchedResultsController != nil)
{
  return __fetchedResultsController;
}
```

Figure 13.9   Sample App: Movie list view controller.

If the fetched results controller is already set up, it is returned. Otherwise, a new fetched results controller is set up, starting with a fetch request:

```
NSFetchRequest *fetchRequest = [[NSFetchRequest alloc] init];
```

The fetch request needs to be associated with an entity from the managed object model, and a managed object context:

```
NSManagedObjectContext *moc = kAppDelegate.managedObjectContext;

NSEntityDescription *entity =
 [NSEntityDescription entityForName:@"Movie"
       inManagedObjectContext:moc];

[fetchRequest setEntity:entity];
```

A batch size can be set up to prevent the fetch request from fetching too many records at once:

```
[fetchRequest setFetchBatchSize:20];
```

Next, the sort order is established for the fetch request using NSSortDescriptor instances. An important point to note is that the attribute used for sections needs to be the first in the sort order so that the records can be correctly divided into sections. The sort order is determined by the order of the sort descriptors in the array of sort descriptors attached to the fetch request.

```
NSSortDescriptor *sortDescriptor =
 [[NSSortDescriptor alloc] initWithKey:@"title"
              ascending:YES];

NSSortDescriptor *sharedSortDescriptor =
 [[NSSortDescriptor alloc] initWithKey:@"lent" ascending:NO];

NSArray *sortDescriptors = [NSArray arrayWithObjects:
             sharedSortDescriptor,sortDescriptor,
             nil];

[fetchRequest setSortDescriptors:sortDescriptors];
```

After the fetch request is ready, the fetched results controller can be initialized. It requires a fetch request, a managed object context, a key path or an attribute name to be used for the table view sections, and a name for a cache (if nil is passed, no caching is done). The fetched results controller can specify a delegate that will respond to any Core Data changes. When this is complete, the fetched results controller is assigned to the view controller's property:

```
NSFetchedResultsController *aFetchedResultsController =
 [[NSFetchedResultsController alloc]
 initWithFetchRequest:fetchRequest
 managedObjectContext:moc
  sectionNameKeyPath:@"lent"
      cacheName:nil];

aFetchedResultsController.delegate = self;
self.fetchedResultsController = aFetchedResultsController;
```

Now that the fetched results controller has been prepared, the fetch can be executed to obtain a result set the table view can display, and the fetched results controller can be returned to the caller:

```
NSError *error = nil;
if (![self.fetchedResultsController performFetch:&error])
{
  NSLog(@"Unresolved error %@, %@", error, [error userInfo]);
  abort();
}

return __fetchedResultsController;
```

Integrating Table View and Fetched Results Controller

Integrating the table view and fetched results controller is just a matter of updating the table view's datasource and delegate methods to use information from the fetched results controller. In `ICFMovieListViewController`, the fetched results controller tells the table view how many sections it has:

```
- (NSInteger)numberOfSectionsInTableView:(UITableView *)tableView
{
  return [[self.fetchedResultsController sections] count];
}
```

The fetched results controller tells the table view how many rows are in each section, using the `NSFetchedResultsSectionInfo` protocol:

```
- (NSInteger)tableView:(UITableView *)tableView
 numberOfRowsInSection:(NSInteger)section
{
  id <NSFetchedResultsSectionInfo> sectionInfo =
   [[self.fetchedResultsController sections]
   objectAtIndex:section];

  return [sectionInfo numberOfObjects];
}
```

The fetched results controller provides section titles, which are the values of the attribute specified as the section name. Since the sample app is using a Boolean attribute for the sections, the values that the fetched results controller returns for section titles are not user-friendly titles: 0 and 1. The sample app looks at the titles from the fetched results controller and returns more helpful titles: Shared instead of 1 and Not Shared instead of 0.

```
- (NSString *)tableView:(UITableView *)tableView
 titleForHeaderInSection:(NSInteger)section
{
  id <NSFetchedResultsSectionInfo> sectionInfo =
   [[self.fetchedResultsController sections]
   objectAtIndex:section];

  if ([[sectionInfo indexTitle] isEqualToString:@"1"])
  {
    return @"Shared";
  }
  else
  {
    return @"Not Shared";
  }
}
```

To populate the table cells, the sample app dequeues a reusable cell, and then calls the `configureView:` method, passing the `indexPath` for the cell:

```
- (UITableViewCell *)tableView:(UITableView *)tableView
    cellForRowAtIndexPath:(NSIndexPath *)indexPath
{
  UITableViewCell *cell =
   [tableView dequeueReusableCellWithIdentifier:@"Cell"];

  [self configureCell:cell atIndexPath:indexPath];

  return cell;
}
```

The fetched results controller knows which movie should be displayed at each index path, so the sample app can get the correct movie to display by calling the `objectAtIndexPath:` method on the fetched results controller. Then, it is simple to update the cell with data from the movie instance.

```
- (void)configureCell:(UITableViewCell *)cell
    atIndexPath:(NSIndexPath *)indexPath
{
  ICFMovie *movie =
   [self.fetchedResultsController objectAtIndexPath:indexPath];

  cell.textLabel.text = [movie cellTitle];

  cell.detailTextLabel.text = [movie movieDescription];
}
```

The last table-view integration detail would typically be handling table cell selection in the `tableView:didSelectRowAtIndexPath:` method. In this case, no integration in that method is needed since selection is handled by storyboard segue. In the `prepareForSegue:sender:` method, selection of a table cell is handled with an identifier called `showDetail`:

```
if ([[segue identifier] isEqualToString:@"showDetail"])
{
NSIndexPath *indexPath =
    [self.tableView indexPathForSelectedRow];

  ICFMovie *movie =
   [[self fetchedResultsController]
     objectAtIndexPath:indexPath];

  ICFMovieDisplayViewController *movieDisplayVC =
   (ICFMovieDisplayViewController *)
    [segue destinationViewController];

  [movieDisplayVC setMovieDetailID:[movie objectID]];
}
```

This method gets the index path of the selected row from the table view, and then gets the movie instance from the fetched results controller using the index path. The method then sets the `movieDetailID` of the `ICFMovieDisplayViewController` instance with the movie instance's `objectID`.

Responding to Core Data Changes

For the fetched results controller to respond to Core Data changes and update the table view, methods from the `NSFetchedResultsControllerDelegate` protocol need to be implemented. First the view controller needs to declare that it will implement the delegate methods:

```
@interface ICFMovieListViewController : UITableViewController
 <NSFetchedResultsControllerDelegate>
```

The fetched results controller delegate will be notified when content will be changed, giving the delegate the opportunity to animate the changes in the table view. Calling the `beginUpdates` method on the table view tells it that all updates until `endUpdates` is called should be animated simultaneously.

```
- (void)controllerWillChangeContent:
  (NSFetchedResultsController *)controller
{
  [self.tableView beginUpdates];
}
```

There are two delegate methods that might be called based on data changes. One method will tell the delegate that changes occurred that affect the table-view sections; the other will tell the delegate that the changes affect objects at specified index paths, so the table view will need to update the associated rows. Because the data changes are expressed by type, the delegate will be notified if the change is an insert, a delete, a move, or an update, so a typical pattern is to build a `switch` statement to perform the correct action by change type. For sections, the sample app will only make changes that can insert or delete a section (if a section name is changed, that might trigger a case in which a section might move and be updated as well).

```
- (void)controller:(NSFetchedResultsController *)controller
 didChangeSection:(id <NSFetchedResultsSectionInfo>)sectionInfo
      atIndex:(NSUInteger)sectionIndex
  forChangeType:(NSFetchedResultsChangeType)type
{
  switch(type)
  {
    case NSFetchedResultsChangeInsert:
      ...
      break;

    case NSFetchedResultsChangeDelete:
      ...
      break;
  }
}
```

Table views have a convenient method to insert new sections, and the delegate method receives all the necessary information to insert new sections:

```
[self.tableView
   insertSections:[NSIndexSet indexSetWithIndex:sectionIndex]
 withRowAnimation:UITableViewRowAnimationFade];
```

Removing sections is just as convenient:

```
[self.tableView
   deleteSections:[NSIndexSet indexSetWithIndex:sectionIndex]
 withRowAnimation:UITableViewRowAnimationFade];
```

For object changes, the delegate will be informed of the change type, the object that changed, the current index path for the object, and a "new" index path if the object is being inserted or moved. Using switch logic to respond by change type works for this method as well.

```
- (void)controller:(NSFetchedResultsController *)controller
  didChangeObject:(id)anObject
    atIndexPath:(NSIndexPath *)indexPath
   forChangeType:(NSFetchedResultsChangeType)type
   newIndexPath:(NSIndexPath *)newIndexPath
{
  UITableView *tableView = self.tableView;

  switch(type)
  {
    case NSFetchedResultsChangeInsert:
      ...
      break;

    case NSFetchedResultsChangeDelete:
      ...
      break;

    case NSFetchedResultsChangeUpdate:
      ...
      break;

    case NSFetchedResultsChangeMove:
      ...
      break;
  }
}
```

Table views have convenience methods to insert rows by index path. Note that the newIndex-Path is the correct index path to use when inserting a row for an inserted object.

```
[tableView
 insertRowsAtIndexPaths:[NSArray arrayWithObject:newIndexPath]
    withRowAnimation:UITableViewRowAnimationFade];
```

To delete a row, use the `indexPath` passed to the delegate method.

```
[tableView
 deleteRowsAtIndexPaths:[NSArray arrayWithObject:indexPath]
    withRowAnimation:UITableViewRowAnimationFade];
```

To update a row, call the `configureCell:atIndexPath:` method for the current `indexPath`. This is the same configure method called from the table view delegate's `tableView:cellFor RowAtIndexPath:` method.

```
[self configureCell:[tableView cellForRowAtIndexPath:indexPath]
    atIndexPath:indexPath];
```

To move a row, delete the row for the current `indexPath` and insert a row for the `newIndexPath`.

```
[tableView
 deleteRowsAtIndexPaths:[NSArray arrayWithObject:indexPath]
    withRowAnimation:UITableViewRowAnimationFade];
```

```
[tableView
 insertRowsAtIndexPaths:[NSArray arrayWithObject:newIndexPath]
    withRowAnimation:UITableViewRowAnimationFade];
```

The fetched results controller delegate will be notified when the content changes are complete, so the delegate can tell the table view there will be no more animated changes by calling the `endUpdates` method. After that method is called, the table view will animate the accumulated changes in the user interface.

```
- (void)controllerDidChangeContent:
  (NSFetchedResultsController *)controller
{
  [self.tableView endUpdates];
}
```

Adding, Editing, and Removing Managed Objects

Although it is useful to be able to fetch and display data, apps often need to add new data, edit existing data, and remove unneeded data at the user's request.

Inserting a New Managed Object

In the sample app, view the Movies tab. To insert a new movie, the user can tap the Add button in the navigation bar. The Add button is wired to perform a segue to the

ICFMovieEditViewController. In the segue logic, a new movie managed object is inserted
into Core Data, and the new movie's object ID is passed to the edit movie view controller.
This approach is used in the sample app to prevent having logic in the edit view controller to
handle both creating new managed objects and editing existing managed objects; however, it
would be perfectly acceptable to create the new movie managed object in the edit view controller if that makes more sense in a different app.

To create a new instance of a movie managed object, a reference to the managed object context
is needed.

```
NSManagedObjectContext *moc =
  [kAppDelegate managedObjectContext];
```

To insert data, Core Data needs to know what entity the new data is for. Core Data has a class
called NSEntityDescription that provides information about entities. Create a new instance
using NSEntityDescription's class method:

```
ICFMovie *newMovie = [NSEntityDescription
 insertNewObjectForEntityForName:@"Movie"
     inManagedObjectContext:moc];
```

Populate the new movie managed object's attributes with data:

```
[newMovie setTitle:@"New Movie"];
[newMovie setYear:@"2012"];
[newMovie setMovieDescription:@"New movie description."];
[newMovie setLent:@NO];
[newMovie setLentOn:nil];
[newMovie setTimesWatched:@0];
```

Prepare an NSError variable to capture any potential errors, and save the managed object
context.

```
NSError *mocSaveError = nil;

if (![moc save:&mocSaveError])
{
  NSLog(@"Save did not complete successfully. Error: %@",
     [mocSaveError localizedDescription]);
}
```

After the managed object context has been successfully saved, the fetched results controller
will be notified if the save affects the results of the controller's fetch, and the delegate methods
described earlier in the chapter will be called.

Removing a Managed Object

On the Movies tab in the sample app, the user can swipe on the right side of a table cell, or
can tap the Edit button to reveal the delete controls for each table cell. When Delete is tapped

on a cell, the table view delegate method `tableView:commitEditingStyle:forRowAtIndex Path:` is called. The method checks whether the editing style is delete. If so, the method gets a reference to the managed object context from the fetched results controller. The fetched results controller keeps a reference to the managed object context it was initialized with, which is needed to delete the object.

```
NSManagedObjectContext *context =
 [self.fetchedResultsController managedObjectContext];
```

The method determines which managed object should be deleted, by asking the fetched results controller for the managed object at the specified index path.

```
NSManagedObject *objectToBeDeleted =
 [self.fetchedResultsController objectAtIndexPath:indexPath];
```

To delete the managed object, the method tells the managed object context to delete it.

```
[context deleteObject:objectToBeDeleted];
```

The deletion is not permanent until the managed object context is saved. After it is saved, the delegate methods described earlier in the chapter will be called and the table will be updated.

```
NSError *error = nil;
if (![context save:&error])
{
    NSLog(@"Error deleting movie, %@", [error userInfo]);
}
```

Editing an Existing Managed Object

On the Movies tab in the sample app, the user can tap a movie to see more detail about it. To change any of the information about the movie, tap the Edit button in the navigation bar, which will present an instance of `ICFMovieEditViewController`. When the view is loaded, it will load an instance of `ICFMovie` using the `objectID` passed in from the display view or list view, will save that instance into the property `editMovie`, and will configure the view using information from the movie managed object.

If the user decides to edit the year of the movie, for example, another view controller will be presented with a `UIPickerView` for the user to select a new year. The `ICFMovieEditViewController` is set up as a delegate for the year chooser, so when the user has selected a new year and taps Save, the delegate method `chooserSelectedYear:` is called. In that method, the `editMovie` is updated with the new date and the display is updated.

```
- (void)chooserSelectedYear:(NSString *)year
{
    [self.editMovie setYear:year];
    [self.movieYearLabel setText:year];
}
```

Note that the managed object context was not saved after `editMovie` was updated. The managed object `editMovie` can keep updates temporarily until the user makes a decision about whether to make the changes permanent, indicated by tapping the Save or Cancel button.

Saving and Rolling Back Your Changes

If the user taps the Save button, he has indicated his intention to keep the changes made to the `editMovie`. In the `saveButtonTouched:` method, the fields not updated with delegate methods are saved to the `editMovie` property:

```
NSString *movieTitle = [self.movieTitle text];
[self.editMovie setTitle:movieTitle];

NSString *movieDesc = [self.movieDescription text];
[self.editMovie setMovieDescription:movieDesc];

BOOL sharedBool = [self.sharedSwitch isOn];
NSNumber *shared = [NSNumber numberWithBool:sharedBool];
[self.editMovie setLent:shared];
```

Then the managed object context is saved, making the changes permanent.

```
NSError *saveError = nil;
[kAppDelegate.managedObjectContext save:&saveError];
if (saveError)
{

  UIAlertView *alert =
    [[UIAlertView alloc]
     initWithTitle:@"Error saving movie"
         message:[saveError localizedDescription]
         delegate:nil
     cancelButtonTitle:@"Dismiss"
     otherButtonTitles:nil];

  [alert show];
}
else
{
  NSLog(@"Changes to movie saved.");
}
```

If the user decides that the changes should be thrown away and not be made permanent, the user will tap the Cancel button, which calls the `cancelButtonTouched:` method. That method will first check whether the managed object context has any unsaved changes. If so, the method will instruct the managed object context to roll back or throw away the unsaved changes. After that is completed, the managed object context will be back to the state it was in before any of the changes were made. Rather than the user interface being updated to reflect throwing away the changes, the view is dismissed.

```
if ([kAppDelegate.managedObjectContext hasChanges])
{
  [kAppDelegate.managedObjectContext rollback];
  NSLog(@"Rolled back changes.");
}

[self.navigationController.presentingViewController
 dismissModalViewControllerAnimated:YES];
```

Summary

This chapter described how to set up a new project to use Core Data and how to set up all the Core Data environment pieces. The chapter detailed how to create a managed object model, including how to add a new entity, add attributes to an entity, and set up relationships between entities. It also described why an NSManagedObject subclass is useful and how to create one.

This chapter explained how to set up some initial data for the project, and demonstrated how to insert new managed objects. Alternative techniques for initial data setup were discussed.

This chapter then detailed how to create a fetch request to get saved managed objects, and how to fetch individual managed objects using an objectID. It described how to display data from managed objects in the user interface of an app. It explained how to use predicates to fetch managed objects that match specific criteria.

This chapter introduced the fetched results controller, a powerful tool for integrating Core Data with the UITableView; described how to set up a UITableView with a fetched results controller; and explained how to set up a fetched results controller delegate to automatically update a table view from Core Data changes.

Lastly, this chapter explained how to add, edit, and delete managed objects, and how to save changes or roll back unwanted changes.

With all of these tools, you should now have a good foundation for using Core Data effectively in your apps.

Exercises

1. For the Friend managed object, there is an attribute specified for email, but the ICFFriendEditViewController does not support editing the email address. Update that view controller to display the friend's email address when the view is displayed, allow the user to edit the email address, and ensure that the email address is saved when the Save button is tapped. Test tapping the Cancel button to make sure that

changes to the email address are thrown away. Then add a Remind Friend button to the `ICFMovieDisplayViewController` that will present an email message composer with the friend's email address.

2. Currently, the friends list is not very helpful, because the user can see which friends have borrowed movies but cannot see which movies the friends have borrowed. Change the accessory selection to edit the friend record instead of row selection, and add a new view controller to display all the movies a friend has borrowed when the row for a friend is selected. Hint: Use a table view controller backed with a fetched results controller to display the list of movies borrowed by a friend.

3. Change the sort order in `ICFMovieListViewController` to sort by year instead of title, without messing up the Shared/Not Shared section headers. Hint: This is a very simple change.

14

Language Features

With the introduction of Objective-C 2.0 in 2006, continued support for Clang and LLVM compiler enhancements, and Xcode 4 in 2011, many useful new features have been added that enhance code readability and reduce the amount of code needed to meet a requirement. This chapter highlights some of the most useful new features that have been added, and some features that have been around a while that are not as well known, including the following:

- Literals, which make declaring numbers, arrays, and dictionaries as easy and simple to read as string declarations.

- Automatic Reference Counting (ARC), which provides an automated way to handle memory management, without many of the drawbacks of garbage collection or manual memory management. Using ARC can reduce the amount of code needed in a project and help avoid common memory management issues.

- Properties, which have been enhanced to the point that declaring instance variables for a class is rarely necessary. The compiler can generate accessor methods that respect memory management, read/write, and threading settings.

- Blocks, which are anonymous functions that can be passed around like parameters and can make use of variables in their local scope. These are very effective tools for simplifying code and improving code readability. Many of the iOS APIs have added support for blocks.

- Fast enumeration, which provides a simple, readable approach to iterating over a collection, and performing actions on each item in a collection.

- Method swizzling, which allows the developer to dynamically swap out method implementations at runtime. This can be used to enhance existing functionality when the source code is not available, and when neither subclassing nor using categories is a good option.

Literals

When Xcode 4.4 was released in July of 2012, the compiler was updated to add support for several new types of literal syntax that make declaring and using NSNumber, NSArray, and NSDictionary much simpler and much more readable. The new syntax follows the lead of NSString literals by using the @ prefix with syntactical elements to define Objective-C objects:

```
NSString *aString = @"This is a string.";
```

Now, an @ symbol followed by numbers, brackets, curly braces, or parentheses has special meaning and represents an Objective-C object:

```
NSNumber *integerNumber = @45;
NSArray *workArray = @[aString, floatNumber, integerNumber];
NSDictionary *workDict = @{ @"float": floatNumber,
                            @"integer" : integerNumber,
                            @"array" : workArray };
NSNumber *radiansPerDegree = @(M_PI / 180);
```

In addition, new syntax has been added to make accessing elements in arrays or dictionaries simpler.

```
NSString *myString = workArray[0];
NSNumber *myNumber = workDict[@"float"];
```

NSNumber

Previously, to declare and instantiate an NSNumber, a developer had to either alloc/init or use a class method with a scalar like so:

```
NSNumber *floatNumber = [NSNumbernumberWithFloat:3.14159];
NSNumber *doubleNumber = [NSNumbernumberWithDouble:3.14159];

NSNumber *integerNumber = [NSNumbernumberWithInteger:45];

NSNumber *unsignedIntegerNumber =
[NSNumbernumberWithUnsignedInteger:45U];

NSNumber *longNumber = [NSNumbernumberWithLong:1234567L];

NSNumber *longLongNumber =
[NSNumbernumberWithLongLong:1234567890LL];

NSNumber *boolNumber = [NSNumbernumberWithBool:YES];
NSNumber *charNumber = [NSNumbernumberWithChar:'Q'];
```

With the new syntax, this is the equivalent of using the class methods on NSNumber:

```
NSNumber *floatNumber = @3.14159F;
NSNumber *doubleNumber = @3.14159;
```

```
NSNumber *integerNumber = @45;
NSNumber *unsignedIntegerNumber = @45U;
NSNumber *longNumber = @1234567L;
NSNumber *longLongNumber = @1234567890LL;

NSNumber *boolNumber = @YES;
NSNumber *charNumber = @'Q';
```

NSArray

To declare and instantiate an NSArray with a known set of elements previously, a class method or equivalent alloc/init needed to be used:

```
NSArray *workArray = [NSArrayarrayWithObjects: aString,
                    floatNumber, integerNumber, nil];
```

With the new syntax, declaring and instantiating an NSArray is much simpler and less verbose, and the nil terminator is no longer required.

```
NSArray *workArray = @[aString, floatNumber, integerNumber];
```

Be sure to note, however, that putting a nil object in the brackets either will cause a warning if the compiler can detect that the value will be nil at compile time, or will generate a runtime exception.

In addition to supporting a new approach to instantiating arrays, a new method of accessing and updating objects in an array is now supported. The previous approach was to call a method on NSArray to access an element.

```
NSString *myString = [workArray objectAtIndex:0];
```

Now C-style subscripting is supported to access elements in an array.

```
NSString *myString = workArray[0];
```

This type of subscripting also works for setting elements in a mutable array.

```
mutableArray[0] = @"Updated Element";
```

These C-style subscripting methods to access array elements are supported by the compiler by translating the expressions into method calls. The objectAtIndexedSubscript: method is how the accessor subscript is implemented.

```
NSString *myString = [workArray objectAtIndexedSubscript:0];
```

The mutator subscript is implemented with the setObject:atIndexedSubscript: method.

```
[mutableArray setObject:@"Updated Element" atIndexedSubscript:0];
```

NSDictionary

To declare and instantiate an NSDictionary with a known set of keys and values previously, a class method or equivalent alloc/init needed to be used:

```
NSDictionary *workDict =
[NSDictionarydictionaryWithObjectsAndKeys:@"float",
floatNumber, @"integer", integerNumber, @"array",
workArray, nil];
```

With the new syntax, declaring and instantiating an NSDictionary is much simpler, much less verbose, and easier to read:

```
NSDictionary *workDict = @{ @"float": floatNumber,
                    @"integer" : integerNumber,
                    @"array" : workArray };
```

Be sure to note, however, that putting a nil object as either a key or a value either will cause a warning if the compiler can detect that the value will be nil at compile time, or will generate a runtime exception.

In addition to supporting a new method to instantiate dictionaries, a new method of accessing and updating objects in a dictionary is now supported. The previous approach was to call a method on NSDictionary to access an element by specifying a key.

```
NSNumber *myNumber = [workDict objectForKey:@"float"];
```

Now elements in a dictionary can be accessed using the key as a subscript.

```
NSNumber *myNumber = workDict[@"float"];
```

Elements in a mutable dictionary can also be set using a key as a subscript.

```
workDict[@"float"] = @3.14159F;
```

These subscripting methods are supported by the compiler by translating the expressions into method calls. The objectForKeyedSubscript: method is how the accessor subscript is implemented.

```
NSNumber *myNumber = [workArray objectForKeyedSubscript:0];
```

The mutator subscript is implemented with the setObject:forKeyedSubscript: method.

```
[mutableDict setObject:@12.345F forKeyedSubscript:@"float"];
```

Boxed Expressions

The compiler also supports boxed C expressions, including scalars, enums, and C string pointer types. A boxed expression will convert the result of the expression contained in parentheses into an appropriate Objective-C object.

```
NSNumber *radiansPerDegree = @(M_PI / 180);
NSNumber *myFavButtonType = @(UIButtonTypeInfoDark);

char *cString = "The quick brown fox...";
NSString *stringFromCString = @(cString);
```

Automatic Reference Counting

Automatic Reference Counting (ARC) is LLVM compiler support for automatically handling memory management for Objective-C objects. Instead of the developer calling `retain`, `release`, and `autorelease` methods for objects created in a project, the compiler will calculate the lifetime of each object created and automatically insert the appropriate `retain`, `release`, and `autorelease` calls as necessary. ARC can completely avoid the error-prone and tedious manual approach to memory management, while reducing the amount of code needed and potentially even make code perform faster. ARC code can also work seamlessly with non-ARC code; for example, if a third-party library that a project depends on is not using ARC, the project can still be updated to take advantage of ARC without updating the third-party library. ARC has matured to the point that Apple recommends using it on all new projects.

Using ARC in a New Project

In Xcode 5, ARC is the default for all new projects. For Xcode 4.6 holdouts, new projects must be enabled for ARC by selecting the option when creating it using Xcode 4.6, as shown in Figure 14.1.

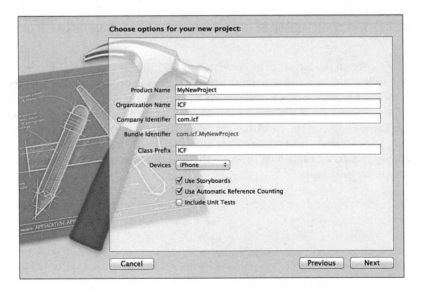

Figure 14.1   Xcode 4 New Project dialog displaying checked Use Automatic Reference Counting option.

Converting an Existing Project to ARC

Existing projects written without ARC can be converted to use ARC by selecting Edit, Refactor, Convert to Objective-C ARC from the menu in Xcode, as shown in Figure 14.2.

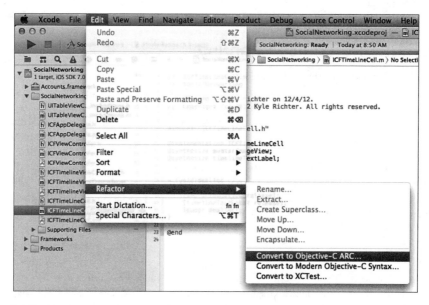

Figure 14.2   Xcode menu, Convert to Objective-C ARC.

Xcode will ask which targets should be converted to ARC, using a dialog as shown in Figure 14.3.

After you have selected the targets to be converted to ARC and clicked Check, Xcode will examine the code in the target to determine whether there will be any issues in converting to ARC. If there are problems, Xcode will present an error dialog, and any errors with the code preventing conversion to ARC will be displayed in Xcode's Issue Navigator. Resolve any outstanding issues and rerun the check process by selecting Convert to Objective-C ARC from Xcode's Edit, Refactor menu, and repeating the steps described. After the issues are all resolved, Xcode will display a dialog explaining the steps that will be taken to convert the project to ARC, as shown in Figure 14.4.

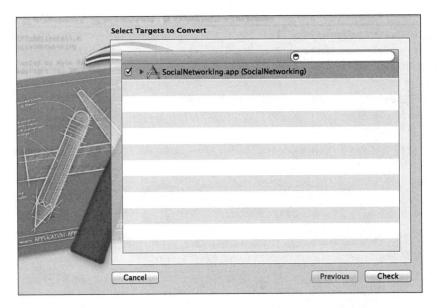

Figure 14.3   Xcode Convert to Objective-C ARC, Select Targets to Convert dialog.

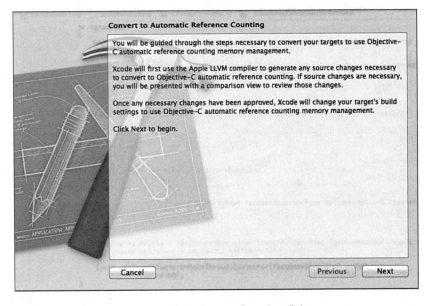

Figure 14.4   Xcode Convert to Automatic Reference Counting dialog.

After you click Next, Xcode will preview the changes that need to be made to convert the project to ARC, as shown in Figure 14.5. Xcode will display each file that will require changes, and each specific change that will be needed. This preview highlights how the amount of code in the project will be reduced.

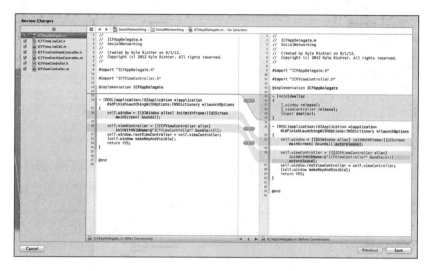

Figure 14.5   Xcode Source Comparison View.

Clicking Save will make the recommended changes to the project.

A project can be set to use ARC manually by specifying a build setting, as shown in Figure 14.6. After this setting is changed, the compiler will issue errors for any non-ARC issues found in the project, and it is up to the developer to address those manually.

Figure 14.6   Xcode Build Settings for Objective-C Automatic Reference Counting.

Basic ARC Usage

There are new coding rules and guidelines to follow for projects using ARC. The compiler will enforce the ARC-specific rules, and generate warnings or errors as appropriate:

- Create instances of variables and properties as normal, using `alloc`/`init`, `new`, `copy`, or class methods.

- Using `retain`, `release`, and `autorelease` is not allowed. The compiler will automatically insert `retain`, `release`, and `autorelease` for objects allocated in project code at compile time. Note that the inserted statements are not visible.

- Use qualifiers for properties (described in more detail in the "Properties" section later in the chapter) or variables to specify ownership and lifecycle. ARC qualifiers, described in the next subsection, tell the compiler when a `retain` is needed to indicate ownership, or when an object is owned somewhere else and a `retain` is not needed. The qualifiers help ARC understand the intended life cycle of an object so that the compiler can properly `release` and/or `nil` an object pointer when it is no longer needed.

- Avoid `dealloc`. The compiler will create `dealloc` methods automatically as needed, and `dealloc` must not be called directly by code. Custom `dealloc` methods can be created to handle special situations or objects not handled directly by ARC; however, [super dealloc] cannot be called from those custom `dealloc` methods.

- Use `@autorelease` blocks instead of `NSAutoreleasePool`. Blocks are described in more detail later in the chapter.

- When using or interacting with Core Foundation objects, use the new qualifiers `__bridge`, `__bridge_retain`, `__bridge_transfer` to indicate ownership intent.

ARC Qualifiers

There are four ARC qualifiers for object ownership that tell the compiler how to handle each object. The qualifiers are specified either implicitly (`__strong` is the default) or explicitly when declaring an object.

- **`__autoreleasing`:** autoreleasing is not the same as `autorelease`; rather, it is used for passing an object by reference, as in this example:

  ```
  __autoreleasing NSError *error = nil;

  self.listArray = [moc executeFetchRequest:fetchReq
                                      error:&error];
  ```

- **`__strong`:** strong is the default, and it indicates that the object should be retained for the lifetime of its current scope. The object will be set to `nil` before it is destroyed.

- **`__weak`:** weak indicates that the object should not be retained. The compiler will automatically set the object to `nil` before it is destroyed.

- **`__unsafe_unretained`:** Same as weak, but the object is not set to `nil` before it is destroyed.

Declaring properties have different qualifiers, which each imply one of the four ARC qualifiers as described in the "Properties" section later in the chapter.

Blocks

Blocks are a new C language feature, made available in Objective-C and in iOS starting with version 4.0. Since then, Apple has added support for blocks in significant portions of the iOS SDK. Blocks are anonymous functions, which can accept parameters and return a value, and are able to capture the state of the runtime when they are executed. In addition, blocks are actually Objective-C objects, so they can be passed around as parameters; can be stored in Foundation arrays, dictionaries, and sets; and can take advantage of manual memory management or ARC. Last but not least, blocks can modify objects in the same lexical scope. All that adds up to the capability for blocks to make previously cumbersome programming patterns simple and readable.

In practice, blocks are widely used to replace delegates and completion handlers. Rather than setting up a property for a delegate, adding a protocol definition, implementing delegate methods, and devising methods to pass state variables to the delegate methods, you can implement delegate logic in a block.

Declaring and Using Blocks

One method of using blocks is to create a block variable, which can be assigned a block and then executed inline in code. A block variable declaration can have a name, can declare parameter types, and can optionally declare a return type (the compiler can infer the return type, but it is good coding form to declare it).

```
NSString* (^repeatString) (int, NSString*);
```

In this case, NSString* at the left of the line of code declares the return type. In parentheses, after the caret symbol (^), repeatString is the name of the declared block. The second set of parentheses declares that two parameters are required for the block, first an int and second an NSString*. After these are declared, the block can be assigned using a block literal, indicated by the caret symbol.

```
repeatString = ^NSString* (int numTimes, NSString *repeat)
{
    NSMutableString *retString = [[NSMutableString alloc] init];

    for (int i=0; i<numTimes; i++)
    {
        [retString appendString:repeat];
    }
    return [NSString stringWithString:retString];
};
```

The block literal requires restating the return type after the caret symbol, and then naming the parameters that must match the declaration. The block code is specified between brackets, and a semicolon after the final bracket indicates that the assignment of the block variable is complete. After the block variable is assigned, it can be used in code just like a function.

```
NSString *repeatTest = repeatString(5,@"Test ");

NSLog(@"The result is: %@",repeatTest);
```

This will log the following result:

```
The result is: Test Test Test Test Test
```

Block definitions can also be established using a `typedef` for simplicity and clarity:

```
typedefvoid (^MyCompletionBlock)(id result, NSError *error);
```

After a block has a type definition, it can be used to create a block variable or in method declarations.

Capturing State with Blocks

When assigning a block literal, variables from the current lexical scope can be used in the block. An important characteristic of this use is that, by default, the value of those variables is "captured" or locked to the value at the time when the block is assigned. Even if the value of that variable is changed before the block is executed, the value at the time of assignment is what is used in the block execution. This example modifies the previous example to use an `NSString*` from the enclosing scope in the block, rather than a parameter.

```
NSString *blockTestString = @"Block Test ";

NSString *(^repeatString) (int);

repeatString = ^NSString* (int numTimes)
{
    NSMutableString *retString = [[NSMutableStringalloc] init];

    for (int i=0; i<numTimes; i++)
    {
        [retString appendString:blockTestString];
    }
return retString;
};

blockTestString = @"Block Test Change";

NSString *repeatTest = repeatString(5);

NSLog(@"The result is: %@",repeatTest);
```

This approach will log the following:

```
The result is: Block Test Block Test Block Test Block Test Block Test
```

If the block needs to be able to use the updated value of the variable, or needs to update the variable directly, that variable can be declared with the __block modifier to indicate that blocks should access the variable directly rather than capturing its value at the time of block assignment. To modify the previous example to demonstrate the block using the current value of a variable from the enclosing scope, and the block updating that variable, first the variable is declared with the __block modifier.

```
__block NSString *blockTestString = @"Block Test ";
```

Then the block is modified to be return type void, and the block literal is changed to update the variable directly rather than return a value.

```
void (^repeatString) (int);

repeatString = ^ (int numTimes)
{
    NSMutableString *retString = [[NSMutableString alloc] init];

    for (int i=0; i<numTimes; i++)
    {
        [retString appendString:blockTestString];
    }
    blockTestString = retString;
};
```

After the block is defined and assigned, the blockTestString variable is changed, and then the block is executed.

```
blockTestString = @"Block Test Change ";

repeatString(5);

NSLog(@"The result is: %@",blockTestString);
```

This logs the following result, indicating that the blockTestString variable was used with the most recent value before the block was executed, and that the blockTestString string was changed by the block:

```
The result is: Block Test Change Block Test Change Block Test Change
 Block Test Change Block Test Change
```

Having both approaches available gives the developer a great deal of flexibility in using blocks to achieve desired results.

Using Blocks as Method Parameters

Another method of using blocks is to use them as method parameters. A common use case for this is a completion handler for a long-running or asynchronous task. To use a block as a completion handler, first a method must be declared with a completion block as a parameter.

```
- (void)longRunningTaskWithCompletionHandler:
    (void(^)(void))completionBlock
{
    ...
    if (completionBlock) {
        completionBlock();
    }
}
```

The syntax might look a bit awkward, but the method declares that it should receive a block with no parameters and no return type as a parameter. When the method has completed, it will execute the passed-in completion block. This allows the caller to avoid having to set up separate delegate methods to handle the completion logic, and thus the caller can specify the starting and completion logic all in one place, making it easy to read and check.

```
[self.submitButton setEnabled:NO];
[self.progressIndicator setHidden:NO];
[self.progressIndicator startAnimating];

ICFViewController* __weak weakSelf = self;

[selflongRunningTaskWithCompletionHandler:^{
    [weakSelf.submitButton setEnabled:YES];
    [weakSelf.progressIndicator stopAnimating];
    [weakSelf.progressIndicator setHidden:YES];
}];
```

In this example, a UIButton called submitButton and a UIActivityIndicatorView called progressIndicator have been set up as properties (described in the next section) in the class. When the Submit button is tapped, a method will disable the button to prevent additional submissions while the long-running task is running. The method will display the progress Indicator and start animation, and then call the long-running task. The completion handler block is assigned directly in the method call to the long-running task as a parameter, so all the completion logic is visible right where the long-running task method call is made. The completion logic will reenable the submitButton and hide the progressIndicator. Although this example is trivial, it should be evident that this pattern can be very useful in common situations, especially when handling error conditions locally.

> **Note**
>
> A subclass of NSOperation called NSBlockOperation has been added, which offers support for using a block in an operation queue. In addition, Grand Central Dispatch offers support for executing blocks on a specific queue. See Chapter 17, "Grand Central Dispatch for Performance," for more information on using operation queues and Grand Central Dispatch.

Memory, Threads, and Blocks

When a block literal is assigned, memory for the block is automatically allocated on the stack. This memory takes a snapshot of the values of any variables from the enclosing scope used in the block, and captures a pointer to any variables that use the __block modifier. While the block exists on the stack, calling retain on that block will have no practical effect. To retain a block in memory either as a property on a class or as a parameter to a method call, the block must be copied, which will move it to the heap. After it's on the heap, normal memory management rules apply.

Because blocks are initially allocated on the stack, there is a practical limit on the number of blocks that can be allocated at once. If blocks are created in a loop, it is possible to create so many blocks at once that the stack is "blown," and a stack overflow condition can be created. If this situation arises, it can be addressed by copying the blocks to the heap as they are allocated.

One special memory management case to be aware of when using blocks is a retain cycle. Presume that a view controller has a custom button, which can be given a block. The view controller has a strong reference to the custom button.

```
@property(nonatomic,strong) IBOutlet ICFCustomButton *customButton;
```

The custom button has a property established for the block, which correctly specifies copy so that the block will be copied to the heap, and will be guaranteed to be available when the button needs it.

```
@property (nonatomic, copy) MyButtonBlock myButtonBlock;
```

Now presume that the view controller would like to update some UI elements when the button executes the block.

```
[self.customButton setMyButtonBlock:^(){
    [self.submitButton setEnabled:YES];
    [self.progressIndicator stopAnimating];
    [self.progressIndicator setHidden:YES];
}];
```

Because the block contains a reference to the enclosing object and the block is copied to the heap, the block will by default retain the enclosing object. In that case it will not be able to be released and a retain cycle will be created. The compiler might pick up this situation and display a warning, as shown in Figure 14.7, but it is important to note that the compiler might not catch all possible retain-cycle situations.

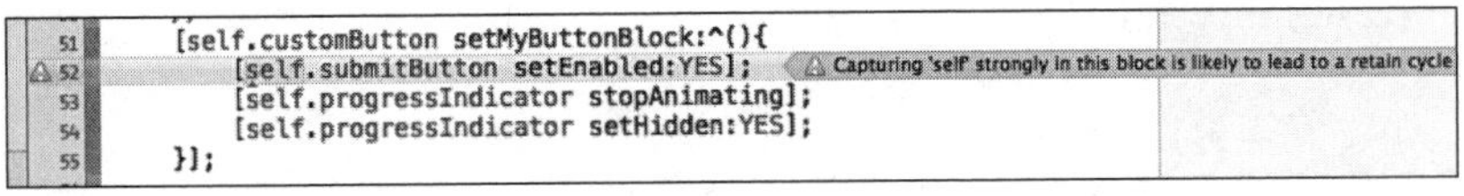

```
51    [self.customButton setMyButtonBlock:^(){
52        [self.submitButton setEnabled:YES];    ⚠ Capturing 'self' strongly in this block is likely to lead to a retain cycle
53        [self.progressIndicator stopAnimating];
54        [self.progressIndicator setHidden:YES];
55    }];
```

Figure 14.7   Xcode warning: potential retain cycle in block.

To prevent this problem, a weak reference to self can be created to be used by the block.

```
ICFViewController* __weak weakSelf = self;
```

```
[self.customButton setMyButtonBlock:^(){
    [weakSelf.submitButton setEnabled:YES];
    [weakSelf.progressIndicator stopAnimating];
    [weakSelf.progressIndicator setHidden:YES];
}];
```

By declaring the reference to self to use __weak, the block will not retain self and the retain cycle will be avoided.

Lastly, when blocks are being used, it is important to understand which thread the block will be executed on. Depending on the consumer of the block, the block might be executed on the main thread or might be executed on a background thread. Not knowing which thread the logic is being executed on can lead to subtle and difficult-to-diagnose bugs. One technique is to put a breakpoint in the block during development to see which thread the block has been executed on, and adjust the block logic accordingly. Another technique is to write the block logic with no assumptions at all about which thread it is being executed on, and use Grand Central Dispatch to execute the block logic on the correct threads as necessary.

Properties

Properties were introduced with Objective-C 2.0. They provide a way to easily declare instance variables for a class, and have the compiler generate accessor methods automatically. In addition, they provide a way to declare ownership intent via qualifiers for both ARC and non-ARC classes; the compiler will generate the correct code for the qualifier specified.

Declaring Properties

Properties are declared in the interface for a class. They can be declared in the header (.h) file for external visibility, or in the implementation file (.m) for properties that should be visible only to the instance. Before properties were available, instance variables were declared like so:

```
@interface ICFViewController : UIViewController
{
IBOutlet UITextView *myTextView;
IBOutlet UILabel *myLabel;
```

```
UIImage *attachmentImage;
UIImagePickerController *picker;
}
```

In the implementation file, accessor methods needed to be written for each instance variable. This code is tedious and repetitive to write, and simple errors in accessor methods can have dire memory management consequences like leaks or crashes.

With properties, adding the equivalent instance variables and accessor methods is as simple as a declaration:

```
@property(nonatomic, strong) IBOutlet UITextView *myTextView;
@property(nonatomic, strong) IBOutlet UILabel *myLabel;
@property(nonatomic, strong) UIImage *attachmentImage;
@property(nonatomic, strong) UIImagePickerController *picker;
```

The compiler will create an instance variable and standard accessor methods according to the qualifiers specified.

There are six memory-related qualifiers that can be used for properties:

- **assign:** `assign` means that the instance variable is not retained, and is not set to `nil` before destruction. It is semantically identical to __unsafe_unretained with ARC. This is the default for non-object properties; for example, c types like `BOOL` or `int`.

- **copy:** `copy` will manage retaining and releasing the instance variable, and will set to `nil` before destruction. In addition, when the instance variable is being set, it will be copied instead of the pointer being directly assigned. Sets the instance variable to __strong ownership with ARC.

- **retain:** `retain` will manage retaining and releasing the instance variable, and will set to `nil` before destruction for non-ARC projects. Although it's not technically meant for usage with ARC (`strong` is the preferred keyword), using `retain` will set an instance variable to __strong ownership with ARC.

- **strong:** `strong` will manage retaining and releasing the instance variable, and will set to `nil` before destruction. It sets the instance variable to __strong ownership with ARC. `strong` is the default for object properties.

- **weak:** `weak` will not retain the instance variable, but will automatically set it to `nil` before destruction. It sets the instance variable to __weak ownership with ARC.

- **unsafe_unretained:** `unsafe_unretained` will not retain the instance variable, and will not set it to `nil` before destruction. It sets the instance variable to __unsafe_ unretained with ARC.

In addition to memory qualifiers, properties can have other qualifiers that drive behavior of the accessor methods:

- **readonly/readwrite:** `readwrite` is the default, and tells the compiler to create both a getter and a setter method for the instance variable. The `readonly` qualifier will tell the compiler to generate only a getter method. There is not an option to generate only a setter method.

- **atomic/nonatomic:** atomic is the default, and tells the compiler to add locks so that the property can be safely accessed by multiple threads simultaneously. If that locking mechanism is not needed, nonatomic can be specified to prevent the compiler from generating the locking code. In that case, the property cannot be safely accessed from multiple threads.

Synthesizing Properties

Formerly, properties needed to be synthesized in the implementation (.m) file for the compiler to generate the accessor methods, like so:

```
@synthesize myImage;
```

As of Xcode 4.4/LLVM 4.0, this is no longer necessary because the compiler will now automatically synthesize accessor methods. If a custom name is desired for the underlying instance variable, that can be accomplished using @synthesize.

```
@synthesize myImage = myImageCustomName;
```

Accessing Properties

If properties have been declared in the header file, they can then be accessed from other classes:

```
NSString *setString = @"Some string...";

ICFObject *anObject = [[ICFObject alloc] init];
[anObject setMyString:setString];

UIImage *anImage = [anObject myImage];

[anObject release];
```

The getter method for a property is simply the name of the property. The setter method for the property is "set" prefixed to the name of the property, in camel case. In the previous code example, the string property myString can be set using the method setMyString:.

To access a property internally, the keyword self can be used:

```
[self setMyString:@"A new string"];

UIImage *image = [self myImage];
```

The underlying instance variable can be accessed directly as well. Instance variables generated automatically are prefixed with an underscore. Special consideration to threading and memory management should be given when the instance variable is being accessed directly.

```
NSLog(@"My String is %@",myStringCustomName);
```

Dot Notation

Introduced with Objective-C 2.0, dot notation provides a simple mechanism for accessing properties that have accessor methods. To get the value of a property, use this:

```
UIImage *image = self.myImage;
```

To set the value of a property, use this:

```
self.myString = @"Another string";
```

Dot notation can be strung together to simplify accessing or updating values for nested objects.

```
self.myView.myLabel.text = @"Label Title";
```

> **Note**
>
> ARC memory qualifiers set on properties do not protect against retain cycles. A retain cycle is when two objects have strong references to each other, and the compiler is never able to release them. An example of this is a delegate relationship, in which a parent object holds a reference to a child object, and the child object keeps a reference to the parent object in order to call delegate methods. If both of the properties used to establish the relationship use the strong qualifier, there will be a retain cycle and the parent will never release the child properly, keeping the memory occupied unnecessarily.

Fast Enumeration

Fast enumeration was added to Objective-C in version 2.0. It is a feature to simplify enumerating the objects in a collection and performing activities on the enumerated objects. Before fast enumeration, there were two approaches to enumerating the objects in a collection. The first approach, which works with collection types such as NSSet, NSArray, and NSDictionary, is to use an NSEnumerator to iterate over the objects (or also keys for an NSDictionary) in a collection.

```
NSArray *myArray = @[@"Item One", @"Item Two", @"Item Three"];

NSEnumerator *enumerator = [myArray objectEnumerator];
NSString *arrayString;
while ((arrayString = [enumerator nextObject]) != nil)
{
    NSLog(@"String is: %@",arrayString);
}
```

For an `NSArray`, a `for` loop can be constructed that will iterate over the indexes of an array instead of using an `NSEnumerator`.

```
NSArray *myArray = @[@"Item One", @"Item Two", @"Item Three"];

int startIndex = 0;
int endingIndex = [myArray count] - 1;

for (int counter = startIndex; counter <= endingIndex; counter++)
{
    NSString *myString = [myArray objectAtIndex:counter];
    NSLog(@"String is: %@",myString);
}
```

With fast enumeration, the amount of code needed to iterate over the elements in a collection can be significantly reduced.

```
NSArray *myArray = @[@"Item One", @"Item Two", @"Item Three"];

for (NSString *myString in myArray)
{
    NSLog(@"String is: %@",myString);
}
```

The new `for` construct specifies an object for each iterated item to be placed in (`NSString *myString` in the example), and the collection to be enumerated. The object does not have to be a specific type; `id` can be used for cases in which the collection contains instances of different classes, which can then be examined in the `for` loop and handled appropriately.

In addition to the new `for` syntax introduced with Objective-C 2.0, block-based enumerator methods have been added to several of the collection classes such as `NSSet`, `NSArray`, and `NSDictionary`. These methods look similar to this example:

```
[myArray enumerateObjectsUsingBlock:
^(NSString *myString, NSUInteger index, BOOL *stop) {
    NSLog(@"String is: %@",myString);
}];
```

The block will have access to the object, the index of the object, and a `BOOL` pointer that can be set to `YES` to stop iterating over the collection. In addition, some of the new methods support passing in options to iterate over an ordered collection in reverse order, or any collection concurrently.

Method Swizzling

The Objective-C runtime is flexible and provides support for dynamically changing object types and methods during execution of code. This support allows the developer to dynamically replace methods on existing classes, called method swizzling. Method swizzling can be used for a wide variety of use cases, but is typically most useful for replacing or augmenting existing methods on built-in classes where subclassing is not an option, or where using a category is not sufficient to achieve the desired results. For example, one project uses method swizzling to replace the `setTitle:` method on the `UIViewController` class to intelligently set either the title label or a custom image. Another project uses method swizzling to test whether calls to UIKit methods are performed on the correct thread. Apple even uses method swizzling to implement key-value observing. Method swizzling can be used for performance testing, to bring out information that debugging and instruments cannot.

To implement method swizzling, select an existing method to replace or augment. Create a replacement method, and then instruct the Objective-C runtime to replace the implementation or swap implementations. Replacing the implementation will completely replace the existing implementation, and the original implementation will no longer be available. Swapping implementations will keep the original implementation available so that it can be called, much like calling `super` on an overridden method in a subclass.

As a contrived example, consider swizzling `setTitle:forState:` on `UIButton`. The swizzled method will automatically update all four control states for a button, and append the name of the control state to the title for visibility. Note that this could easily be achieved by subclassing the button and overriding that method, but this example shows how the same result can be achieved with method swizzling. The new method is added to a category on `UIButton`.

```objc
- (void)setButtonTitle:(NSString *)buttonTitle
      forControlState:(UIControlState)controlState
{
    NSString *normTitle =
    [buttonTitle stringByAppendingString:@"-Normal"];

    [self setButtonTitle:normTitle
        forControlState:UIControlStateNormal];

    NSString *selTitle =
    [buttonTitle stringByAppendingString:@"-Selected"];

    [self setButtonTitle:selTitle
        forControlState:UIControlStateSelected];

    NSString *highTitle =
    [buttonTitle stringByAppendingString:@"-Highlighted"];

    [self setButtonTitle:highTitle
        forControlState:UIControlStateHighlighted];

    NSString *disTitle =
    [buttonTitle stringByAppendingString:@"-Disabled"];

    [self setButtonTitle:disTitle
        forControlState:UIControlStateDisabled];
}
```

An odd side effect of this approach to method swizzling is that calling the original implementation of the method from the new implementation requires using the new method name, which makes it look recursive. In reality, calling the new method name from the new method calls the original method implementation, much like calling super would from an overridden method in a subclass.

Another method is created in the same category to complete the actual method swizzle. Note that the Objective-C runtime library must be imported in order for the method-swapping functions to be recognized by the compiler.

```
#import <objc/runtime.h>
```

The method is called swizzleTitleMethod. It first gets a reference to the class and selector of the original method.

```
- (void)swizzleTitleMethod
{
    Class thisClass = [self class];

    SEL originalTitleSelector = @selector(setTitle:forState:);


    . . .

}
```

The swizzleTitleMethod method then gets a reference to the method represented by the selector from the class definition. Note that this is just the method definition, not the actual implementation of the method.

```
Method originalTitleMethod =
class_getInstanceMethod(thisClass,originalTitleSelector);
```

Next, references for the new selector and method definition are obtained.

```
SEL newTitleSelector =
@selector(setButtonTitle:forControlState:);

Method newTitleMethod =
class_getInstanceMethod(thisClass, newTitleSelector);
```

Finally, the methods are swapped using a function from the Objective-C runtime library.

```
method_exchangeImplementations(originalTitleMethod,
                               newTitleMethod);
```

The swizzleTitleMethod method can be called at any point before it is needed to swap methods, and could even be reversed at some point during execution due to the dynamic nature of the Objective-C runtime.

If the original implementation of the method is not needed, the Objective-C runtime function class_replaceMethod can be used instead to completely replace the method on the class.

Note that this function requires a reference to the actual implementation (IMP) of the new method.

Summary

This chapter covered several new features that have been introduced to iOS development since the introduction of Objective-C 2.0, LLVM, and Xcode 4.

New, much simpler literal syntax for NSNumber, NSArray, and NSDictionary instantiations was introduced. In addition, new syntax for accessing and updating elements of NSArray, NSMutableArray, NSDictionary, and NSMutableDictionary variables using subscripts was described. The new syntax can make code much shorter and more readable.

Automatic Reference Counting was discussed. The chapter covered how to create a new project to use ARC and how to convert an existing project to ARC. New memory management qualifiers and new coding rules required by ARC were explained. Proper use of ARC can reduce the amount of code needed in a project, improve memory management, and avoid memory leaks.

Blocks were introduced, with instructions on how to declare a block, how to create a block using a block literal, and how blocks are able to make use of surrounding state. Usage of blocks as parameters was described, as well as some memory management considerations specific to blocks.

Properties, which simplify declaration of instance variables and provide automatic accessor method generation, were described. New syntax for accessing properties using dot notation was demonstrated. Use of properties can greatly reduce the amount of code needed in a custom class, and proper use of qualifiers can standardize usage and avoid bugs in writing boilerplate code.

New fast enumeration capabilities, including new for-in syntax and block-based object iteration, were described. These capabilities simplify and greatly reduce the amount of code needed to iterate over a collection of objects.

Method swizzling, which is a technique for dynamically swapping method implementations at runtime, was introduced. Method swizzling can be used to augment or replace methods on built-in classes when subclassing or categorization are not sufficient.

All these techniques provide many opportunities to reduce the amount of code needed to meet requirements, improve code readability, prevent errors, and generally improve the quality of code.

Exercises

1. Find an old project using manual memory management and convert it to use ARC.

2. Use Xcode's tool to convert an old project to use modern Objective-C syntax, by selecting Edit, Refactor, Convert to Modern Objective-C Syntax from the menu.

15

Integrating Twitter and Facebook Using Social Framework

Social Integration

Social networking is here to stay, and users want to be able to access their social media accounts on everything from the newest iOS game to their refrigerators (Samsung Model RF4289HARS). Before iOS 5, adding Twitter and Facebook to an app was a frustrating and challenging endeavor; third-party libraries written by people who didn't understand the platform were rampant, often not even compiling. Starting with iOS 5, Apple introduced Social Framework, which allowed developers to directly integrate Twitter services into their apps with little effort. With iOS 6, Apple expanded the Social Framework functionality to include Facebook and Sina Weibo (China's leading social network).

Not only are users craving social integration in just about everything with a screen, but social integration can be highly beneficial to the app developer as well. When a user tweets a high score from your game or shares a Facebook message about an app, it will reach a market that a developer would not be able to penetrate. Not only is the app reaching new customers, but it is getting a personalized endorsement from a potential new customer's friends. There are few apps that could not benefit from the inclusion of social media and, with iOS 6, it has become easier than ever to add this functionality.

The Sample App

The sample app for this chapter is called SocialNetworking (see Figure 15.1). The app features a single text view with a character-count label and a button to attach an image. There are two buttons on the title bar as well that allow the user to access Twitter and Facebook functionality. The sample app enforces a 140-character count on Facebook posts and Twitter; in reality, Facebook supports much longer text posts.

Figure 15.1   A first look at the sample app, SocialNetworking, for this chapter.

Tapping the buttons for each of the services brings up three options: composer, auto-post, and timeline. The composer option will take you to the built-in SLComposeViewController and is the easiest and fastest way to post a message to a social service. The auto-post option will post the text and optional image from the main screen without the user needing to take any additional steps; this step can also be considered programmatic posting. The timeline option will bring up the user's Twitter timeline or Facebook feed. The sample app does not include functionality for Sina Weibo, although either service can be adapted with relative ease.

Logging In

The Social Framework uses a centralized login system for Facebook and Twitter, which can be found under the Settings.app, as shown in Figure 15.2.

In the event that a user is not currently logged in to Twitter or Facebook and attempts to access Twitter and Facebook functionality, he will be prompted to set up a new account, as shown in Figure 15.3. This system works only when the SLComposeViewController is being used; otherwise, a simple access-denied message is presented if no accounts are configured. In addition to the no-accounts message, you might occasionally see an Error 6 returned if the accounts in Settings.app are not properly configured. This is typically caused by an account set with incorrect credentials.

Figure 15.2   Logging in to a social service on iOS requires the user to leave the app and visit the settings app.

Figure 15.3   The user being prompted to configure a Twitter account for the device.

> **Note**
>
> There is currently no Apple-approved method of loading the user directly into the configure screen for Twitter and Facebook outside of the `SLComposeViewController` built-in message.

Using `SLComposeViewController`

The easiest way to post a new message to Twitter or Facebook is to use the `SLComposeViewController`. It requires no fiddling with permissions and, if the user has not set up an account, it prompts them to configure one. The downside of `SLComposeViewController` is that there is no way to customize the appearance of the view that the user is presented with, as shown in Figure 15.4.

Figure 15.4   Posting a new tweet with an image using the `SLComposeViewController`.

Before anything can be done with `SLComposeViewController`, the Social.framework must first be imported into the project. In addition, the header file `"Social/Social.h"` will need to be imported; note the capitalization of the header files.

The following code is the most effortless method of presenting a `SLComposeViewController` for Twitter. The first step is a call to `isAvailableForServiceType`; in the event that the device is not capable of posting to Twitter, it will gracefully exit here. A new SLComposeViewController is created and a new block is made to handle the results of the action. The completion handler for the SLComposeViewController is set to the newly created block and it is presented with presentViewController. These are the bare minimum steps that need to be completed in order to post from an iOS app to Twitter. This option is demonstrated in the sample app as the Composer option under the Twitter menu.

```
if([SLComposeViewController
➥isAvailableForServiceType:SLServiceTypeTwitter])
{

    SLComposeViewController *controller =
    ➥[SLComposeViewController
    ➥composeViewControllerForServiceType: SLServiceTypeTwitter];

    SLComposeViewControllerCompletionHandler myBlock =
    ^(SLComposeViewControllerResult result){
        if (result == SLComposeViewControllerResultCancelled)
        {
            NSLog(@"Cancelled");
        }

        else
        {
            NSLog(@"Done");
        }

        [controller dismissViewControllerAnimated:YES
        ➥completion:nil];
    };

    controller.completionHandler = myBlock;

    [self presentViewController:controller animated:YES
    ➥completion:nil];
}

else
{
    NSLog(@"Twitter Composer is not available.");
}
```

You can also customize an SLComposeViewController by setting the initial text, images, and URLs.

```
[controller setInitialText:@"Check out my app:"];
[controller addImage:[UIImage imageNamed:@"Kitten.jpg"]];
[controller addURL:[NSURL URLWithString:@"http://amzn.to/Um85L0"]];
```

Multiple images and URLs can also be added.

```
[controller addImage:[UIImage imageNamed:@"Kitten1.jpg"]];
[controller addImage:[UIImage imageNamed:@"Kitten2.jpg"]];
```

In the event that it is necessary to remove URLs or images from the
SLComposeViewController after they have been added, it can be done with a single
method call.

```
[controller removeAllImages];
[controller removeAllURLs];
```

The approach for SLComposeViewController with Facebook is identical to Twitter
with one exception: Both uses of SLServiceTypeTwitter should be replaced with
SLServiceTypeFacebook.

Posting with a Custom Interface

It might become necessary to move beyond the capabilities of the SLComposeViewController
and implement a ground-up solution. Luckily, Social Framework fully supports this kind of
interaction. When SLComposeViewController was used, the differences between posting to
Facebook and posting Twitter were minor, but this will no longer be the case when dealing
with customized interfaces. Twitter and Facebook support when working at a lower level are
almost entirely different. This section is broken into two subsections: one for Twitter and one
for Facebook. Twitter support is the simpler of the two, so that is covered first.

Posting to Twitter

In addition to importing the Social.framework and importing the "Social/Social.h"
header from the SLComposeViewController, the "Accounts/Accounts.h" header will also
need to be imported. To begin working with more direct access to Twitter's APIs, two new
objects first need to be created.

```
ACAccountStore *account = [[ACAccountStore alloc] init];
ACAccountType *accountType = [account
➥accountTypeWithAccountTypeIdentifier: ACAccountTypeIdentifierTwitter];
```

The ACAccountStore will allow the code base to access the Twitter account that has been
configured in the Settings.app, and the ACAccountType contains the information needed for a
particular type of account. The accountType object can be queried to see whether access has
already been granted to the user.

```
if (accountType.accessGranted)
{
    NSLog(@"User has already granted access to this service");
}
```

To prompt the user to grant access to the Twitter account information, a call on the ACAccountStore for requestAccessToAccountsWithType:options:completion: is required. If the account has already been authorized, the completion block will return YES for granted without prompting the user again.

```
[account requestAccessToAccountsWithType:accountType options:nil
➥completion:^(BOOL granted, NSError *error)
```

If the user grants access or if access has already been granted, a list of the user's Twitter accounts will need to be retrieved. A user can add multiple Twitter accounts to his device and you cannot determine which one he will want to post from. In the event that multiple accounts are found, the user should be prompted to specify which account he would like to use.

```
if (granted == YES)
{
    NSArray *arrayOfAccounts = [account accountsWithAccountType:
    ➥accountType];
}
```

In the sample app, after it checks to make sure that there is at least one properly configured account, the last one found in the array is simply selected. In an App Store app it will be important to present the user with an option to select which account she wants to use if more than one is found.

```
if ([arrayOfAccounts count] > 0)
{
    ACAccount *twitterAccount = [arrayOfAccounts lastObject];
}
```

After a reference to the account is created and stored in an ACAccount, the post data can be configured. Depending on whether the post will include an image or other media, a different post URL is used.

```
NSURL *requestURL = nil;

if(hasAttachmentedImage)
{
    requestURL = [NSURL URLWithString:
    ➥@"https://upload.twitter.com/1.1/statuses/
    ➥update_with_media.json"];
}

else
{
    requestURL = [NSURL URLWithString:
    ➥@"http://api.twitter.com/1.1/statuses/update.json"];
}
```

> **Warning**
>
> Posting a tweet to the improper URL will result in its failing. You cannot post an image tweet to the `update.json` endpoint, and you cannot post a non-image tweet to the `update_with_media.json` endpoint.

After the endpoint URL has been determined, a new `SLRequest` object is created. The `SLRequest` is the object that will contain all the information needed to post the full tweet details to Twitter's API.

```
SLRequest *postRequest = [SLRequest
➥requestForServiceType:SLServiceTypeTwitter
➥requestMethod:SLRequestMethodPOST
➥URL:requestURL parameters:nil];
```

After the `SLRequest` has been created, an account must be defined for it. Using the account that was previously determined, the account property is set.

```
postRequest.account = twitterAccount;
```

To add text to this tweet, a call on the `postRequest` to `addMultipartData:withName:type:filename:` is used. The text is a simple string with `NSUTF8StringEncoding`. The name used here correlates to the Twitter API documentation; for text it is `status`. For `type`, `multipart/form-data` is used in accordance with the Twitter API. No filename is required for text.

```
[postRequest addMultipartData:[socialTextView.text dataUsingEncoding:
➥NSUTF8StringEncoding] withName:@"status"
➥type:@"multipart/form-data"filename:nil];
```

> **Note**
>
> For more information on Twitter's API and where these constants are pulled from, visit https://dev.twitter.com/docs.

If the tweet has an image associated with it, add it next. A `UIImage` first needs to be converted to `NSData` using `UIImageJPEGRepresentation`. This example is similar to the preceding text-based example except that a filename is specified.

```
NSData *imageData = UIImageJPEGRepresentation(self.attachmentImage, 1.0);

[postRequest addMultipartData:imageData withName:@"media"
type:@"image/jpeg" filename:@"Image.jpg"];
```

> **Note**
>
> Multiple images can be added with repetitive calls to `addMultipartData:withName:type:filename:`.

After the `postRequest` has been fully populated with all the information that should appear in the tweet, it is time to post it to Twitter's servers. This is done with a call to `performRequest WithHandler:`. A `URLResponse` code of `200` indicates a success; every other response code indicates a type of failure. A successful post from the sample is shown in Figure 15.5.

Figure 15.5   A successful tweet to Twitter using a custom interface as shown in the sample app.

> **Note**
>
> It is important to remember that `UIAlertViews` cannot be shown from within a completion block, since the completion block will not necessarily be executed on the main thread. In the sample app error messages are passed to a main thread method to display alerts.

```
[postRequest performRequestWithHandler:^(NSData *responseData,
➥NSHTTPURLResponse *urlResponse, NSError *error)
{
    if(error != nil)
    {
        [self performSelectorOnMainThread:
        ➥@selector(reportSuccessOrError:) withObject:[error
        ➥localizedDescription] waitUntilDone:NO];
    }
```

```
    if([urlResponse statusCode] == 200)
    {
        [self performSelectorOnMainThread:
        ➥@selector(reportSuccessOrError:) withObject:@"Your
        ➥message has been posted to Twitter" waitUntilDone:NO];
    }

}];
```

This concludes all the required steps to post a string and an image to Twitter using a custom interface. In the following subsection, Facebook posting will be fully explored.

> **Tip**
>
> Inside of the sample app, the process of posting to Twitter is fully laid out in the method `twitterPost`.

Posting to Facebook

The same basic principles apply when working with a Facebook post as with Twitter. There are, however, multiple additional steps required to deal with a number of authentication and permission requirements. Unlike Twitter, Facebook has various levels of permissions. If a user authorizes an app to access her feed, she might not want the app to be able to publish to her feeds. To make matters more complex, permissions have to be requested in certain orders, and requests for read and write permission cannot be made at the same time.

Creating a Facebook App

To post or interact with Facebook from a mobile app, a Facebook app that corresponds to the mobile app must first be created.

Log in to https://developers.facebook.com/apps using a Facebook account that you want to have ownership of the app.

Select the button + Create New App, as shown in Figure 15.6. Enter values for App Name and App Namespace. Clicking the question mark icon next to any field will provide additional details.

After a new Facebook App has been created (see Figure 15.7), copy down the App ID number. Browse through all the pages for the new app and ensure that it is configured to suit the needs of the iOS app. By default, there are no options that need to be changed to continue working through this section.

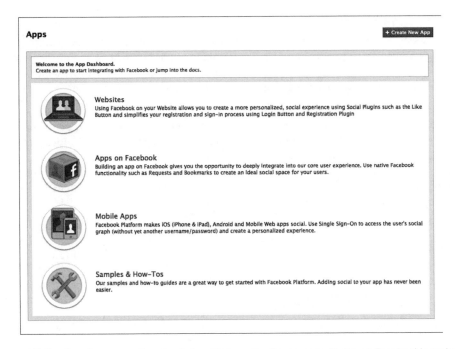

Figure 15.6   Creating a new Facebook App ID from the Developers Portal on Facebook's website.

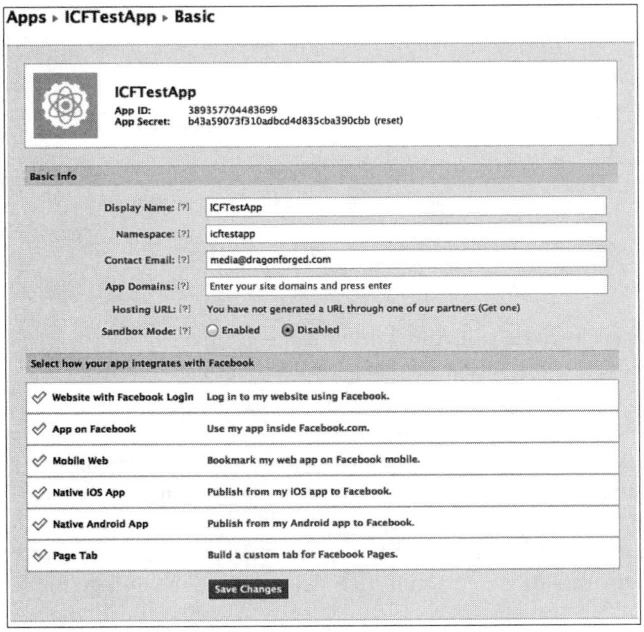

Figure 15.7   A newly created Facebook App. The App ID will be needed to make any Facebook calls from within an iOS app.

Basic Facebook Permissions

The first group of permissions that every Facebook-enabled app needs to request (except if you are using only the `SLComposeViewController`) is basic profile access. This is done by requesting any of the following attributes: id, name, `first_name`, `last_name`, link, username, gender, or locale. Requesting any of these items grants access to all the remaining items.

If the app has not yet been set up according to the instructions from the preceding section for Twitter, the proper headers and frameworks need to be first imported. Basic permission is requested upon app launch or entering into the section of the app that requires Facebook interaction. It is not recommended to access basic permissions after the user has already attempted to make a post; this will create a chain of pop-up alerts that a user will have trouble understanding. The following code is part of the `viewDidLoad:` method of `ICFViewController.m` in the sample app:

```
ACAccountStore *accountStore = [[ACAccountStore alloc] init];
ACAccountType *facebookAccountType = [accountStore
➡accountTypeWithAccountTypeIdentifier: ACAccountTypeIdentifierFacebook];


NSDictionary *options = @{
ACFacebookAudienceKey : ACFacebookAudienceEveryone,
ACFacebookAppIdKey : @"363120920441086",
ACFacebookPermissionsKey : @[@"email"]};


[accountStore requestAccessToAccountsWithType:facebookAccountType
➡options:options completion:^(BOOL granted, NSError *error)
{
     if (granted)
     {
          NSLog(@"Basic access granted");
     }

     else
     {
          NSLog(@"Basic access denied");
     }
}];
```

The `ACAccountStore` and `ACAccountType` are configured in the same fashion as for Twitter, as described in the preceding section. A new dictionary called options is created; this will be used to supply the API parameters for whatever call is to be made. For basic permissions `ACFacebookAudienceEveryone` is passed for `ACFacebookAudienceKey`. The `ACFacebookAppIdKey` is the App ID that was created in the section "Creating a Facebook App." Since any of the basic permissions can be used to request access to all basic permissions, the email attribute is used for the `ACFacebookPermissionsKey`. A call of `requestAccessT oAccountWithType:options:completion:` is made on the `accountStore`. The user will be presented with a dialog similar to the one shown in Figure 15.8. The result of the user granting or denying permissions is logged.

Figure 15.8   A user being prompted to allow the sample app SocialNetworking to access basic profile information.

Publishing to Stream Permissions

Before an app can post to a user's stream, it first needs to request write permissions. This step must be done after basic permissions have been authorized. Requesting publish permissions is nearly identical to requesting permissions to the basic profile information. Instead of requesting access to `email` for `ACFacebookPermissionsKey`, permission is requested for `publish_stream`. The user will be prompted as shown in Figure 15.9. After a user has granted permission, he will not be prompted again unless he removes the app's permissions from within Facebook.

```
ACAccountStore *accountStore = [[ACAccountStore alloc] init];
ACAccountType *facebookAccountType = [accountStore
➥accountTypeWithAccountTypeIdentifier:ACAccountTypeIdentifierFacebook];

NSDictionarvy *options = @{
ACFacebookAudienceKey : ACFacebookAudienceEveryone,
ACFacebookAppIdKey : @"363120920441086",
ACFacebookPermissionsKey : @[@"publish_stream"]};

[accountStore requestAccessToAccountsWithType:facebookAccountType
➥options:options completion:^(BOOL granted, NSError *error)
```

```
{
    if (granted)
    {
        NSLog(@"Publish permission granted");
    }

    else
    {
        NSLog(@"Publish permission denied");
    }
}];
```

Figure 15.9   A user being prompted to allow the sample app SocialNetworking to access
publishing privileges.

Note

Important: Do not forget to change the `ACFacebookAppIdKey` to match the ID of the Facebook
App that you will be publishing under.

Posting to the Facebook Stream

After the user has granted permission to publish to her timeline on her behalf, the app is ready to create a new post. The first step to creating a new Facebook post is to create an NSDictionary that will store a single object under the key @"message". This key/value pair will hold the text that will appear in the post.

```
NSDictionary *parameters = [NSDictionary
➥dictionaryWithObject:socialTextView.text forKey:@"message"];
```

If the post does not contain any media such as images, the message is posted to https://graph.facebook.com/me/feed; however, if the new post will contain photos or media, it will need to be posted to https://graph.facebook.com/me/photos. These URLs cannot be mixed; for example, posting a feed item with no image to https://graph.facebook.com/me/photos will result in a failure. The sample app performs a simple check to determine which endpoint to use.

```
if(self.attachmentImage)
{
    feedURL = [NSURL URLWithString:
    ➥@"https://graph.facebook.com/me/photos"];
}

else
{
    feedURL = [NSURL URLWithString:
    ➥@"https://graph.facebook.com/me/feed"];
}
```

After the proper URL for posting has been determined, a new SLRequest object is created specifying the URL and the parameters.

```
SLRequest *feedRequest = [SLRequest

requestForServiceType:SLServiceTypeFacebook
                        requestMethod:SLRequestMethodPOST
                        URL:feedURL
                        parameters:parameters];
```

In the event that the post contains an image, that data needs to be added to the feedRequest. This is done using the addMultipartData:withName:type:filename: method.

```
if(self.attachmentImage)
{
    NSData *imageData =
    ➥UIImagePNGRepresentation(self.attachmentImage);
    ➥[feedRequest addMultipartData:imageData withName:@"source"
    ➥type:@"multipart/form-data" filename:@"Image"];
}
```

After the optional image data is added, a `performRequestWithHandler:` is called in the same
fashion as Twitter. Facebook will return a `urlResponse` code of `200` if the post was successful.

```
[feedRequest performRequestWithHandler:^(NSData *responseData,
➥NSHTTPURLResponse *urlResponse, NSError *error)
{
     NSLog(@"Facebook post statusCode: %u", [urlResponse
     ➥statusCode]);

     if([urlResponse statusCode] == 200)
     {
        [self performSelectorOnMainThread:@selector
        ➥(reportSuccessOrError:) withObject:@"Your message has
        ➥been posted to Facebook" waitUntilDone:NO];
     }

     else if(error != nil)
     {
        [self performSelectorOnMainThread:
        ➥@selector(faceBookError:) withObject:error
        ➥waitUntilDone:NO];
     }
}];
```

Additional information about formatting posts and embedding media for Facebook can be
found through the documentation at http://developers.facebook.com.

Accessing User Timelines

There might be times when posting a status update is not enough to satisfy an app's social
interaction requirements. Accessing a timeline on Twitter or Facebook is complex, and there
is an abundance of tricky edge cases and data types to support, from Twitter's retweets to
Facebook embedded data. This section takes a cursory look at accessing the raw data from a
timeline and displaying it to a tableview. It has been left simple because the subject of time-
lines is a rabbit hole that can very well occupy a book in and of itself.

Twitter

As shown in previous sections, Twitter has been easier to interact with than the more complex
Facebook APIs, due mainly to the multiple permission hierarchy implemented with Facebook.
Accessing a user's Twitter timeline begins in the same fashion as posting new a tweet; refer-
ences to `ACAccountStore` and `ACAccountType` are created.

```
ACAccountStore *account = [[ACAccountStore alloc] init];

ACAccountType *accountType = [account
➥accountTypeWithAccountTypeIdentifier: ACAccountTypeIdentifierTwitter];
```

Continuing in the same fashion as posting a new tweet, a call to `requestAccessToAccount WithType:` is performed on the account object. Basic error handling is also set up here.

```
[account requestAccessToAccountsWithType:accountType options:nil
➥completion:^(BOOL granted, NSError *error)
{
    if(error != nil)
    {
        [self
performSelectorOnMainThread:@selector(reportSuccessOrError:)
➥withObject:[error localizedDescription]
➥waitUntilDone:NO];
    }

}];
```

If no errors are returned and access is granted, a copy of the `ACAccount` object for the user is obtained. The sample app, once again, just uses the last object in the count array; however, it is important to keep in mind that some users might be logged in to several Twitter accounts at once and should be given the option of selecting which account they want to use. The request URL used to retrieve a copy of the users timeline is http://api.twitter.com/1.1/statuses/ home_timeline.json. A number of options are also required to be supplied. The first option, `count`, specifies the number of tweets that will be retrieved per call. The second option is a Boolean value used to specify whether tweet entities should be included. A tweet entity will include additional details such as users mentioned, hashtags, URLs, and media.

After it has been created, the `SLRequest` is submitted in the same fashion used when posting to a new status update. The `performRequestWithHandler` success block will contain the `responseData` that can then be displayed. The following code is part of the twitterTimeline method of `ICFViewController.m`:

```
if (granted == YES)
{
    NSArray *arrayOfAccounts = [account
    ➥accountsWithAccountType:accountType];

    if ([arrayOfAccounts count] > 0)
    {
        ACAccount *twitterAccount = [arrayOfAccounts
        ➥lastObject];

        NSURL *requestURL = [NSURL URLWithString:
        @"http://api.twitter.com/1.1/statuses/home_timeline.json"];

        NSDictionary *options = @{
        @"count" : @"20",
        @"include_entities" : @"1"};
```

```
SLRequest *postRequest = [SLRequest
requestForServiceType:SLServiceTypeTwitter
requestMethod:SLRequestMethodGET
URL:requestURL parameters:options];

postRequest.account = twitterAccount;

[postRequest performRequestWithHandler:^(NSData
➥*responseData, NSHTTPURLResponse *urlResponse, NSError
➥*error)
{
    if(error != nil)
    {
        [self performSelectorOnMainThread:@selector
          ➥(reportSuccessOrError:) withObject:[error
          ➥localizedDescription] waitUntilDone:NO];
    }

     [self performSelectorOnMainThread:
     ➥ @selector(presentTimeline:) withObject:
       ➥[NSJSONSerialization JSONObjectWithData:responseData
     ➥ options:NSJSONReadingMutableLeaves error:&error]
     ➥ waitUntilDone:NO];
}];
}
}
```

Provided is a sample of the `responseData` with tweet entities enabled from a typical Twitter timeline fetch; in addition, a sample of how this tweet shows up on the Twitter website is shown in Figure 15.10. As shown in the following console output, Twitter provides a considerable amount of information to which the developer has access. For more information on working with JSON data, refer to Chapter 7, "Working with and Parsing JSON."

Figure 15.10　A fully rendered tweet as seen on the Twitter website. The data that makes up this tweet can be seen in the log statements earlier in this section.

```
2013-02-27 21:50:54.562 SocialNetworking[28672:4207] (
        {
        contributors = "<null>";
        coordinates = "<null>";
        "created_at" = "Thu Feb 28 02:50:41 +0000 2013";
```

```
        entities =           {
            hashtags =              (
                            {
                    indices =                   (
                        63,
                        76
                    );
                    text = bluesjamtime;
                }
            );
            media =               (
                            {
                    "display_url" = "pic.twitter.com/CwoYlbWaQJ";
                    "expanded_url" =
➥"http://twitter.com/neror/status/306959580582248448/photo/1";
                    id = 306959580586442753;
                    "id_str" = 306959580586442753;
                    indices =                   (
                        77,
                        99
                    );
                    "media_url" =
➥"http://pbs.twimg.com/media/BEKKHLlCAAEUQ6x.jpg";
                    "media_url_https" =
➥"https://pbs.twimg.com/media/BEKKHLlCAAEUQ6x.jpg";
                    sizes =                    {
                        large =                    {
                            h = 768;
                            resize = fit;
                            w = 1024;
                        };
                        medium =                     {
                            h = 450;
                            resize = fit;
                            w = 600;
                        };
                        small =                    {
                            h = 255;
                            resize = fit;
                            w = 340;
                        };
                        thumb =                    {
                            h = 150;
                            resize = crop;
                            w = 150;
                        };
                    };
```

```
                    type = photo;
                    url = "http://t.co/CwoYlbWaQJ";
              }
         );
         urls =                  (
         );
         "user_mentions" =               (
         );
    };
    favorited = 0;
    geo = "<null>";
    id = 306959580582248448;
    "id_str" = 306959580582248448;
    "in_reply_to_screen_name" = "<null>";
    "in_reply_to_status_id" = "<null>";
    "in_reply_to_status_id_str" = "<null>";
    "in_reply_to_user_id" = "<null>";
    "in_reply_to_user_id_str" = "<null>";
    place =           {
         attributes =              {
         };
         "bounding_box" =                {
              coordinates =                 (
                                       (
                                            (
                        "-95.90998500000001",
                        "29.537034"
                   ),
                                            (
                        "-95.01449599999999",
                        "29.537034"
                   ),
                                            (
                        "-95.01449599999999",
                        "30.110792"
                   ),
                                            (
                        "-95.90998500000001",
                        "30.110732"
                   )
                   )
              );
              type = Polygon;
         };
         country = "United States";
         "country_code" = US;
         "full_name" = "Houston, TX";
```

```
            id = 1c69a67ad480e1b1;
            name = Houston;
            "place_type" = city;
            url =
➥"http://api.twitter.com/1/geo/id/1c69a67ad480e1b1.json";
        };
        "possibly_sensitive" = 0;
        "retweet_count" = 0;
        retweeted = 0;
        source = "<a href=\http://tapbots.com/software/tweetbot/mac\
➥rel=\"nofollow\">Tweetbot for Mac</a>";
        text = "Playing my strat always gets the creative coding juices
➥going. #bluesjamtime http://t.co/CwoYlbWaQJ";
        truncated = 0;
        user =            {
            "contributors_enabled" = 0;
            "created_at" = "Mon Sep 04 02:05:35 +0000 2006";
            "default_profile" = 0;
            "default_profile_image" = 0;
            description = "Dad, iOS & Mac game and app developer,
➥Founder of Free Time Studios, Texan";
            "favourites_count" = 391;
            "follow_request_sent" = "<null>";
            "followers_count" = 2254;
            following = 1;
            "friends_count" = 865;
            "geo_enabled" = 1;
            id = 5250;
            "id_str" = 5250;
            "is_translator" = 0;
            lang = en;
            "listed_count" = 182;
            location = "Houston, Texas";
            name = "Nathan Eror";
            notifications = "<null>";
            "profile_background_color" = 1A1B1F;
            "profile_background_image_url" =
➥"http://a0.twimg.com/images/themes/theme9/bg.gif";
            "profile_background_image_url_https" =
➥"https://si0.twimg.com/images/themes/theme9/bg.gif";
            "profile_background_tile" = 0;
            "profile_image_url" =
➥"http://a0.twimg.com/profile_images/1902659692/36A2FDF8-72F4-
➥485E-B574-892C1FF16534_normal";
            "profile_image_url_https" =
➥"https://si0.twimg.com/profile_images/1902659692/36A2FDF8-72F4-
➥485E-B574-892C1FF16534_normal";
```

```
                "profile_link_color" = 2FC2EF;
                "profile_sidebar_border_color" = 181A1E;
                "profile_sidebar_fill_color" = 252429;
                "profile_text_color" = 666666;
                "profile_use_background_image" = 1;
                protected = 0;
                "screen_name" = neror;
                "statuses_count" = 5091;
                "time_zone" = "Central Time (US & Canada)";
                url = "http://www.freetimestudios.com";
                "utc_offset" = "-21600";
                verified = 0;
            };
        }
    )
```

Facebook

Retrieving a Facebook timeline is done through the endpoint https://graph.facebook.com/me/
feed. To begin, a new NSURL is created and then used to generate a new SLRequest. The following example assumes that the app has previously authenticated a user for permissions and was
granted. See the earlier section on Facebook permissions for more details.

```
NSURL *feedURL = [NSURL URLWithString:
➥@"https://graph.facebook.com/me/feed"];

SLRequest *feedRequest = [SLRequest

requestForServiceType:SLServiceTypeFacebook
                          requestMethod:SLRequestMethodGET
                          URL:feedURL
                          parameters:nil];

feedRequest.account = self.facebookAccount;
```

After the SLRequest has been set up, a call to performRequestWithHandler: is invoked on
the feedRequest object. In the event of a success, Facebook will return a urlResponse status
code of 200; any other status code indicates a failure.

```
[feedRequest performRequestWithHandler:^(NSData *responseData,
➥NSHTTPURLResponse *urlResponse, NSError *error)
{
    NSLog(@"Facebook post statusCode: %u", [urlResponse
    ➥statusCode]);

    if([urlResponse statusCode] == 200)
    {
```

```
    NSLog(@"%@", [[NSJSONSerialization
    ➡JSONObjectWithData:responseData
    ➡options:NSJSONReadingMutableLeaves error:&error]
    ➡objectForKey:@"data"]);

    [self performSelectorOnMainThread:
    ➡@selector(presentTimeline:) withObject:
    ➡[[NSJSONSerialization JSONObjectWithData:responseData
    ➡options:NSJSONReadingMutableLeaves error:&error]
    ➡objectForKey:@"data"] waitUntilDone:NO];
}

else if(error != nil)
{
    [self performSelectorOnMainThread:
    ➡@selector(faceBookError:) withObject:error
    ➡waitUntilDone:NO];
}
}];
```

Facebook supports many types of post updates, from likes, comments, and new friends, to wall updates. Many of these dictionaries use different key sets for the information that is typically displayed. The sample app will handle the most common types of Facebook posts. Following are three standard post types with all the accompanying data. The first is a message indicating that a new Facebook friend has been connected. The second item in the array represents a post in which the user likes a link. The final example shows the user adding a comment to a post by another user. It is important to thoroughly test any use of Facebook timeline parsing on a wide selection of Facebook events to ensure proper compatibility. More information on the formatting and behavior of Facebook posts can be found at http://developers.facebook.com. For more information on working with JSON data, refer to Chapter 7.

```
(
    {
    actions =          (
                    {
            link =
➡"http://www.facebook.com/1674990377/posts/4011976152528";
            name = Comment;
        },
                    {
            link =
➡"http://www.facebook.com/1674990377/posts/4011976152528";
            name = Like;
        }
    );
    comments =          {
        count = 0;
```

```
    };
    "created_time" = "2013-02-10T18:26:44+0000";
    from =              {
        id = 1674990377;
        name = "Kyle Richter";
    };
    id = "1674990377_4011976152528";
    privacy =           {
        value = "";
    };
    "status_type" = "approved_friend";
    story = "Kyle Richter and Kirby Turner are now friends.";
    "story_tags" =             {
        0 =             (
                            {
                id = 1674990377;
                length = 12;
                name = "Kyle Richter";
                offset = 0;
                type = user;
            }
        );
        17 =             (
                            {
                id = 827919293;
                length = 12;
                name = "Kirby Turner";
                offset = 17;
                type = user;
            }
        );
    };
    type = status;
    "updated_time" = "2013-02-10T18:26:44+0000";
},
    {
    comments =          {
        count = 0;
    };
    "created_time" = "2013-01-03T00:58:41+0000";
    from =              {
        id = 1674990377;
        name = "Kyle Richter";
    };
    id = "1674990377_3785554092118";
    privacy =           {
        value = "";
    };
```

```
        story = "Kyle Richter likes a link.";
        "story_tags" =             {
            0 =                    (
                                       {
                    id = 1674990377;
                    length = 12;
                    name = "Kyle Richter";
                    offset = 0;
                    type = user;
                }
            );
        };
        type = status;
        "updated_time" = "2013-01-03T00:58:41+0000";
    },
        {
        application =            {
            id = 6628568379;
            name = "Facebook for iPhone";
            namespace = fbiphone;
        };
        comments =            {
            count = 0;
        };
        "created_time" = "2013-01-02T19:20:59+0000";
        from =            {
            id = 1674990377;
            name = "Kyle Richter";
        };
        id = "1674990377_3784462784836";
        privacy =             {
            value = "";
        };
        story = "\"Congrats!\" on Dan Burcaw's link.";
        "story_tags" =            {
            15 =               (
                                       {
                    id = 10220084;
                    length = 10;
                    name = "Dan Burcaw";
                    offset = 15;
                    type = user;
                }
            );
        };
        type = status;
        "updated_time" = "2013-01-02T19:20:59+0000";
})
```

Summary

This chapter covered the basics of integrating both Twitter and Facebook into an iOS app. Topics ranged from working with the built-in composer to writing highly customized posting engines. In addition, readers learned how to pull down the timeline and feed data and display it for consumption.

Social media integration has never been an easy topic, but with the enhancements made to Social Framework as well as Apple's commitment to bring social intergeneration to more third-party apps, it continues to get easier. The skills required to build a rich social app that includes Twitter and Facebook interaction should now be much clearer.

Exercises

1. Build out the timeline views for both Twitter and Facebook, adding things such as shared images, usernames, dates, and tappable links.

2. Add additional support to Facebook postings such as captions, attached links, location, and tags.

3. Expand the functionality of the sample code by adding support for the user to select which account the user would like to use if they happen to be logged into multiple accounts.

16

Working with Background Tasks

When iOS was first introduced in 2008, only one third-party app at a time could be active—the foreground app. This meant that any tasks that the app needed to complete had to finish while the app was in the foreground being actively used, or those tasks had to be paused and resumed the next time the app was started. With the introduction of iOS 4, background capabilities were added for third-party apps. Since iOS devices have limited system resources and battery preservation is a priority, background processing has some limitations to prevent interference with the foreground app and to prevent using too much power. An app can accomplish a lot with correct usage of backgrounding capabilities. This chapter explains what options are available and how to use them.

There are two approaches to background task processing supported by iOS:

- *The first approach is finishing a long-running task in the background. This method is appropriate for completing things like large downloads or data updates that stretch beyond the time the user spends interacting with the app.*

- *The second approach is supporting very specific types of background activities allowed by iOS, such as playing music, interacting with Bluetooth devices, monitoring the GPS for large changes, or maintaining a persistent network connection to allow VoIP-type apps to work.*

> **Note**
>
> The term "background task" is frequently used interchangeably for two different meanings: executing a task when the app is not in the foreground (described in this chapter), and executing a task asynchronously off the main thread (described in Chapter 17, "Grand Central Dispatch for Performance").

The Sample App

The sample app for this chapter is called BackgroundTasks. This app demonstrates the two backgrounding approaches: completing a long-running task while the app is in the background, and playing audio continuously while the app is in the background. The user interface is very simple—it presents a button to start and stop background music, and a button to start the background task (see Figure 16.1).

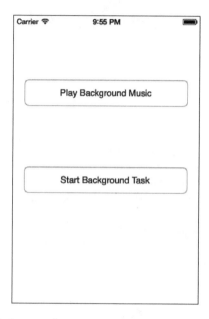

Figure 16.1   BackgroundTasks sample app.

Checking for Background Availability

All devices capable of running iOS 6 or iOS 5 support performing activities in the background, referred to as multitasking in Apple's documentation. If the target app needs to support iOS 4, note that there are a few devices that do not support multitasking. Any code written to take advantage of multitasking should check to ensure that multitasking is supported by the device. When the user taps the Start Background Task button in the sample app, the `startBackgroundTaskTouched:` method in `ICFViewController` will be called to check for multitasking support.

```
- (IBAction)startBackgroundTaskTouched:(id)sender
{
    UIDevice* device = [UIDevice currentDevice];
```

```
if (! [device isMultitaskingSupported])
{
    NSLog(@"Multitasking not supported on this device.");
    return;
}

[self.backgroundButton setEnabled:NO];
NSString *buttonTitle =@"Background Task Running";

[self.backgroundButton setTitle:buttonTitle
                       forState:UIControlStateNormal];

dispatch_queue_t background =
dispatch_get_global_queue(DISPATCH_QUEUE_PRIORITY_DEFAULT, 0);

dispatch_async(background, ^{
    [self performBackgroundTask];
});

}
```

To check for multitasking availability, use the class method `currentDevice` on `UIDevice` to get information about the current device. Then call the `isMultitaskingSupported` method to determine whether multitasking is supported. If multitasking is supported, the user interface is updated and the `performBackgroundTask` method is called asynchronously to start the background task (refer to Chapter 17 for more info on executing tasks asynchronously).

Finishing a Task in the Background

To execute a long-running task in the background, the application needs to be informed that the task should be capable of running in the background. Consideration should also be given to the amount of memory needed for the task, and the total amount of time needed to complete the task. If the task will be longer than 10 to 15 minutes, it is very likely that the app will be terminated before the task can complete. The task logic should be able to handle a quick termination, and be capable of being restarted when the app is relaunched. Apps are given a set amount of time to complete their background tasks, and can be terminated earlier than the given amount of time if the operating system detects that resources are needed.

To see the background task in action, start the sample app as shown in Figure 16.1 from Xcode. Tap the Start Background Task button, and then tap the Home button to exit the app. Observe the console in Xcode to see log statements generated by the app; this will confirm that the app is running in the background.

```
Background task starting, task ID is 1.
Background Processed 0. Still in foreground.
Background Processed 1. Still in foreground.
```

```
Background Processed 2. Still in foreground.
Background Processed 3. Still in foreground.
Background Processed 4. Still in foreground.
Background Processed 5. Still in foreground.
Background Processed 6. Time remaining is: 599.579052
Background Processed 7. Time remaining is: 598.423525
Background Processed 8. Time remaining is: 597.374849
Background Processed 9. Time remaining is: 596.326780
Background Processed 10. Time remaining is: 595.308253
```

The general process to execute a background task is as follows:

- Request a background task identifier from the application, specifying a block as an expiration handler.

  The expiration handler will get called only if the app runs out of background time or the system determines that resource usage is too high and the app should be terminated.

- Perform the background task logic.

  Any code between the request for background task identifier and the background task end will be included.

- Tell the application to end the background task, and invalidate the background task identifier.

Background Task Identifier

To start a task that can complete running in the background, a background task identifier needs to be obtained from the application. The background task identifier helps the application keep track of which tasks are running and which are complete. The background task identifier is needed to tell the application that a task is complete and background processing is no longer required. The performBackgroundTask method in ICFViewController obtains the background task identifier before beginning the work to be done in the background.

```
__block UIBackgroundTaskIdentifier bTask =
[[UIApplication sharedApplication]
beginBackgroundTaskWithExpirationHandler:
^{
    ...
}];
```

When obtaining a background task, an expiration handler block should be specified. The reason the __block modifier is used when declaring the background task identifier is that the background task identifier is needed in the expiration handler block, and needs to be modified in the expiration handler block.

Expiration Handler

The expiration handler for a background task will get called if the operating system decides the app has run out of time and/or resources and needs to be shut down. The expiration handler will get called on the main thread before the app is about to be shut down. Not much time is provided (at most it is a few seconds), so the handler should do a minimal amount of work.

```
__block UIBackgroundTaskIdentifier bTask =
[[UIApplication sharedApplication]
beginBackgroundTaskWithExpirationHandler:
^{
    NSLog(@"Background Expiration Handler called.");
    NSLog(@"Counter is: %d, task ID is %u.",counter,bTask);

    [[UIApplication sharedApplication]
    endBackgroundTask:bTask];

    bTask = UIBackgroundTaskInvalid;
}];
```

The minimum that the expiration handler should do is to tell the application that the background task has ended by calling the `endBackgroundTask:` method on the shared application instance, and invalidate the background task ID by setting the `bTask` variable to `UIBackgroundTaskInvalid` so that it will not inadvertently be used again.

```
Background Processed 570. Time remaining is: 11.482063
Background Processed 571. Time remaining is: 10.436456
Background Processed 572. Time remaining is: 9.394706
Background Processed 573. Time remaining is: 8.346616
Background Processed 574. Time remaining is: 7.308527
Background Processed 575. Time remaining is: 6.260324
Background Processed 576. Time remaining is: 5.212251
Background Expiration Handler called.
Counter is: 577, task ID is 1.
```

Completing the Background Task

After a background task ID has been obtained, the actual work to be done in the background can commence. In the `performBackgroundTask` method some variables are set up to know where to start counting, to keep count of iterations, and to know when to stop. A reference to `NSUserDefaults standardUserDefaults` is established to retrieve the last counter used, and store the last counter with each iteration.

```
NSInteger counter = 0;

NSUserDefaults *userDefaults =
[NSUserDefaults standardUserDefaults];
```

```
NSInteger startCounter =
[userDefaults integerForKey:kLastCounterKey];

NSInteger twentyMins = 20 * 60;
```

The background task for the sample app is trivial—it puts the thread to sleep for a second in a loop to simulate lots of long-running iterations. It stores the current counter for the iteration in NSUserDefaults so that it will be easy to keep track of where it left off if the background task expires. This logic could be modified to handle keeping track of any repetitive background task.

```
NSLog(@"Background task starting, task ID is %u.",bTask);
for (counter = startCounter; counter<=twentyMins; counter++)
{
    [NSThread sleepForTimeInterval:1];
    [userDefaults setInteger:counter
                    forKey:kLastCounterKey];

    [userDefaults synchronize];

    NSTimeInterval remainingTime =
    [[UIApplication sharedApplication] backgroundTimeRemaining];

    NSLog(@"Background Processed %d. Time remaining is: %f",
    counter,remainingTime);
}
```

When each iteration is complete, the time remaining for the background task is obtained from the application. This can be used to determine whether additional iterations of a background task should be started.

Note
The background task is typically expired when there are a few seconds remaining to give it time to wrap up, so any decision to start a new iteration should take that into consideration.

After the background task work is done, the last counter is updated in NSUserDefaults so that it can start over correctly, and the UI is updated to allow the user to start the background task again.

```
NSLog(@"Background Completed tasks");

[userDefaults setInteger:0
                forKey:kLastCounterKey];

[userDefaults synchronize];

dispatch_sync(dispatch_get_main_queue(), ^{
    [self.backgroundButton setEnabled:YES];
```

```
    [self.backgroundButton setTitle:@"Start Background Task"
                           forState:UIControlStateNormal];
});
```

Finally there are two key items that need to take place to finish the background task: tell the application to end the background task, and invalidate the background task identifier. Every line of code between obtaining the background task ID and ending it will execute in the background.

```
[[UIApplication sharedApplication] endBackgroundTask:self.backgroundTask];

self.backgroundTask = UIBackgroundTaskInvalid;
```

Implementing Background Activities

iOS supports a very specific set of background activities that can continue processing without the limitations of the background task identifier approach. These activities can continue running or being available without a time limit, and need to avoid using too many system resources to keep the app from getting terminated.

Types of Background Activities

These are the background activities:

- Playing background audio
- Tracking device location
- Supporting a Voice over IP app
- Downloading new Newsstand app content
- Communication with an external or Bluetooth accessory
- Fetching content in the background
- Initiating a background download with a push notification

To support any of these background activities, the app needs to declare which background activities it supports in the Info.plist file. To do this, select the app target in Xcode, and select the Capabilities tab. Turn "Background Modes" to On, then check the desired modes to support. Xcode will add the entries to the Info.plist file for you. Or, edit the Info.plist file directly by selecting the app target in Xcode, then select the Info tab. Look for the Required Background Modes entry in the list; if it is not present, hover over an existing entry and click the plus sign to add a new entry, and then select Required Background Modes. An array entry will be added with one empty NSString item. Select the desired background mode, as shown in Figure 16.2.

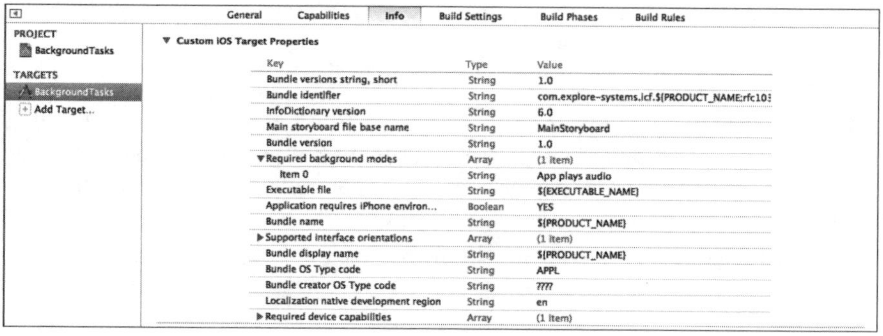

Figure 16.2   Xcode's Info editor showing required background modes.

After the Required Background Modes entry is established, activity-specific logic can be built into the app and it will function when the app is in the background.

Playing Music in the Background

To play music in the background, the first step is to adjust the audio session settings for the app. By default, an app uses the AVAudioSessionCategorySoloAmbient audio session category. This ensures that other audio is turned off when the app is started, and that the app audio is silenced when the screen is locked or the ring/silent switch on the device is set to silent. This session will not work, since audio will be silenced when the screen is locked or when another app is brought to the foreground. The viewDidLoad method in ICFViewController adjusts the audio session category to AVAudioSessionCategoryPlayback, which will ensure that the audio will continue playing when the app is in the background or the ring/silent switch is set to silent.

```
AVAudioSession *session = [AVAudioSession sharedInstance];

NSError *activeError = nil;
if (![session setActive:YES error:&activeError])
{
    NSLog(@"Failed to set active audio session!");
}


NSError *categoryError = nil;
if (![session setCategory:AVAudioSessionCategoryPlayback
                error:&categoryError])
{
    NSLog(@"Failed to set audio category!");
}
```

The next step in playing audio is to initialize an audio player. This is also done in the `viewDidLoad` method so that the audio player is ready whenever the user indicates that audio should be played.

```
NSError *playerInitError = nil;

NSString *audioPath =
[[NSBundle mainBundle] pathForResource:@"16_audio"
                               ofType:@"mp3"];

NSURL *audioURL = [NSURL fileURLWithPath:audioPath];

self.audioPlayer = [[AVAudioPlayer alloc]
                    initWithContentsOfURL:audioURL
                    error:&playerInitError];
```

The Play Background Music button is wired to the `playBackgroundMusicTouched:` method. When the user taps that button, the logic checks to see whether audio is currently playing. If audio is currently playing, the method stops the audio and updates the title of the button.

```
if ([self.audioPlayer isPlaying])
{
    [self.audioPlayer stop];

    [self.audioButton setTitle:@"Play Background Music"
                      forState:UIControlStateNormal];

}
else
{ ...
}
```

If music is not currently playing, the method starts the audio and changes the title of the button.

```
[self.audioPlayer play];

[self.audioButton setTitle:@"Stop Background Music"
                  forState:UIControlStateNormal];
```

While the audio is playing, the user can press the lock button on the device or the home button to background the app, and the audio will continue playing. A really nice feature when audio is playing and the screen is locked is to display the currently playing information on the lock screen. To do this, first set up a dictionary with information about the playing media.

```
UIImage *lockImage = [UIImage imageNamed:@"book_cover"];

MPMediaItemArtwork *artwork =
[[MPMediaItemArtwork alloc] initWithImage:lockImage];
```

```
NSDictionary *mediaDict =
@{
    MPMediaItemPropertyTitle: @"BackgroundTask Audio",
    MPMediaItemPropertyMediaType: @(MPMediaTypeAnyAudio),
    MPMediaItemPropertyPlaybackDuration:
    @(self.audioPlayer.duration),
    MPNowPlayingInfoPropertyPlaybackRate: @1.0,
    MPNowPlayingInfoPropertyElapsedPlaybackTime:
    @(self.audioPlayer.currentTime),
    MPMediaItemPropertyAlbumArtist: @"Some User",
    MPMediaItemPropertyArtist: @"Some User",
    MPMediaItemPropertyArtwork: artwork };
```

There are a number of options that can be set. Note that a title and an image are specified; these will be displayed on the lock screen. The duration and current time are provided and can be displayed at the media player's discretion, depending on the state of the device and the context in which it will be displayed. After the media information is established, the method starts the audio player, then informs the media player's MPNowPlayingInfoCenter about the playing media item info. It sets self to be the first responder, since the media player's info center requires the view or view controller playing audio to be the first responder in order to work correctly. It tells the app to start responding to "remote control" events, which will allow the lock screen controls to control the audio in the app with delegate methods implemented.

```
[[MPNowPlayingInfoCenter defaultCenter]
 setNowPlayingInfo:mediaDict];

[self becomeFirstResponder];

[[UIApplication sharedApplication]
 beginReceivingRemoteControlEvents];
```

Now when the audio is playing in the background, the lock screen will display information about it, as shown in Figure 16.3.

In addition, the Control Center will display information about the audio, as shown in Figure 16.4.

Figure 16.3   Lock screen showing sample app playing background audio.

Figure 16.4   Lock screen control center showing sample app playing background audio.

Summary

This chapter illuminated two approaches to executing tasks while the app is in the background, or while it is not the current app that the user is interacting with.

The first approach to background task processing described was finishing a long-running task in the background. The sample app demonstrated how to check whether the device is capable of running a background task, showed how to set up and execute a background task, and explained how to handle the case when iOS terminates the app and notifies the background task that it will be ended (or expired).

The second approach to background tasks described was supporting very specific types of background activities allowed by iOS, like playing music, interacting with Bluetooth devices, monitoring the GPS for large changes, or maintaining a persistent network connection to allow VoIP-type apps to work. The chapter explained how to configure an Xcode project to allow a background activity to take place, and then the sample app demonstrated how to play audio in the background while displaying information about the audio on the lock screen.

Exercises

1. Enhance the background task processing to download a series of images, or download and process a large JSON file in the background.

2. Add the capability to monitor the GPS for large location changes while the app is in the background, and log the changes as they happen. Refer to Chapter 2, "Core Location, MapKit, and Geofencing," for more information on location information.

3. Update the audio handling to support the controls shown on the lock screen and Control Center. Hint: Implement the `remoteControlReceivedWithEvent:` method in the view controller that becomes the first responder.

Grand Central Dispatch for Performance

Many apps have challenging performance requirements, involving multiple processor-intensive and high-latency tasks that need to take place simultaneously. This chapter demonstrates the negative effects of blocking the main queue, which makes the user interface slow or completely unusable—not at all desirable for a good user experience. It then examines tools supported by iOS that allow the programmer to perform tasks "in the background," meaning that a processing task will take place and not directly delay updating the user interface. Apple provides several tools with varying degrees of control over how background tasks are accomplished.

Concurrent programming is frequently done using threads. It can be very challenging to get the desired performance improvements from a multicore device by managing threads directly in an app, because effective thread management requires real-time monitoring and management of system resources and usage. To address this problem, Apple introduced Grand Central Dispatch, or GCD. GCD manages queues, which are an abstracted level above threads. Queues can operate concurrently or serially, and can automatically handle thread management and optimization at a system level.

This chapter introduces several approaches to background processing of long-running tasks, and highlights the benefits and drawbacks of each.

The Sample App

The sample app is called LongRunningTasks. It will demonstrate a trivial long-running task on the main thread, and then several different techniques for handling the same long-running task off the main thread. The trivial long-running tasks are five loops to add 10 items each with a time delay to an array, which can then be displayed in a table view. The sample app has a table view, which will present a list of the available approaches. Selecting an approach will present a table view for the approach. The table view has 5 starting items, so it is clear when attempting to scroll whether the main thread is being interrupted by the long-running task. The long-running tasks will then create 50 more items in batches of 10 to display in the table view. The table view will be notified upon completion to update the UI on the main thread, and the new items will appear.

The sample app (as shown in Figure 17.1) will illustrate the following techniques:

- **performSelectorInBackground:withObject:** This is the simplest approach to running code off the main thread and it works well when the task has simple and straightforward requirements. The system does not perform any additional management of tasks performed this way, so this is best suited to nonrepetitive tasks.

- **NSOperationQueue:** This is a slightly more complex method to running code off the main thread, and it provides some additional control capabilities, like running serially, concurrently, or with dependencies between tasks. Operation queues are implemented with and are a higher level of abstraction of GCD queues. Operation queues are best suited to repetitive, well-defined asynchronous tasks; for example, network calls or parsing.

- **GCD Queues:** This is the most "low-level" approach to running code off the main thread, and it provides the most flexibility. The sample app will demonstrate running tasks serially and concurrently using GCD queues. GCD can be used for anything from just communicating between the background and the main queue, to quickly performing a block of code for each item in a list, to processing large, repetitive asynchronous tasks.

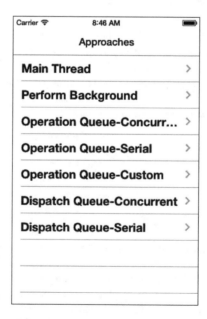

Figure 17.1   Sample app, long-running task approach list.

Introduction to Queues

Some of the terminology related to concurrent processing can be a bit confusing. A "thread" is a commonly used term; in the context of an iOS app, a thread is a standard POSIX thread. Technically, a thread is just a set of instructions that can be handled independently within a process (an app is a process), and multiple threads can exist within a process, sharing memory and resources. Since threads function independently, work can be split across threads to get it done more quickly. It is also possible to run into problems when multiple threads need access to the same resource or data. All iOS apps have a main thread that handles the run loop and updating the UI. For an app to remain responsive to user interaction, the main thread must be given only tasks that can be completed in less than 1/60 of a second.

A "queue" is a term that Apple uses to describe the contexts provided by Grand Central Dispatch. A queue is managed by GCD as a group of tasks to be executed. Depending on the current system utilization, GCD will dynamically determine the right number of threads to use to process the tasks in a queue. The main queue is a special queue managed by GCD that is associated with the main thread. So when you run a task on the main queue, GCD executes that task on the main thread.

People will frequently toss around the terms "thread" and "queue" interchangeably; just remember that a queue is really just a managed set of threads, and "main" is just referring to the thread that handles the main run loop and UI.

Running on the Main Thread

Run the sample app and select the row called Main Thread. Notice that the five initial items in the table view are initially visible, but they cannot be scrolled and the UI is completely unresponsive while the additional items are being added. There is logging to demonstrate that the additional items are being added while the UI is frozen—view the debugging console while running the app to see the logging. The frozen UI is obviously not a desirable user experience, and it is unfortunately easy to get a situation like this to happen in an app. To see why this is happening, take a look at the ICFMainThreadLongRunningTaskViewController class. First, the array to store display data is set up and given an initial set of data:

```
- (void)viewDidLoad
{
    [super viewDidLoad];

    self.displayItems =
    [[NSMutableArray alloc] initWithCapacity:45];

    [self.displayItems addObject:@[@"Item Initial-1",
    @"Item Initial-2",@"Item Initial-3",
    @"Item Initial-4",@"Item Initial-5"]];

}
```

After the initial data is set up and the view is visible, the long-running task is started:

```
- (void)viewDidAppear:(BOOL)animated
{
    [super viewDidAppear:animated];

    for (int i=1; i<=5; i++)
    {
        NSNumber *iteration = [NSNumber numberWithInt:i];
        [self performLongRunningTaskForIteration:iteration];
    }
}
```

The app is calling the `performLongRunningTaskForIteration:` method five times to set up additional table data. This does not appear to be doing anything that would slow down the main thread. Examine the `performLongRunningTaskForIteration:` method to see what is hanging the main thread. The intention is for the long-running task to add ten items to an array, which will then be added to the `displayItems` array, which is the data source for the table view.

```
- (void)performLongRunningTaskForIteration:(id)iteration
{
    NSNumber *iterationNumber = (NSNumber *)iteration;

    NSMutableArray *newArray =
    [[NSMutableArray alloc] initWithCapacity:10];

    for (int i=1; i<=10; i++)
    {

        [newArray addObject:
        [NSString stringWithFormat:@"Item %@-%d",
        iterationNumber,i]];

        [NSThread sleepForTimeInterval:.1];

        NSLog(@"Main Added %@-%d",iterationNumber,i);
    }

    [self.displayItems addObject:newArray];
    [self.tableView reloadData];
}
```

Since the main thread is responsible for keeping the user interface updated, any activity that takes longer than 1/60 of a second can result in noticeable delays. In this case, notice that the method is calling `sleepForTimeInterval:` on `NSThread` for every iteration. Obviously, this is not something that would make sense to do in a typical app, but it clearly illustrates the point that a single method call that takes a little bit of time and blocks the main thread can cause severe performance issues.

> **Note**
>
> Finding the method calls that take up an appreciable amount of time is rarely as clear as this example. Refer to Chapter 25, "Debugging and Instruments," for techniques to discover where performance issues are taking place.

In this case, the `sleepForTimeInterval:` method call is quickly and frequently blocking the main thread, so even after the `for` loop is complete, the main thread does not have enough time to update the UI until all the calls to `performLongRunningTaskForIteration:` are complete.

Running in the Background

Run the sample app, and select the row called Perform Background. Notice that the five initial items in the table view are initially visible, and they are scrollable while the long-running tasks are being processed (view the debugging console to confirm that they are being processed while scrolling the table view). After the tasks are completed, the additional rows become visible.

This approach sets up the initial data in exactly the same way as the Main Thread approach. View `ICFPerformBackgroundViewController` in the sample app source code to see how it is set up. After the initial data is set up and the view is visible, the long-running task is started; this is where performing the task in the background is specified.

```
- (void)viewDidAppear:(BOOL)animated
{
    [super viewDidAppear:animated];

    SEL taskSelector =
    @selector(performLongRunningTaskForIteration:);

    for (int i=1; i<=5; i++)
    {

        NSNumber *iteration = [NSNumber numberWithInt:i];

        [self performSelectorIn Background:taskSelector
                            withObject:iteration];

    }
}
```

A selector is set up; this is just the name of the method to perform in the background. `NSObject` defines the method `performSelectorInBackground:withObject:`, which requires an Objective-C object to be passed as the parameter `withObject:`. This method will spawn a

new thread, execute the method with the passed parameter in that new thread, and return to
the calling thread immediately. This new thread is the developer's responsibility to manage, so
it is entirely possible to create too many new threads and overwhelm the system. If testing indicates that this is a problem, an operation queue or dispatch queue (both described later in the
chapter) can be used to provide more precise control over the execution of the tasks and better
management of system resources.

The method `performLongRunningTaskForIteration:` performs exactly the same task as in
the Main Thread approach; however, instead of adding the `newArray` to the `displayItems`
array directly, the method calls the `updateTableData:` method using `NSObject`'s method
`performSelectorOnMainThread:withObject:waitUntilDone:`. Using that approach is
necessary for two reasons. First, UIKit objects, including our table view, will update the UI
only if they are updated on the main thread. Second, the property `displayItems` is declared
as `nonatomic`, meaning that the getter and setter methods generated are not thread-safe. That
could be "fixed" by declaring the `displayItems` property `atomic`, but that would add some
performance overhead to lock the array before updating it. If the property is updated on the
main thread, locking is not required.

```
- (void)performLongRunningTaskForIteration:(id)iteration
{
    NSNumber *iterationNumber = (NSNumber *)iteration;

    NSMutableArray *newArray =
    [[NSMutableArray alloc] initWithCapacity:10];

    for (int i=1; i<=10; i++)
    {

        [newArray addObject:
         [NSString stringWithFormat:@"Item %@-%d",
          iterationNumber,i]];

        [NSThread sleepForTimeInterval:.1];

        NSLog(@"Background Added %@-%d",iterationNumber,i);
    }

    [self performSelectorOnMainThread:@selector(updateTableData:)
                           withObject:newArray
                        waitUntilDone:NO];
}
```

The `updateTableData:` method simply adds the newly created items to the `displayItems`
array and informs the table view to reload and update the UI.

An interesting side effect is that the order in which the additional rows are added is not deterministic—it will potentially be different every time the app is run.

```
10:51:09.324 LongRunningTasks[29382:15903] Background Added 3-1
10:51:09.324 LongRunningTasks[29382:16303] Background Added 5-1
10:51:09.324 LongRunningTasks[29382:15207] Background Added 1-1
10:51:09.324 LongRunningTasks[29382:15e03] Background Added 4-1
10:51:09.324 LongRunningTasks[29382:15107] Background Added 2-1
10:51:09.430 LongRunningTasks[29382:15207] Background Added 1-2
10:51:09.430 LongRunningTasks[29382:16303] Background Added 5-2
10:51:09.430 LongRunningTasks[29382:15e03] Background Added 4-2
10:51:09.430 LongRunningTasks[29382:15107] Background Added 2-2
10:51:09.430 LongRunningTasks[29382:15903] Background Added 3-2
. . .
```

This is a symptom of the fact that using this technique makes no promises about when a task will be completed or in what order it will be processed, since the tasks are all performed on different threads. If the order of operation is not important, this technique can be just fine; if order matters, an operation queue or dispatch queue is needed to process the tasks serially (both described later, in the sections "Serial Operations" and "Serial Dispatch Queues").

Running in an Operation Queue

Operation queues (NSOperationQueue) are available to manage a set of tasks or operations (NSOperation). An operation queue can specify how many operations can run concurrently, can be suspended and restarted, and can cancel all pending operations. Operations can be a simple method invocation, a block, or a custom operation class. Operations can have dependencies established to make them run serially. Operations and operation queues are actually managed by Grand Central Dispatch, and are implemented with dispatch queues.

The sample app illustrates three approaches using an operation queue: concurrent operations, serial operations with dependencies, and custom operations to support cancellation.

Concurrent Operations

Run the sample app, and select the row called Operation Queue-Concurrent. The five initial items in the table view are visible, and they are scrollable while the long-running tasks are being processed (view the debugging console to confirm that they are being processed while scrolling the table view). After the tasks are completed, the additional rows become visible.

Examine the ICFOperationQueueConcurrentViewController in the sample app source code to see how this approach is set up. Before operations are added, the operation queue needs to be set up in the viewDidLoad: method:

```
self.processingQueue = [[NSOperationQueue alloc] init];
```

This approach sets up the initial data in exactly the same way as the Main Thread approach. After the initial data is set up and the view is visible, the long-running tasks are added to the operation queue as instances of NSInvocationOperation:

```
- (void)viewDidAppear:(BOOL)animated
{
    [super viewDidAppear:animated];

    SEL taskSelector =
    @selector(performLongRunningTaskForIteration:);

    for (int i=1; i<=5; i++)
    {

        NSNumber *iteration = [NSNumber numberWithInt:i];

        NSInvocationOperation *operation =
        [[NSInvocationOperation alloc] initWithTarget:self
        selector:taskSelector object:iteration];

        [operation setCompletionBlock:^{
            NSLog(@"Operation #%d completed.",i);
        }];

        [self.processingQueue addOperation:operation];
    }
}
```

Each operation is assigned a completion block that will run when the operation is finished processing. The method performLongRunningTaskForIteration: performs exactly the same task as in the Perform Background approach; in fact, the method is not changed in this approach. The updateTableData: method is also not changed. The results will be very similar to the Perform Background approach in that the items will not be added in a deterministic order.

```
21:00:16.165 LongRunningTasks[31009] OpQ Concurrent Added 1-1
21:00:16.165 LongRunningTasks[31009] OpQ Concurrent Added 3-1
21:00:16.165 LongRunningTasks[31009] OpQ Concurrent Added 4-1
21:00:16.165 LongRunningTasks[31009] OpQ Concurrent Added 2-1
21:00:16.165 LongRunningTasks[31009] OpQ Concurrent Added 5-1
...
21:00:17.107 LongRunningTasks[31009] Operation #4 completed.
21:00:17.108 LongRunningTasks[31009] Operation #2 completed.
21:00:17.107 LongRunningTasks[31009] Operation #5 completed.
21:00:17.108 LongRunningTasks[31009] Operation #3 completed.
21:00:17.109 LongRunningTasks[31009] Operation #1 completed.
```

The main difference here is that the NSOperationQueue is managing the threads, and will process only up to the default maximum concurrent operations for the queue. This can be very important when your app has many different competing tasks that need to happen concurrently and need to be managed to avoid overloading the system.

> **Note**
>
> The default maximum concurrent operations for an operation queue is a dynamic number deter-mined in real time by the system. It can vary based on the current system load. The maximum number of operations can also be specified for an operation queue, in which case the queue will process only up to the specified number of operations simultaneously.

Serial Operations

Visit the sample app, and select the row called Operation Queue-Serial. The five initial items in the table view are visible, and they are scrollable while the long-running tasks are being processed (view the debugging console to confirm that they are being processed while scrolling the table view). After the tasks are completed, the additional rows become visible.

The setups of the initial data and operation queue are identical to the Operation Queue-Concurrent approach. To have the operations process serially in the correct order, they need to be set up with dependencies. To accomplish this task, the `viewDidAppear:` method adds an array to store the operations as they are created, and an `NSInvocationOperation` (`prevOperation`) to track the previous operation created.

```
NSMutableArray *operationsToAdd = [[NSMutableArray alloc] init];

NSInvocationOperation *prevOperation = nil;
```

While the operations are being created, the method keeps track of the previously created opera-tion. The newly created operation adds a dependency to the previous operation so that it cannot run until the previous operation completes. The new operation is added to the array of operations to add to the queue.

```
for (int i=1; i<=5; i++)
{

    NSNumber *iteration = [NSNumber numberWithInt:i];

    NSInvocationOperation *operation =
    [[NSInvocationOperation alloc] initWithTarget:self
    selector:taskSelector object:iteration];

    if (prevOperation)
    {
        [operation addDependency:prevOperation];
    }

    [operationsToAdd addObject:operation];

    prevOperation = operation;
}
```

After all the operations are created and added to the array, they are added to the queue. Because an operation will start executing as soon as it is added to an operation queue, the operations need to be added all at once to ensure that the queue can respect the dependencies.

```
for (NSInvocationOperation *operation in operationsToAdd)
{
    [self.processingQueue addOperation:operation];
}
```

The operation queue will analyze the added operations and dependencies, and determine the optimum order in which to execute them. Observe the debugging console to see that the operations execute in the correct order serially.

```
16:51:45.216 LongRunningTasks[29554:15507] OpQ Serial Added 1-1
16:51:45.318 LongRunningTasks[29554:15507] OpQ Serial Added 1-2
16:51:45.420 LongRunningTasks[29554:15507] OpQ Serial Added 1-3
16:51:45.522 LongRunningTasks[29554:15507] OpQ Serial Added 1-4
16:51:45.625 LongRunningTasks[29554:15507] OpQ Serial Added 1-5
16:51:45.728 LongRunningTasks[29554:15507] OpQ Serial Added 1-6
16:51:45.830 LongRunningTasks[29554:15507] OpQ Serial Added 1-7
16:51:45.931 LongRunningTasks[29554:15507] OpQ Serial Added 1-8
16:51:46.034 LongRunningTasks[29554:15507] OpQ Serial Added 1-9
16:51:46.137 LongRunningTasks[29554:15507] OpQ Serial Added 1-10
16:51:46.246 LongRunningTasks[29554:14e0b] OpQ Serial Added 2-1
16:51:46.349 LongRunningTasks[29554:14e0b] OpQ Serial Added 2-2
16:51:46.452 LongRunningTasks[29554:14e0b] OpQ Serial Added 2-3
16:51:46.554 LongRunningTasks[29554:14e0b] OpQ Serial Added 2-4
16:51:46.657 LongRunningTasks[29554:14e0b] OpQ Serial Added 2-5
16:51:46.765 LongRunningTasks[29554:14e0b] OpQ Serial Added 2-6
...
```

The serial approach increases the total amount of time needed to complete all the tasks, but successfully ensures that the tasks execute in the correct order.

Canceling Operations

Back in the sample app, select the row called Operation Queue-Concurrent. Quickly tap the Cancel button at the top of the table while the operations are running. Notice that nothing appears to happen after the Cancel button has been tapped, and the operations will finish. When the Cancel button is touched, the operation queue is instructed to cancel all outstanding operations:

```
- (IBAction)cancelButtonTouched:(id)sender
{
    [self.processingQueue cancelAllOperations];
}
```

The reason this does not work as expected is because Cancelled is just a flag on an operation object—the logic of the operation must dictate how the operation behaves when it is canceled. The call to cancelAllOperations: dutifully sets the flag on all the outstanding operations, and since they are not checking their own cancellation status while running, they proceed until they complete their tasks.

To properly handle cancellation, a subclass of NSOperation must be created, or a weak reference to an instance of NSBlockOperation must be checked like so:

```
NSBlockOperation *blockOperation =
        [[NSBlockOperation alloc] init];

__weak NSBlockOperation *blockOperationRef = blockOperation;
[blockOperation addExecutionBlock:^{
    if (![blockOperationRef isCancelled])
    {
        NSLog(@"...not canceled, execute logic here");
    }
}];
```

In the next section, creating a custom NSOperation subclass with cancellation handling is discussed.

Custom Operations

Return to the sample app, and select the row called Operation Queue-Custom. The five initial items in the table view are visible, and they are scrollable while the long-running tasks are being processed (view the debuggving console to confirm that they are being processed while scrolling the table view). Quickly hit the Cancel button at the top of the table before the operations complete. Notice that this time the tasks stop immediately.

The setups of the initial data and operation queue are nearly identical to the Operation Queue-Serial approach. The only difference is the use of a custom NSOperation subclass called ICFCustomOperation:

```
- (void)viewDidAppear:(BOOL)animated
{
    [super viewDidAppear:animated];

    NSMutableArray *operationsToAdd =
    [[NSMutableArray alloc] init];

    ICFCustomOperation *prevOperation = nil;
    for (int i=1; i<=5; i++)
    {

        NSNumber *iteration = [NSNumber numberWithInt:i];
```

```
            ICFCustomOperation *operation =
            [[ICFCustomOperation alloc] initWithIteration:iteration
                                        andDelegate:self];

            if (prevOperation)
            {
                [operation addDependency:prevOperation];
            }

            [operationsToAdd addObject:operation];

            prevOperation = operation;
        }

        for (ICFCustomOperation *operation in operationsToAdd)
        {
            [self.processingQueue addOperation:operation];
        }
    }
```

ICFCustomOperation is declared as a subclass of NSOperation, and declares a protocol so that it can inform a delegate that processing is complete and pass back the results.

```
@protocol ICFCustomOperationDelegate <NSObject>

- (void)updateTableWithData:(NSArray *)moreData;

@end
```

An NSOperation subclass needs to implement the main method. This is where the processing logic for the operation should go:

```
- (void)main
{
    NSMutableArray *newArray =
    [[NSMutableArray alloc] initWithCapacity:10];

    for (int i=1; i<=10; i++)
    {

        if ([self isCancelled])
        {
            break;
        }

        [newArray addObject:
         [NSString stringWithFormat:@"Item %@-%d",
          self.iteration,i]];
```

```
        [NSThread sleepForTimeInterval:.1];
        NSLog(@"OpQ Custom Added %@-%d",self.iteration,i);
    }

    [self.delegate updateTableWithData:newArray];
}
```

At the beginning of the `for` loop, the cancellation status is checked:

```
if ([self isCancelled])
{
    break;
}
```

This check allows the operation to respond immediately to a cancellation request. When designing a custom operation, give careful consideration to how cancellations should be processed, and whether any rollback logic is required.

Properly handling cancellations is not the only benefit to creating a custom operation subclass; it is a very effective way to encapsulate complex logic in a way that can be run in an operation queue.

Running in a Dispatch Queue

Dispatch queues are provided by Grand Central Dispatch to execute blocks of code in a managed environment. GCD is designed to maximize concurrency and take full advantage of multicore processing power by managing the number of threads allocated to a queue dynamically based on the status of the system.

GCD offers three types of queues: the main queue, concurrent queues, and serial queues. The main queue is a special queue created by the system, which is tied to the application's main thread. In iOS, three concurrent queues are available: the high-, normal-, and low-priority queues. Serial queues can be created by the application and must be managed like any other application resource. The sample app demonstrates using concurrent and serial GCD queues, and how to interact with the main queue from those queues.

Note

As of iOS 6, created dispatch queues are managed by ARC, and do not need to be retained or released.

Concurrent Dispatch Queues

Open the sample app, and select the row called Dispatch Queue-Concurrent. The five initial items in the table view are visible, and they are scrollable while the long-running tasks are being processed (view the debugging console to confirm that they are being processed while scrolling the table view). After the tasks are completed, the additional rows become visible. Notice that this approach completes significantly faster than any of the previous approaches.

To start the long-running tasks in the `viewDidAppear:` method, the app gets a reference to the high-priority concurrent dispatch queue:

```
dispatch_queue_t workQueue =
dispatch_get_global_queue(DISPATCH_QUEUE_PRIORITY_HIGH, 0);
```

Using `dispatch_get_global_queue` provides access to the three global, system-maintained concurrent dispatch queues. References to these queues do not need to be retained or released. After a reference to the queue is available, logic can be submitted to it for execution inside a block.

```
for (int i=1; i<=5; i++)
{

    NSNumber *iteration = [NSNumber numberWithInt:i];

    dispatch_async(workQueue, ^{
        [self performLongRunningTaskForIteration:iteration];
    });
}
```

The use of `dispatch_async` indicates that the logic should be performed asynchronously. In that case, the work in the block will be submitted to the queue, and the call to do that will return immediately without blocking the main thread. Blocks can also be submitted to the queue synchronously using `dispatch_sync`, which will cause the calling thread to wait until the block has completed processing.

In the `performLongRunningTaskForIteration:` method, there are a few differences from previous approaches that need to be highlighted. The `newArray` used to keep track of created items needs a `__block` modifier so that the block can update it.

```
__block NSMutableArray *newArray =
[[NSMutableArray alloc] initWithCapacity:10];
```

The method then gets a reference to the low-priority concurrent dispatch queue.

```
dispatch_queue_t detailQueue =
dispatch_get_global_queue(DISPATCH_QUEUE_PRIORITY_LOW, 0);
```

The low-priority dispatch queue is then used for a powerful GCD technique: processing an entire enumeration simultaneously.

```
dispatch_apply(10, detailQueue, ^(size_t i)
{
    [NSThread sleepForTimeInterval:.1];
```

```
        [newArray addObject:[NSString stringWithFormat:
                            @"Item %@-%zu",iterationNumber,i+1]];

        NSLog(@"Dispatch Q Added %@-%zu",iterationNumber,i+1);
});
```

With `dispatch_apply`, all that is needed is a number of iterations, a reference to a dispatch queue, a variable to express which iteration is being processed (it must be `size_t`), and a block to be processed for each iteration. GCD will fill the queue with all the possible iterations, and they will be processed as close to simultaneously as possible, within the constraints of the system. This is the technique that allows this approach to process so much more quickly than the other approaches, and it can be very effective if order is not important.

> ### Note
> There are methods on collection classes that can achieve a similar effect at a higher level of abstraction. For example, `NSArray` has a method called `enumerateObjectsWithOptions: usingBlock:`. This method can enumerate the objects in an array serially, serially in reverse, or concurrently.

After the iterations are complete and the array of new items has been created, the method needs to inform the UI to update the table view.

```
dispatch_async(dispatch_get_main_queue(), ^{
    [self updateTableData:newArray];
});
```

This `dispatch_async` call uses the function `dispatch_get_main_queue` to access the main queue. Note that this technique can be used from anywhere to get to the main queue, and can be a very handy way to update the UI to report status on long-running tasks.

Serial Dispatch Queues

Run the sample app, and select the row called Dispatch Queue-Serial. The five initial items in the table view are visible, and they are scrollable while the long-running tasks are being processed (view the debugging console to confirm that they are being processed while scrolling the table view). After the tasks are completed, the additional rows become visible. This approach is not as fast as the Concurrent Dispatch Queue approach, but it will process the items in the order in which they are added to the queue.

To start the long-running tasks in the `viewDidAppear:` method, the app creates a serial dispatch queue:

```
dispatch_queue_t workQueue =
dispatch_queue_create("com.icf.serialqueue", NULL);
```

Blocks of work can be added to the serial queue asynchronously:

```
for (int i=1; i<=5; i++)
{

    NSNumber *iteration = [NSNumber numberWithInt:i];

    dispatch_async(workQueue, ^{
        [self performLongRunningTaskForIteration:iteration];
    });
}
```

The method performLongRunningTaskForIteration: performs exactly the same task as in the Main Thread, Perform Background, and Concurrent Operation Queue approach; however, the method calls the updateTableData: method using dispatch_async to the main queue.

```
- (void)performLongRunningTaskForIteration:(id)iteration
{
    NSNumber *iterationNumber = (NSNumber *)iteration;

    NSMutableArray *newArray =
    [[NSMutableArray alloc] initWithCapacity:10];

    for (int i=1; i<=10; i++)
    {

        [newArray addObject:[NSString stringWithFormat:
                            @"Item %@-%d",iterationNumber,i]];

        [NSThread sleepForTimeInterval:.1];
        NSLog(@"DispQ Serial Added %@-%d",iterationNumber,i);
    }

    dispatch_async(dispatch_get_main_queue(), ^{
        [self updateTableData:newArray];
    });
}
```

The serial dispatch queue will execute the long-running tasks in the order in which they are added to the queue, first in, first out. The debugging console will show that the operations execute in the correct order.

```
20:41:00.340 LongRunningTasks[30650:] DispQ Serial Added 1-1
20:41:00.444 LongRunningTasks[30650:] DispQ Serial Added 1-2
20:41:00.546 LongRunningTasks[30650:] DispQ Serial Added 1-3
20:41:00.648 LongRunningTasks[30650:] DispQ Serial Added 1-4
20:41:00.751 LongRunningTasks[30650:] DispQ Serial Added 1-5
```

```
20:41:00.852 LongRunningTasks[30650:] DispQ Serial Added 1-6
20:41:00.955 LongRunningTasks[30650:] DispQ Serial Added 1-7
20:41:01.056 LongRunningTasks[30650:] DispQ Serial Added 1-8
20:41:01.158 LongRunningTasks[30650:] DispQ Serial Added 1-9
20:41:01.261 LongRunningTasks[30650:] DispQ Serial Added 1-10
20:41:01.363 LongRunningTasks[30650:] DispQ Serial Added 2-1
20:41:01.465 LongRunningTasks[30650:] DispQ Serial Added 2-2
20:41:01.568 LongRunningTasks[30650:] DispQ Serial Added 2-3
20:41:01.671 LongRunningTasks[30650:] DispQ Serial Added 2-4
20:41:01.772 LongRunningTasks[30650:] DispQ Serial Added 2-5
...
```

Again, the serial approach increases the total amount of time needed to complete all the tasks, but successfully ensures that the tasks execute in the correct order. Using a dispatch queue to process tasks serially is simpler than managing dependencies in an operation queue, but does not offer the same high-level management options.

Summary

This chapter introduced several techniques to process long-running tasks without interfering with the UI, including `performSelectorInBackground:withObject:`, operation queues, and Grand Central Dispatch queues.

Using the `performSelectorInBackground:withObject:` method on `NSObject` to execute a task in the background is the simplest approach, but provides the least support and management.

Operation queues can process tasks concurrently or serially, using a method call, a block, or a custom operation class. Operation queues can be managed by specifying a maximum number of concurrent operations, they can be suspended and resumed, and all the outstanding operations can be canceled. Operation queues can handle custom operation classes. Operation queues are implemented by Grand Central Dispatch.

Dispatch queues can also process tasks concurrently or serially. There are three global concurrent queues, and applications can create their own serial queues. Dispatch queues accept blocks to be executed, and can execute blocks synchronously or asynchronously.

None of these techniques is described as "the best," because each technique has pros and cons relative to the requirements of an application, and testing should be done to understand which technique is most appropriate.

Exercises

1. Compare the thread handling of the Perform Background, Operation Queue-Concurrent, and Dispatch Queue-Concurrent approaches by cranking up the number of tasks to be performed from 5 to 100, and determine how that affects UI responsiveness and the total time to complete all the tasks by approach.

2. Replace the trivial long-running task with a real task, like parsing lots of JSON files or some image processing. Determine which approach is most effective for the type of task selected.

18

Using Keychain to Secure Data

Securing sensitive user data is a critical and often-overlooked step of software development. The technology news is constantly plagued by stories of large companies storing password or credit card information in plain text. Users put their trust in developers to treat sensitive information with the care and respect it deserves. This includes encrypting local copies of that information to prevent unauthorized access. It is the duty of every developer to treat users' data as they would like their own secure information to be handled.

Apple has provided a security framework called Keychain to store encrypted information on an iOS device. The Keychain also has several additional benefits beyond standard application and data security. Information stored in the Keychain persists even after an app has been deleted from the device, and Keychain information can even be shared among multiple apps by the same developer.

This chapter demonstrates the use of Apple's KeychainItemWrapper *class to secure and retrieve sensitive information. Although it is completely acceptable and occasionally required to write a Keychain wrapper from the ground up, leveraging Apple's libraries can be a tremendous timesaver and will often provide all the functionality required. This chapter does not cover creating a custom Keychain wrapper class but leverages Apple's provided code to quickly add Keychains to an iOS app.*

> **Tip**
>
> The most up-to-date version of Apple's KeychainItemWrapper class can be found at http://developer.apple.com/library/ios/#samplecode/GenericKeychain/Listings/ Classes_KeychainItemWrapper_m.html.

It is important to remember that while securing information on disk, it is only a small part of complete app security; other factors such as transmitting data over a network and password enforcement are just as critical in providing a well-rounded secure app.

Introduction to the Sample App

The Keychain sample app is a single-view app that will secure a credit card number along with relevant user information, such as name and expiration date. To access the information, the user sets a PIN on first launch. Both the PIN and the credit card information are secured using the Keychain.

> **Note**
>
> The Keychain does not work on the iOS simulator as of iOS 7. The wrapper class provided by Apple and used in this chapter does make considerable efforts to properly simulate the Keychain behaviors. In addition, since code being executed on the simulator is not code signed, it is important to keep in mind that there are no restrictions on which apps can access Keychain items. It is highly recommended that Keychain development be thoroughly debugged on the device after it's working correctly on the simulator.

The sample app itself is really quite simple. It consists of four text fields and a button. The majority of the sample code not directly relating to the Keychain handles laying out information.

> **Note**
>
> Deleting the app from a device does not remove the Keychain for that app, which can make debugging considerably more difficult. The simulator does have a Reset Contents and Settings option, which will wipe the Keychain. It is highly recommended that a Keychain app not be debugged on a device until it is functional on the simulator.

Setting Up and Using Keychain

Keychain is part of the Security.framework and has been available for iOS starting with the initial SDK release. Keychain has its roots in Mac OS X development, where it was first introduced with OS X 10.2. However, Keychain's history predates even OS X with roots back into OS 8.6. Keychain was initially developed for Apple's email system called PowerTalk.

Keychain can be used to secure small amounts of data such as passwords, keys, certificates, and notes. However, if an app is securing large amounts of information such as encoded images or videos, implementing a third-party encryption library is usually a better fit than Keychain. Core data also provides encryption capabilities, and is worth exploring if the app will be Core Data–based.

Before working with Keychain, the Security.framework must be added to the project and `<Security/Security.h>` needs to be imported to any classes directly accessing Keychain methods and functions.

Setting Up a New `KeychainItemWrapper`

On iOS Keychains are unlocked based on the code signing of the app that is requesting it. Since there is no systemwide password as seen on OS X, there needs to be an additional step to secure data. Since the app controls which Keychain data can be accessed to truly secure information, the app itself should be password protected. This is done through the sample app using a PIN entry system.

When the app is launched for the first time, it will prompt the user to enter a new PIN and repeat it. To securely store the PIN, a new `KeychainItemWrapper` is created.

```
pinWrapper = [[KeychainItemWrapper
➥alloc]initWithIdentifier:@"com.ICF.Keychain.pin" accessGroup:nil];
```

Creating a new `KeychainItemWrapper` is done using two attributes. The first attribute is an identifier for that Keychain item. It is recommended that a reverse DNS approach be used here such as com.company.app.id. `accessGroup` is set to `nil` in this example, and the `accessGroup` parameter is used for sharing Keychains across multiple apps. Refer to the section "Sharing a Keychain Between Apps" for more information on `accessGroups`.

The next attribute that should be set on a new `KeychainItemWrapper` is the `kSecAttrAccessible`. This controls when the data will be unlocked. In the sample app the data becomes available when the device is unlocked, securing the data for a locked device. There are several possible options for this parameter, as detailed in Table 18.1.

```
[pinWrapper setObject:kSecAttrAccessibleWhenUnlocked forKey:
➥(id)kSecAttrAccessible];
```

Table 18.1 **All Possible Constants and Associated Descriptions to Be Supplied to `kSecAttrAccessible`**

Constant	Description
`kSecAttrAccessibleAfterFirstUnlock`	This Keychain will unlock data on the first device unlock after a restart; items will remain locked until the device is restarted. This setting is recommended for items that might be required by background tasks. These items will move to a new device when the user upgrades.
`kSecAttrAccessibleAfterFirst UnlockThisDeviceOnly`	This setting will duplicate the functionality described in `kSecAttrAccessibleAfterFirstUnlock` but will not transfer to a new device if the user upgrades or restores from a backup.
`kSecAttrAccessibleAlways`	This item is always unlocked whether or not the device is unlocked; it is not recommended to be used to secure information. These items will migrate when a user upgrades his device.

Constant	Description
`kSecAttrAccessibleAlwaysThis DeviceOnly`	This setting will duplicate the functionality described in `kSecAttrAccessibleAlways` but will not transfer to a new device if the user upgrades or restores from a backup.
`kSecAttrAccessibleWhenUnlocked`	This item is unlocked only when the user has unlocked the device. This parameter is recommended when an app needs access to secure information when it is in the foreground. This is also the most common setting for `kSecAttrAccessible`. This item will also migrate when a user upgrades his device.
`kSecAttrAccessibleWhenUnlocked ThisDeviceOnly`	This setting will duplicate the functionality described in `kSecAttrAccessibleWhenUnlocked` but will not transfer to a new device if the user upgrades or restores from a backup.

The app now knows the identifier for the Keychain as well the security level that is required of it. However, an additional parameter needs to be set before data can begin to be stored. The `kSecAttrService` is used to store a username for the password pair that will be used for the PIN. A PIN does not have an associated password; for the purposes of the sample app, `pinIdentifer` is used here. Although Keychains will often work while the `kSecAttrService` is omitted, having a value set here corrects many hard-to-reproduce failures.

```
[pinWrapper setObject:@"pinIdentifer" forKey: (id)kSecAttrAccount];
```

Storing and Retrieving the PIN

After a new `KeychainItemWrapper` has been configured in the manner described in the preceding section, data can be stored into it. Storing information in a Keychain is very similar to storing data in a dictionary. The sample app first checks to make sure that both of the PIN text fields match; then it calls `setObject:` on the `pinWrapper` that was created in the preceding section. For the key identifier `kSecValueData` is used. This item is covered more in depth in the section "Keychain Attribute Keys"; for now, however, it is important to use this constant.

```
if([pinField.text isEqualToString: pinFieldRepeat.text])
{
    [pinWrapper setObject:[pinField text] forKey:kSecValueData];
}
```

After a new value has been stored into the Keychain, it can be retrieved in the same fashion. To test whether the user has entered the correct PIN in the sample app, the following code is used:

```
if([pinField.text isEqualToString: [pinWrapper
➥objectForKey:kSecValueData]])
```

After the PIN number being entered has been confirmed as the PIN number stored in the Keychain, the user is allowed to access the next section of the app, described in the section "Securing a Dictionary."

Keychain Attribute Keys

Keychains are stored much like NSDictionaries; however, they have very specific keys that can be associated with them. Unlike an NSDictionary, a Keychain cannot use any random string for a key value. Each Keychain is associated with a Keychain Class; if using Apple's `KeychainItemWrapper`, it defaults to using `CFTypeRef kSecClassGenericPassword`. However, other options exist for `kSecClassInternetPassword`, `kSecClassCertificate`, `kSecClassKey`, and `kSecClassIdentity`. Each class has different associated values attached to it. For the purposes of this chapter as well as for the `KeychainItemWrapper`, the focus will be on `kSecClassGenericPassword`.

`kSecClassGenericPassword` contains 14 possible keys for storing and accessing data, as described in Table 18.2. It is important to keep in mind that these keys are optional and are not required to be populated in order to function correctly.

Table 18.2 **Keychain Attribute Keys Available When Working with `kSecClassGenericPassword`**

Attribute	Description
`kSecAttrAccessible`	The locking behavior key, discussed in Table 18.1.
`kSecAttrAccessGroup`	The string for the access group as seen during a new Keychain initialized and discussed in depth in the section "Sharing a Keychain Between Apps."
`kSecAttrCreationDate`	A `CFDateRef` representing the date the Keychain item was created.
`kSecAttrModificationDate`	A `CFDateRef` representing the date the Keychain item was last modified.
`kSecAttrDescription`	A string that represents a user-visible description for the Keychain, such as `Twitter Password`.
`kSecAttrComment`	A string that corresponds to a user-editable comment for the Keychain item.
`kSecAttrCreator`	A four-digit `CFNumberRef` representation of character code that reflects the creator code for the Keychain, such as `aCrt`. This will identify the creator of the Keychain if needed for custom implementations.

Attribute	Description
kSecAttrType	A four-digit `CFNumberRef` representation of character code that reflects the item type for the Keychain, such as `aTyp`. This will identify the type for a Keychain if needed for custom implementations.
kSecAttrLabel	A string that represents a user-visible label for the Keychain item.
kSecAttrIsInvisible	A `CFBooleanRef` representation of whether the item is invisible. `kCFBooleanTrue` represents invisible.
kSecAttrIsNegative	A `CFBooleanRef` indicating whether a valid password is associated with this item. This is useful if you do not want to store a password and force a user to enter it each time.
kSecAttrAccount	The account name attribute as discussed in the section "Setting up a New `KeychainItemWrapper`."
kSecAttrService	A `CFStringRef` that represents the service associated with this item.
kSecAttrGeneric	A generic attribute key that can be used to store a user-defined attribute.

Securing a Dictionary

Securing a more complex data type such as a dictionary follows the same approach taken to secure the PIN in earlier sections. The Keychain wrapper only allows for the storage of strings; to secure a dictionary, it is first turned into a string. The approach chosen for the sample code is to first save the dictionary to a JSON string using the `NSJSONSerialization` class. (See Chapter 7, "Working with and Parsing JSON," for more info.)

```
NSMutableDictionary *secureDataDict = [[[NSMutableDictionary alloc]
➡init] autorelease];

NSError *error = nil;

if(numberTextField.text)
    [secureDataDict setObject:numberTextField.text
    ➡forKey:@"numberTextField"];

if(expDateTextField.text)
    [secureDataDict setObject:expDateTextField.text
    ➡forKey:@"expDateTextField"];
```

```
if(CV2CodeTextField.text)
    [secureDataDict setObject:CV2CodeTextField.text
    ➥forKey:@"CV2CodeTextField"];

if(nameTextField.text)
    [secureDataDict setObject:nameTextField.text
    ➥forKey:@"nameTextField"];

NSData *rawData = [NSJSONSerialization
➥dataWithJSONObject:secureDataDict
            options:0
              error:&error];

if(error != nil)
{
    NSLog(@"An error occurred: %@", [error localizedDescription]);
}

NSString *dataString = [[[NSString alloc] initWithData:rawData
➥encoding:NSUTF8StringEncoding] autorelease];
```

After the value of the dictionary has been converted into a string representation of the dictionary data, it can be added to the Keychain in the same fashion as previously discussed.

```
KeychainItemWrapper *secureDataKeychain = [[KeychainItemWrapper alloc]
➥initWithIdentifier:@"com.ICF.keychain.securedData" accessGroup:nil];

[secureDataKeychain setObject:@"secureDataIdentifer" forKey:
➥(id)kSecAttrAccount];

[secureDataKeychain setObject:kSecAttrAccessibleWhenUnlocked forKey:
➥(id)kSecAttrAccessible];

[secureDataKeychain setObject:dataString forKey:kSecValueData];

[secureDataKeychain release];
```

To retrieve the data in the form of a dictionary, the steps must be followed in reverse. Starting with an NSString from the Keychain, it is turned into a NSData value. The NSData is used with NSJSONSerialization to retrieve the original dictionary value. After the dictionary is re-created, the text fields that display the user's credit card information are populated.

```
KeychainItemWrapper *secureDataKeychain = [[KeychainItemWrapper alloc]
➥initWithIdentifier:@"com.ICF.keychain.securedData" accessGroup:nil];

NSString *secureDataString = [secureDataKeychain
➥objectForKey:kSecValueData];
```

```objc
if([secureDataString length] != 0)
{
    NSData* data = [secureDataString
    ➥dataUsingEncoding:NSUTF8StringEncoding];

    NSError *error = nil;

    NSDictionary *secureDataDictionary = [NSJSONSerialization
    ➥JSONObjectWithData:data
    options:NSJSONReadingMutableContainers
    error:&error];

    if(error != nil)
    {
        NSLog(@"An error occurred: %@", [error localizedDescription]);
    }

    numberTextField.text = [secureDataDictionary
    ➥objectForKey:@"numberTextField"];

    expDateTextField.text = [secureDataDictionary
    ➥objectForKey:@"expDateTextField"];

    CV2CodeTextField.text = [secureDataDictionary
    ➥objectForKey:@"CV2CodeTextField"];

    nameTextField.text = [secureDataDictionary
    ➥objectForKey:@"nameTextField"];
}

else
{
    NSLog(@"No Keychain data stored yet");
}
```

Resetting a Keychain Item

At times it might be necessary to wipe out the data in a Keychain while not replacing it
with another set of user data. This can be done using Apple's library by invoking the
resetKeyChainItem method on the Keychain wrapper that needs to be reset.

```objc
[pinWrapper resetKeychainItem];
```

Sharing a Keychain Between Apps

A Keychain can be shared across multiple iOS apps if they are published by the same developer and under certain conditions. The most important requirement for sharing Keychain data between two apps is that both apps must have the same bundle seed. For example, consider two apps with the bundle identifiers 659823F3DC53.com.ICF.firstapp and 659823F3DC53.com. ICF.secondapp. These apps would be able to access and modify each other's Keychain data. Keychain sharing with a wildcard ID does not seem to work, although the official documentation remains quiet on this situation. Bundle seeds can be configured from the developer portal when new apps are created.

When you have two apps that share the same bundle seed, each app will need to have its entitlements configured to allow for a Keychain access group. Starting with Xcode 4.5, Keychain Groups are configured from the summary tab of the target, as shown in Figure 18.1. Before Xcode 4.5, the bundle ID with seed needed to be added to the entitlements file under the array for the key `keychain-access-groups`. When using the newer Keychain Group entries, you should omit the bundle seed.

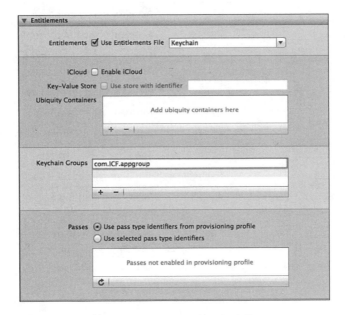

Figure 18.1   Setting up a new Keychain Group using Xcode 4.5 or newer.

For the shared Keychain to be accessed, the Keychain group first needs to be set. With a modification of the PIN example from earlier in the chapter, it would look like the following code snippet:

```
[pinWrapper setObject:@"659823F3DC53.com.ICF.appgroup"
➥forKey:(id)kSecAttrAccessGroup];
```

> **Note**
>
> Remember that when setting the access group in Xcode, you do not need to specify the bundle seed. However, when you are setting the `kSecAttrAccessGroup` property, the bundle seed needs to be specified and the bundle seed of both apps must match.

After an access group has been set on a `KeychainItemWrapper`, it can be created, modified, and deleted in the typical fashion discussed throughout this chapter.

Keychain Error Codes

The Keychain can return several specialized error codes depending on any issues encountered at runtime. These errors are described in Table 18.3.

Table 18.3 **Keychain Error Codes and Their Descriptions**

Code	Value	Description
errSecSuccess	0	No error encountered.
errSecUnimplemented	-4	Function or operation not implemented.
errSecParam	-50	One or more parameters passed to the function were not valid.
errSecAllocate	-108	Failed to allocate memory.
errSecNotAvailable	-25291	No trust results are available.
errSecAuthFailed	-25293	Authorization/authentication failed.
errSecDuplicateItem	-25299	The item already exists.
errSecItemNotFound	-25300	The item cannot be found.
errSecInteractionNotAllowed	-25308	Interaction with the Security Server is not allowed.
errSecDecode	-26275	Unable to decode the provided data.

Summary

This chapter covered using Keychain to secure small amounts of app data. The sample app covered setting and checking a PIN number for access to an app on launch. It also covered the storage and retrieval of multiple fields of credit card data.

Keychain and data security is a large topic, and this chapter merely touches the tip of the iceberg. The development community is also seeking security professionals, especially in the mobile marketplace. Keychain is an exciting and vast topic that should now be much less intimidating. Hopefully this introduction to securing data with Keychain will set you as a developer down a path of conscious computer security and prevent yet another story in the news about the loss of confidential information by a careless developer.

Exercises

1. Modify the sample app to not only store one set of credit card data but also allow the user to create and retrieve multiple cards.

2. Create two new apps that share a Keychain Group, and experiment with sharing Keychain data between the two apps.

Working with Images and Filters

Images and image handling are central to many iOS apps. At a basic level, images are a necessary part of customizing the user interface, from custom view backgrounds to custom buttons and view elements. Beyond that, iOS 6 added very sophisticated support for customizing user-provided images with the Core Image library. Previous to iOS 6, doing image manipulations required custom image-handling code using Quartz or custom C libraries. With the addition of Core Image, many complex image-editing functions demonstrated by successful apps, like Instagram, can now be handled by iOS with minimal effort.

This chapter describes basic image handling: how to load and display an image, how to handle images on devices with different capabilities, and some basic image display techniques. It also describes how to acquire an image from the device's image library or camera. In addition, this chapter demonstrates and describes how to use the Core Image library to apply effects to user-provided images.

The Sample App

The sample app for this chapter is called ImagePlayground. The app demonstrates selecting an image from the device's photo library or acquiring an image from the camera to be used as a source image, which the app then resizes to a smaller size. The user can select and chain filters to apply to the source image to alter how it looks, with the effect of each filter displayed in a table alongside the name of each selected filter. The filter selection process demonstrates how Core Image filters are organized into categories, and enables the user to customize a selected filter and preview its effect.

Basic Image Data and Display

Some basic image-handling techniques are required to support the images displayed in the sample app. This section describes different techniques for displaying images in a view and for handling stretchable images that can be used in buttons of different sizes, and it explains the basic approach needed to acquire an image from the user's photo library or camera.

Instantiating an Image

To use an image in an app, iOS provides a class called `UIImage`. This class supports many image formats:

- Portable Network Graphic (PNG): `.png`
- Tagged Image File Format (TIFF): `.tiff, .tif`
- Joint Photographic Experts Group (JPEG): `.jpeg, .jpg`
- Graphic Interchange Format (GIF): `.gif`
- Windows Bitmap Format (DIB): `.bmp, .BMPf`
- Windows Icon Format: `.ico`
- Windows Cursor: `.cur`
- XWindow bitmap: `.xbm`

When using images for backgrounds, buttons, or other elements in the user interface, Apple recommends using the PNG format. `UIImage` has a class method called `imageNamed:` that can be used to instantiate an image. This method provides a number of advantages:

- Looks for and loads the image from the app's main bundle without needing to specify the path to the main bundle.
- Automatically loads a PNG image with no file extension. So specifying `myImage` will load `myImage.png` if that exists in the app's main bundle.
- Takes into consideration the scale of the screen when loading the image, and `@2x` is automatically appended to the image name if the scale is 2.0. In addition, it will check for `~ipad` and `~iphone` versions of the images and use those if available.
- Supports in-memory caching. If the same image has already been loaded and is requested again, it will return the already-loaded image and not reload it. This is very useful when the same image is used multiple times in the user interface.

For images that are not present in the app's main bundle, when the `imageNamed:` method is not appropriate, there are several other approaches to instantiate images. A `UIImage` can be instantiated from a file, as in this code example, which will load `myImage.png` from the app's `Documents` directory:

```
NSArray *pathForDocuments =
NSSearchPathForDirectoriesInDomains(NSDocumentDirectory,
                                    NSUserDomainMask, YES);
```

```
NSString *imagePath =
[[pathForDocuments lastObject]
stringByAppendingPathComponent:@"myImage.png"];

UIImage *myImage =
[UIImage imageWithContentsOfFile:imagePath];
```

A UIImage can be instantiated from NSData, as in the next code example. NSData can be from any source; typically it is from a file or from data pulled from a network connection.

```
NSData *imageData = [NSData dataWithContentsOfFile:imagePath];

UIImage *myImage2 = [UIImage imageWithData:imageData];
```

A UIImage can be created from Core Graphics images, as in this code example, which uses Core Graphics to take a sample rectangle from an existing image:

```
CGImageRef myImage2CGImage = [myImage2 CGImage];
CGRect subRect = CGRectMake(20, 20, 120, 120);

CGImageRef cgCrop =
CGImageCreateWithImageInRect(myImage2CGImage, subRect);

UIImage *imageCrop = [UIImage imageWithCGImage:cgCrop];
```

A UIImage can be created from Core Image images, as described in detail later in the chapter in "Core Image Filters," in the subsection "Rendering a Filtered Image."

Displaying an Image

After an instance of UIImage is available, there are a few ways to display it in the user interface. The first is UIImageView. When an instance of UIImageView is available, it has a property called image that can be set:

```
[self.sourceImageView setImage:scaleImage];
```

UIImageView can also be instantiated with an image, which will set the bounds to the size of the image:

```
UIImageView *newImageView =
[[UIImageView alloc] initWithImage:myImage];
```

For images displayed in a UIImageView, setting the contentMode can have interesting and useful effects on how the image is displayed, as shown in Figure 19.1.

The content mode setting tells the view how to display its contents. Aspect fit and fill modes will preserve the aspect ratio of the image, whereas scale to fill mode will skew the image to fit the view. Modes such as center, top, bottom, left, and right will preserve the dimensions of the image while positioning it in the view.

Figure 19.1   Sample app: content mode effects.

Several other UIKit items support or use images, for example, `UIButton`. A useful technique for buttons especially is to utilize the resizable image capability provided by the `UIImage` class. This can be used to provide the same style for buttons of different sizes, without warping or distorting the edges of the button image, as shown in Figure 19.2.

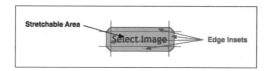

Figure 19.2   Sample app: custom button using resizable background image.

The source image for the button is only 28 pixels by 28 pixels. The resizable image used at the background is created from the original image by specifying edge insets to indicate what parts of the image should be kept static, and which parts can be stretched or tiled to fill in the additional space.

```
UIImage *startImage =
[UIImage imageNamed:@"ch_20_stretch_button"];

CGFloat topInset = 10.0f;
CGFloat bottomInset = 10.0f;
CGFloat leftInset = 10.0f;
CGFloat rightInset = 10.0f;

UIEdgeInsets edgeInsets =
UIEdgeInsetsMake(topInset, leftInset, bottomInset, rightInset);
```

```
UIImage *stretchImage =
[startImage resizableImageWithCapInsets:edgeInsets];

[self.selectImageButton setBackgroundImage:stretchImage
                             forState:UIControlStateNormal];

[self.selectImageButton setBackgroundImage:stretchImage
                             forState:UIControlStateSelected];

[self.selectImageButton setBackgroundImage:stretchImage
                             forState:UIControlStateHighlighted];

[self.selectImageButton setBackgroundImage:stretchImage
                             forState:UIControlStateDisabled];
```

> **Tip**
>
> Update old projects in Xcode 5 to use the Asset Catalog, which can automatically support stretchable images with no code.

Using the Image Picker

It is very common for apps to make use of images provided by the user. To allow an app access to the user's photos in the camera roll and photo albums, iOS provides two approaches: the `UIImagePickerController` and the asset library. The `UIImagePickerController` provides a modal user interface to navigate through the user's albums and photos, so it is appropriate to use when Apple's provided styling works for the app and there are no special requirements for photo browsing and selection. The asset library provides full access to the photos and albums, so it is appropriate to use when there are specific user-interface and styling requirements for navigating and selecting images. The asset library is fully described in Chapter 23, "Accessing Photo Libraries."

To see how to use a `UIImagePickerController`, refer to the `selectImageTouched:` method in `ICFViewController` in the sample app. The method starts by allocating and initializing an instance of `UIImagePickerController`.

```
UIImagePickerController *imagePicker =
[[UIImagePickerController alloc] init];
```

The method then customizes the picker. The `UIImagePickerController` can be customized to acquire images or videos from the camera, from the photo library, or from the saved photos album. In this case, the photo library is specified.

```
[imagePicker setSourceType:
 UIImagePickerControllerSourceTypePhotoLibrary];
```

A `UIImagePickerController` can be customized to select images, videos, or both, by specifying an array of media types. Note that the media types which can be specified are constants that are defined in the MobileCoreServices framework, so it is necessary to add that framework to the project and import it in the view controller. For the sample app, only photos are desired, so the `kUTTypeImage` constant is used.

```
[imagePicker setMediaTypes:@[(NSString*)kUTTypeImage]];
```

The picker can be customized to allow or prevent editing of the selected image. If editing is allowed, the user will be able to pinch and pan the image to crop it within a square provided in the user interface.

```
[imagePicker setAllowsEditing:YES];
```

Lastly, the picker receives a delegate. The delegate is informed when the user has selected an image or has cancelled image selection according to the `UIImagePickerControllerDelegate` protocol. The delegate is responsible for dismissing the image picker view controller.

```
[imagePicker setDelegate:self];
```

In the sample app, the image picker is presented in a popover view controller using the source image container view as its anchor view.

```
self.imagePopoverController = [[UIPopoverController alloc]
initWithContentViewController:imagePicker];

[self.imagePopoverController
presentPopoverFromRect:self.sourceImageContainer.frame
inView:self.view
permittedArrowDirections:UIPopoverArrowDirectionAny
animated:YES];
```

When the user has selected an image and cropped it, the delegate method is called.

```
- (void)imagePickerController:(UIImagePickerController *)picker
didFinishPickingMediaWithInfo:(NSDictionary *)info
{
...
}
```

The delegate is provided with a dictionary of information about the selected media. If editing occurred during the selection process, information about the editing that the user performed is included in the dictionary. The keys and information contained in the info dictionary are described in Table 19.1.

Table 19.1 **`UIImagePickerControllerDelegate` Media Info Dictionary**

Key	Value
`UIImagePickerControllerMediaType`	Contains an `NSString` constant indicating whether the user selected an image (`kUTTypeImage`) or a video (`kUTTypeMovie`).
`UIImagePickerControllerOriginalImage`	A `UIImage` containing the image selected by the user with no cropping or editing applied.
`UIImagePickerControllerEditedImage`	A `UIImage` containing the image selected by the user, with cropping or editing applied. If the image was not edited, this will not be available in the dictionary.
`UIImagePickerControllerCropRect`	An `NSValue` containing a `CGRect` of the cropping rectangle applied to the original image. If the image was not edited, this will not be available in the dictionary.
`UIImagePickerControllerMediaURL`	An `NSURL` pointing to the location of the data for a movie in the device's filesystem. This URL is accessible to the app and can be used to upload the movie data or use in a movie player. This will not be available if the media type is `image`.
`UIImagePickerControllerReferenceURL`	An `NSURL` representing the corresponding `ALAsset`. This can be used to interact with the asset directly using the asset library as described in Chapter 23.
`UIImagePickerControllerMediaMetadata`	An `NSDictionary` containing metadata for a photo taken from the camera. This is not available for images or movies from the photo library.

In the sample app, the selected image is resized to 200px by 200px so that it will be easy to work with and will fit nicely in the display. First, a reference to the editing image is acquired.

```
UIImage *selectedImage =
[info objectForKey:UIImagePickerControllerEditedImage];
```

Then a `CGSize` is created to indicate the desired size, and a scale method in a category set up for `UIImage` is called to resize the image. The resized image is then set as the image to display in the user interface.

```
CGSize scaleSize = CGSizeMake(200.0f, 200.0f);

UIImage *scaleImage =
[selectedImage scaleImageToSize:scaleSize];

[self.sourceImageView setImage:scaleImage];
```

After the image is set, the popover with the image picker is dismissed.

Resizing an Image

When images are being displayed, it is advisable to work with the smallest image possible while still maintaining a beautiful user interface. Although the sample app certainly could use the full-size selected image, performance will be affected if a larger image is used and there will be increased memory requirements to handle a larger image. Therefore, the sample app will resize a selected image to work with the image at the exact size needed for the user interface and no larger. To scale an image in iOS, the method will need to use Core Graphics. The sample app includes a category called Scaling on UIImage (in UIImage+Scaling), with a method called scaleImageToSize:. The method accepts a CGSize parameter, which is a width and a height.

The first step in resizing an image is to create a Core Graphics context, which is a working area for images.

```
UIGraphicsBeginImageContextWithOptions(newSize, NO, 0.0);
```

UIKit provides the convenience function UIGraphicsBeginImageContextWithOption, which will create a Core Graphics context with the options provided. The first parameter passed in is a CGSize, which specifies the size of the context; in this case, the method uses the size passed in from the caller. The second parameter is a BOOL, which tells Core Graphics whether the context and resulting image should be treated as opaque (YES) or should include an alpha channel for transparency (NO). The final parameter is the scale of the image, where 1.0 is nonretina and 2.0 is retina. Passing in 0.0 will tell the function to use the scale of the current device's screen. After a context is available, the method draws the image into the context using the drawInRect: method.

```
CGFloat originX = 0.0;
CGFloat originY = 0.0;

CGRect destinationRect =
CGRectMake(originX, originY, newSize.width, newSize.height);

[self drawInRect:destinationRect];
```

The drawInRect: method will draw the content of the image into the Core Graphics context, using the position and dimensions specified in the destination rectangle. If the width and height of the source image are different from the new dimensions, the drawInRect: method will resize the image to fit in the new dimensions.

Note that it is important to take the aspect ratios of the source image and destination into consideration when doing this. The aspect ratio is the ratio of the width to the height of the image. If the aspect ratios are different, the `drawInRect:` method will stretch or compress the image as needed to fit into the destination context, and the resulting image will appear distorted.

Next the method creates a new `UIImage` from the context, ends the context since it is no longer required, and returns the newly resized image.

```
UIImage *newImage = UIGraphicsGetImageFromCurrentImageContext();
UIGraphicsEndImageContext();
return newImage;
```

Core Image Filters

The sample app allows the user to select a starting image, and select a sequence of filters to apply to that image to arrive at a final image. As a general rule, Core Image filters require an input image (except in cases in which the filter generates an image) and some parameters to customize the behavior of the filter. When requested, Core Image will process the filter against the input image to provide an output image. Core Image is very efficient in the application of filters. A list of filters will be applied only when the final output image is requested, not when each filter is specified. In addition, Core Image will combine the filters mathematically wherever possible so that a minimum of calculations are performed to process the filters.

Note
To use Core Image in a project, add the Core Image framework to the project and import `<CoreImage/CoreImage.h>` in each class that requires it.

Filter Categories and Filters

Core Image filters are organized into categories internally. A filter can belong to more than one category; for example, a color effect filter like Sepia Tone belongs to six categories, including `CICategoryColorEffect`, `CICategoryVideo`, `CICategoryInterlaced`, `CICategoryNonSquarePixels`, `CICategoryStillImage`, and `CICategoryBuiltIn`. These categories are useful to the developer to determine what Core Image filters are available for a desired task, and can be used as in the sample app to allow the user to browse and select available filters.

In the sample app, when a user taps the Add Filter button, a popover segue is initiated. This segue will initialize a `UIPopoverController`, a `UINavigationController`, and an instance of `ICFFilterCategoriesViewController` as the top view controller in the navigation controller. The instance of `ICFViewController` implements `ICFFilterProcessingDelegate` and is set as the delegate so that it will be notified when a filter is selected or when the selection process is cancelled. The instance of `ICFFilterCategoriesViewController` sets up a dictionary of user-readable category names in the `viewDidLoad` method to correspond with Core Image's category keys for presentation in a table.

```
self.categoryList = @{
    @"Blur" : kCICategoryBlur,
    @"Color Adjustment" : kCICategoryColorAdjustment,
    @"Color Effect" : kCICategoryColorEffect,
    @"Composite" : kCICategoryCompositeOperation,
    @"Distortion" : kCICategoryDistortionEffect,
    @"Generator" : kCICategoryGenerator,
    @"Geometry Adjustment" : kCICategoryGeometryAdjustment,
    @"Gradient" : kCICategoryGradient,
    @"Halftone Effect" : kCICategoryHalftoneEffect,
    @"Sharpen" : kCICategorySharpen,
    @"Stylize" : kCICategoryStylize,
    @"Tile" : kCICategoryTileEffect,
    @"Transition" : kCICategoryTransition
};
self.categoryKeys = [self.categoryList allKeys];
```

The table looks as shown in Figure 19.3.

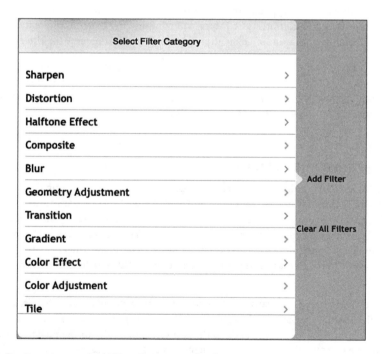

Figure 19.3   Sample app: Add Filter, Category selection.

When the user selects a category, a segue is initiated. In the `prepareForSegue:sender:` method the destination instance of `ICFFiltersViewController` is updated with the Core Image constant for the selected category, and is assigned the `ICFFilterProcessingDelegate` delegate. In the `viewDidLoad` method, the `ICFFiltersViewController` will get a list of available filters for the filter category.

```
self.filterNameArray =
[CIFilter filterNamesInCategory:self.selectedCategory];
```

The filters are displayed in a table as shown in Figure 19.4.

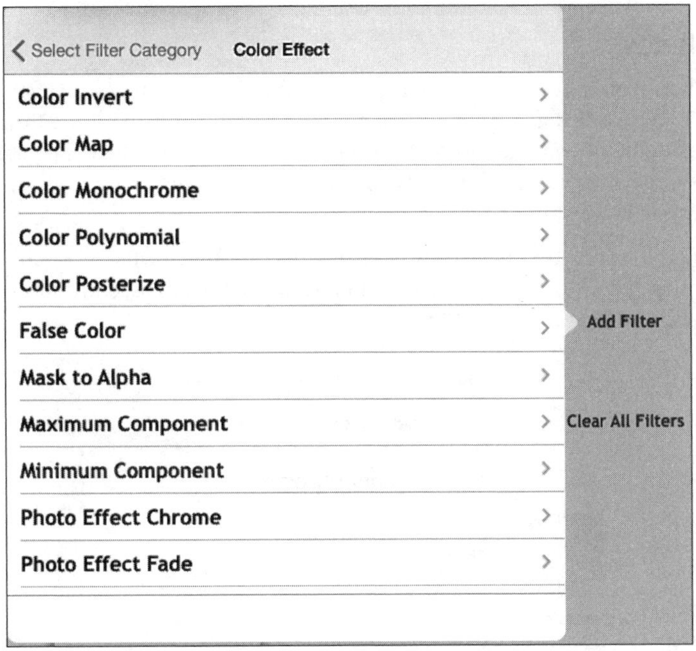

Figure 19.4   Sample app: Add Filter, Filter selection.

Core Image filters can be instantiated by name, so the `tableView:cellForRowAtIndexPath:` method instantiates a `CIFilter`, and examines the filter's attributes to get the display name of the filter.

```
NSString *filterName =
[self.filterNameArray objectAtIndex:indexPath.row];

CIFilter *filter = [CIFilter filterWithName:filterName];
NSDictionary *filterAttributes = [filter attributes];
```

```
NSString *categoryName =
[filterAttributes valueForKey:kCIAttributeFilterDisplayName];

[cell.textLabel setText:categoryName];
```

When the user selects a filter, a segue is initiated. In the `prepareForSegue:sender:` method the destination instance of `ICFFilterViewController` is updated with an instance of `CIFilter` for the selected filter, and is assigned the `ICFFilterProcessingDelegate` delegate. When the `ICFFilterViewController` instance appears, it will display the customizable attributes for the selected filter.

Filter Attributes

Core Image filters have a flexible approach to customization. All instances of `CIFilter` have a dictionary property called `attributes` that contains information about the filter and all the customizations to the filter. Instances of `CIFilter` have a property called `inputKeys`, which lists the keys of each customizable input item, and a property called `outputKeys`, which lists the output items from the filter.

The sample app has specialized table cells to enable the user to see what attributes are available for a selected filter, adjust those attributes, and preview the image based on the current attribute parameters, as shown in Figure 19.5.

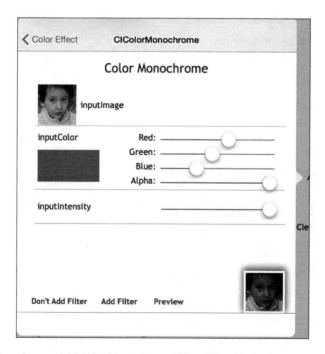

Figure 19.5   Sample app: Add Color Monochrome Filter, Filter Attributes.

Each attribute has information that can be used to determine how to display and edit the attribute in the user interface. In `ICFFilterViewController`, the `tableView:cellForRowAt IndexPath:` method determines which attribute to look at based on the index path.

```
NSString *attributeName =
[[self.selectedFilter inputKeys] objectAtIndex:indexPath.row];
```

Using the attribute name from the filter's `inputKeys` property, the method can then get an `NSDictionary` of info about the attribute.

```
NSDictionary *attributeInfo =
[[self.selectedFilter attributes] valueForKey:attributeName];
```

With the attribute info available, the method can inspect what type the attribute is and what class the filter expects the attribute information to be expressed in. With that info the method can dequeue the correct type of custom cell to use to edit the attribute. `ICFInputInfoCell` is a superclass with several subclasses to handle images, colors, numbers, vectors, and transforms.

```
NSString *cellIdentifier =
[self getCellIdentifierForAttributeType:attributeInfo];


ICFInputInfoCell *cell = (ICFInputInfoCell *)
[tableView dequeueReusableCellWithIdentifier:cellIdentifier
                            forIndexPath:indexPath];
```

The custom `getCellIdentifierForAttributeType:` method uses the attribute type and class to determine what type of cell to return. Note that the filters are not completely consistent with attribute types and classes; one filter might specify an attribute type of `kCIAttributeTypeColor`, whereas another might specify an attribute class of `CIColor`. The method corrects for this by allowing either approach.

```
NSString *attributeType = @"";
if ([attributeInfo objectForKey:kCIAttributeType])
{
    attributeType =
    [attributeInfo objectForKey:kCIAttributeType];
}


NSString *attributeClass =
[attributeInfo objectForKey:kCIAttributeClass];


NSString *cellIdentifier = @"";

if ([attributeType isEqualToString:kCIAttributeTypeColor] ||
    [attributeClass isEqualToString:@"CIColor"])
{
    cellIdentifier = kICSInputColorCellIdentifier;
}
```

```
if ([attributeType isEqualToString:kCIAttributeTypeImage] ||
    [attributeClass isEqualToString:@"CIImage"])
{
    cellIdentifier = kICSInputImageCellIdentifier;
}

if ([attributeType isEqualToString:kCIAttributeTypeScalar] ||
    [attributeType isEqualToString:kCIAttributeTypeDistance] ||
    [attributeType isEqualToString:kCIAttributeTypeAngle] ||
    [attributeType isEqualToString:kCIAttributeTypeTime])
{
    cellIdentifier = kICSInputNumberCellIdentifier;
}

if ([attributeType isEqualToString:kCIAttributeTypePosition] ||
    [attributeType isEqualToString:kCIAttributeTypeOffset] ||
    [attributeType isEqualToString:kCIAttributeTypeRectangle])
{
    cellIdentifier = kICSInputVectorCellIdentifier;
}

if ([attributeClass isEqualToString:@"NSValue"])
{
    cellIdentifier = kICSInputTransformCellIdentifier;
}

return cellIdentifier;
```

Each of the cell subclasses can accept the attribute dictionary, configure the cell display with provided or default values, manage editing of the parameter values, and then return an instance of the expected class when requested.

Initializing an Image

To apply a filter to an image, Core Image requires an image to be an instance of CIImage. To get an instance of CIImage from a UIImage, a conversion to CGImage and then to CIImage is needed. In ICFFilterViewController, the tableView:cellForRowAtIndexPath: method handles the inputImage by checking with the filter delegate to get either the starting image or the image from the previous filter. The filter delegate keeps an array of UIImages, which it will use to return the last image from the imageWithLastFilterApplied method.

If the starting image is provided, it is converted to CGImage and then used to create a CIImage. If the input image is from another filter, it is safe to assume that UIImage has an associated CIImage (asking a UIImage for a CIImage works only when the UIImage has been created from a CIImage; otherwise, it returns nil).

```
if ([attributeName isEqualToString:@"inputImage"])
{
    UIImage *sourceImage =
    [self.filterDelegate imageWithLastFilterApplied];

    [[(ICFInputImageTableCell *)cell inputImageView]
     setImage:sourceImage];

    CIImage *inputImage = nil;
    if ([sourceImage CIImage])
    {
        inputImage = [sourceImage CIImage];
    }
    else
    {
        CGImageRef inputImageRef = [sourceImage CGImage];
        inputImage = [CIImage imageWithCGImage:inputImageRef];
    }

    [self.selectedFilter setValue:inputImage
                           forKey:attributeName];
}
```

Rendering a Filtered Image

To render a filtered image, all that is required is to request the `outputImage` from the filter's attributes, and to call one of the available methods to render it to a context, an image, a bitmap, or a pixel buffer. At that point the filter operations will be applied to the `inputImage` and the `outputImage` will be produced. In the sample app, this occurs in two instances: if the user taps Preview in the filter view controller (as shown in Figure 19.5), or if the user taps Add Filter. When the user taps the Preview button in `ICFFilterViewController`, the `previewButtonTouched:` method is called. This method begins by initializing a Core Image context (note that the context can be initialized once as a property, but is done here to illustrate it all in one place).

```
CIContext *context = [CIContext contextWithOptions:nil];
```

The method then gets a reference to the `outputImage` from the filter, and sets up a rectangle that will be used to tell the context what part of the image to render. In this case the rectangle is the same size as the image and might seem superfluous; however, note that there are some filters that generate infinitely sized output images (see the Generator category of filters), so it is prudent to specify desired dimensions.

```
CIFilter *filter = self.selectedFilter;
CIImage *resultImage = [filter valueForKey:kCIOutputImageKey];
CGRect imageRect = CGRectMake(0, 0, 200, 200);
```

The method then asks the context to create a Core Graphics image using the `outputImage` and the rectangle.

```
CGImageRef resultCGImage =
[context createCGImage:resultImage fromRect:imageRect];
```

The Core Graphics result image can then be used to create a `UIImage` to display on the screen.

```
UIImage *resultUIImage =
[UIImage imageWithCGImage:resultCGImage];

[self.previewImageView setImage:resultUIImage];
```

The preview image is displayed in the lower-right corner of the filter view, as shown in Figure 19.5.

Chaining Filters

Chaining filters is the process of applying more than one filter to a source image. With the combination of filters applied to a source image, interesting effects can be produced, as shown in Figure 19.6.

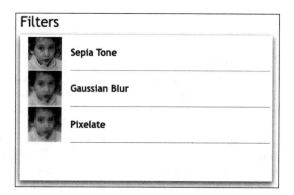

Figure 19.6   Sample app: filter list.

When a user taps Add Filter (refer to Figure 19.5), the `addFilter:` method of the `ICFFilterProcessing` protocol gets called in `ICFViewController`. The method checks to see whether the filter to be added is the first filter, in which case it leaves the source image as the `inputImage` for the filter. If it is not the first filter, the method uses the `outputImage` of the last filter as the `inputImage` for the filter to be added.

```
CIFilter *lastFilter = [self.filterArray lastObject];

if (lastFilter)
{
```

```
    if ([[filter inputKeys] containsObject:@"inputImage"] )
    {
        [filter setValue:[lastFilter outputImage]
                forKey:@"inputImage"];
    }
}
```

```
[self.filterArray addObject:filter];
```

Using this technique, any number of filters can be chained together. With the last filter, the method renders the final image.

```
CIContext *context = [CIContext contextWithOptions:nil];
CIImage *resultImage = [filter valueForKey:kCIOutputImageKey];

CGImageRef resultCGImage =
[context createCGImage:resultImage
            fromRect:CGRectMake(0, 0, 200, 200)];

UIImage *resultUIImage =
[UIImage imageWithCGImage:resultCGImage];
```

The final image is added to the list of images, and the filter list table is reloaded to display the images for each filter step.

```
[self.resultImageView setImage:resultUIImage];

[self.filteredImageArray addObject:self.resultImageView.image];
[self.filterList reloadData];

[self.filterPopoverController dismissPopoverAnimated:YES];
```

Core Image will automatically optimize the filter chain to minimize the number of calculations necessary; in other words, Core Image will not process each step in the filter individually; rather, it will combine the math operations indicated by the filters and perform the filter operation in one step.

Face Detection

Core Image provides the capability to detect faces and facial features in an image or a video. Face detection can be used for a number of useful things; for example, the standard Camera app in iOS 6 can highlight faces in the viewfinder. Face locations and dimensions can be used in filters to make faces anonymous or highlight faces in a number of engaging ways. The sample app contains functionality to detect and highlight faces and face features in the source image.

Setting Up a Face Detector

To use a face detector, Core Image needs an instance of CIImage as a source image to analyze. In the detectFacesTouched: method in ICFViewController, an instance of CIImage is created from the source image displayed.

```
UIImage *detectUIImage = [self.sourceImageView image];
CGImageRef detectCGImageRef = [detectUIImage CGImage];

CIImage *detectImage =
[CIImage imageWithCGImage:detectCGImageRef];
```

Face detection in Core Image is provided by the CIDetector class. There is currently only one type of detector, specified by the constant CIDetectorTypeFace. The class method to create a detector accepts a dictionary of options; in this case, a face detector can use either high- or low-accuracy setting. The high-accuracy setting is more accurate but takes more time to complete, so it is appropriate for cases in which performance is not the primary consideration. The low-accuracy setting is appropriate for cases like a real-time video feed in which performance is more important than precision. A Core Image context can be provided but is not required.

```
NSDictionary *options =
@{CIDetectorAccuracy : CIDetectorAccuracyHigh};

CIDetector *faceDetector =
[CIDetector detectorOfType:CIDetectorTypeFace
                   context:nil
                   options:options];
```

After the detector is created, calling the featuresInImage: method will provide an array of features detected in the source image.

```
NSArray *features = [faceDetector featuresInImage:detectImage];
```

Features discovered will be returned as instances of CIFaceFeature, which is a subclass of CIFeature. Instances of CIFeature have a bounds property, which is a rectangle outlining the feature's relative position inside the source image.

Processing Face Features

The detectFacesTouched: method in ICFViewController will iterate over the found faces, and will visually highlight them in the source image, as shown in Figure 19.7. The method will also log detailed information about each face feature to a text view in the display.

For each face, the method first gets a rectangle to position the red square around the face.

```
CGRect faceRect =
[self adjustCoordinateSpaceForMarker:face.bounds
                          andHeight:detectImage.extent.size.height];
```

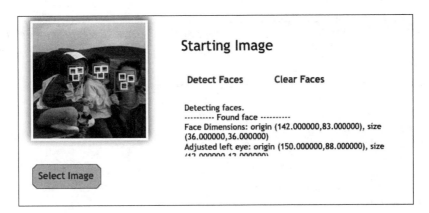

Figure 19.7   Sample app: detect faces.

To determine where to draw the rectangle for a face, the method needs to adjust the positions provided by Core Image, which uses a different coordinate system than UIKit. Core Image's coordinate system is flipped in the Y or vertical direction so that position zero is at the bottom of an image instead of the top. The adjustCoordinateSpaceForMarker:andHeight: method will adjust a marker rectangle by shifting the marker by the height of the image and flipping it, so the new coordinates are expressed the same way as in UIKit's coordinate system.

```
CGAffineTransform scale = CGAffineTransformMakeScale(1, -1);

CGAffineTransform flip =
CGAffineTransformTranslate(scale, 0, -height);

CGRect flippedRect = CGRectApplyAffineTransform(marker, flip);
return flippedRect;
```

With the correct coordinates, the method will add a basic view with a red border to the source image view to highlight the face.

```
UIView *faceMarker = [[UIView alloc] initWithFrame:faceRect];
faceMarker.layer.borderWidth = 2;
faceMarker.layer.borderColor = [[UIColor redColor] CGColor];
[self.sourceImageView addSubview:faceMarker];
```

The CIFaceFeature class has methods to indicate whether a face has detected a left eye, a right eye, and a mouth. As of iOS 7, it has methods to indicate whether a detected face is smiling (hasSmile), or whether either of the eyes is blinking (leftEyeClosed and rightEyeClosed).

```
if (face.hasLeftEyePosition)
{
    ...
}
```

If an eye or a mouth has been detected, a position will be available for that face feature expressed as a `CGPoint`. Since only a position is provided for each face feature (and not dimensions), the method uses a default width and height for the rectangles to indicate the location of a face feature.

```
CGFloat leftEyeXPos = face.leftEyePosition.x - eyeMarkerWidth/2;
CGFloat leftEyeYPos = face.leftEyePosition.y - eyeMarkerWidth/2;

CGRect leftEyeRect =
CGRectMake(leftEyeXPos, leftEyeYPos, eyeMarkerWidth, eyeMarkerWidth);

CGRect flippedLeftEyeRect =
[self adjustCoordinateSpaceForMarker:leftEyeRect
andHeight:self.sourceImageView.bounds.size.height];
```

With the calculated and adjusted rectangle, the method adds a yellow square to the source image view to highlight the left eye.

```
UIView *leftEyeMarker =
[[UIView alloc] initWithFrame:flippedLeftEyeRect];

leftEyeMarker.layer.borderWidth = 2;

leftEyeMarker.layer.borderColor =
[[UIColor yellowColor] CGColor];

[self.sourceImageView addSubview:leftEyeMarker];
```

The same approach is repeated for the right eye and the mouth.

Summary

This chapter described basic image handling, including how to load and display an image, how to specify a content mode to adjust how an image is displayed, and how to create a stretchable image to reuse a source image for elements of different sizes. It demonstrated how to get an image from the user's photo library or from the camera, and how to customize the image picker with options such as which albums to use and whether to allow cropping the selected image. It also explained how to resize an image.

Then, this chapter explained how to make use of Core Image filters, including how to get information about the available filters and filter categories, how to apply a filter to an image, and how to chain filters together to achieve interesting effects. Finally, this chapter described how to utilize Core Image's face detection.

Exercises

1. The sample app demonstrates using a Core Image context that does not display in real time; rather, the user has to tap the Preview button to view a preview of the filter applied to the input image. Core Image is capable of providing real-time image updates from a filter using an EAGL context. In `ICFFilterViewController` create a property for an `EAGLContext` and a `CIContext`. Use these snippets of code to create the context, and then modify `ICFFilterViewController` to process the preview in real time. Hint: Use a `GLKView` instead of a `UIImageView`, and add logic to the `updateFilterAttribute:with Value:` method to update the live preview when parameters change.

```
self.previewEAGLContext =
[[EAGLContext alloc] initWithAPI:kEAGLRenderingAPIOpenGLES2];

NSDictionary *options =
@{kCIContextWorkingColorSpace : [NSNull null]};

self.previewCIContext =
[CIContext contextWithEAGLContext:self.previewEAGLContext
                          options:options];
```

2. Transitions are really just filters applied a number of times over a period of time. The transition filters support time parameters to calculate what the transition image should look like as time progresses. Enhance the preview function to display a full transition over time.

20

Collection Views

Collection views were added in iOS 6 to provide a convenient new way to display scrollable cell-based information in a view with arbitrary layouts. Consider the iOS 6 version of Photos.app, which presents thumbnails of images in a scrollable grid. Before iOS 6, implementing a grid view would require setting up a table view with logic to calculate which thumbnail (or "cell") should go in each position in each table row, or would require custom logic to place thumbnails in a scroll view and manage them all as scrolling occurs. Both approaches are challenging, time-consuming, and error prone to implement. Collection views address this situation by providing a cell management architecture that is very similar to row management in a table view, while abstracting the layout of cells.

There is a default collection view layout called flow layout, which can be used to quickly and easily implement many common grid-style layouts for both horizontal and vertical scrolling. Custom layouts can be created to implement specialized grids or any nongrid layout that can be visualized and calculated at runtime.

Collection views can be organized into sections, with section header and section footer views that depend on section data. In addition, decoration views not related to content data can be specified to enhance the look of the collection view.

Last but not least, collection views support lots of types of animation, including custom states while cells are scrolling, animations for inserting or removing cells, and transitioning between layouts.

The Sample App

The sample app for this chapter is called PhotoGallery. The app demonstrates presenting the user's photo library in a few different implementations of a collection view:

- The first implementation is a basic collection view of thumbnails, organized by album, that can be scrolled vertically. It has section headers displaying album names, and can be created with a minimum of custom code.
- The second implementation uses a custom subclass of the flow layout so that it can display decoration views.
- The third implementation uses a custom layout to present items in a nongrid layout, and includes the capability to change to another layout with a pinch gesture.

Introducing Collection Views

A collection view needs a few different classes in order to work. The base class is called `UICollectionView` and is a subclass of `UIScrollView`. It will manage the presentation of cells provided by the datasource (which can be any class implementing the `UICollectionViewDataSource` protocol), according to the layout referenced by the collection view, which will be an instance of `UICollectionViewLayout`. A delegate conforming to the `UICollectionViewDelegate` protocol can be specified to manage selection and highlighting of cells.

The class that conforms to the `UICollectionViewDataSource` protocol will return configured cells to the collection view, which will be instances of `UICollectionViewCell`. If the collection view is configured to use section headers and/or section footers, the data source will return configured instances of `UICollectionReusableView`.

In the sample app, refer to the Basic Flow Layout to see these classes all working together as shown in Figure 20.1.

Figure 20.1   Sample app: Basic Flow Layout.

Setting Up a Collection View

The Basic Flow Layout example in the sample app demonstrates setting up a collection view with a minimum of customization, to show how quickly and easily a collection view can be created. Instead of using a basic `UIViewController` subclass, the basic flow used a `UICollectionViewController` subclass called `PHGBasicFlowViewController`, which conforms to the `UICollectionViewDataSource` and `UICollectionViewDelegate` protocols. This approach is not required; it is convenient when the collection view is all that is being displayed for a view controller. A collection view can be used with a standard view controller with no issues:

1. In the MainStoryboard, examine the Basic Flow View Controller–Basic Scene.

2. Expand the scene to see the collection view controller, as shown in Figure 20.2.

3. With the collection view controller selected, note the custom class specified in the identity inspector.

This ensures that the collection view controller will use the custom subclass `PHGBasicFlowViewController`.

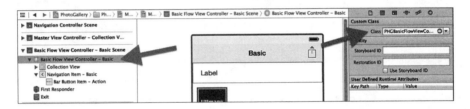

Figure 20.2   Xcode storyboard: specify custom class for collection view controller.

`UICollectionViewController` instances have a property called `collectionView`, which is represented in Interface Builder as the collection view object. With the collection view object selected, note that several settings can be configured: the type of layout, the scrolling direction, and whether a section header and/or section footer should be used, as shown in Figure 20.3.

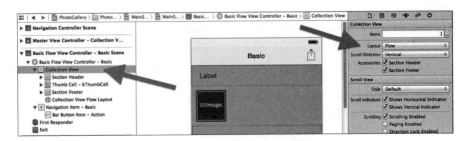

Figure 20.3   Xcode storyboard: custom collection view settings.

Interface Builder will present objects for the section header, collection view cell, and section footer that can be customized as well. For each of these, a custom subclass has been set up to simplify managing the subviews that need to be configured at runtime. This is not required; the UICollectionViewCell and UICollectionReusableView classes can be used directly if preferred.

The collection view cell subclass is called PHGThumbCell, and has one property called thumbImageView, which will be used to display the thumbnail image. The collection view object in Interface Builder is configured to use the custom subclass in the identity inspector, and references a UIImageView object for the thumbImageView property. The key item to set up for the collection view cell is the identifier, as shown in Figure 20.4; this is how the data source method will identify the type of cell to be configured and displayed.

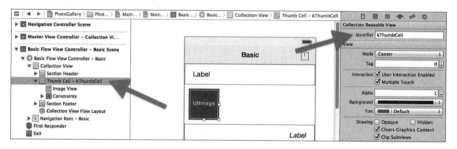

Figure 20.4   Xcode storyboard: collection view cell identifier.

The collection view section header subclass is called PHGSectionHeader, and the section footer subclass is called PHGSectionFooter. Each subclass has a property for a label that will be used to display the header or footer title for the section. Both objects in Interface Builder are configured to use their respective custom subclasses in the identity inspector, and reference UILabel objects for their title properties. Just as the collection view cell "identifier" was specified for the collection view cell, separate identifiers are specified for the section header and section footer.

Implementing the Collection View Data Source Methods

After all the objects are configured in Interface Builder, the data source methods need to be implemented for the collection view to work. Confirm that the collection view object in the storyboard has the data source set to the basic flow view controller, as shown in Figure 20.5.

The sample app is a gallery app that displays photos from the user's photo library, so there is logic implemented in the viewDidLoad method that builds an array of image assets (organized as an array containing asset arrays, in which each asset array holds the assets for a group/album) and an array of photo album titles. Refer to Chapter 23, "Accessing Photo Libraries," for more details on that process.

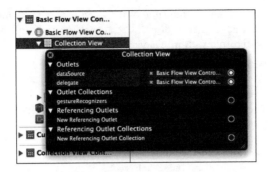

Figure 20.5   Xcode storyboard: collection view data source setting.

The collection view needs to know how many sections to present, which is returned in the `numberOfSectionsInCollectionView:` method. The method is set up to return the count of albums (or groups) from the array of asset groups built in `viewDidLoad`.

```
- (NSInteger)numberOfSectionsInCollectionView:(UICollectionView *)collectionView
{
    return [self.assetGroupArray count];
}
```

Next the collection view needs to know how many cells to present in each section. This method is called `collectionView:numberOfItemsInSection:`. The method has been built to find the correct asset array for the section index, and then return the count of assets in that array.

```
- (NSInteger)collectionView:(UICollectionView *)view
      numberOfItemsInSection:(NSInteger)section;
{
    NSArray *sectionAssets = self.assetArray[section];
    return [sectionAssets count];
}
```

After the collection view has the counts of sections and items, it can determine how to lay out the view. Depending on where in the scrollable bounds the current view is, the collection view will request section headers, footers, and cells for the visible area of the view. Section headers and footers are requested from the `collectionView:viewForSupplementary ElementOfKind:atIndexPath:` method. Section headers and footers both need to be instances (or subclasses) of `UICollectionReusableView`. The method declares a `nil` instance of `UICollectionReusableView`, which will be populated with either a configured section header or a section footer.

```
UICollectionReusableView *supplementaryView = nil;
```

The logic in the method must check the value of the `kind` parameter (which will be either `UICollectionElementKindSectionHeader` or `UICollectionElementKindSectionFooter`) to determine whether to return a section header or section footer.

```
if ([kind isEqualToString:UICollectionElementKindSectionHeader]) {

    PHGSectionHeader *sectionHeader =
    [collectionView dequeueReusableSupplementaryViewOfKind:kind
    withReuseIdentifier:kSectionHeader forIndexPath:indexPath];

    [sectionHeader.headerLabel
     setText:self.assetGroupArray[indexPath.section]];

    supplementaryView = sectionHeader;
}
```

To get an instance of the custom `PHGSectionHeader`, the collection view is asked to provide a supplementary view for the specified index path, using the dequeue with reuse identifier method. Note that the reuse identifier must be the same as specified in Interface Builder previously for the section header. This method will either instantiate a new view or reuse an existing view that is no longer being displayed. Then the title of the section is looked up in the group array, and put in the header's title label.

For cells, the `collectionView:cellForItematIndexPath:` method is called. In this method, a cell is dequeued for the reuse identifier specified (this must match the reuse identifier specified for the cell in Interface Builder).

```
PHGThumbCell *cell =
[cv dequeueReusableCellWithReuseIdentifier:kThumbCell
                             forIndexPath:indexPath];
```

The cell is then configured to display the thumbnail image for the asset at the `indexPath` and returned for display.

```
ALAsset *assetForPath =
self.assetArray[indexPath.section][indexPath.row];

UIImage *assetThumb =
[UIImage imageWithCGImage:[assetForPath thumbnail]];

[cell.thumbImageView setImage:assetThumb];

return cell;
```

If setting up the cells and section header/footer object in a storyboard is not the preferred approach, they can be set up in nibs or in code. In that case, it is necessary to register the class or nib for the reuse identifier for cells using either the `registerClass:forCellWithReuse Identifier:` method or the `registerNib:forCellWithReuseIdentifier:` method. For section headers and footers the methods `registerClass:forSupplementaryViewOfKind:` `withReuseIdentifier:` or `registerNib:forSupplementaryViewOfKind:withReuse` `Identifier:` can be used.

Implementing the Collection View Delegate Methods

The collection view delegate can manage selection and highlighting of cells, can track removal of cells or sections, and can be used to display the Edit menu for items and perform actions from the Edit menu. The basic flow in the sample app demonstrates cell selection and highlighting. Confirm that the delegate for the collection view object is set to the basic flow view controller, as shown in Figure 20.5.

Collection view cells are designed to be able to change visually when they are selected or highlighted. A collection view cell has a subview called `contentView` where any content to be displayed for the cell should go. It has a `backgroundView`, which can be customized and which is always displayed behind the `contentView`. In addition, it has a `selectedBackgroundView`, which will be placed behind the `contentView` and in front of the `backgroundView` when the cell is highlighted or selected.

For the custom `PHGThumbCell` class, the `selectedBackgroundView` is instantiated and customized in the cell's `initWithCoder:` method, since the cell is instantiated from the storyboard. Be sure to use the appropriate init method to customize the `backgroundView` and `selectedBackgroundView` depending on how your cells will be initialized.

```
- (id)initWithCoder:(NSCoder *)aDecoder
{
    self = [super initWithCoder:aDecoder];
    if (self) {

        self.selectedBackgroundView =
        [[UIView alloc] initWithFrame:CGRectZero];

        [self.selectedBackgroundView
         setBackgroundColor:[UIColor redColor]];
    }
    return self;
}
```

By default, collection views support single selection. To enable a collection view to support multiple selection, use the following:

```
[self.collectionView setAllowsMultipleSelection:YES];
```

For cell selection, there are four delegate methods that can be implemented. Two methods indicate whether a cell should be selected or deselected, and two methods indicate whether a cell was selected or deselected. For this example only the methods indicating whether a cell was selected or deselected are implemented.

```objc
- (void)collectionView:(UICollectionView *)collectionView
didSelectItemAtIndexPath:(NSIndexPath *)indexPath
{
    NSLog(@"Item selected at indexPath: %@",indexPath);
}

- (void)collectionView:(UICollectionView *)collectionView
didDeselectItemAtIndexPath:(NSIndexPath *)indexPath
{
    NSLog(@"Item deselected at indexPath: %@",indexPath);
}
```

Note that there is no logic in either method to actually manage the list of items selected—this is handled by the collection view. The selection delegate methods are then needed only for any customizations to manage when cells are selected, or to respond to a selection or deselection. The collection view maintains an array of index paths for selected cells, which can be used for any custom logic. The sample demonstrates tapping an action button in the navigation bar to display how many cells are selected, as shown in Figure 20.6; this could easily be enhanced to display an activity view for the selected cells.

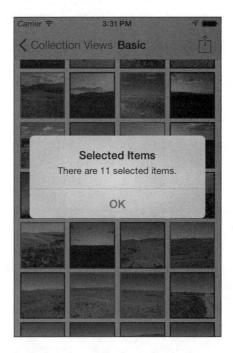

Figure 20.6   Sample app: basic flow demonstrating cell selection.

Customizing Collection View and Flow Layout

Various customizations are possible for a flow layout collection view. The size of each cell can be customized individually, as well as the size of each section header and section footer. Guidelines can be provided to ensure that a minimum amount of spacing is respected between cells, as well as between cells, section headers and footers, and section boundaries. In addition, decoration views, which are views that enhance the collection view aesthetically but are not directly related to the collection view's data, can be placed anywhere in the collection view.

Basic Customizations

The flow layout provided in the SDK can be customized to provide a wide variety of grid-based layouts. The flow layout has logic built in to calculate, based on scrolling direction and all the parameters set for cell size, spacing and sections, how many cells should be presented per row, and then how big the scroll view should be. When these parameters are manipulated, collection views can be created that display one cell per row (or even per screen), multiple cells packed tightly together in a row (as in iOS7's Photos.app), or anything in between. These parameters are illustrated in Figure 20.7.

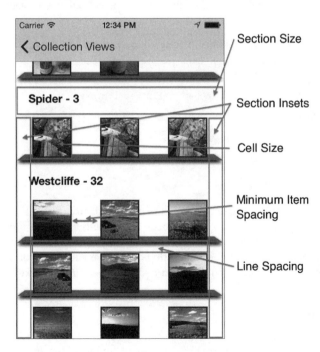

Figure 20.7   Collection view customizable parameters.

There are a few approaches to performing basic customizations on a flow layout collection view. The simplest approach is to set the defaults for the collection view in Interface Builder, by selecting the collection view object (or collection view flow layout object) and using the Size Inspector, as shown in Figure 20.8. Note that adjustments to these values affect the flow layout object associated with the collection view.

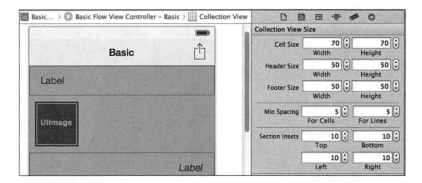

Figure 20.8   Xcode Interface Builder: Size Inspector for the collection view object.

Another approach is to update the items in code, in an instance or a subclass of `UICollectionViewFlowLayout`. In `PHGCustomFlowLayout`, the attributes for the custom flow layout are set in the `init` method.

```
self.scrollDirection = UICollectionViewScrollDirectionVertical;

self.itemSize = CGSizeMake(60, 60);
self.sectionInset = UIEdgeInsetsMake(10, 26, 10, 26);
self.headerReferenceSize = CGSizeMake(300, 50);
self.minimumLineSpacing = 20;
self.minimumInteritemSpacing = 40;
```

Finally, the collection view's delegate can implement methods from the `UICollectionViewDelegateFlowLayout` protocol. These methods can be used to customize dimensions for individual cells based on data, or individual section headers or footers based on data. For example, photos with a higher user rating could be made bigger, or a section header or footer could be expanded as needed to accommodate an extra row of text for a long title.

Decoration Views

Decoration views can be used to enhance the visual look of the collection view, independently of cells and section headers and footers. They are intended to be independent of collection view data, and as such are not handled by the collection view's data source or delegate. Since decoration views can be placed anywhere in a collection view, logic must be provided to tell the collection view where the decoration views should go. This necessitates creating a subclass of `UICollectionViewFlowLayout` to calculate locations for decoration views and to place them in the collection view when they should be visible in the currently displayed area.

In the sample app, tap the Custom Flow Layout option from the top menu to view an example that uses decoration views. The tilted shelf with a shadow below each row of photos is a decoration view, as shown in Figure 20.9.

Figure 20.9   Sample App: Custom Flow Layout example.

The first step in using a decoration view is to register a class or nib that can be used for decoration view. In `PHGCCustomFlowLayout`, a subclass of `UICollectionReusableView` called `PHGRowDecorationView` is registered in the `init` method.

```
[self registerClass:[PHGRowDecorationView class]
forDecorationViewOfKind:[PHGRowDecorationView kind]];
```

The `PHGCCustomFlowLayout` class has custom drawing logic to draw the shelf and shadow. Note that multiple types of decoration views can be registered for a collection view if desired; they can be distinguished using the `kind` parameter. After a decoration view class or nib is registered, the layout needs to calculate where the decoration views should be placed. To do this, the custom layout overrides the `prepareLayout` method, which gets called every time the layout needs to be updated. The method will calculate frame `rects` for each needed decoration view and store them in a property so that they can be pulled as needed.

In the `prepareLayout` method, `[super prepareLayout]` is called first to get the base layout. Then some calculations are performed to determine how many cells can fit in each row, presuming that they are uniform in size.

```
[super prepareLayout];

NSInteger sections = [self.collectionView numberOfSections];

CGFloat availableWidth = self.collectionViewContentSize.width -
(self.sectionInset.left + self.sectionInset.right);

NSInteger cellsPerRow =
floorf((availableWidth + self.minimumInteritemSpacing) /
       (self.itemSize.width + self.minimumInteritemSpacing));
```

A mutable dictionary to store the calculated frames for each decoration is created, and a float to track the current y position in the layout while performing calculations is created.

```
NSMutableDictionary *rowDecorationWork =
[[NSMutableDictionary alloc] init];

CGFloat yPosition = 0;
```

With that established, the method will iterate over the sections to find rows needing decoration views.

```
for (NSInteger sectionIndex = 0; sectionIndex < sections; sectionIndex++)
{
...
}
```

Within each section, the method will calculate how much space the section header takes up, and how much space is needed between the section and the top of the cells in the first row. Then the method will calculate how many rows there will be in the section based on the number of cells.

```
yPosition += self.headerReferenceSize.height;
yPosition += self.sectionInset.top;

NSInteger cellCount =
[self.collectionView numberOfItemsInSection:sectionIndex];

NSInteger rows = ceilf(cellCount/(CGFloat)cellsPerRow);
```

Then the method will iterate over each row, calculate the frame for the decoration view for that row, create an index path for the row and section, store the frame rectangle in the work dictionary using the index path as the key, and adjust the current y position to account for minimum line spacing unless it is the final row of the section.

```
for (int row = 0; row < rows; row++)
{
    yPosition += self.itemSize.height;

    CGRect decorationFrame = CGRectMake(0,
    yPosition-kDecorationYAdjustment,
    self.collectionViewContentSize.width,
    kDecorationHeight);

    NSIndexPath *decIndexPath = [NSIndexPath
    indexPathForRow:row inSection:sectionIndex];

    rowDecorationWork[decIndexPath] =
    [NSValue valueWithCGRect:decorationFrame];

    if (row < rows - 1)
        yPosition += self.minimumLineSpacing;
}
```

> **Note**
>
> The index path for the decoration item does not need to be strictly correct because the layout uses it only for a unique identifier for the decoration view. The developer can use any scheme that makes sense for the decoration view's index path, and is unique for the decoration views of the same type in the collection view. Non-unique index paths will generate an assertion failure.

The method will then adjust for any space required at the end of the section, including the section inset and footer.

```
yPosition += self.sectionInset.bottom;
yPosition += self.footerReferenceSize.height;
```

After all the sections have been iterated, the dictionary of decoration view frames will be stored in the layout's property for use during layout.

```
self.rowDecorationRects =
[NSDictionary dictionaryWithDictionary:rowDecorationWork];
```

Now that the decoration view frames have been calculated, the layout can use them when the collection view asks for layout attributes for the visible bounds in the overridden `layoutAttributesForElementsInRect:` method. First the method gets the attributes for the cells and section headers from the superclass, and then it will update those attributes to ensure that the cells are presented in front of the decoration views.

```
NSArray *layoutAttributes =
[super layoutAttributesForElementsInRect:rect];
```

```
for (UICollectionViewLayoutAttributes *attributes
     in layoutAttributes)
{
    attributes.zIndex = 1;
}
```

The method will set up a mutable copy of the attributes so that it can add the attributes needed for the decoration views. It will then iterate over the dictionary of the calculated decoration view frames, and check to see which frames are in the collection view's visible bounds. Layout attributes will be created for those decoration views, and adjusted to ensure that they are presented behind the cell views. The updated array of attributes will be returned.

```
NSMutableArray *newLayoutAttributes =
[layoutAttributes mutableCopy];

[self.rowDecorationRects enumerateKeysAndObjectsUsingBlock:
 ^(NSIndexPath *indexPath, NSValue *rowRectValue, BOOL *stop) {

    if (CGRectIntersectsRect([rowRectValue CGRectValue], rect))
    {
        UICollectionViewLayoutAttributes *attributes =
        [UICollectionViewLayoutAttributes
        layoutAttributesForDecorationViewOfKind:
        [PHGRowDecorationView kind] withIndexPath:indexPath];

        attributes.frame = [rowRectValue CGRectValue];
        attributes.zIndex = 0;
        [newLayoutAttributes addObject:attributes];
    }
}];

layoutAttributes = [NSArray arrayWithArray:newLayoutAttributes];

return layoutAttributes;
```

With the attributes for the decoration views being included in the whole set of layout attributes, the collection view will display the decoration views, as shown in Figure 20.9.

Creating Custom Layouts

Custom layouts can be created for collection views that do not fit well into a grid format. In the sample app tap Custom Layout from the main menu to see an example of a layout that is more complex than a grid format. This layout presents images from the photo library in a continuous sine curve, even between section breaks as shown in Figure 20.10.

Figure 20.10   Sample app: custom layout example.

To create a subclass of `UICollectionViewLayout`, several methods need to be implemented:

- The `collectionViewContentSize` method tells the collection view how to size the scroll view.

- The `layoutAttributesForElementsInRect:` method tells the collection view all the layout attributes necessary for cells, section headers and footers, and decoration views in the rectangle specified.

- The `layoutAttributesForItemAtIndexPath:` method returns the layout attributes for a cell at an index path.

- The `layoutAttributesForSupplementaryViewOfKind:atIndexPath:` method returns the layout attributes for a section header or footer at the index path. Does not need to be implemented if section headers or footers are not used in the collection view.

- The `layoutAttributesForDecorationViewOfKind:atIndexPath:` method returns the layout attributes for a decoration view at the index path. Does not need to be implemented if decoration views are not used in the collection view.

- The `shouldInvalidateLayoutForBoundsChange:` method is used for animation of items in the layout. If this method returns `yes`, the collection view will recalculate all the layout attributes for the visible bounds. This will allow layout attributes to change based on their position on the screen.

- The `prepareLayout` method, though optional, is a good place to calculate the layout since it gets called every time the layout needs to be updated.

In `PHGCustomLayout`, the `prepareLayout` method begins by determining the number of sections to be displayed, creates a float variable to track the current y position during the calculations, creates a dictionary to store the center points of the cells, and creates an array to store the frames of the section headers.

```
NSInteger numSections = [self.collectionView numberOfSections];

CGFloat currentYPosition = 0.0;
self.centerPointsForCells = [[NSMutableDictionary alloc] init];
self.rectsForSectionHeaders = [[NSMutableArray alloc] init];
```

The method then iterates over the sections. For each section it will calculate and store the frame for the section header, and then update the current y position from the top of the calculated section header to the vertical center of the first cell to be displayed. It will then determine the number of cells to be presented for the section.

```
for (NSInteger sectionIndex = 0; sectionIndex < numSections;
    sectionIndex++)
{
    CGRect rectForNextSection = CGRectMake(0, currentYPosition,
    self.collectionView.bounds.size.width, kSectionHeight);

    self.rectsForSectionHeaders[sectionIndex] =
    [NSValue valueWithCGRect:rectForNextSection];

    currentYPosition +=
    kSectionHeight + kVerticalSpace + kCellSize / 2;

    NSInteger numCellsForSection =
    [self.collectionView numberOfItemsInSection:sectionIndex];
    ...
}
```

Next the method will iterate over the cells. It will calculate the horizontal center of the cell using the sine function, and store the center point in the dictionary with the index path for the cell as the key. The method will update the current vertical position and continue.

```
for (NSInteger cellIndex = 0; cellIndex < numCellsForSection;
    cellIndex++)
{
    CGFloat xPosition =
    [self calculateSineXPositionForY:currentYPosition];

    CGPoint cellCenterPoint =
    CGPointMake(xPosition, currentYPosition);
```

```
NSIndexPath *cellIndexPath = [NSIndexPath
indexPathForItem:cellIndex inSection:sectionIndex];

self.centerPointsForCells[cellIndexPath] =
[NSValue valueWithCGPoint:cellCenterPoint];

currentYPosition += kCellSize + kVerticalSpace;
}
```

After all the section header frames and cell center points have been calculated and stored, the method will calculate and store the content size of the collection view in a property so that it can be returned from the collectionViewContentSize method.

```
self.contentSize =
CGSizeMake(self.collectionView.bounds.size.width,
          currentYPosition + kVerticalSpace);
```

When the collection view is displayed, the layoutAttributesForElementsInRect: method will be called for the visible bounds of the collection view. That method will create a mutable array to store the attributes to be returned, and will iterate over the section frame array to determine which section headers should be displayed. It will call the layoutAttributesFor SupplementaryViewOfKind:atIndexPath: method for each section header to be displayed to get the attributes for the section headers, and store the attributes in the work array.

```
NSMutableArray *attributes = [NSMutableArray array];
for (NSValue *sectionRect in self.rectsForSectionHeaders)
{
    if (CGRectIntersectsRect(rect, sectionRect.CGRectValue))
    {
        NSInteger sectionIndex =
        [self.rectsForSectionHeaders indexOfObject:sectionRect];

        NSIndexPath *secIndexPath =
        [NSIndexPath indexPathForItem:0 inSection:sectionIndex];

        [attributes addObject:
         [self layoutAttributesForSupplementaryViewOfKind:
          UICollectionElementKindSectionHeader
          atIndexPath:secIndexPath]];
    }
}
```

The method will then iterate over the dictionary containing index paths and cell center points to determine which cells should be displayed, will fetch the necessary cell attributes from the layoutAttributesForItemAtIndexPath: method, and will store the attributes in the work array.

```
[self.centerPointsForCells enumerateKeysAndObjectsUsingBlock:
 ^(NSIndexPath *indexPath, NSValue *centerPoint, BOOL *stop) {

    CGPoint center = [centerPoint CGPointValue];

    CGRect cellRect = CGRectMake(center.x - kCellSize/2,
    center.y - kCellSize/2, kCellSize, kCellSize);

    if (CGRectIntersectsRect(rect, cellRect)) {
        [attributes addObject:
        [self layoutAttributesForItemAtIndexPath:indexPath]];
    }
}];
```

To determine the layout attributes for each section header, the `layoutAttributesFor SupplementaryViewOfKind:atIndexPath:` method will begin by getting a default set of attributes for the section header by calling the `UICollectionViewLayoutAttributes` class method `layoutAttributesForSupplementaryViewOfKind:withIndexPath:`. Then the method will update the size and center point of the section header using the frame calculated in the `prepareLayout` method earlier, and return the attributes.

```
UICollectionViewLayoutAttributes *attributes =
[UICollectionViewLayoutAttributes
 layoutAttributesForSupplementaryViewOfKind:
 UICollectionElementKindSectionHeader withIndexPath:indexPath];

CGRect sectionRect =
[self.rectsForSectionHeaders[indexPath.section] CGRectValue];

attributes.size =
CGSizeMake(sectionRect.size.width, sectionRect.size.height);

attributes.center =
CGPointMake(CGRectGetMidX(sectionRect),
            CGRectGetMidY(sectionRect));

return attributes;
```

To determine the layout attributes for each cell, the `layoutAttributesForItemWithIndex Path:` method will get a default set of attributes for the cell by calling the `UICollectionView LayoutAttributes` class method `layoutAttributesForCellWithIndexPath:`. Then the method will update the size and center point of the cell using the point calculated in the `prepareLayout` method earlier, and return the attributes.

```
UICollectionViewLayoutAttributes *attributes =
[UICollectionViewLayoutAttributes
 layoutAttributesForCellWithIndexPath:path];
```

```
attributes.size = CGSizeMake(kCellSize, kCellSize);

NSValue *centerPointValue = self.centerPointsForCells[path];

attributes.center = [centerPointValue CGPointValue];
return attributes;
```

With all those methods implemented, the collection view is able to calculate the positions for all the items in the view, and properly retrieve the positioning information as needed to display the custom layout shown in Figure 20.10.

Collection View Animations

Collection views have extensive built-in support for animations. A collection view can change layouts, and animate all the cells from the positions in the first layout to the positions in the new layout. Within a layout, collection views can animate each cell individually by adjusting the layout attributes as scrolling occurs. Changes to the cells in the layout, including insertions and deletions, can all be animated.

Collection View Layout Changes

In the sample app, tap the Custom Flow item in the menu. Perform a pinch-out gesture on any image in the view, and observe the layout changing to a new layout with animations. The cells will all move from their original positions to the new positions, and the collection view will be scrolled to display the pinched cell in the center of the view. The logic to do this is set up in the PHGCustomLayoutViewController. When the view controller is loaded, two pinch gesture recognizers are created and stored in properties. The gesture recognizer for a pinch out is added to the collection view. For more information on gesture recognizers, refer to Chapter 22, "Gesture Recognizers."

```
self.pinchIn = [[UIPinchGestureRecognizer alloc]
            initWithTarget:self
            action:@selector(pinchInReceived:)];

self.pinchOut = [[UIPinchGestureRecognizer alloc]
            initWithTarget:self
            action:@selector(pinchOutReceived:)];

[self.collectionView addGestureRecognizer:self.pinchOut];
```

When a pinch out is received, the pinchOutReceived: method is called. That method will check the state of the gesture to determine the correct course of action. If the state is UIGestureRecognizerStateBegan, the method will determine which cell the user has pinched over and will store that in order to navigate to it after the transition has occurred.

```
if (pinchRecognizer.state == UIGestureRecognizerStateBegan)
{
    CGPoint pinchPoint =
    [pinchRecognizer locationInView:self.collectionView];

    self.pinchedIndexPath =
    [self.collectionView indexPathForItemAtPoint:pinchPoint];
}
```

When the pinch gesture is completed, the method will be called again, and the method will check whether the state is ended. If so, the method will remove the pinch recognizer from the view to prevent any additional pinches from accidentally occurring during the transition, and will then create the new layout and initiate the animated transition. The method defines a completion block to execute when the transition to the new layout is complete. This completion block will add the pinch in gesture recognizer so that the user can pinch and return to the previous view, and will perform the animated navigation to the cell that the user pinched over.

```
[self.collectionView removeGestureRecognizer:self.pinchOut];

UICollectionViewFlowLayout *individualLayout =
[[PHGAnimatingFlowLayout alloc] init];

__weak UICollectionView *weakCollectionView = self.collectionView;
__weak UIPinchGestureRecognizer *weakPinchIn = self.pinchIn;
__weak NSIndexPath *weakPinchedIndexPath = self.pinchedIndexPath;
void (^finishedBlock)(BOOL) = ^(BOOL finished) {

    [weakCollectionView scrollToItemAtIndexPath:weakPinchedIndexPath
    atScrollPosition:UICollectionViewScrollPositionCenteredVertically
    animated:YES];

    [weakCollectionView addGestureRecognizer:weakPinchIn];
};
[self.collectionView setCollectionViewLayout:individualLayout
                                    animated:YES
                                  completion:finishedBlock];
```

> **Note**
>
> All the animations are handled by the collection view. No custom logic was required to perform any calculations for the animations.

Collection View Layout Animations

After a pinch out has occurred on the custom layout, the newly presented layout has a unique feature. The cells in each row are larger the closer they are to the center of the view along the y axis, as shown in Figure 20.11.

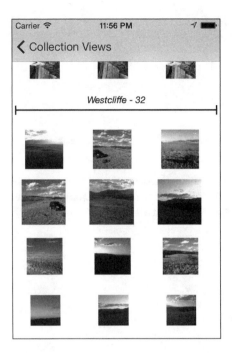

Figure 20.11   Sample app: custom layout example.

As the user scrolls, the size of the cells will change dynamically depending on their proximity to the center of the view. To achieve this effect, some custom logic is implemented in the PHGAnimatingFlowLayout class. The first piece is required to tell the layout that it should recalculate the layout attributes of each cell when scrolling occurs. This is done by returning YES from the shouldInvalidateLayoutForBoundsChange: method.

```
- (BOOL)shouldInvalidateLayoutForBoundsChange:(CGRect)oldBounds
{
    return YES;
}
```

When the flow layout has invalidated the layout during a scroll, it will call the layout AttributesForElementsInRect: method to get new layout attributes for each visible cell. This method will determine which layout attributes are for cells in the visible rect so that they can be modified.

```
NSArray *layoutAttributes =
[super layoutAttributesForElementsInRect:rect];

CGRect visibleRect;
visibleRect.origin = self.collectionView.contentOffset;
visibleRect.size = self.collectionView.bounds.size;
```

```
for (UICollectionViewLayoutAttributes *attributes
    in layoutAttributes)
{
    if (attributes.representedElementCategory ==
        UICollectionElementCategoryCell &&
        CGRectIntersectsRect(attributes.frame, rect))
    {
        ...
    }
}
```

For each cell, the method will calculate how far away from the center of the view the cell is along the y axis. The method will then calculate how much to scale up the cell based on how far away from the center it is. The layout attributes are updated with the 3D transform and returned.

```
CGFloat distanceFromCenter =
CGRectGetMidY(visibleRect) - attributes.center.y;

CGFloat distancePercentFromCenter =
distanceFromCenter / kZoomDistance;

if (ABS(distanceFromCenter) < kZoomDistance) {
    CGFloat zoom =
    1 + kZoomAmount * (1 - ABS(distancePercentFromCenter));

    attributes.transform3D =
    CATransform3DMakeScale(zoom, zoom, 1.0);
}
else
{
    attributes.transform3D = CATransform3DIdentity;
}
```

Collection View Change Animations

Collection views offer support for animations when items are being inserted or deleted. This animation is not demonstrated in the sample app, but can be covered with some discussion. To build support for animating insertions and deletions, there are a few methods in the collection view layout subclass to implement. First is the `prepareForCollectionViewUpdates:` method, which can be used for any preparation needed before animations occur. That method receives an array of updates that can be inspected so that the method can be customized to perform preparations by individual items and by type of update.

For insertions, the `initialLayoutAttributesForAppearingItemAtIndexPath:` method can be implemented. This method can be used to tell the layout where to display the item before putting it in the calculated position in the layout with animation. In addition, any other initial attributes assigned to the item will animate to the final layout attributes, meaning that an item can be scaled, can be rotated, or can make any other change as it flies in.

For deletions, the `finalLayoutAttributesForDisappearingItemAtIndexPath:` method can be implemented. This method can be used to tell the layout where the final position for an item should be as it is pulled out of the layout with animation. Again, any other final attributes can be assigned to the item for additional animation.

Finally, the `finalizeCollectionViewUpdates` method can be implemented. This method will be executed when all the inserts and deletes have completed, so it can be used to clean up any state saved during the preparations.

Summary

This chapter covered collection views. It described how to implement a basic collection view with minimal custom code, and then explored some more advanced customizations to collection views, including customizations to the flow layout, decoration views, and completely custom layouts. The chapter discussed what animation options are supported by collection views, and how to implement animations while changing layouts, while scrolling through a collection view, and while inserting or deleting items.

Exercises

1. The sample app demonstrates how to transition from one layout to another with the Custom Flow menu option. Create a new layout that will display an image that fills the full width of the screen, and scrolls horizontally. Set the pinch-in gesture to display the new layout. Hint: Use a `UICollectionViewFlowLayout` subclass to implement the new layout, and be sure to adjust the logic in the collection view data source to display the full-screen-size image instead of the thumbnail.

2. Implement a method to add and delete items from the collection view (but not the actual asset library). Add support for insert and delete animations.

21

Introduction to TextKit

Both the iPhone and, later, the iPad have supported a number of text presentation elements from their inception. Text fields, labels, text views, and Web views have been with the OS since its release. Over time these classes have been expanded and improved with the goal of giving developers more flexibility with rich text.

In the beginning the only practical way to display attributed text was to use a UIWebView and use HTML to render custom attributes; however, this was slow and carried with it terrible performance. iOS 3.2 introduced Core Text, which brought the full power of NSAttributedString *to the platform from the Mac. Core Text, however, was complex and unwieldy and was largely shunned by developers who were not coming from the Mac or did not have an abundance of time to invest in text rendering for their apps.*

Enter TextKit. Announced as part of iOS 7, TextKit is not a framework in the traditional sense. Instead, TextKit is the nomenclature for a set of enhancements to existing text-displaying objects to easily render and work with attributed strings. Although TextKit adds several new features and functionalities beyond what Core Text offered, a lot of that functionality is re-created in TextKit, albeit in a much easier fashion. Existing Core Text code likewise is easily portable to TextKit, often needing no changes or only very minor changes through the use of toll-free bridges.

An introduction to TextKit is laid out over the following pages. It will demonstrate some of the basic principles of text handling on iOS 7; however, working with text on modern devices is a vast topic, worthy of its own publication. Apple has put considerable time and effort into making advanced text layout and rendering easier than it has ever been in the past. The techniques and tools described will provide a stepping stone into a world of virtually limitless text presentation.

Sample App

The sample app (Figure 21.1) is a simple table view–based app that will allow the user to explore four of the many features of iOS 7's TextKit. There is very little overhead for the sample app not directly related to working with the new TextKit functionality. It consists of a main view built on a `UINavigationController` and a table view that allows the selection of one of four items. The sample app provides demos for Dynamic Link Detection, which will automatically detect and highlight various data types; Hit Detection, which enables the user to select a word from a UITextView; and Content Specific Highlighting, which demos TextKit's capability to work with attributed strings. Lastly, the sample app exhibits Exclusion Paths, which exhibits the capability to wrap text around objects or bezier paths.

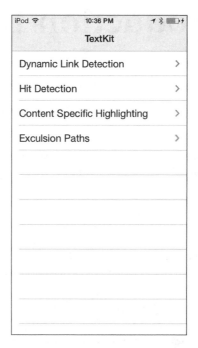

Figure 21.1   A look at the sample app showing a table view with options for different TextKit functionalities.

Introducing **NSLayoutManager**

NSLayoutManger was first introduced with iOS 7. It can be used to coordinate the layout and display of characters held in an NSTextStore, which is covered in the following section. NSLayoutManager can be used to render multiple NSTextViews together to create a complex text layout. NSLayoutManager contains numerous classes for adding, removing, aligning, and otherwise working with NSTextContainer that are covered more in depth in a later section.

NSTextStore

Each NSLayoutManager has an associated NSTextStorage that acts as a subclass of NSMutableAttributedString. Readers familiar with Core Text or Mac OS X text rendering might be familiar with an attributed string, which is used for storage of stylized text. An `NSTextStorage` provides an easy-to-interact-with wrapper for easily adding and removing attributes from text.

`NSTextStorage` can be used `setAttributes:range:` to add new attributes to a string; for a list of attributes see Table 21.1. Polling the text for currently enabled attributes can be done using `attributesAtIndex:effectiveRange:`.

Table 21.1   **Available Text Attributes**

Attribute	Description
`NSFontAttributeName`	The font name for the text; defaults to `Helvetica(Neue) 12`.
`NSParagraphStyleAttributeName`	The paragraph style of the text; accepts `NSParagraphStyle` constants. Defaults to `defaultParagraphStyle`.
`NSForegroundColorAttributeName`	The color of the text lettering; accepts a `UIColor`, defaults to `blackColor`.
`NSBackgroundColorAttributeName`	The color of the background behind the text; accepts a `UIColor`. Defaults to `nil`, which is used for no color.
`NSLigatureAttributeName`	An `NSNumber` representing whether the text has ligatures turned on (1) or off (0); defaults to no ligatures.
`NSKernAttributeName`	Controls kerning. Although this property is available on iOS, values other than off (0) are not supported.
`NSStrikethroughStyleAttributeName`	An `NSNumber` representing whether the text is strikethrough (1) or nonstrikethrough (0); defaults to off.
`NSUnderlineStyleAttributeName`	An `NSNumber` representing whether the text is underlined (1) or nonunderlined (0); defaults to off.
`NSStrokeColorAttributeName`	A `UIColor` representing the text stroke coloring; defaults to `nil`, which uses the same color set in `NSForegroundColorAttributeName`.
`NSStrokeWidthAttributeName`	A floating `NSNumber` representing the width in percent of font point size. This is often used to create an outline effect. Defaults to 0 for no stroke. Negative values represent a stroke and fill, and positive values will create a hollow stroke.

Attribute	Description
NSShadowAttributeName	The amount of shadow to be applied to the text; accepts constants from NSShadow and defaults to no shadow.
NSTextEffectAttributeName	The text effect; as of iOS 7 there is only one possible value other than nil for off, NSTextEffectLetterpressStyle.
NSAttachmentAttributeName	An NSTextAttachment, which is NSData represented by an UIImage; defaults to nil.
NSLinkAttributeName	An NSURL or NSString representing a link.
NSBaselineOffsetAttributeName	NSNumber containing a floating point value in points for a baseline offset; defaults to 0.
NSUnderlineColorAttributeName	A UIColor representing the color of the underline stroke; defaults to nil for same as foreground color.
NSStrikethroughColorAttributeName	A UIColor representing the color of the strikethrough stroke; defaults to nil for same as foreground color.
NSObliquenessAttributeName	An NSNumber floating-point value controlling the skew applied to glyphs. Defaults to 0 for no skew.
NSExpansionAttributeName	An NSNumber floating-point value controlling the expansion applied to glyphs. Defaults to 0 for no expansion.
NSWritingDirectionAttributeName	Accepts masking from NSWritingDirection and NSTextWritingDirection.
NSVerticalGlyphFormAttributeName	An NSNumber representing either horizontal text (0) or vertical text (1).

NSLayoutManagerDelegate

NSLayoutManager also has an associated delegate that can be used to handle how the text is rendered. One of the most useful sets of methods deals with the handling of line fragments that can be used to specify exactly how the line and paragraphs break. Additionally, methods are available when the text has finished rendering.

NSTextContainer

The NSTextContainer is another important new addition to iOS 7's TextKit. An NSTextContainer defines a region in which text is laid out; NSLayoutManagers discussed in the preceding section can control multiple NSTextContainers. NSTextContainers have support for number of lines, text wrapping, and resizing in a text view. Additional support for exclusion paths is discussed in the section "Exclusion Paths."

Detecting Links Dynamically

Dynamic Link Detection is very easy to implement and provides a great user experience if the user is working with addresses, URLs, phone numbers, or dates in a text view. The easiest way to turn on these properties is through Interface Builder (shown in Figure 21.2).

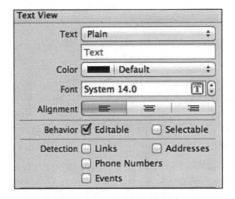

Figure 21.2   Dynamic Link Detection controls in Xcode 5.

These properties can also be toggled on and off using code.

```
[textView setDataDetectorTypes: UIDataDetectorTypePhoneNumber |
➥UIDataDetectorTypeLink | UIDataDetectorTypeAddress |
➥UIDataDetectorTypeCalendarEvent];
```

iOS 7 added a new delegate method as part of `UITextViewDelegate` to intercept the launching of events. The following example detects the launch URL event on a URL and provides an alert to the user:

```
- (BOOL)textView:(UITextView *)textView shouldInteractWithURL:(NSURL
➥*)URL inRange:(NSRange)characterRange
{
    toBeLaunchedURL = URL;

    if([[URL absoluteString] hasPrefix:@"http://"])
    {
        UIAlertView *alert = [[UIAlertView alloc]
        ➥initWithTitle:@"URL Launching" message:[NSString
        ➥stringWithFormat:@"About to launch %@", [URL
```

```
    ➥absoluteString]] delegate:self
    ➥cancelButtonTitle:@"Cancel"
    ➥otherButtonTitles:@"Launch", nil];

        [alert show];
        [alert release];

        return NO;
    }


    return YES;
}
```

Detecting Hits

Hit detection has always been complex to implement and often required for elaborate text-driven apps. iOS 7 added support for per-character hit detection. In order to support this functionality a subclassed `UITextView` is created, called `ICFCustomTextView` in the sample project. The `UITextView` implements a `touchesBegan` event method.

When a touch begins, the location in the view is captured and it is adjusted down the y axis by ten to line up with the text elements. A method is invoked on the layoutManager that is a property of the text view, `characterIndexForPoint: inTextContainer: fractionOf DistanceBetweenInsertionPoints:`. This returns the index of the character that was selected.

After the character index has been determined, the beginning and end of the word that it is contained within are calculated by searching forward and backward for the next white-space character. The full word is then displayed in a `UIAlertView` to the user.

```
- (void)touchesBegan:(NSSet *)touches withEvent:(UIEvent *)event
{
    UITouch *touch = [touches anyObject];
    CGPoint touchPoint = [touch locationInView:self];

    touchPoint.y -= 10;

    NSInteger characterIndex = [self.layoutManager
    ➥characterIndexForPoint:touchPoint
    ➥inTextContainer:self.textContainer
    ➥fractionOfDistanceBetweenInsertionPoints:0];

    if(characterIndex != 0)
    {
```

```
    NSRange start = [self.text
    ➥rangeOfCharacterFromSet:[NSCharacterSet
    ➥whitespaceAndNewlineCharacterSet]
    ➥options:NSBackwardsSearch range:NSMakeRange(0,characterIndex)];

    NSRange stop = [self.text rangeOfCharacterFromSet:
    ➥[NSCharacterSet whitespaceAndNewlineCharacterSet]
    ➥options:NSCaseInsensitiveSearch
    ➥range:NSMakeRange(characterIndex,self.text.length-
    ➥characterIndex)];

    int length =  stop.location - start.location;

    NSString *fullWord = [self.text
    ➥substringWithRange:NSMakeRange (start.location, length)];


    UIAlertView *alert = [[UIAlertView alloc]
    ➥initWithTitle:@"Selected Word"
    ➥message:fullWord
    ➥delegate:nil
    ➥cancelButtonTitle:@"Dismiss"
    ➥otherButtonTitles: nil];

    [alert show];
    [alert release];
  }

  [super touchesBegan: touches withEvent: event];
}
```

Exclusion Paths

Exclusion Paths (shown in Figure 21.3) allow text to wrap around images or other objects that appear inline. iOS 7 added a simple property in order to add an exclusion path to any text container.

Figure 21.3   Text wrapping around a UIImage using iOS 7's exclusion paths.

To specify an exclusion path, a `UIBezierPath` representing the area to be excluded is first created. To set an exclusion path, an array of the avoided areas is passed to the `exclusion Paths` property of a `textContainer`. The text container can be found as a property of the `UITextView`.

```
- (void)viewDidLoad
{
    [super viewDidLoad];

    UIBezierPath *circle = [UIBezierPath
    ➥bezierPathWithOvalInRect:CGRectMake(110, 100, 100, 102)];

    UIImageView *imageView = [[[UIImageView alloc]
    ➥initWithFrame:CGRectMake(110, 110, 100, 102)] autorelease];

    [imageView setImage: [UIImage imageNamed: @"DF.png"]];
    [imageView setContentMode:UIViewContentModeScaleToFill];
    [self.myTextView addSubview: imageView];

    self.myTextView.textContainer.exclusionPaths = @[circle];
}
```

Content Specific Highlighting

One of the most interesting features of TextKit is Content Specific Highlighting. Before iOS 7, using CoreText to modify the appearance of specific strings inside of a text view was elaborate and cumbersome. iOS 7 brings many improvements to rich text rendering and definition.

To work with custom attributed text, a subclass of an NSTextStorage is created, called ICFDynamicTextStorage in the sample project. This approach will allow the developer to set tokens for different attributed strings to be rendered per string encountered. A classwide NSMutableAttributedString is created, which will hold on to all the associated attributes for the displayed text.

```
- (id)init
{
    self = [super init];

    if (self)
    {
        backingStore = [[NSMutableAttributedString alloc] init];
    }

    return self;
}
```

A convenience method for returning the string is also created, as well as one for returning the attributes at an index.

```
- (NSString *)string
{
    return [backingStore string];
}

- (NSDictionary *)attributesAtIndex:(NSUInteger)location
▶effectiveRange:(NSRangePointer)range
{
    return [backingStore attributesAtIndex:location
    ▶effectiveRange:range];
}
```

The next four methods deal with the actual inputting and setting of attributes, from replacing the characters to making sure that text is being properly updated.

```
- (void)replaceCharactersInRange:(NSRange)range withString:(NSString
▶*)str
{
    [self beginEditing];
    [backingStore replaceCharactersInRange:range withString:str];
```

```objc
    [self edited:NSTextStorageEditedCharacters|
    ➦NSTextStorageEditedAttributes range:range
    ➦changeInLength:str.length - range.length];

    textNeedsUpdate = YES;
    [self endEditing];
}


- (void)setAttributes:(NSDictionary *)attrs range:(NSRange)range
{
    [self beginEditing];
    [backingStore setAttributes:attrs range:range];

    [self edited:NSTextStorageEditedAttributes range:range
    ➦changeInLength:0];

    [self endEditing];
}


- (void)performReplacementsForCharacterChangeInRange:
➦(NSRange)changedRange
{
    NSRange extendedRange = NSUnionRange(changedRange, [[self
    ➦string] lineRangeForRange:NSMakeRange(changedRange.location,
    ➦0)]);

    extendedRange = NSUnionRange(changedRange, [[self string]
    ➦lineRangeForRange:NSMakeRange(NSMaxRange(changedRange), 0)]);

    [self applyTokenAttributesToRange:extendedRange];
}


-(void)processEditing
{
    if(textNeedsUpdate)
    {
        textNeedsUpdate = NO;
        [self performReplacementsForCharacterChangeInRange:[self
        ➦editedRange]];
    }

    [super processEditing];
}
```

The last method in the subclassed NSTextStore applies the actual tokens that will be set using a property on the NSTextStore to the string. The tokens are passed as an NSDictionary, which defines the substring they should be applied for. When the substring is detected using the `enumerateSubstringsInRange:` method, the attribute is applied using the previous `addAttribute:range:` method. This system also allows for default tokens to be set when a specific attribute has not been set.

```
- (void)applyTokenAttributesToRange:(NSRange)searchRange
{
    NSDictionary *defaultAttributes = [self.tokens
    ➥objectForKey:defaultTokenName];

    [[self string] enumerateSubstringsInRange:searchRange
    ➥options:NSStringEnumerationByWords usingBlock:^(NSString
    ➥*substring, NSRange substringRange, NSRange enclosingRange,
    ➥BOOL *stop)
    {
        NSDictionary *attributesForToken = [self.tokens
        ➥objectForKey:substring];

        if(!attributesForToken)
        {
            attributesForToken = defaultAttributes;
        }

        [self addAttributes:attributesForToken
        ➥range:substringRange];

    }];
}
```

After the subclass of `NSTextStore` is written, modifying text itself becomes fairly trivial, the results of which are shown in Figure 21.4. A new instance of the customized text store is allocated and initialized, followed by a new instance of `NSLayoutManager`, and lastly an `NSTextContainer` is created. The text container is set to share its frame and bounds with the text view, and is then added to the `layoutManager`. The text store then adds the layout manager.

A new `NSTextView` is created and set to the frame of the view, and its text container is set to the previously created one. Next, the auto-resizing mask for the text view is configured to be scalable for screen sizes and other adjustments. Finally, scrolling and keyboard behavior for the text view are configured, and the text view is added as a subview of the main view.

The `tokens` property of the customized text field is used to set a dictionary of dictionaries for the attributes to be assigned to each substring encountered. The first example, "Mary", will set the `NSForegroundColorAttributeName` attribute to red. A complete list of attributes was given earlier in Table 21.1. The sample demonstrates multiple types of attributes on various keywords. The example for "was" shows how to add multiple attributes together using a custom font, color, and underlining the text. A default token is also set that specifies how text not specifically assigned will be displayed.

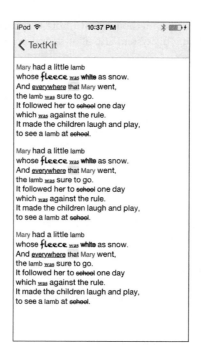

Figure 21.4   Content Specific Highlighting showing updated attributes for several keywords.

After the attributes have been set, some static text is added to the text view in the form of the poem "Mary Had a Little Lamb;" the resulting attributed text appears in Figure 21.4. Typing into the text view will update the attributes in real time and can be seen by typing out any of the substrings in which special attributes were configured.

```
- (void)viewDidLoad
{
    [super viewDidLoad];

    ICFDynamicTextStorage *textStorage = [[[ICFDynamicTextStorage
    ➥alloc] init] autorelease];

    NSLayoutManager *layoutManager = [[[NSLayoutManager alloc] init]
    ➥autorelease];

    NSTextContainer *container = [[[NSTextContainer alloc]
    ➥initWithSize:CGSizeMake(myTextView.frame.size.width,
    ➥CGFLOAT_MAX)] autorelease];

    container.widthTracksTextView = YES;
    [layoutManager addTextContainer:container];
    [textStorage addLayoutManager:layoutManager];
```

```
myTextView = [[[UITextView alloc] initWithFrame:self.view.frame
➥textContainer:container] autorelease];

myTextView.autoresizingMask = UIViewAutoresizingFlexibleHeight |
➥UIViewAutoresizingFlexibleWidth;

myTextView.scrollEnabled = YES;

myTextView.keyboardDismissMode =
UIScrollViewKeyboardDismissModeOnDrag;

[self.view addSubview:myTextView];

textStorage.tokens = @{ @"Mary":@{ NSForegroundColorAttributeName:
➥[UIColor redColor]},
➥@"lamb":@{ NSForegroundColorAttributeName:[UIColor blueColor]},
➥@"everywhere":@{ NSUnderlineStyleAttributeName:@1},
➥@"that":@{NSBackgroundColorAttributeName : [UIColor yellowColor]},
➥@"fleece":@{NSFontAttributeName:[UIFont
➥fontWithName:@"Chalkduster" size:14.0f]},
➥@"school":@{NSStrikethroughStyleAttributeName:@1},
➥@"white":@{NSStrokeWidthAttributeName:@5},
➥@"was":@{NSFontAttributeName:[UIFont fontWithName:@"Palatino-Bold"
➥size:10.0f], NSForegroundColorAttributeName:[UIColor purpleColor],
➥NSUnderlineStyleAttributeName:@1}, defaultTokenName:@{
➥NSForegroundColorAttributeName : [UIColor blackColor],
➥NSFontAttributeName: [UIFont systemFontOfSize:14.0f],
➥NSUnderlineStyleAttributeName : @0,
➥NSBackgroundColorAttributeName : [UIColor whiteColor],
➥NSStrikethroughStyleAttributeName : @0,
➥NSStrokeWidthAttributeName : @0}};

NSString *maryText = @"Mary had a little lamb\nwhose fleece was
➥white as snow.\nAnd everywhere that Mary went,\nthe lamb was sure
➥to go.\nIt followed her to school one day\nwhich was against the
➥rule.\nIt made the children laugh and play,\nto see a lamb at
➥school.";

[myTextView setText:[NSString stringWithFormat:@"%@\n\n%@\n\n%@",
➥maryText, maryText, maryText]];
}
```

Changing Font Settings with Dynamic Type

iOS 7 added support for Dynamic Type, which enables the user to specify a font size at an OS level. Users can access the Dynamic Type controls under the general section of iOS 7's Settings.

app (shown in Figure 21.5). When the user changes the preferred font size, the app will receive a notification named `UIContentSizeCategoryDidChangeNotification`. This notification should be monitored to handle updating the font size.

Figure 21.5   Changing the systemwide font size using Dynamic Type settings in iOS 7's Settings.app.

```
[[NSNotificationCenter defaultCenter] addObserver:self
➥selector:@selector(preferredSizeDidChange:)
➥name:UIContentSizeCategoryDidChangeNotification object:nil];
```

To display text at the user's preferred font settings, the font should be set using one of the attributes from Font Text Styles, which are described in Table 21.2.

```
self.textLabel.font = [UIFont
➥preferredFontForTextStyle:UIFontTextStyleBody];
```

This will return a properly sized font based on the user settings.

Table 21.2   **Font Text Styles as Defined in iOS 7**

Attribute	Description
`UIFontTextStyleHeadline1`	A first-order headline
`UIFontTextStyleHeadline2`	A second-order headline
`UIFontTextStyleBody`	Body text
`UIFontTextStyleSubheadline1`	A first-order subheadline
`UIFontTextStyleSubheadline2`	A second-order subheadline
`UIFontTextStyleFootnote`	A footnote
`UIFontTextStyleCaption1`	A standard caption
`UIFontTextStyleCaption2`	An alternative caption

Summary

Text rendering on iOS is a deep and complex topic made vastly easier with the introduction of TextKit. This chapter merely broke the surface of what is possible with TextKit and text rendering in general. Hopefully it has created a topic not nearly as intimidating as text render has been in the past.

Several examples were explored in this chapter, from hit detection to working with attributed strings. In addition, the building blocks that make up text rendering objects should now be much clearer. Although text rendering is a vast topic, worthy of its own dedicated book, the information in this chapter should provide a strong foot forward.

Exercises

1. Modify the Exclusion Paths demo to add a pan gesture to allow the image to be dragged around the screen and update the exclusion paths in real time.

2. Explore the Content Specific Highlighting in more depth, and see how different attributes discussed in Table 21.1 work together. Add the capability to detect a username beginning with an @ symbol and color or otherwise denote it.

22

Gesture Recognizers

What if an app needed a quick and easy way to handle taps, swipes, pinches, and rotations? Back in the Dark Ages (before the iPad was released), a developer had to subclass UIView, *implement the* touchesBegan:/touchesMoved:/touchesEnded: *methods, and write custom logic to determine when any of these actions was taking place. It could take all day!*

Apple introduced UIGestureRecognizers *to address this need with iOS 3.2 when the original iPad was released.* UIGestureRecognizer *is an abstract class that puts a common architecture around handling gestures. There are several concrete implementations to handle the everyday gestures that are commonly used, and even subclassing guidelines to create your own gestures using the same architecture. With these new classes, complex gesture handling can be implemented much more quickly than in the past.*

Types of Gesture Recognizers

Gesture recognizers fall into two general categories, as defined by Apple:

- **Discrete:** Discrete gesture recognizers are intended to handle cases in which the interaction is quick and simple, like a tap. In that case, the app really needs to know only that the tap occurred, and then can complete the desired action.

- **Continuous:** Continuous gesture recognizers handle cases in which the interaction needs to keep getting information as the gesture proceeds, as in a pinch or rotation. In those cases, the app will likely require information during the interaction to handle UI changes. For example, it might need to know how far a user has pinched so that it can resize a view accordingly, or it might want to know how far a user has rotated her fingers and rotate a view to match.

Six predefined gesture recognizers are available, as listed in Table 22.1. They are actually versatile, and can handle pretty much all the standard touch interactions that are familiar in iOS.

Table 22.1   **List of Built-In `UIGestureRecognizers`**

Class Name	Type
`UITapGestureRecognizer`	Discrete
`UIPinchGestureRecognizer`	Continuous
`UIPanGestureRecognizer`	Continuous
`UISwipeGestureRecognizer`	Discrete
`UIRotationGestureRecognizer`	Continuous
`UILongPressGestureRecognizer`	Continuous

Basic Gesture Recognizer Usage

A basic gesture recognizer is simple to set up. Typically, a gesture recognizer would be set up in a view controller where there is visibility to the view of interest, and a logical place to put a method that can accomplish what is wanted. All that needs to be determined is what view the tap recognizer should belong to, and what method should be called when the recognizer has succeeded.

```
UITapGestureRecognizer *tapRecognizer =
[[UITapGestureRecognizer alloc] initWithTarget:self
action:@selector(myGestureViewTapped:)];

[myGestureView addGestureRecognizer:tapRecognizer];
[tapRecognizer release];
```

Some gesture recognizers will accept more parameters to refine how they act, but for the most part, all that is needed is a view and a method to get going. When the gesture has been recognized in the specified view, the method will get called with a reference to the gesture recognizer if desired.

Introduction to the Sample App

The sample app for this chapter is called Gesture Playground. It has only one view, called `myGestureView` (shown in Figure 22.1), which will be manipulated by the gestures as they are introduced in the chapter. All the code needed is present in the project; certain sections will need to be commented or uncommented as described to see each gesture. To get started, open the project in Xcode.

Figure 22.1   View of Gesture Playground's view controller in Interface Builder.

Tap Recognizer in Action

The code to set up the tap gesture recognizer is in the `viewDidLoad` method in the sample app's view controller.

Now, all that is left to do is something interesting after a tap is received—let's just present a `UIAlertView`, as follows:

```
(void)myGestureViewTapped:(UIGestureRecognizer *)tapGestureRecognizer
{
    UIAlertView *alert = [[UIAlertView alloc] initWithTitle:@"Tap
      Received"
    message:@"Received tap in myGestureView"
    delegate:nil
    cancelButtonTitle:@"OK Thanks"
    otherButtonTitles:nil];

    [alert show];
    [alert release];
}
```

Run the project and tap the view. An alert view will be presented, as shown in Figure 22.2.

Figure 22.2   Single tap received.

Try tapping around the outside of the view. Notice that the alert view does not get displayed unless a tap actually occurs in the view.

Tap Recognizer Versus Button

So why couldn't a button be used for that? It's quicker and easier, and could be set up in Interface Builder with no code! True. In a lot of cases, using a UIButton is the best approach. However, there are times when a tap recognizer is ideal. One example is when there are several input text fields that need to slide up and down with the keyboard, and you want to be able to tap anywhere to dismiss the keyboard. If you place all the fields in a UIView, a tap recognizer can be added to that view to easily dismiss the keyboard.

Pinch Recognizer in Action

The tap recognizer was pretty simple. Now, let's do something more interesting with a pinch recognizer. A pinch recognizer will be set up to resize myGestureView. In the viewDid Load method for the view controller, comment out the code that sets up the tap gesture, and uncomment the following code to set up the pinch gesture recognizer:

```
UIPinchGestureRecognizer *soloPinchRecognizer =
[[UIPinchGestureRecognizer alloc] initWithTarget:self
action:@selector(myGestureViewSoloPinched:)];

[myGestureView addGestureRecognizer:soloPinchRecognizer];

[soloPinchRecognizer release];
```

Next, create the method specified as the target for the pinch recognizer. Note that the method will have to inspect the pinch gesture recognizer to know how far a user has pinched. Happily, iOS will pass a reference to the gesture recognizer to your method, so an instance variable or property is not needed to store it. `UIPinchGestureRecognizer` instances also have a method called `scale`, which turns out to be perfect for setting up a scale affine transform on your view:

```
- (void)myGestureViewSoloPinched:(UIPinchGestureRecognizer
*)pinchGesture {
    CGFloat pinchScale = [pinchGesture scale];

    CGAffineTransform scaleTransform =
     CGAffineTransformMakeScale(pinchScale, pinchScale);

    [myGestureView setTransform:scaleTransform];
}
```

Run the project, pinch in and out over the view, and note that it resizes with the pinch.

> **Note**
>
> To perform a two-finger pinch in the iOS Simulator, hold down the Option key and notice that two circles appear, which represent fingers. As the mouse pointer is moved, the fingers will get closer or farther apart. The center point between the fingers will be the center of the app's view. In Gesture Playground, this is a little inconvenient, because `myGestureView` is near the bottom of the screen. To reposition the center point, just hold down the Shift key while still holding the Option key and move the mouse pointer.

What if the view is small and hard to pinch on? Add the gesture recognizer to the parent view, and it will pick up the pinch anywhere in that view. Just change the setup like so:

```
UIPinchGestureRecognizer *soloPinchRecognizer =
[[UIPinchGestureRecognizer alloc] initWithTarget:self

action:@selector(myGestureViewSoloPinched:)];

// [myGestureView addGestureRecognizer:soloPinchRecognizer];
[[self view] addGestureRecognizer:soloPinchRecognizer];
[soloPinchRecognizer release];
```

Run the project, and notice that you can pinch anywhere in the app and your view will scale. That is one of gesture recognizer's underrated features: the capability to easily decouple the touch action from the view that you want to affect. A touch can be detected anywhere in the app, and the touch data can be used or transformed to affect other views. To be more precise with this method, the touch location for the gestures can be examined using the `locationInView:` method, to determine whether it is close enough to the view to process.

Multiple Recognizers for a View

There are times when more than one recognizer will be needed on a view; for example, if the user wants to be able to scale and rotate `myGestureView` at the same time. To illustrate this, add a rotation gesture recognizer to see how it interacts with a pinch gesture recognizer. In the Gesture Playground sample app, view controller `viewDidLoad` method, comment out the current code to set up the pinch gesture recognizer. Then uncomment the following code to set up both the pinch recognizer and the rotation gesture recognizer:

```
UIPinchGestureRecognizer *pinchRecognizer =
[[UIPinchGestureRecognizer alloc] initWithTarget:self

action:@selector(myGestureViewPinched:)];

    //[pinchRecognizer setDelegate:self];
[myGestureView addGestureRecognizer:pinchRecognizer];
[pinchRecognizer release];

UIRotationGestureRecognizer *rotateRecognizer =
[[UIRotationGestureRecognizer alloc] initWithTarget:self
action:@selector(myGestureViewRotated:)];

    //[rotateRecognizer setDelegate:self];
[myGestureView addGestureRecognizer:rotateRecognizer];
[rotateRecognizer release];
```

Now, to handle both rotation and scaling at the same time, a new method to build a concatenated affine transform to apply to our view is needed. For that method to work, the last and current scale and rotation factors will need to be stored so that nothing is lost between gestures. Notice that these properties have been established in the view controller.

```
@property (nonatomic, assign) CGFloat scaleFactor;
@property (nonatomic, assign) CGFloat rotationFactor;
@property (nonatomic, assign) CGFloat currentScaleDelta;
@property (nonatomic, assign) CGFloat currentRotationDelta;
```

Back in `viewDidLoad`, initialize the `scaleFactor` and `rotationFactor:` to prevent flickering when the view is initially resized.

```
[self setScaleFactor:1.0];
[self setRotationFactor:0.0];
```

Set up the method to handle the rotation recognizer, which conveniently has a property called rotation to let you know how far the user has rotated his fingers:

```
- (void)myGestureViewRotated:(UIRotationGestureRecognizer
➥*)rotateGesture {
CGFloat newRotateRadians = [rotateGesture rotation];

    [self updateViewTransformWithScaleDelta:0.0
    ➥andRotationDelta:newRotateRadians];
    if ([rotateGesture state] == UIGestureRecognizerStateEnded) {
        CGFloat saveRotation = [selfrotationFactor] +
        newRotateRadians;
        [self setRotationFactor:saveRotation];
        [self setCurrentRotationDelta:0.0];
    }
}
```

This method will get the amount of rotation from the gesture recognizer, expressed in radians. It will then call a custom method to create a scale and rotate affine transformation to apply to the view. If the touch is ended, the method will calculate the last rotation amount based on the current state and new rotation amount, and save it in the rotation factor property. Then the method will clear the calculated rotation delta amount—which is used to keep the rotation transformation from getting out of whack between touches. The method to create the scale and rotate transformation looks like this:

```
- (void)updateViewTransformWithScaleDelta:(CGFloat)scaleDelta
➥andRotationDelta:(CGFloat)rotationDelta;
{
    if (rotationDelta != 0) {
        [self setCurrentRotationDelta:rotationDelta];
    }
    if (scaleDelta != 0) {
        [self setCurrentScaleDelta:scaleDelta];
    }
    CGFloat scaleAmount = [self scaleFactor]+[self currentScaleDelta];

    CGAffineTransform scaleTransform =
    CGAffineTransformMakeScale(scaleAmount, scaleAmount);

    CGFloat rotationAmount =
    [self rotationFactor]+[self currentRotationDelta];

    CGAffineTransform rotateTransform =
    CGAffineTransformMakeRotation(rotationAmount);

    CGAffineTransform newTransform =
    CGAffineTransformConcat(scaleTransform, rotateTransform);

    [myGestureView setTransform:newTransform];
}
```

This method will properly account for scale changes and rotation changes from touches. The method will check to see whether the amount of scale or rotation change is not equal to zero, since the gesture recognizer will return the scale or rotation as the amount of change from where the touch began. That amount is called the delta. Since the view should maintain its current state when a touch begins, the method cannot immediately apply the reported touch delta; rather, it must add the delta to the current state to prevent the view from jumping around.

Run Gesture Playground, touch with two fingers and rotate, and watch how the view turns. Also note that pinching still works, but that pinching and rotating at the same time does not. We will explain that later in the chapter. First a bit more about how gesture recognizers handle touches.

Gesture Recognizers: Under the Hood

Now that basic gesture recognizers have been demonstrated in action and the first issue has been encountered with them, it is a good time to walk through, in a little more detail, how gesture recognizers work.

The first thing to understand is that gesture recognizers operate outside the normal view responder chain. The UIWindow will send touch events to gesture recognizers first, and they must indicate that they cannot handle the event in order for touches to get forwarded to the view responder chain by default.

Next, it is important to understand the basic sequence of events that takes place when an app is trying to determine whether a gesture has been recognized:

The window will send touch events to gesture recognizer(s).

The gesture recognizer will enter UIGestureRecognizerStatePossible state.

For discrete gestures, the gesture recognizer will determine whether the gesture is UIGestureRecognizerStateRecognized or UIGestureRecognizerStateFailed.

If it is UIGestureRecognizerStateRecognized, the gesture recognizer consumes that touch event and calls the delegate method specified.

If it is UIGestureRecognizerStateFailed, the gesture recognizer forwards the touch event back to the responder chain.

For continuous gestures, the gesture recognizer will determine whether the gesture is UIGestureRecognizerStateBegan or UIGestureRecognizerStateFailed.

If the gesture is UIGestureRecognizerStateBegan, the gesture recognizer consumes the touch events and calls the delegate method specified. It will then update to UIGestureRecognizerStateChanged every time there is a change in the gesture and keep calling the delegate method until the last touch ends, at which point it will become UIGestureRecognizerStateEnded. If the touch pattern no longer matches the expected gesture, it can change to UIGestureRecognizerStateCancelled.

If it is `UIGestureRecognizerStateFailed`, the gesture recognizer forwards the touch event(s) back to the responder chain.

It is important to note that the time elapsed between `UIGestureRecognizerStatePossible` and `UIGestureRecognizerStateFailed` states can be significant and noticeable. If there is a gesture recognizer in the user interface that is experiencing an unexplained slowdown with touches, that is a good place to look. The best approach is to add logging into the gesture handling methods—log the method and state each time the method is called. Then, there will be a clear picture of the state transitions with timestamps from the logging so that it is clear where any delays are taking place.

Multiple Recognizers for a View: Redux

Now that the chapter has explained how the gesture recognizers receive and handle touches, it is clear that only one of the gesture recognizers is receiving and handling touches at a time. To get them both to handle touches simultaneously, there is a `UIGestureRecognizerDelegate` protocol that can be implemented to have a little more control over how touches are delivered to gesture recognizers. This protocol specifies three methods:

- `(BOOL)gestureRecognizerShouldBegin:(UIGestureRecognizer *)gestureRecognizer`: Use this method to indicate whether the gesture recognizer should transition from `UIGestureRecognizerStatePossible` to `UIGestureRecognizerStateBegan`, depending on the state of the application. If `YES` is returned, the gesture recognizer will proceed; otherwise, it will transition to `UIGestureRecognizerStateFailed`.

- `(BOOL)gestureRecognizer:(UIGestureRecognizer *)gestureRecognizer shouldReceiveTouch:(UITouch *)touch`: Use this method to indicate whether the gesture recognizer should receive a touch. This provides the opportunity to prevent a gesture recognizer from receiving a touch based on developer-defined criteria.

- `(BOOL)gestureRecognizer:(UIGestureRecognizer *)gestureRecognizer shouldRecognizeSimultaneouslyWithGestureRecognizer:(UIGestureRecognizer *)otherGestureRecognizer`: Use this method when there is more than one gesture recognizer that should simultaneously receive touches. Return `YES` to have everything operate simultaneously, or test the incoming gesture recognizers to decide whether they meet criteria for simultaneous handling.

To get the gestures to handle touches simultaneously in Gesture Playground, implement the `shouldRecognizeSimultaneously...` method:

```
- (BOOL)gestureRecognizer:(UIGestureRecognizer *)gestureRecognizer
shouldRecognizeSimultaneouslyWithGestureRecognizer:

(UIGestureRecognizer *)otherGestureRecognizer
{
    return YES;
}
```

Be sure to set the delegate for each of the gesture recognizers, by uncommenting the `setDelegate` calls in the project.

```
UIPinchGestureRecognizer *pinchRecognizer =
[[UIPinchGestureRecognizer alloc] initWithTarget:self

action:@selector(myGestureViewPinched:)];

[pinchRecognizer setDelegate:self];
[[self view] addGestureRecognizer:pinchRecognizer];
[pinchRecognizer release];

UIRotationGestureRecognizer *rotateRecognizer =
[[UIRotationGestureRecognizer alloc] initWithTarget:self
action:@selector(myGestureViewRotated:)];

[rotateRecognizer setDelegate:self];
[[self view] addGestureRecognizer:rotateRecognizer];
[rotateRecognizer release];
```

Then, run Gesture Playground and touch with two fingers to pinch and rotate. The view will now resize and rotate smoothly (see Figure 22.3).

Figure 22.3   Simultaneously rotating and scaling.

Requiring Gesture Recognizer Failures

In some cases, a gesture recognizer needs to fail in order to meet an app's requirements. A great example is when a tap and a double tap need to work on the same view. By default, if a single-tap gesture recognizer and a double-tap gesture recognizer are attached to the same view, the single-tap recognizer will fire even if a double tap occurs—so both the single-tap and the double-tap target methods will get called. To see this in action, comment out the initial tap recognizer in `viewDidLoad` in the sample project.

```
/*
UITapGestureRecognizer *tapRecognizer =
[[UITapGestureRecognizer alloc] initWithTarget:self
action:@selector(myGestureViewTapped:)];

[myGestureView addGestureRecognizer:tapRecognizer];
[tapRecognizer release];
*/
```

Then, in `viewDidLoad` uncomment out the following lines:

```
UITapGestureRecognizer *doubleTapRecognizer =
[[UITapGestureRecognizer alloc] initWithTarget:self

action:@selector(myGestureViewDoubleTapped:)];

[doubleTapRecognizer setNumberOfTapsRequired:2];
[myGestureView addGestureRecognizer:doubleTapRecognizer];

UITapGestureRecognizer *singleTapRecognizer =
[[UITapGestureRecognizer alloc] initWithTarget:self
action:@selector(myGestureViewTapped:)];

//[singleTapRecognizer
➥requireGestureRecognizerToFail:doubleTapRecognizer];
[myGestureView addGestureRecognizer:singleTapRecognizer];
[singleTapRecognizer release];
[doubleTapRecognizer release];
```

Note that the handling methods now being called in the project are using `NSLog` statements for illustration instead of `UIAlertView`, which will block the UI.

```
- (void)myGestureViewSingleTapped:(UIGestureRecognizer
➥*)tapGestureRecognizer {
    NSLog(@"Single Tap Received");
}

- (void)myGestureViewDoubleTapped:(UIGestureRecognizer
➥*)doubleTapGestureRecognizer {
    NSLog(@"Double Tap Received");
}
```

Both the single-tap and the double-tap methods get called with a double tap:

```
2012-02-29 15:53:51.460 Gesture Playground[7911:fe03] Single Tap Received
2012-02-29 15:53:51.644 Gesture Playground[7911:fe03] Double Tap Received
```

If that is not desired, the double-tap recognizer would need to fail before calling the single-tap target method. There is a method on `UIGestureRecognizer` called `requireGesture RecognizerToFail`. To prevent both from firing, carry out these steps:

1. Set up the double-tap recognizer.

2. Set up the single-tap recognizer.

3. Call `requireGestureRecognizerToFail` from the single-tap recognizer, passing the double-tap recognizer as the parameter.

Here is the code (just uncomment the `requireGestureRecognizerToFail` line):

```
UITapGestureRecognizer *doubleTapRecognizer =
[[UITapGestureRecognizer alloc] initWithTarget:self

action:@selector(myGestureViewDoubleTapped:)];

[doubleTapRecognizer setNumberOfTapsRequired:2];
[myGestureView addGestureRecognizer:doubleTapRecognizer];

UITapGestureRecognizer *singleTapRecognizer =
[[UITapGestureRecognizer alloc] initWithTarget:self
action:@selector(myGestureViewTapped:)];

[singleTapRecognizer requireGestureRecognizerToFail:doubleTapRecognizer];

[myGestureView addGestureRecognizer:singleTapRecognizer];
[singleTapRecognizer release];
[doubleTapRecognizer release];
```

Try it with a double tap first, and the single-tap method no longer fires on a double tap.

```
2012-02-29 16:00:11.854 Gesture Playground[7965:fe03] Double Tap Received
```

Custom `UIGestureRecognizer` Subclasses

When an app needs to recognize a gesture that falls outside of the standard gestures provided by Apple, `UIGestureRecognizer` needs to be subclassed. The first decision to be made is whether the custom recognizer should follow the discrete or continuous pattern. With that in mind, the subclass will need to implement the following methods:

```
- (void) reset;
- (void) touchesBegan: (NSSet *) touches withEvent: (UIEvent *) event;
- (void) touchesMoved: (NSSet *) touches withEvent: (UIEvent *) event;
- (void) touchesEnded: (NSSet *) touches withEvent: (UIEvent *) event;
- (void) touchesCancelled: (NSSet *) touches withEvent: (UIEvent *) event;
```

In the subclass, build logic in the `touchesBegan:`/`touchesMoved:`/`touchesEnded:` methods that recognize the gesture, and then update the subclass to the right state as the touches proceed. Remember to set the state to `UIGestureRecognizerStateFailed` as soon as possible to avoid UI delays, and to check the state in those methods to avoid doing any unnecessary logic. For example, if two touches are needed for the gesture, immediately fail in `touchesBegan:` if there are more or fewer touches. If the state is already `UIGestureRecognizerStateFailed`, return immediately from `touchesMoved:` and `touchesEnded:`.

In the reset method, update any instance variables used to track the gesture to their initial state so that the recognizer is ready to go with the next touch.

> **Note**
>
> For more detail on creating `UIGestureRecognizer` subclasses, check out Apple's Event Handling Guide for iOS: Gesture Recognizers at https://developer.apple.com/library/ios/#DOCUMENTATION/EventHandling/Conceptual/EventHandlingiPhoneOS/GestureRecognizers/GestureRecognizers.html. It has all the detail needed, and links to the relevant class references as well.

Summary

In this chapter, gesture recognizers were introduced, including the difference between a discrete and a continuous gesture recognizer, as were the six gesture recognizers that are available in iOS. The chapter walked through basic usage of a gesture recognizer, and then dived into some more advanced use cases with multiple gesture recognizers. Lastly, the concept of a custom gesture recognizer was introduced.

At this point, the reader should be comfortable creating and using the built-in gesture recognizers, and exploring some of the features that were not discussed (for example, how to handle a three-finger swipe). The reader should also understand the basics of how gesture recognizers work under the hood, and be ready to attempt a custom subclass.

Exercise

Create a `UIGestureRecognizer` subclass that will recognize a Z gesture (like Zorro!). (Hint: This should be a discrete gesture, but you'll need to have logic in all three touch methods to get it to work. Don't forget your state changes!)

23

Accessing Photo Libraries

All current iOS devices come with at least one camera capable of taking photos and videos. In addition, all iOS devices can sync photos from iTunes on a computer to the Photos app and organize them in albums and events. Before iOS 4, the only method for developers to access user photos was `UIImagePickerController`. *This approach has some drawbacks; namely, you can select only one photo at a time, and you have no control over the appearance of the UI. With the addition of the* `AssetsLibrary` *classes, Apple provides much more robust access to the user's photos, videos, albums, and events in your app.*

Sample App

The sample app, Asset Navigator, is a minimal reproduction of the iOS Photos app. The sample app will display a table of all the albums available on the device, including the album name, number of photos, and videos included in the album, and a representative image. If you tap an album, it will show thumbnails of all the photos and videos in the album. Tapping a thumbnail will show a large representation of the photo. Before running the sample app, prepare your device by syncing some photos to it and taking some photos. That way, you will have photos in albums and the Camera Roll. If you use iCloud, turn on Photo Stream as well.

> **Note**
>
> To use the `AssetsLibrary` classes, add the `AssetsLibrary` framework to the project, and import the asset classes as needed.

The Assets Library

The Assets Library consists of a group of classes to navigate through the albums and photos on the device:

- **ALAssetsLibrary:** The base class for accessing all groups and assets. It provides methods for enumerating groups, directly accessing groups and assets with URLs, and writing new assets to the Saved Photos album. Any ALAsset or ALAssetsGroup instances accessed through an instance of ALAssetsLibrary are valid only while that instance of ALAssetsLibrary remains a valid object.

- **ALAssetsGroup:** Represents a group of photos and videos. It can either be synced from a photo album in iTunes, or can be the user's Camera Roll or Saved Photos album. It provides methods for enumerating assets in the group, displaying a poster image, filtering assets in the groups (ALAssetsFilter), and getting information about the group.

- **ALAsset:** Represents a photo or video. It provides methods to get available ALAssetRepresentation instances for the asset, thumbnails, and information about the asset, such as date, location, type, and orientation.

- **ALAssetRepresentation:** An ALAsset can have more than one "representation" or format. For example, there might be a RAW version and a JPEG version of the same photo. This class represents one representation of an asset. It provides methods to get images (full resolution, full size, or sized to your specifications); raw data; and image information, such as scale, orientation, and filename.

> **Note**
>
> Do not release your instance of ALAssetsLibrary until you are done with your Assets Library processing. Doing so will create some challenging bugs.

Enumerating Asset Groups and Assets

A common design pattern when dealing with ALAssetsLibrary is enumeration. Because the user's permission is required to access asset groups and assets, you typically need to enumerate the groups and assets to put them in a data structure to use in your user interface. The sample app will enumerate the groups on the device first to gather information about them to present in ICFAssetLibraryViewController. To do this, create an instance of ALAssetsLibrary, and then call the method to enumerate groups.

```
ALAssetsLibrary *al =
[[[ALAssetsLibrary alloc] init] autorelease];

...
```

```
[al enumerateGroupsWithTypes:ALAssetsGroupAll
              usingBlock:enumerateAssetGroupsBlock
             failureBlock:assetGroupEnumErrorBlock];
```

> **Note**
>
> Many of the `AssetsLibrary` methods return void, and accept success and failure blocks. The reason for this is that these methods require explicit user permission, since the images can contain location information. So these methods all act asynchronously, and return the success block if permission is granted, or the failure block without permission.

Permissions

The first time an app tries to access the `ALAssetsLibrary`, the device will ask the user for permission (as shown in Figure 23.1).

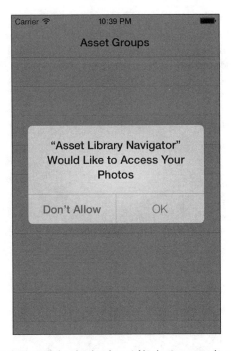

Figure 23.1   Access Permission dialog in the Asset Navigator sample app.

If permission is granted, the `enumerateAssetGroupsBlock` block will be executed; this is described in detail later in the section "Groups." If permission is not granted, the `assetGroupEnumErrorBlock` block will be executed.

```
void (^assetGroupEnumErrorBlock)(NSError*) =
^(NSError* error) {

    NSString *msgError =
    @"Cannot access asset library groups. \n"
    "Visit Privacy | Photos in Settings.app \n"
    "to restore permission.";

    UIAlertView* alertView =
    [[UIAlertView alloc] initWithTitle:nil
                              message:msgError
                             delegate:self
                    cancelButtonTitle:@"OK"
                    otherButtonTitles:nil];

    [alertView show];
    [alertView release];
};
```

If the user denies permission to access the photo library, the alert view presented will explain to the user how to restore permission later if desired. To restore permissions, the user would need to navigate to the right spot in Settings.app (see Figure 23.2).

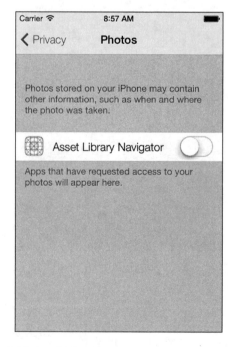

Figure 23.2   Settings.app: photo privacy.

When the user changes the setting, iOS will kill the sample app so that it will launch again rather than coming out of the background and requiring an adjustment to the new privacy setting.

Groups

When permission has been granted by the user, the `enumerateAssetGroupsBlock` block will be executed. The block will be executed on the main thread, but there is no guarantee when the block will be called since it might be waiting for permission. So any logic in that block needs to take that into consideration. The block signature accepts an instance of `ALAssetsGroup` and a pointer to a `BOOL`. If you want to immediately stop iterating, set the `BOOL` pointer `stop` to `YES`.

```
void (^enumerateAssetGroupsBlock)(ALAssetsGroup*, BOOL*) =
^(ALAssetsGroup* group, BOOL* stop)
{
    if (group)
    {
        ...
    }

    else
    {
        [self setAssetGroupArray:
         [NSArray arrayWithArray:setupArray]];

        [setupArray release];
        [assetGroupTableView reloadData];
    }
};
```

The block will be executed once for each available group, and then one additional time. So the method needs to check for an instance of `ALAssetsGroup`, since the last iteration of the block will be executed without one. In that case the method knows that the enumeration is complete, so the array used as the data source for the `assetGroupTableView` can be initialized using the `setupArray`.

The sample app will display several pieces of information about each group, such as the name of the group, the number of photos and videos in the group, and a representative image for the group. Capture each of those pieces of data from each group, and create an `NSDictionary` for each group to store in the table view data source array.

```
NSUInteger numAssets = [group numberOfAssets];
```

First, capture the number of assets in the group. This is the total number of photos and videos in that group.

> **Note**
>
> An asset can belong to more than one group, so adding up the photos and videos in the groups might not give you the true total number of photos and videos.

```
NSString *groupName =
[group valueForProperty:ALAssetsGroupPropertyName];

NSURL *groupURL =
[group valueForProperty:ALAssetsGroupPropertyURL];

NSString *groupLabelText =
[NSString stringWithFormat:@"%@ (%d)",groupName, numAssets];
```

Next, the sample app gets the name of the group and the URL for the group, and then formats the name with the number of assets for display. The URL will be used later to directly access the group without having to enumerate all of them.

```
UIImage *posterImage =
[UIImage imageWithCGImage:[group posterImage]];
```

The group exposes a poster image, which you can use as a representative thumbnail for the group. The `posterImage` is returned as a `CGImageRef`, which can be used to create an instance of `UIImage`.

```
[group setAssetsFilter:[ALAssetsFilter allPhotos]];
NSInteger groupPhotos = [group numberOfAssets];

[group setAssetsFilter:[ALAssetsFilter allVideos]];
NSInteger groupVideos = [group numberOfAssets];

NSString *info = @"%d photos, %d videos in group";
NSString *groupInfoText =
[NSString stringWithFormat:info, groupPhotos, groupVideos];
```

To determine how many videos and photos are in a group, use `ALAssetsFilter`. `ALAssetsFilter` provides three class methods to filter photos, videos, or all assets. To utilize the filter, call `setAssetsFilter:` on the group instance, and then call `numberOfAssets` to get the filtered number of assets. The group can be enumerated using a filter as well if only photos or videos are desired.

```
NSDictionary *groupDict =
@{kGroupLabelText: groupLabelText,
  kGroupURL:groupURL,
  kGroupPosterImage:posterImage,
  kGroupInfoText:groupInfoText};

[setupArray addObject:groupDict];
```

After all the information about the group has been gathered, create an NSDictionary and add it to the setupArray. This will be the data source for the table view. After all the groups have been enumerated and all the data has been collected in the assetGroupArray, the table view is ready to display (see Figure 23.3).

Figure 23.3   Asset Groups in the Asset Navigator sample app.

The sample app implements the UITableViewDataSource protocol method tableView :numberOfRowsInSection: to tell the UITableView to display one row per item in the assetGroupArray.

```objectivec
- (NSInteger)tableView:(UITableView *)tableView
 numberOfRowsInSection:(NSInteger)section
{
    NSInteger returnCount = 0;

    if (assetGroupArray)
    {
        returnCount = [assetGroupArray count];
    }
    return returnCount;
}
```

The sample app implements the `UITableViewDataSource` protocol method `tableView:cellForRowAtIndexPath:` to populate group information in each cell.

```objc
- (UITableViewCell *)tableView:(UITableView *)tableView
        cellForRowAtIndexPath:(NSIndexPath *)indexPath
{
    NSString *cellID = @"ICFAssetLibraryTableCell";
    ICFAssetLibraryTableCell *cell = (ICFAssetLibraryTableCell *)
    [tableView dequeueReusableCellWithIdentifier:cellID];

    NSDictionary *cellDict =
    [assetGroupArray objectAtIndex:indexPath.row];

    [cell.assetGroupNameLabel
     setText:[cellDict objectForKey:kGroupLabelText]];

    [cell.assetGroupInfoLabel
     setText:[cellDict objectForKey:kGroupInfoText]];

    [cell.assetGroupTopImageView
     setImage:[cellDict objectForKey:kGroupPosterImage]];

    return cell;
}
```

This will display the customized label including the group name and total number of images, the number of photos and videos in the group, and the poster image for the group.

When the user touches a group, the sample app will display all the assets for that group. Since the sample project uses storyboarding for navigation, a segue is set up from the table cell to the `ICFAssetGroupViewController`. The segue is named `ViewAssetGroup` (see Figure 23.4).

In `ICFAssetLibaryViewController` implement the `prepareForSegue:sender:` method to set up the destination view controller.

```objc
- (void)prepareForSegue:(UIStoryboardSegue *)segue
                 sender:(id)sender
{
    if ([segue.identifier isEqualToString:@"ViewAssetGroup"])
    {
        NSIndexPath *indexPath =
        [assetGroupTableView indexPathForSelectedRow];

        NSDictionary *selectedDict =
        [assetGroupArray objectAtIndex:indexPath.row];

        [self setSelectedGroupURL:
         [selectedDict objectForKey:kGroupURL]];
```

```
ICFAssetGroupViewController *aVC =
segue.destinationViewController;

[aVC setAssetGroupURL:[self selectedGroupURL]];

[aVC setAssetGroupName:
  [selectedDict objectForKey:kGroupLabelText]];

[assetGroupTableView
  deselectRowAtIndexPath:indexPath animated:NO];
}
}
```

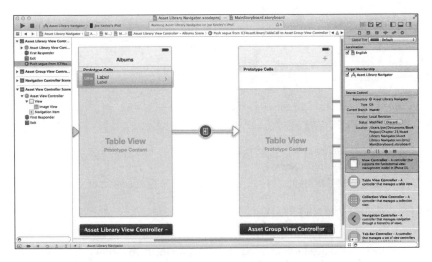

Figure 23.4   View Asset Group storyboard segue.

In the prepareForSegue:sender: method, first check that the segue's identifier is equal to ViewAssetGroup, since this method will be called for any segue set up for ICFAssetLibrary ViewController. Then, determine the index path for the tapped row in the table—use the row to get the associated dictionary of group information. Set the group URL and group name in the destination view controller, and then deselect the tapped row so that it does not stay selected.

Assets

In the ICFAssetGroupViewController viewDidLoad method, start by displaying the group name as the view title, and set up an ALAssetsLibrary property so that it will be available throughout the life cycle of the view controller. Prepare an empty mutable array that will be populated with ALAsset instances. Also check whether the selected group is the Camera Roll; if so, enable the Add button so that the user can take a picture with the camera and see it.

```
- (void)viewDidLoad
{
    [super viewDidLoad];

    [self setTitle:self.assetGroupName];

    NSRange cameraRollLoc =
    [self.assetGroupName rangeOfString:@"Camera Roll"];

    if (cameraRollLoc.location == NSNotFound)
    {
        [self.addButton setEnabled:NO];
    }

    ALAssetsLibrary *setupAssetsLibrary =
    [[ALAssetsLibrary alloc] init];

    [self setAssetsLibrary:setupAssetsLibrary];
    [setupAssetsLibrary release];

    NSMutableArray *setupArray = [[NSMutableArray alloc] init];
    [self setAssetArray:setupArray];
    [setupArray release];

    [self retrieveAssetGroupByURL];
}
```

Next, retrieve the selected asset group using the URL provided. To retrieve the asset group by URL, you need to set up a result block and an error block. The result block accepts an ALAssetsGroup instance, and the error block accepts an NSError instance.

```
- (void)retrieveAssetGroupByURL
{
    void (^retrieveGroupBlock)(ALAssetsGroup*) =
    ^(ALAssetsGroup* group)
    {
        if (group)
        {
            [self enumerateGroupAssetsForGroup:group];
        }
        else
        {
            NSLog(@"Error. Can't find group!");
        }
    };
```

```objc
void (^handleAssetGroupErrorBlock)(NSError*) =
^(NSError* error)
{
    NSString *errMsg = @"Error accessing group";

    UIAlertView* alertView =
    [[UIAlertView alloc] initWithTitle:nil
                              message:errMsg
                              delegate:nil
                    cancelButtonTitle:@"OK"
                    otherButtonTitles:nil];

    [alertView show];
    [alertView release];
};

[self.assetsLibrary groupForURL:self.assetGroupURL
                    resultBlock:retrieveGroupBlock
                   failureBlock:handleAssetGroupErrorBlock];
}
```

If the group cannot be found, a log entry will be written to the console. If permission has been denied, the error block will present an alert view. If no error is encountered and the group is found, the block will call the `enumerateAssetsForGroup:` method.

```objc
- (void)enumerateGroupAssetsForGroup:(ALAssetsGroup *)group
{
    NSInteger lastIndex = [group numberOfAssets] - 1;

    void (^addAsset)(ALAsset*, NSUInteger, BOOL*) =
    ^(ALAsset* result, NSUInteger index, BOOL* stop)
    {
        if (result != nil)
        {
            [self.assetArray addObject:result];
        }

        if (index == lastIndex)
        {
            [self.assetTableView reloadData];
        }
    };

    [group enumerateAssetsUsingBlock:addAsset];
}
```

In this method, you calculate the last index to know when it is time to reload the table view's data. While the block enumerates the assets, add each `ALAsset` to the view controller's `assetArray` property.

Displaying Assets

Asset Navigator will display the assets in a group in a `UITableView`, similar to the way that Apple's Photos app does with four images per row. To do this, determine how many rows are needed.

```
- (NSInteger)tableView:(UITableView *)tableView
 numberOfRowsInSection:(NSInteger)section
{
    NSInteger returnCount = 0;

    if (assetArray && ([assetArray count] > 0))
    {
        if ([assetArray count] % 4 == 0)
        {
            returnCount = ([assetArray count] / 4);
        }
        else
        {
            returnCount = ([assetArray count] / 4) + 1;
        }
    }
    return returnCount;
}
```

If the number of assets in the group is evenly divisible by four, divide the number of assets by four. Otherwise, divide by four and add one to get the right number of rows. Since you are using integer division, you will always have at least one row.

When setting up the table view cells, you can safely assume with this logic that each row will have at least one image. A custom `UITableViewCell` subclass is used, called `ICFAssetGroupTableCell`. This custom table cell has four images and four buttons:

```
- (UITableViewCell *)tableView:(UITableView *)tableView
        cellForRowAtIndexPath:(NSIndexPath *)indexPath
{
    NSString *cellID = @"ICFAssetGroupTableCell";
    ICFAssetGroupTableCell *cell = (ICFAssetGroupTableCell *)
    [tableView dequeueReusableCellWithIdentifier:cellID];
```

```
ALAsset *firstAsset =
[assetArray objectAtIndex:indexPath.row * 4];

[cell.assetButton1 setImage:
 [UIImage imageWithCGImage:[firstAsset thumbnail]]
                    forState:UIControlStateNormal];

[cell.assetButton1 setTag:indexPath.row * 4];

if (indexPath.row * 4 + 1 < [assetArray count])
{
    ALAsset *secondAsset =
    [assetArray objectAtIndex:indexPath.row * 4 + 1];

    [cell.assetButton2 setImage:
     [UIImage imageWithCGImage:[secondAsset thumbnail]]
                        forState:UIControlStateNormal];

    [cell.assetButton2 setTag:indexPath.row * 4 + 1];
    [cell.assetButton2 setEnabled:YES];
}
else
{
    [cell.assetButton2 setImage:nil
                        forState:UIControlStateNormal];

    [cell.assetButton2 setEnabled:NO];
}

if (indexPath.row * 4 + 2 < [assetArray count])
{
    ALAsset *thirdAsset =
    [assetArray objectAtIndex:indexPath.row * 4 + 2];

    [cell.assetButton3 setImage:
     [UIImage imageWithCGImage:[thirdAsset thumbnail]]
                        forState:UIControlStateNormal];

    [cell.assetButton3 setTag:indexPath.row * 4 + 2];
    [cell.assetButton3 setEnabled:YES];
}
else
{
```

```
                [cell.assetButton3 setImage:nil
                                 forState:UIControlStateNormal];

                [cell.assetButton3 setEnabled:NO];
        }

        if (indexPath.row * 4 + 3 < [assetArray count])
        {
            ALAsset *fourthAsset =
            [assetArray objectAtIndex:indexPath.row * 4 + 3];

            [cell.assetButton4 setImage:
             [UIImage imageWithCGImage:[fourthAsset thumbnail]]
                             forState:UIControlStateNormal];

            [cell.assetButton4 setTag:indexPath.row * 4 + 3];
            [cell.assetButton4 setEnabled:YES];
        }
        else
        {
            [cell.assetButton4 setImage:nil
                             forState:UIControlStateNormal];

            [cell.assetButton4 setEnabled:NO];
        }

        return cell;
}
```

For the second, third, and fourth images, check to see whether the `assetArray` has an entry. If so, set the image from the `ALAsset`, enable the button, and set the tag to the index of the asset; otherwise, set the corresponding image to `nil` and disable the button. Note that `ALAsset` has a method called `thumbnail` that returns a `CGImageRef`. This method returns a 75-pixel-by-75-pixel thumbnail. You can use this to create a `UIImage` and populate the `UIImageView` in the cell (see Figure 23.5).

Next, you need to set up navigation to the full-screen view for an asset. Since the sample project uses storyboarding for navigation, a segue is set up from each of the four buttons in the table cell to the `ICFAssetViewController`. The segues are named `ViewAssetImage` (see Figure 23.6).

Figure 23.5   Asset Groups: Camera Roll.

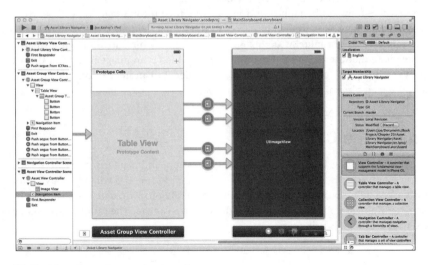

Figure 23.6   View Asset Image storyboard segue.

In `ICFAssetGroupViewController` implement the `prepareForSegue:` method.

```
- (void)prepareForSegue:(UIStoryboardSegue *)segue
                sender:(id)sender
{
    if ([segue.identifier isEqualToString:@"ViewAssetImage"])
    {
        NSInteger indexForAsset = [sender tag];

        ALAsset *selectedAsset =
        [assetArray objectAtIndex:indexForAsset];

        ICFAssetViewController *aVC =
        segue.destinationViewController;

        ALAssetRepresentation *rep =
        [selectedAsset defaultRepresentation];

        UIImage *img =
        [UIImage imageWithCGImage:[rep fullScreenImage]];

        [aVC setAssetImage: img];
    }
}
```

In that method, first check that the segue's identifier is equal to `ViewAssetImage`. Then, determine the asset's index for the tapped button by using the button's tag. You will get the default representation for the asset, from which you can then get a full-screen image to display. Each `ALAsset` can have one or more `ALAssetRepresentations`, which are different formats of the same asset. Note that the default representation for a video is an image instead of the actual video. Set that image on the destination view controller. Tap an image from the group view to see the full-screen view of an image (see Figure 23.7).

Saving to the Camera Roll

To save an image so that the user can see it in Photos.app, an image first needs to be acquired. The simplest approach is to utilize `UIImagePickerController`. iOS will allow saving an image only to the Saved Photos album, which is called "Saved Photos" on a device that does not have a camera, or "Camera Roll" on a device that does have a camera. The sample app assumes that a device with a camera is being used.

Figure 23.7   Asset detail view.

In `ICFAssetGroupViewController` there is a `UIButton` called `addButton` that is wired in the storyboard to call `addButtonTouched:` when it is touched. This button is made visible only when viewing the Camera Roll album. When tapped, the method will present an instance of `UIImagePickerController` that is configured to only access the camera. If the device does not have a camera, a `UIAlertView` is presented.

```
- (IBAction)addButtonTouched:(id)sender
{
    if ([UIImagePickerController isSourceTypeAvailable:
        UIImagePickerControllerSourceTypeCamera])
    {

        UIImagePickerController *ip =
        [[UIImagePickerController alloc] init];

        [ip setSourceType:
        UIImagePickerControllerSourceTypeCamera];

        [ip setDelegate:self];
```

```
        [self presentViewController:ip
                            animated:YES
                          completion:nil];

        [ip release];
    }
    else
    {
        NSString *errMsg = @"Camera Not Available";

        UIAlertView* alertView =
        [[UIAlertView alloc] initWithTitle:nil
                                   message:errMsg
                                  delegate:nil
                         cancelButtonTitle:@"Dismiss"
                         otherButtonTitles:nil];

        [alertView show];
        [alertView release];
    }
}
```

When the user picks an image, the UIImagePickerController delegate method will be called
with an NSDictionary of information. Note that the user might have edited the image in
the picker, so the method needs to check whether there is an edited image in the returned
NSDictionary. If not, the original image provided can be used.

```
- (void)imagePickerController:(UIImagePickerController *)picker
didFinishPickingMediaWithInfo:(NSDictionary *)info
{
    UIImage *selectedImage =
    [info objectForKey:UIImagePickerControllerEditedImage];

    if (!selectedImage)
    {

        selectedImage =
        [info objectForKey:UIImagePickerControllerOriginalImage];

    }

    UIImageWriteToSavedPhotosAlbum(selectedImage, self,
     @selector(image:didFinishSavingWithError:contextInfo:),
     NULL);
```

```
    [self dismissModalViewControllerAnimated:YES];
}
```

After an image is obtained, call the `UIImageWriteToSavedPhotosAlbum` function. Specify an image, and if desired a delegate, selector, and context information. In the sample app, a delegate is specified to refresh the list of assets and update the table view with the newly saved image.

```
- (void)image:(UIImage *)image
didFinishSavingWithError:(NSError *)error
  contextInfo:(void *)contextInfo
{

    if(error != nil)
    {
        NSLog(@"Error Saving:%@",[error localizedDescription]);
        return;
    }
    [self.assetArray removeAllObjects];
    [self retrieveAssetGroupByURL];
}
```

Dealing with Photo Stream

Photo Stream is a photo-syncing feature that is part of Apple's iCloud service. When an iCloud user adds a photo to a Photo Stream–enabled device, that photo is instantly synced to all the user's other Photo Stream–enabled devices. For example, if the user has an iPhone, an iPad, and a Mac, and takes a photo on the iPhone, the photo will be visible immediately on the iPad (in the Photos app) and the Mac (in iPhoto or Aperture) with no additional effort required.

To use Photo Stream, the user needs to have an iCloud account. An iCloud account can be created free on an iOS device. Visit Settings, iCloud. Create a new account or enter iCloud account information. After the iCloud account information is entered on the device, Photo Stream can be turned on (see Figure 23.8).

When Photo Stream is enabled, a new album called My Photo Stream will be visible in the list of albums (see Figure 23.9). No additional code is required in the sample app to display or handle the Photo Stream group.

If you take a photo on your device, it will be visible both in the Camera Roll album and in the Photo Stream album.

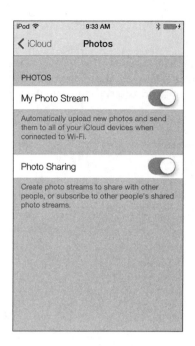

Figure 23.8   Settings: iCloud.

Figure 23.9   Asset Groups, including Photo Stream.

Summary

This chapter explained how to access the photo libraries using the Asset Library classes. It showed how to enumerate asset groups, and display asset group names and counts of photos and videos inside an asset group. This chapter demonstrated how to enumerate the assets in an asset group, and display the thumbnail associated with an asset, as well as the full-screen image for an asset.

In addition, the chapter explained how to save an acquired image into the Saved Photos/ Camera Roll album, and how to enable Photo Stream and view the Photo Stream asset group.

Exercises

1. Add a Play icon to the center of thumbnails for videos in the asset group view, and play videos in the asset detail view.

2. Add the capability to add an album (group), and add assets to the new album.

24

Passbook and PassKit

With iOS 6 Apple introduced a new standard app called Passbook, which is a place to keep and have easy access to a user's event tickets, traveling tickets, coupons, and store cards (like gift cards, prepaid cards, or rewards cards). Passbook is currently available only on iPhone and iPod touch devices, not on iPad devices.

Passbook has special access to the lock screen. If a user is within a geofence, defined by a location or set of locations listed in the pass, on a relevant date specified in a pass, the pass will be displayed on the lock screen so that the user can slide and open it directly in the Passbook app.

The Passbook app displays passes like a stack so that the user can see the top part of each pass. The top section contains a logo and colored background, and can contain some custom information. When a user taps on the top part of a pass, the pass will expand to display the entire pass, which can contain several areas of custom fields, a background graphic, and a barcode. The user can delete a pass when it is no longer needed, and Passbook will delete it with a shredder animation. The Passbook app has support built in to leverage a Web service and push notifications to handle seamless updates to a pass already in Passbook.

Using Passbook requires building a "pass" in a prescribed format and delivering the pass to a user. The pass needs to be built somewhere other than the user's device, typically on a server, since it is a signed archive of files including icons and logos for display, a file with information about the pass, a signature file, and a manifest.

There are a few options available to deliver the pass to the user. Mail.app and Safari.app can recognize a pass and import it into Passbook, or a custom app can utilize PassKit to add a new pass or update an existing pass. For testing passes, the iOS Simulator can display a pass when it is dropped onto it.

PassKit is part of the iOS SDK that can be used by custom apps to import or update a pass in Passbook, check whether a pass is new or updated, and display some information about existing passes.

This chapter describes the design considerations relevant to different pass types, and how to build and test passes for Passbook. It demonstrates how to use PassKit to interact with passes from an app. Lastly, it describes how Passbook can handle updates from a Web service.

The Sample App

The sample app is called Pass Test. It includes pre-signed sample passes for each pass type (see Figure 24.1). The user can add a new pass to Passbook in the app using PassKit, can simulate updating an existing pass with new information, can view the pass directly in Passbook, and can remove the pass from Passbook all from the app. The sample app is covered in more detail in the section "Interacting with Passes in an App."

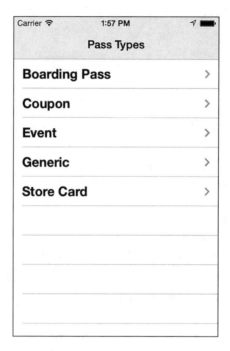

Figure 24.1   Pass Test sample app.

Designing the Pass

Before a pass can be sent to any users, the pass needs to be designed and configured. The pass provider needs to determine what type of pass should be used and how the pass should look. This includes figuring out what fields of information should be presented on the pass, where the fields should be placed, whether a barcode should be used, and what information will be provided to determine whether the pass should be displayed on the lock screen. An individual pass is actually a signed bundle of files, including some images, a JSON file called pass.json with information about the pass and display information, and a signature and manifest.

Pass Types

Apple has provided several standard pass types, each of which can be customized:

- **Boarding Pass:** A boarding pass is intended to cover travel situations, such as an airline boarding pass, train ticket, bus pass, shuttle voucher, or any other ticket required to board a conveyance with a defined departure location and destination.

- **Coupon:** A coupon is a pass that handles a discount for a vendor. The coupon is designed to be flexible enough to handle a wide variety of permutations, such as percentage or dollar-off discounts, or discounts specific to a product or group of products, or no product at all, at a specific location, group of locations, or any location for a vendor.

- **Event:** An event pass is a ticket for entry to any event, such as a theater production, movie, sporting event, or special museum event—anything with limited access granted by a ticket.

- **Store Card:** A store card pass is similar to a gift card, in that the user can buy a preset amount of money on the pass, display the pass to the vendor for payment, and have the payment amount decremented from the pass. The vendor might allow refilling the pass or might require the purchase of a new pass when the amount has been fully depleted. Store cards can also be used as reward or loyalty cards, in which points are collected with each purchase until a threshold is reached and a reward is given.

- **Generic:** A generic pass can be used for anything that does not fit into the prebuilt pass types, or where the prebuilt pass types are not sufficient. Generic passes include a thumbnail image so that they can be used for an organization-specific ID card like a gym membership card.

Each pass type has a specialized layout to be considered when designing the pass. Passes are divided into sections where fields of data can be presented: header, primary, secondary, auxiliary, and back. Passes can also use custom images in some instances. The following sections describe the layouts for each pass type.

Pass Layout—Boarding Pass

A boarding pass has the layout shown in Figure 24.2.

For a boarding pass, the departure location and destination are typically specified as the primary fields (a boarding pass can have up to two primary fields). Secondary and auxiliary fields are laid out beneath the primary fields. The footer image is optional.

Pass Layout—Coupon

A coupon pass has the layout shown in Figure 24.3.

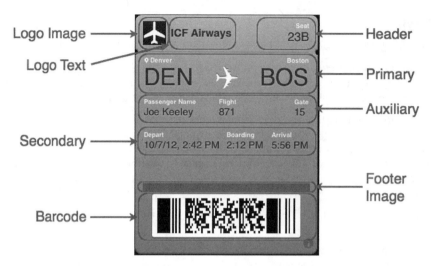

Logo Image ⟶

Logo Text

Secondary ⟶

Barcode ⟶

Header

Primary

Auxiliary

Footer
Image

Figure 24.2   Boarding pass layout.

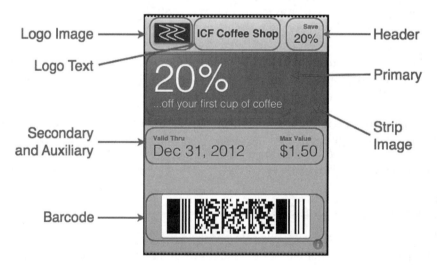

Logo Image ⟶

Logo Text

Secondary
and Auxiliary ⟶

Barcode ⟶

Header

Primary

Strip
Image

Figure 24.3   Coupon pass layout.

A coupon can have only one primary field, and can optionally display a strip image behind the primary field. A coupon can have up to four total secondary and auxiliary fields.

Pass Layout—Event

An event pass has the layout shown in Figure 24.4.

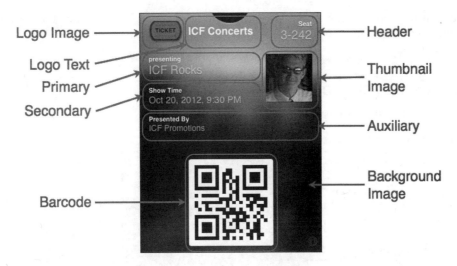

Figure 24.4   Event pass layout.

An event pass can have only one primary field, and can optionally display a background image behind all the fields and the barcode. If provided, the background image is automatically cropped and blurred. An event can also optionally display a thumbnail image to the right of the primary and secondary fields.

Pass Layout—Generic

A generic pass has the layout shown in Figure 24.5.

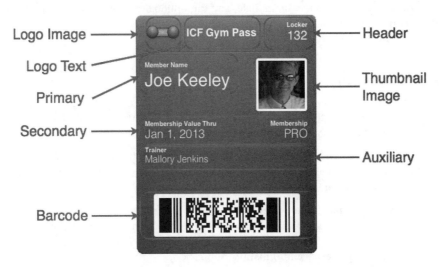

Figure 24.5   Generic pass layout.

A generic pass can have only one primary field, and can optionally display a thumbnail image to the right of the primary field. Secondary and auxiliary fields are presented below the primary field.

Pass Layout—Store Card

A store card pass has the layout shown in Figure 24.6.

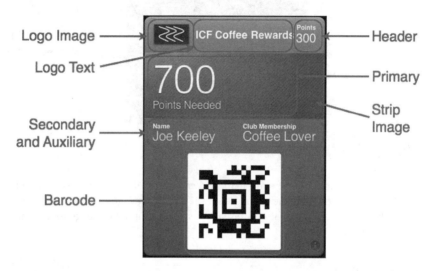

Figure 24.6   Store card pass layout.

A store card can have only one primary field, and can optionally display a strip image behind the primary field. A store card can have up to four total secondary and auxiliary fields, presented below the primary field.

Pass Presentation

Passes are presented to users in several situations outside Passbook, and it is important to understand which parts of the pass can be customized to handle that presentation. When a pass is distributed to a user via email, it looks like the screenshot displayed in Figure 24.7.

The image presented is icon.png from the pass bundle. The top line of text in blue is derived automatically from the type of pass as specified in the pass.json file, and the bottom line of text is the organization name specified in the pass.json file.

When the device is near a relevant location specified in the pass, or the date is a relevant date specified in the pass, the pass is visible on the device's lock screen much like a push notification, as shown in Figure 24.8. More information about this is available in the section "Building the Pass," in the "Pass Relevance Information" subsection.

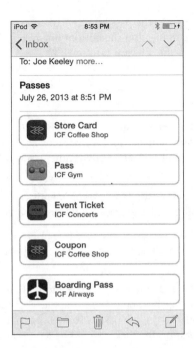

Figure 24.7   Passes distributed in email.

Figure 24.8   Pass displayed on the lock screen.

The image presented is `icon.png` in the pass bundle. The top line of text is the organization name specified in the `pass.json` file, and the bottom line of text is the `relevantText` specified in the `pass.json` file, with the relevant locations.

Building the Pass

A pass will typically be built by an automated server. This section and the next section of the chapter describe building a pass manually so that the steps necessary are clear; automating the process would depend on the choice of server environment and is left as an exercise for the reader.

Several steps are required to build a pass. Apple recommends creating a folder to hold all the files required for an individual pass, for example, a folder called `Boarding Pass.raw`.

Place all the required and desired images in the pass folder. Passes support retina and nonretina versions of images using standard "@2x" naming syntax. The images that need to be provided are these:

- **`icon.png` (required):** A 29×29-pixel PNG image (and retina version), which will be displayed in any PassKit-capable app (like Mail.app or Safari.app) when the app has detected a pass and is displaying the pass as something that can be used. The image is also displayed for the pass on the lock screen. The icon is automatically given rounded edges and a shine effect like an app icon.

- **`logo.png` (required):** A logo PNG image, with maximum dimensions of 160×50 pixels (and retina version), that will be placed on the header of the pass in Passbook. Apple recommends using only an image in the logo, and recommends avoiding any stylized text in the logo. When the logo is presented, it will be presented with the standardized header (with customizable text) that will look uniform in Passbook.app.

- **`background.png` (optional, available only for event passes):** A PNG image with maximum dimensions of 180×220 pixels can be specified for the entire background of the front of the pass. This image is automatically cropped and blurred.

- **`strip.png` (optional, available only for coupon, event, and store card passes):** A PNG image can be specified to go behind the primary fields on the pass. The strip image has shine applied by default, which can be turned off. Maximum dimensions are 312×84 pixels for Event passes, 312×110 pixels for Coupons and Store Card passes with a square barcode, and 312×123 pixels for Coupons and Store Cards with a rectangular barcode.

- **`thumbnail.png` (optional, available only on event and generic passes):** A PNG image can be displayed on the front of the pass. Apple recommends this for a person's image for a membership card, but it could also be used as a membership level indicator or graphical way of presenting pass data.

- **`footer.png` (optional, available only for boarding passes):** A PNG image can be specified to go just above the barcode on the pass.

The majority of work building an individual pass is in creating the `pass.json` file. This file defines all the information for the pass, including unique identification of the pass, type of pass, relevance information, and layout and visual customizations for the pass in a JSON hash. Create a plain text file called `pass.json` in the pass folder, and prepare it with all the desired information for a pass.

> **Note**
>
> Refer to Chapter 7, "Working with and Parsing JSON," for more information on building a JSON hash. Also note that you can unzip any existing pass and examine its `pass.json` file for a starting point.

Basic Pass Identification

The pass requires several fields to identify it, as shown the following example from a pass:

```
"description" : "Event Ticket",
"formatVersion" : 1,
"passTypeIdentifier" : "pass.explore-systems.icfpasstest.event",
"serialNumber" : "12345",
"teamIdentifier" : "59Q54EHA9F",
"organizationName" : "ICF Concerts",
```

The required fields are:

- **description (required):** A localizable string used by iOS accessibility to describe the pass.

- **formatVersion (required):** The Passbook format version, which must be the number 1 currently.

- **passTypeIdentifier (required):** An identifier, provided by Apple, for the pass type. See section "Signing and Packaging the Pass," specifically the subsection "Creating the Pass Type ID," for more info on how to obtain a Pass Type ID.

- **serialNumber (required):** A unique identifier for the Pass Type ID. The combination of Pass Type ID and serial number makes an individual pass unique.

- **teamIdentifier (required):** A team identifier provided by Apple for the organization. It can be found in the Developer Member Center, under Organization Profile, in Company/ Organization ID.

- **organizationName (required):** A localizable string for the name of the organization providing the pass. This is displayed when the pass is presented in Mail.app on an iOS 6 device, and when the pass is displayed on the lock screen as being relevant.

Pass Relevance Information

A pass can optionally supply relevance information, including locations that are relevant to the pass, and a date that is relevant to the pass as shown in this example from a pass:

```
"locations" : [
  {
    "latitude" : 39.749484,
    "longitude" : -104.917513,
    "relevantText" : "...is nearby, stop by for 20% off a coffee!"
  }
],
"relevantDate" : "2012-10-20T19:30:00-08:00"
```

The relevance fields that can be used are:

- **locations (optional):** An array of relevant location information. A location can have latitude, longitude, altitude, and relevantText. The relevantText will be displayed on the lock screen when the device is in proximity to a relevant location. The size of the radius used for the proximity check depends on the pass type.

- **relevantDate (optional):** An ISO 8601 date expressed as a string.

Different rules are applied depending on the pass type:

- **Boarding pass:** Uses a wide radius for the location check. Relevant if a location or date matches.

- **Coupon:** Uses a small radius for the location check and ignores the relevant date.

- **Event:** Uses a wide radius for the location check. Relevant if a location and date match.

- **Generic:** Uses a small radius for the location check. Relevant if a location and date match, or if a location matches and no date is provided.

- **Store card :**Uses a small radius for the location check and ignores the relevant date.

Barcode Identification

To display a barcode on the pass, provide a message, a barcode format, and a message encoding parameter. Optionally, provide an alternative text parameter that will display a human-readable version of the message.

```
"barcode" : {
  "message" : "123456789",
  "format" : "PKBarcodeFormatQR",
  "messageEncoding" : "iso-8859-1"
  "altText" : "123456789",
},
```

The fields used to display a barcode are:

- **format (required):** A string representing a PassKit constant specifying the barcode format the barcode should be displayed in. Passbook currently supports QR (PKBarcodeFormatQR), PDF 417 (PKBarcodeFormatPDF417), and Aztec (PKBarcodeFormatAztec). PDF 417 is a rectangular barcode format, whereas QR and Aztec present square barcodes.

- **message (required):** A string message that will be encoded into a barcode.

- **messageEncoding (required):** A string representing the IANA character set used to convert the message from a string to data. Typically, iso-8859-1.

- **altText (optional):** Human-readable representation of the message encoded, which will be displayed near the barcode.

Pass Visual Appearance Information

A pass can customize the colors of the background, field values, and field labels, as well as the text displayed with the logo.

```
"logoText" : "ICF Concerts",
"foregroundColor" : "rgb(79, 16, 1)",
"backgroundColor" : "rgb(199, 80, 18)",
"labelColor" : "rgb(0,0,0)",
```

The fields that can be used to customize the appearance of the pass are:

- **logoText (optional):** A localizable string, displayed in the header to the right of the logo image.

- **foregroundColor (optional):** A string specifying a CSS-style RGB color to be used for the field values on the pass.

- **backgroundColor (optional):** A string specifying a CSS-style RGB color to be used for the background of the pass. Ignored on an Event pass where a background image is specified.

- **labelColor (optional):** A string specifying a CSS-style RGB color to be used for the field labels on the pass. Apple recommends using white to give passes a degree of uniformity.

- **suppressStripShine (optional):** A Boolean (true or false) indicating whether to suppress applying shine effects to a strip image (available only for a couple, event, or store pass). The default value is false, meaning shine effects are applied.

Pass Fields

Pass fields are specified in an element with a key indicating the type or style of pass; options are boardingPass, coupon, eventTicket, generic, and storeCard. Inside that element are additional elements that organize the fields on the pass.

```
"boardingPass" : {
  "transitType" : "PKTransitTypeAir",
  "headerFields" : [
      ...
  ],
  "primaryFields" : [
      ...
  ],
  "secondaryFields" : [
      ...
  ],
  "auxiliaryFields" : [
      ...
  ],
  "backFields" : [
      ...
  ]
}
```

The fields that can be used to convey pass specific information are:

- **transitType (required for boarding pass, not allowed for other passes):** Identifies the type of transit for a boarding pass, using a string representing a pass kit constant. Choices are PKTransitTypeAir, PKTransitTypeTrain, PKTransitTypeBus, PKTransitTypeBoat, and PKTransitTypeGeneric. The pass will display an icon specific to the transit type.

- **headerFields (optional):** Header fields are displayed on the front of the pass at the very top. This section is also visible when the pass is in a stack, so it is important to be picky about what is shown here.

- **primaryFields (optional):** Primary fields are displayed on the front of the pass just below the header, and typically in a larger, more prominent font.

- **secondaryFields (optional):** Secondary fields are displayed on the front of the pass just below the primary fields, and typically in a normal font size.

- **auxiliaryFields (optional):** Auxiliary fields are displayed on the front of the pass just below the secondary fields, and typically in a smaller, less prominent font.

- **backFields (optional):** Back fields are displayed on the back of the pass.

Inside each of the fields elements is an array of fields. A field at minimum requires a key, value, and label.

```
{
  "key" : "seat",
  "label" : "Seat",
  "value" : "23B",
  "textAlignment" : "PKTextAlignmentRight"
}
```

For each field, the following information can be provided:

- **key (required):** The key must be a string identifying a field that is unique within the pass; for example, `"seat"`.

- **value (required):** The value of the field, for example `"23B"`. The value can be a localizable string, a number, or a date in ISO 8601 format.

- **label (optional):** A localizable string label for the field.

- **textAlignment (optional):** A string representing a pass kit text alignment constant. Choices are `PKTextAlignmentLeft`, `PKTextAlignmentCenter`, `PKTextAlignmentRight`, `PKTextAlignmentJustified`, and `PKTextAlignmentNatural`.

- **changeMessage (optional):** A message describing the change to a field, for example `"Changed to %@"`, where `%@` is replaced with the new value. This is described in more detail later in the chapter, in "Interacting with Passes in an App," in the subsection "Simulate Updating a Pass."

For a date and/or time field, a date style and time style can be specified. Both the date and the time style must be specified in order to display a date or time.

```
{
  "key" : "departuretime",
  "label" : "Depart",
  "value" : "2012-10-7T13:42:00-07:00",
  "dateStyle" : "PKDateStyleShort",
  "timeStyle" : "PKDateStyleShort",
  "isRelative" : false
},
```

The fields needed to specify a date and time are:

- **dateStyle (optional):** Choices are `PKDateStyleNone` (corresponding to `NSDateFormatterNoStyle`), `PKDateStyleShort` (corresponding to `NSDateFormatterShortStyle`), `PKDateStyleMedium` (corresponding to `NSDateFormatterMediumStyle`), `PKDateStyleLong` (corresponding to `NSDateFormatterLongStyle`), and `PKDateStyleFull` (corresponding to `NSDateFormatterFullStyle`).

- **timeStyle (optional):** Choices are `PKDateStyleNone` (corresponding to `NSDateFormatterNoStyle`), `PKDateStyleShort` (corresponding to `NSDateFormatterShortStyle`), `PKDateStyleMedium` (corresponding to `NSDateFormatterMediumStyle`), `PKDateStyleLong` (corresponding to `NSDateFormatterLongStyle`), and `PKDateStyleFull` (corresponding to `NSDateFormatterFullStyle`).

- **isRelative (optional):** `true` displays as a relative date, `false` as an absolute date.

For a number, a currency code or number style can be specified.

```
{
  "key" : "maxValue",
  "label" : "Max Value",
  "value" : 1.50,
  "currencyCode" : "USD"
}
```

The fields used to specify a number or currency style are:

- **currencyCode (optional)**: An ISO 4217 currency code, which will display the number as the currency represented by the code.

- **numberStyle (optional)**: Choices are PKNumberStyleDecimal, PKNumberStylePercent, PKNumberStyleScientific, and PKNumberStyleSpellOut.

> **Tip**
>
> When constructing a pass.json file, test the JSON to confirm that it is valid. This can prevent lots of trial-and-error testing and frustration. Visit www.jslint.com and paste the JSON into the source area. Click the JSLint button and the site will validate the pasted JSON, and highlight any errors. If it says "JSON: good," the JSON is valid; otherwise, an error message will be presented.

After the pass.json file is ready and the other graphics are available, the pass can be signed and packaged for distribution.

Signing and Packaging the Pass

Passbook requires passes be cryptographically signed to ensure that a pass was built by the provider and has not been modified in any way. To sign a pass, a Pass Type ID needs to be established in the iOS Provisioning Portal and a pass signing certificate specific to the Pass Type ID needs to be generated. After the Pass Type ID and certificate are available, passes can be signed. For each unique pass instance a manifest file with checksums for each file in the pass needs to be built so that Passbook can verify each file.

Creating the Pass Type ID

The Pass Type ID identifies the type or class of pass that a provider wants to distribute. For example, if a provider wants to distribute a coupon and a rewards card, the provider would create two Pass Type IDs, one for the coupon and one for the rewards card. To create a Pass Type ID, visit the iOS Dev Center (https://developer.apple.com/devcenter/ios/index.action), and choose Certificates, Identifiers & Profiles in the menu titled iOS Developer Program on the right side of the screen. Click Identifiers and then the Pass Type IDs item in the left menu (see Figure 24.9).

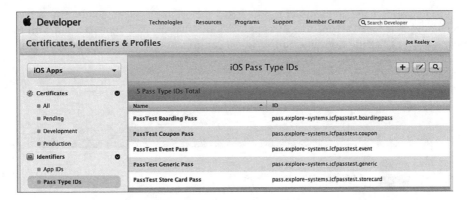

Figure 24.9   iOS Provisioning Portal: Pass Type IDs.

To register a new Pass Type ID, click on the button with the plus sign in the upper-right corner. A form to register a new Pass Type ID will be presented (see Figure 24.10).

Figure 24.10   iOS Provisioning Portal: register a Pass Type ID.

Specify a description and an identifier for the Pass Type ID. Apple recommends using a reverse DNS naming style for Pass Type IDs, and Apple requires that the Pass Type ID begin with the string `"pass."`. Click the Continue button, and a confirmation screen will be presented, as shown in Figure 24.11.

Figure 24.11   iOS Provisioning Portal: confirm Pass Type ID.

Click the Register button to confirm the pass type settings and register the Pass Type ID. After the Pass Type ID has been registered, a certificate must be generated in order to sign passes with the new ID.

Creating the Pass Signing Certificate

To see whether a Pass Type ID has a certificate configured, click on the Pass Type ID in the list, and then click the Edit button. If a certificate has been created for the Pass Type ID, it will be displayed in the Production Certificates section. There will also be an option to create a new certificate for the Pass Type ID, as shown in Figure 24.12.

Click the Create Certificate button to start the certificate generation process. The iOS Provisioning Portal will present instructions to generate the certificate request (see Figure 24.13).

Figure 24.12   iOS Provisioning Portal: Pass Type ID list.

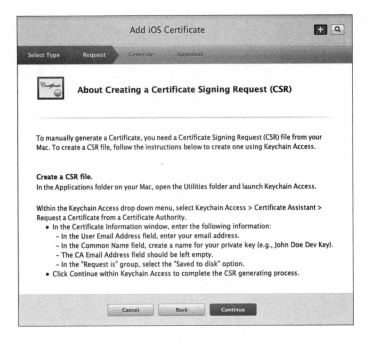

Figure 24.13   iOS Provisioning Portal: Pass Certificate Assistant, generate a Certificate Signing Request.

To generate a certificate request, leave the Pass Certificate Assistant open in your browser, and open Keychain Access (in Applications, Utilities). Select Keychain Access, Certificate Assistant, Request a Certificate from a Certificate Authority from the application menu. You will see the form shown in Figure 24.14.

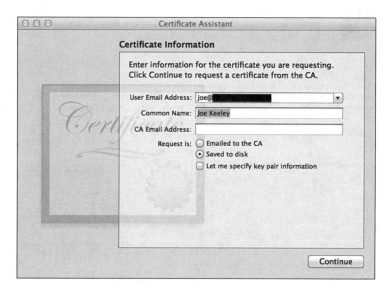

Figure 24.14   Keychain Access Certificate Assistant.

Enter your email address and common name (typically your company name or entity name—it's safe to use whatever name you use for your Apple Developer account), and then select Saved to Disk. Click Continue, and specify where you would like the request saved. After that step is complete, return to the iOS Provisioning Portal and click Continue. The assistant will ask you to select the request that you just saved, as shown in Figure 24.15.

After you have selected your saved request, click Generate and your SSL certificate will be generated, as shown in Figure 24.16.

After your certificate has been generated, you need to download it so that you can use it to sign passes. Click the Download button to download your certificate. After it has successfully downloaded, you can hit the Done button to dismiss the Certificate Assistant. Double-click the downloaded certificate file, and it will automatically be installed in Keychain Access. It should be visible in your list of certificates in Keychain Access, as shown in Figure 24.17. Click on the triangle to confirm that your private key was delivered with the certificate.

Figure 24.15   iOS Provisioning Portal: Pass Certificate Assistant, submit a Certificate Signing Request.

Figure 24.16   iOS Provisioning Portal: Pass Certificate Assistant, generate your Pass Certificate.

| ▼🔲 Pass Type ID: pass.explore-systems.icfpasstest.example | certificate | Jul 26, 2014 9:31:00 PM | login |
| 🔑 Joe Keeley | private key | -- | login |

Figure 24.17   Keychain Access: pass certificate and private key.

To use the certificate for signing from the command line, it must be exported and converted to PEM format. Note that the certificate as displayed in Keychain Access actually contains a private key and a public key. The private key is what is used for signing the pass, and must be kept secret to prevent fraudulent signatures. The public key is used for external verification of the signature. To export the certificate, highlight it, right-click, and select Export; then select a destination for the file. Keychain Access will prompt for a password to protect the file—if it is to be used locally and deleted when done, it is acceptable to skip the password. If the file will be distributed at all, it is highly recommended to protect it with a strong password. Keychain Access will then export the private and public key into a file with a `.p12` extension. Execute the following command to extract the public key and save it in PEM format:

```
$ openssl pkcs12 -in BoardingPassCerts.p12 -clcerts -nokeys -out
➥boardcert.pem -passin pass:
```

Execute this command to extract the private key and save it in PEM format. Select a password to replace `mykeypassword`.

```
$ openssl pkcs12 -in BoardingPassCerts.p12 -nocerts -out boardkey.pem
➥-passin pass: -passout pass:mykeypassword
```

The last item needed to sign is the Apple Worldwide Developer Relations Certification Authority certificate. The certificate will already be available in Keychain Access (under Certificates) if Xcode has been used to build and deploy an app to a device (see Figure 24.18).

Figure 24.18   Keychain Access: Apple Worldwide Developer Relations Certification Authority certificate.

If that certificate is not visible in Keychain Access, download it from www.apple.com/certificateauthority/ and install in Keychain Access. Right-click on the certificate, and select Export. Give the certificate a short name (like `AppleWWDRCert`), select PEM format, and save the certificate.

Creating the Manifest

A manifest file must be created for each individual pass. The manifest is a JSON file called `manifest.json`. It contains an entry for each file that makes up a pass with a corresponding `SHA1` checksum. To create the manifest, create a new file in a text editor. Since the file represents a JSON array, it should start with an open bracket and end with a close bracket. For each file, put the file in quotation marks, a colon, the `SHA1` checksum in quotation marks, and separate items with a comma. To get the `SHA1` checksum for a file, perform the following command in a terminal window from the directory where the pass files exist:

```
$ openssl sha1 pass.json
SHA1(pass.json)= b636f7d021372a87ff2c130be752da49402d0d7f
```

The manifest file should look like this example when complete:

```
{
  "pass.json" : "09040451676851048cf65bcf2e299505f9eef89d",
  "icon.png" : "153cb22e12ac4b2b7e40d52a0665c7f6cda75bed",
  "icon@2x.png" : "7288a510b5b8354cff36752c0a8db6289aa7cbb3",
  "logo.png" : "8b1f3334c0afb2e973e815895033b266ab521af9",
  "logo@2x.png" : "dbbdb5dca9bc6f997e010ab5b73c63e485f22dae"
}
```

Signing and Packaging the Pass

The manifest file must be signed so that Passbook can validate the contents of the pass. To sign the manifest, use `openssl` from a terminal prompt. Specify the `certfile` as the Apple Worldwide Developer Relations certificate, the PEM version of the certificate created earlier as the signer, the PEM version of the key created earlier as the key, and the password set for the private key in place of `mykeypassword`.

```
$ openssl smime -binary -sign -certfile ../AppleWWDRCert.pem
➥-signer ../boardcert.pem -inkey ../boardkey.pem -in manifest.json
➥-out signature -outform DER -passin pass:mykeypassword
```

A file called `signature` will be created (`-out signature`). Any changes to any of the files listed in the manifest require updating the SSA signature for that file in the manifest and re-signing the manifest.

To package the pass, use the `zip` command from a terminal prompt, from the raw directory of pass files. Specify the destination file for the pass, and list the files to be included in the pass.

```
$ zip -r ../boarding_pass.pkpass manifest.json pass.json
➥signature icon.png icon@2x.png logo.png logo@2x.png footer.png
➥footer@2x.png
```

That will zip up all the files listed in an archive called `boarding_pass.pkpass` in the parent directory.

> **Note**
>
> Apple provides a tool called signpass with the Passbook information in the iOS Developer Portal. It comes in an Xcode project—just build the project and put the build product where it can be found in the terminal path. Then execute signpass, providing a pass directory, and it will automatically create and sign the manifest and package the pass in one step. It will utilize your keychain for all the needed certificates, so the steps to export all those are not needed during development. For example, `$ ./signpass -p Event.raw` will produce `Event.pkpass`.

Testing the Pass

To test the pass, drag and drop the file called `boarding_pass.pkpass` into the running Simulator. The Simulator will attempt to load the pass in Safari. If there is a problem with the pass, Safari will present an error message, as shown in Figure 24.19.

Safari will log any problems with the pass to the console. To find out what is wrong with the pass, open Applications, Utilities, Console and look for an error message, as shown in Figure 24.20.

In this example, the error indicates that the pass must contain a key called `transitType`. This key is required for boarding passes, and is not allowed for any other types of passes. Ensure that there is a key called `transitType` inside the boardingPass section of `pass.json`, re-sign the pass, and drop it into the Simulator again to determine whether the error is fixed.

Be certain to tap Add to add the pass to Passbook in the Simulator, because not all pass errors are caught by just displaying the pass. There will be an animation when Add is tapped indicating that the pass has been added to Passbook. If that animation does not occur and the pass just fades away, there was an error with the pass and it will not be added to Passbook. Check the console for any additional errors.

Interacting with Passes in an App

Passes can exist completely outside the confines of an app—in fact, a custom app is not needed at all for the life cycle of a Pass. However, there are use cases in which a custom app is appropriate for getting new passes, handling updates to existing passes, and removing existing passes. The sample app demonstrates how to perform all these tasks.

Carrier
10:15 AM
Yahoo!
m.yahoo.com/?.tsrc=yah
Download Failed
Safari cannot download this file.
OK
go of the past, argues Yahoo!'s Jeff Macke.
» Disney's example
‹ prev
1 / 48
next ›
CUSTOM HOME SALES MANAGER

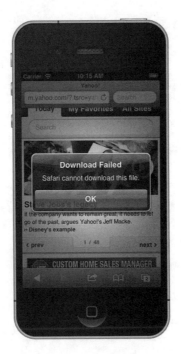

Figure 24.19 Safari in iOS Simulator: error loading pass.

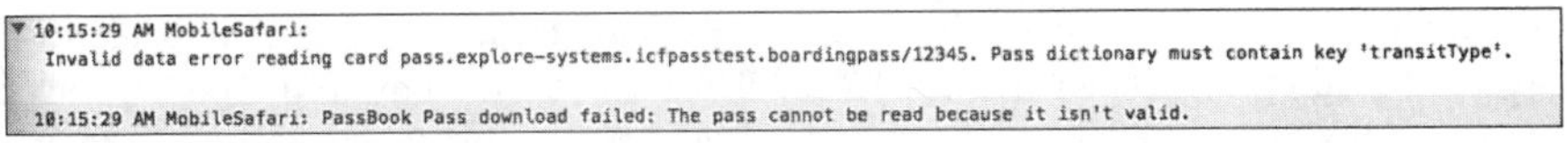
10:15:29 AM MobileSafari:
Invalid data error reading card pass.explore-systems.icfpasstest.boardingpass/12345. Pass dictionary must contain key 'transitType'.
10:15:29 AM MobileSafari: PassBook Pass download failed: The pass cannot be read because it isn't valid.

Figure 24.20 Console: displaying pass error.

Preparing the App

Several steps need to be completed to prepare the app to interact with Passbook. First ensure that `PassKit.framework` has been added to the project, and import `PassKit/PassKit.h` in any classes that need to use the PassKit classes. Next return to the iOS Provisioning Portal and click the App IDs item in the left menu. Click the button with a plus sign to create a new App ID, as shown in Figure 24.21.

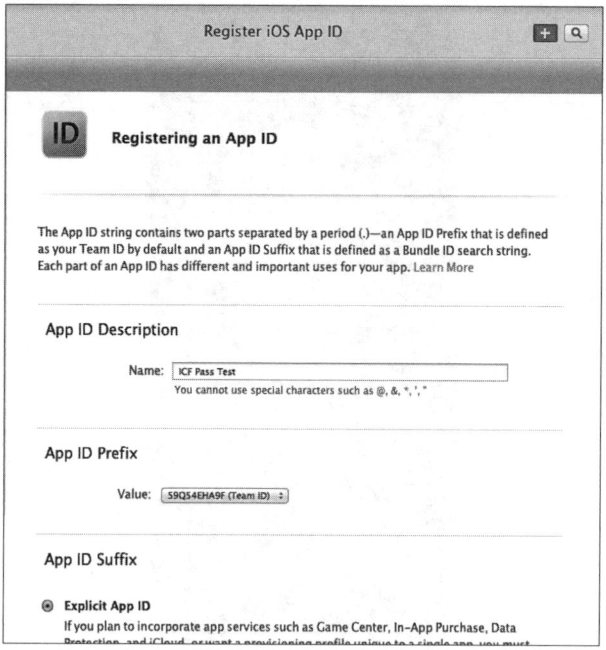

Figure 24.21   iOS Provisioning Portal: create a new App ID.

The new app can be set to enable Passbook while it is being created, or can be updated to enable Passbook after it has been created. To enable Passbook for an existing App ID, click on the App ID on the list, and click the Edit button. Check the Enable Passes option. The iOS Provisioning Portal will present a dialog warning that any existing provisioning profiles created for the App ID must be regenerated in order to be enabled for passes, as shown in Figure 24.22.

Figure 24.22   iOS Provisioning Portal: App ID enabled for passes.

In Xcode, select the project, then the target, and then the Capabilities tab, as shown in Figure 24.23. Setting Passbook to On will have Xcode check that the PassKit framework is linked to the project, the entitlements needed are configured correctly, and the needed provisioning profiles are set up correctly.

Figure 24.23   Xcode showing the Passbook section on the Capabilities tab.

> **Note**
>
> These steps to prepare the app are required only for running the app on a device. Interacting with Passbook works fine in the Simulator without completing these steps.

Now the app is set up to access passes in Passbook. The sample app includes samples of each type of pass in the main bundle for demonstration. Passes would typically not be distributed this way; rather, a pass would more likely be downloaded from a server after some information was provided about the pass recipient. To see how to programmatically interact with Passbook, start the sample app and tap any pass type (this example will demonstrate the boarding pass). The app will check how many passes it can see in Passbook, and will determine whether the selected pass is already in Passbook (see Figure 24.24).

To get this information, the view controller needs to communicate with the pass library. For convenience, a property is set up to keep an instance of `PKPassLibrary`, which is instantiated in the `viewDidLoad` method.

```
- (void)viewDidLoad
{
    [super viewDidLoad];
```

```
    self.passLibrary = [[PKPassLibrary alloc] init];
    [self refreshPassStatusView];
}
```

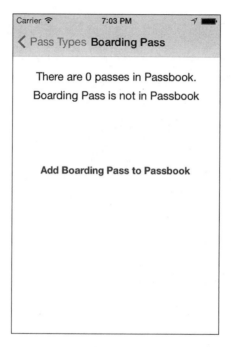

Figure 24.24   Pass Test sample app: boarding pass.

In the `refreshPassStatusView` method, the view controller first checks whether the pass library is available.

```
if (![PKPassLibrary isPassLibraryAvailable])
{
    [self.passInLabel setText:@"Pass Library not available."];

    [self.numPassesLabel setText:@""];
    [self.addButton setHidden:YES];
    [self.updateButton setHidden:YES];
    [self.showButton setHidden:YES];
    [self.deleteButton setHidden:YES];
    return;
}
```

If the pass library is not available, no further action can be taken, so the method updates the UI and hides all the buttons. If the pass library is available, the method gets the information from the `passLibrary` to update the UI. To determine how many passes are in the library, access the `passes` property on the `passLibrary`.

```
NSArray *passes = [self.passLibrary passes];

NSString *numPassesString =
[NSString stringWithFormat:
 @"There are %d passes in Passbook.",[passes count]];

[self.numPassesLabel setText:numPassesString];
```

The `passLibrary` provides a method to access a specific pass using a pass type identifier and a pass serial number. This can be used to determine whether a specific pass is in the pass library.

```
PKPass *currentBoardingPass =
[self.passLibrary passWithPassTypeIdentifier:self.passIdentifier
                            serialNumber:self.passSerialNum];
```

If the pass is present in the library, `currentBoardingPass` will be a valid instance of `PKPass`; otherwise, it will be `nil`. The `refreshPassStatusView` method will check that and update the UI accordingly.

Adding a Pass

Tap on the Add Boarding Pass to Passbook button, which will call the `addPassTouched:` method. This method will first load the pass from the main bundle (again, this would typically be loaded from an external source).

```
NSString *passPath =
[[NSBundle mainBundle] pathForResource:self.passFileName
                            ofType:@"pkpass"];

NSData *passData = [NSData dataWithContentsOfFile:passPath];

NSError *passError = nil;
PKPass *newPass = [[PKPass alloc]
                initWithData:passData error:&passError];
```

PassKit will evaluate the pass data and return an error in `passError` if there is anything wrong with the pass. If the pass is valid and does not already exist in the pass library, the method will present a `PKAddPassesViewController`, which will display the pass as it will appear in Passbook, and manage adding it to the library based on whether the user chooses Add or Cancel (see Figure 24.25). Otherwise, the method will display an alert view with an appropriate error message.

```
if (!passError && ![self.passLibrary containsPass:newPass])
{
    PKAddPassesViewController *newPassVC =
    [[PKAddPassesViewController alloc] initWithPass:newPass];
```

```
    [newPassVC setDelegate:self];

    [self presentViewController:newPassVC
                       animated:YES
                     completion:^(){}];

}
else
{
    NSString *passUpdateMessage = @"";

    if (passError)
    {

        passUpdateMessage =
        [NSString stringWithFormat:@"Pass Error: %@",
         [passError localizedDescription]];

    }
    else
    {
        passUpdateMessage = [NSString stringWithFormat:
                            @"Your %@ has already been added.",
                            self.passTypeName];
    }

    UIAlertView *alert =
    [[UIAlertView alloc] initWithTitle:@"Pass Not Added"
                               message:passUpdateMessage
                              delegate:nil
                     cancelButtonTitle:@"Dismiss"
                     otherButtonTitles:nil];
    [alert show];
}
```

After the user has chosen to add the pass, the PKAddPassesViewController will call the delegate method if a delegate is set.

```
-(void)addPassesViewControllerDidFinish:
(PKAddPassesViewController *)controller
{
    [self dismissViewControllerAnimated:YES completion:^{
        [self refreshPassStatusView];
    }];
}
```

The delegate is responsible for dismissing the PKAddPassesViewController. After it is dismissed, the UI is updated to reflect the addition of the pass, as shown in Figure 24.26.

Figure 24.25   Sample app displaying PassKit Add Passes View Controller.

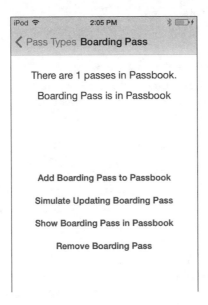

Figure 24.26   Pass Test sample app: boarding pass in the pass library.

Simulate Updating a Pass

Tap on the Simulate Updating Boarding Pass button, which will call the `updatePassTouched` method. This method will first load the updated pass data from the main bundle (this is simulated in that the updated pass would typically be loaded from a server in response to a change), and then instantiate a `PKPass` object.

```
NSString *passName =
[NSString stringWithFormat:@"%@-Update",self.passFileName];

NSString *passPath =
[[NSBundle mainBundle] pathForResource:passName ofType:@"pkpass"];

NSData *passData = [NSData dataWithContentsOfFile:passPath];

NSError *passError = nil;

PKPass *updatedPass = [[PKPass alloc] initWithData:passData
                                            error:&passError];
```

The method will check whether there are any errors instantiating the pass, and whether the pass library already contains the pass. If there are no errors and the pass exists, it will replace the existing pass with the updated pass.

```
if (!passError && [self.passLibrary containsPass:updatedPass])
{

    BOOL updated = [self.passLibrary
                    replacePassWithPass:updatedPass];

    if (updated)
    {
        NSString *passUpdateMessage = [NSString stringWithFormat:
        @"Your %@ has been updated.",self.passTypeName];

        UIAlertView *alert =
        [[UIAlertView alloc] initWithTitle:@"Pass Updated"
                                   message:passUpdateMessage
                                  delegate:nil
                         cancelButtonTitle:@"Dismiss"
                         otherButtonTitles:nil];
        [alert show];
    }
    else
    {
        NSString *passUpdateMessage = [NSString stringWithFormat:
        @"Your %@ could not be updated.",self.passTypeName];
```

```
            UIAlertView *alert =
            [[UIAlertView alloc] initWithTitle:@"Pass Not Updated"
                                      message:passUpdateMessage
                                     delegate:nil
                            cancelButtonTitle:@"Dismiss"
                            otherButtonTitles:nil];
            [alert show];
        }
}
```

The `replacePassWithPass:` method will indicate whether the pass was successfully updated, and an appropriate alert will be displayed to the user.

If the update is time sensitive and critical information for the user to be aware of immediately, a `changeMessage` can be specified in the `pass.json` of the updated pass.

```
"headerFields" : [
  {
     "key" : "seat",
     "label" : "Seat",
     "value" : "14C",
     "textAlignment" : "PKTextAlignmentRight",
     "changeMessage" : "New Seat: %@"
  }
],
```

When a change message is specified, Passbook will display a notification to the user when the pass has been updated (as shown in Figure 24.27). The notification will display the icon included in the pass, the organization name specified in the pass, and a message. If `%@` is specified in the `changeMessage`, then the `changeMessage` specified will be presented in the notification to the user, and `%@` will be replaced with the new value of the field. If `%@` is not in the `changeMessage`, a generic message like `"Boarding Pass changed"` will be presented.

That notification will also remain in Notification Center until removed by the user.

Showing a Pass

To show an existing pass, tap on the Show Boarding Pass in Passbook button, which will call the `showPassTouched` method. Since PassKit does not support displaying a pass inside an app, the method needs to get the pass's public URL, and ask the application to open it. That will open the desired pass directly in Passbook.

```
PKPass *currentBoardingPass =
[self.passLibrary passWithPassTypeIdentifier:self.passIdentifier
                              serialNumber:self.passSerialNum];

if (currentBoardingPass)
{
```

```
[[UIApplication sharedApplication]
 openURL:[currentBoardingPass passURL]];
}
```

Figure 24.27   Pass change notification.

Removing a Pass

To remove a pass directly from the app, tap on the Remove Boarding Pass button, which will call the `deletePassTouched` method. The method will get the pass using the pass identifier and serial number, and remove it from Passbook.

```
PKPass *currentBoardingPass =
[self.passLibrary passWithPassTypeIdentifier:self.passIdentifier
                             serialNumber:self.passSerialNum];

if (currentBoardingPass)
{
    [self.passLibrary removePass:currentBoardingPass];

    [self refreshPassStatusView];
```

```
    NSString *passUpdateMessage =
    [NSString stringWithFormat:@"Your %@ has been removed.",
    self.passTypeName];

    UIAlertView *alert =
    [[UIAlertView alloc] initWithTitle:@"Pass Removed"
                             message:passUpdateMessage
                            delegate:nil
                   cancelButtonTitle:@"Dismiss"
                   otherButtonTitles:nil];
    [alert show];
}
```

Updating Passes Automatically

One of the key features of Passbook is the capability to automatically update passes without the use of an app. This is an overview of the feature, since implementing it requires a server capable of building and updating passes and is beyond the scope of this chapter to fully illustrate.

If updating a pass will be supported, the `pass.json` needs to specify a `webServiceURL` and an `authenticationToken`. When the pass is first added, Passbook will call the `webServiceURL` to register the device and pass with the server, and will provide a push token for use in the next step.

When information related to a pass is updated on the server, the server needs to notify the device with the pass that an update is available. To do this, the server sends a push notification utilizing the push token received in the registration step to the device with the pass, and includes the pass type ID in the push.

> **Note**
>
> Refer to Chapter 9, "Notifications," for more information on sending push notifications.

After the device receives the push notification, Passbook will request a list of passes that have been changed from the server for the specified pass type ID and last updated tag. The server will respond with a list of serial numbers and a new last-updated tag.

The device will then iterate through the serial numbers, and request updated versions of passes from the server for each serial number. If the updated pass includes a `changeMessage` (described in more detail in the earlier section "Simulate Updating a Pass"), then Passbook will display a notification to the user for it.

Using this mechanism, a user's passes can be kept up-to-date with the latest information, and users can selectively be notified when critical, time-sensitive information is changed.

Summary

This chapter provided an in-depth look at Passbook. It covered what Passbook is and what types of passes are supported by Passbook. It explained how to design and build a pass, and the steps needed to sign and package an individual pass. The chapter demonstrated how to interact with passes and Passbook using PassKit from an app, and discussed how to use a Web server to keep passes up-to-date.

Exercises

1. In the sample app, minimal information is displayed about each pass. Enhance the app to display more detail about each pass when it exists in Passbook, utilizing the `localizedName`, `localizedDescription`, `localizedValueForFieldKey`, `relevantDate`, and `organizationName` methods of a `PKPass` object.

2. Create custom passes for each type. Start with a new design, implement the design, sign and package the pass, and test it in the Simulator.

25

Debugging and Instruments

Unlike most other chapters in this book, this chapter has no associated sample code and there is no project. Throughout this book the target has been implementing advanced features and functionality of the iOS SDKs. This chapter focuses on what to do when everything goes wrong. Debugging and increasing performance of any piece of software is a vital and sometimes overlooked step of development. Users expect an app to perform quickly, smoothly, consistently, and without errors or crashes. Regardless of the skill level of a developer, bugs will happen, crashes will be introduced, and performance won't be everything it can be. The material covered here will assist in developing software that gets the most out of the system and performs to the highest possible standards.

Introduction to Debugging

> *"If debugging is the process of removing bugs, then programming must be the process of putting them in." –Edsger W. Dijkstra*

Computers are complex—so complex that very few, if any, people understand how they work on all levels. Very few developers understand programming in binary or assembly, even though that is what the machine itself understands. This complexity means that things will go wrong even if everything is seemingly done correctly. Bugs relating to issues such as race conditions and thread safety are hard to plan for and can be even harder to troubleshoot.

When we leverage the technology provided by the debugger, the difficulty of debugging software becomes drastically easier. From using custom breakpoints to parameters such as NSZombies, most of the hard work of debugging can be turned into a quick task.

The First Computer Bug

In 1947, the first computers were making their rounds through large corporations, universities, and government institutes. Grace Murray Hopper was working on one of these early systems at Harvard University, a Mark II Aiken Relay Calculator. On the 9th of September of 1947, the machine began to exhibit problems and the engineers investigated. What they found was surprising but not entirely unexpected when computers were large machines taking up entire rooms. A simple household moth had become trapped between the points of Relay #70 in Panel F of the Mark II Aiken Relay Calculator. The moth was preventing the relay from functioning as expected, and the machine was quite literally debugged. The engineers knew they had a piece of history and they preserved the moth with a piece of tape and the handwritten note, "First actual case of bug being found" (see Figure 25.1). Today, the first computer bug can be found at the Naval Surface Warfare Center Computer Museum at Dahlgren, Virginia.

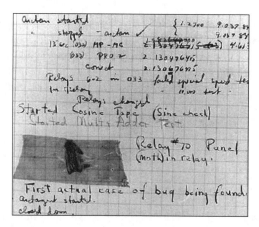

Figure 25.1   The first ever computer bug removed from a Mark II Aiken Relay Calculator in 1947.

Debugging Basics with Xcode

Like most modern IDEs, Xcode has a debugger built into it—in fact, two debuggers, lldb and gdb. Computers execute code very quickly, so quickly that it is nearly impossible to see all the steps as they are happening. This is where a debugger comes in handy; it enables the developer to slow down the execution of code and inspect elements as they change. The debug view might initially be hidden, but it can be accessed with the center view button, as shown in Figure 25.2. The debugger is available only when an app is being executed from within Xcode.

Figure 25.2   Accessing the debugging area in Xcode is done through the lower view area.

The debug view (see Figure 25.3) consists of three primary parts. On the left-hand side is the variable view, which is used to inspect detail information about the objects currently within the scope of memory. The right-hand side is composed of the console, which also contains the debugger prompt. On the top of the view lays the debugging command bar for interacting with the debugger.

Figure 25.3   The debug view.

The debugger will automatically show whenever an exception is encountered, and at any time the developer can also pause the current execution and bring up the debugger, as well using the Pause button in the debugging toolbar.

It is often possible, if the debugger has stopped at an exception, to be able to continue the execution. This can be achieved by using the Resume button in the toolbar. On the toolbar, from left to right, the Step Over command will move to the next line of execution while remaining paused. The Step Into command will move into a new method or function that the debugger is currently stopped on. Likewise, the Step Out Of button will move back outside of the current method or function.

Additionally, from the debugger toolbar each thread in execution can be inspected, showing the stack trace. The stack trace will provide the sequence of events leading up to the current point in execution. This same information can be accessed with the Debug Navigator, which can be accessed from the left-most pane of the Xcode window, shown in Figure 25.4.

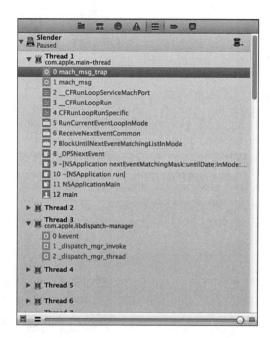

Figure 25.4   The Debug Navigator showing a backtrace across several threads.

Breakpoints

Most developers begin debugging by printing log statements to the console to get an insight into how the code is executing or behaving. Log statements are very useful but they are very limited in their functionality. Breakpoints inform the debugger that the code being executed should be paused to allow for more thorough debugging. To create a new breakpoint, click on the line number where the code should pause. A blue indicator will appear, representing a new breakpoint; to remove the breakpoint, drag the blue indicator off the line number bar. To temporarily disable a breakpoint, toggle it off by clicking on it, and the breakpoint will become a transparent blue.

After a breakpoint has been hit, the code execution will pause. The variable view will populate with all the in-scope variables and the stack trace will show the path of methods and calls that lead to the breakpoint. Calls that are in code written by the developer will appear in black, and system calls appear in a lighter gray. The developer can click through the stack trace to show the line of code that was responsible for calling the following item (see Figure 25.5).

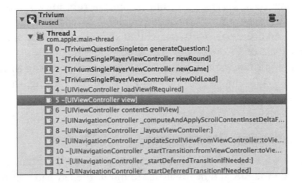

Figure 25.5   A common stack trace. The code is frozen at item 0 in the method `generateQuestion:`. The events that lead to this method can also be seen, from `viewDidLoad` to `newGame` to `newRound`. The lighter gray methods are system calls that were not directly invoked by the developer's code.

Customizing Breakpoints

Breakpoints are highly customizable. Right-clicking on a breakpoint will reveal the edit view shown in Figure 25.6. The first property that can be customized is adding a condition for the breakpoint, such as x == 0. This can be useful when the breakpoint should be fired only under certain circumstances, such as x being equal to 0.

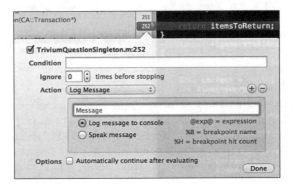

Figure 25.6   Customizing a breakpoint.

The developer might also have cause to ignore the breakpoint the first several times it is hit. A bug might present itself only after a line of code is executed a certain number of times, and this can remove the need for continuously hitting the Continue button.

Breakpoints can also have actions attached to them, such as running an AppleScript, executing a debugger command, performing a shell command, logging a message, or even playing a sound. Playing a sound can be particularly useful as an audio indicator of an event happening, such as a network call or a Core Data merge. Under certain conditions, such as playing audio, the developer might not want to pause the code execution during the breakpoint. If the preferred action is to log a message or play a sound without pausing, the Automatically Continue after Evaluating option can be enabled.

Symbolic and Exception Breakpoints

In addition to user-set breakpoints, there are two types of breakpoints that can be enabled. These are done through the Breakpoint Navigator found in the left pane of the Xcode window.

Symbolic breakpoints can be used to catch all instances of a method or a function being run. For example, to log every instance of `imageNamed:` being called, a new symbolic breakpoint can be created for the symbol `+[UIImage imageNamed:]`. Figure 25.7 shows a symbolic breakpoint that will log each use of `imageNamed:` by playing a sound.

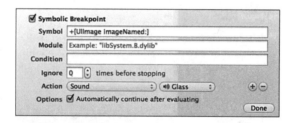

Figure 25.7   A symbolic breakpoint that will play a sound and continue every time a new image is created using the method `imageNamed:`.

Exception breakpoints work very much like symbolic breakpoints except that they are thrown whenever any exception occurs. Often, setting a global exception breakpoint will provide a better stack trace than is typically provided by a crash. This is because the stack trace is provided based on the breakpoint, whereas a crash can be a result of an exception but does not necessarily point back to the root cause. It is considered by many developers to be best practice to always keep a global exception breakpoint on while debugging.

Breakpoint Scope

You can also set the scope of a breakpoint (see Figure 25.8) by right-clicking on a breakpoint in the Breakpoint Navigator. The available scope options are project, workspace, and user. In addition to specifying a scope, the user also has the option of creating a shared breakpoint. A shared breakpoint is helpful when working on a project with multiple developers across a version control system in which it is important that breakpoints are turned on for all users.

Additionally, users can enable breakpoints as a user breakpoint that will be active on all new projects they create.

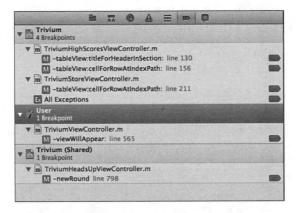

Figure 25.8   Setting up various breakpoints' scope including user and shared breakpoints in Xcode.

Working with the Debugger

Xcode features two debuggers, gdb debugger (GNU Debugger) and LLDB. The debugger can be accessed anytime code execution is currently paused. A gdb or an lldb prompt will appear at the bottom of the console window. Although both debuggers are very large and complex systems, there are several commands that are important for the iOS developer to be familiar with. Apple has begun recommending that LLDB be used for all new projects.

> **Note**
>
> As of Xcode 5, gdb is no longer available and projects will automatically be converted to LLDB if they were set to use gdb from earlier versions of Xcode.

> **Note**
>
> To change the debugger that is being used, edit the scheme for the target that is being executed. This menu can be accessed from the Xcode toolbar next to the run and stop controls.

The first command to turn to when in doubt is the help or h command. The help command will print a root-level help menu, and help followed by any command will print information specific to that command.

The most common debugger commands that will be required by an iOS developer are `p` or `print` and `po` or `print object`. The `print` command will print the value of a scalar expression such as `x + y` or structs such as `CGRect`. Using the `print` command, it is also possible to change the value of variables while in the debugger.

```
(gdb) p scaleStage2
$2 = 0.600000024
(gdb) p scaleStage2 = 0
$3 = 0
(gdb) p scaleStage2
$4 = 0
```

The `print object` (po) command will ask an objective-C object to print its description. For example, to see the contents of a memory address, you can type the following command into the `gdb` or `lldb` prompt:

```
(gdb) po 0x8360580
➡<UIImageView: 0x8360580; frame = (0 0; 320 480); opaque = NO;
 autoresize = RM+BM; userInteractionEnabled = NO; layer = <CALayer:
➡0x83605e0>>
```

Alternatively, an object name can be used, such as this:

```
(gdb) po backgroundView
➡<UIImageView: 0x8360580; frame = (0 0; 320 480); opaque = NO;
 autoresize = RM+BM; userInteractionEnabled = NO; layer = <CALayer:
➡0x83605e0>>
```

The `list` command can be helpful as well. `list` will print the code surrounding the breakpoint line. In addition, `list` takes the parameter of +/- X to specify lines before or after the breakpoint in which to display.

There are times when it is required for a developer in the process of debugging a method or function to override the return value or provide an early return. This can be done using the `return x` command. For example, typing `return 0` followed by `continuing` will simulate the code returning successfully at the breakpoint.

The `backtrace` command, or `bt`, can be used to print the current backtrace to the console. Although this can be helpful for debugging, this information is typically available in a more user-friendly format in the Debug Navigator.

In addition to these commands, the basic toolbar commands can be executed from the debugger prompt, which is often easier than navigating to the very small button in the toolbar. `step` or `s` will move to the next line of code in execution. `continue` or `c` will continue past the breakpoint and resume executing code. `fin` will continue until the end of the method, a useful command that does not have a toolbar equivalent. Finally, `kill` will terminate the program.

`gdb` is a very powerful tool that can provide a tremendous amount of power and flexibility to debugging. To read more about what can be done in gdb, see the official GNU documentation (www.gnu.org/software/gdb/documentation/). Additional information can be found on the lldb debugger at (http://llvm.org/docs/).

> **Tip**
>
> The gdb debugger does not support using dot notation as part of its input; however, the lldb debugger handles dot notation as expected.

Instruments

"Instruments" refers collectively to the 15 profiling and analyzing tools that come bundled with Xcode. See Table 25.1 for a complete list. Although the exact details and behaviors of these instruments warrant a book in and of itself, the basics of how to read and interact with instruments is enough to cover the vast majority of what will be needed by the ordinary iOS developer.

Table 25.1   **Instruments Provided in Xcode and Their Functionality**

Instrument	Description
Allocations	Measures heap memory usage by tracking allocations.
Leaks	Measures general memory usage, checks for leaked memory, and provides statistics on object allocations.
Activity Monitor	Monitors system activity including CPU, memory, disk, network, and statistics.
Zombies	Measures general memory usage while focusing on the detection of over-released "zombie" objects. Also provides statistics on object allocations by class, as well as memory address histories for all active allocations.
Time Profiler	Performs low-overhead time-based sampling of processes running on the system's CPU.
System Trace	Provides information about system behavior by showing when threads are scheduled and showing all their transitions from user into system code.
Automation	Executes a script that simulates UI interaction for an iOS application launched from Instruments.
File Activity	Monitors file and directory activity, including file open/close calls, file permission modifications, directory creation, file moves, etc.
Core Data	Traces Core Data filesystem activity, including fetches, cache misses, and saves.
Energy Diagnostics	Provides diagnostics regarding energy usage, as well as basic on/off state of major device components.

Instrument	Description
Network	Analyzes the usage of TCP/IP and UDP/IP connections.
System Usage	Records I/O system activity related to files, sockets, and shared memory for a single process launched via instruments.
Core Animation	Monitors graphic performance and CPU usage of processes using Core Animation.
OpenGL ES Driver	Measures OpenGL ES graphics performance, as well as CPU usage of a process.
OpenGL ES Analysis	Measures and analyzes OpenGL ES activity to detect OpenGL ES correctness and performance problems. It also offers recommendations for addressing these problems.

Note

It is important to realize that not all instruments are available under certain circumstances. For example, the Core Data instrument is available only when running on the simulator, and the Network instrument is available only while running on a physical device.

The Instruments Interface

To access the instruments interface in Xcode, select the build target, either a simulator or a device, and select the Profile option from the Product menu. A new window (see Figure 25.9) will appear, enabling the user to select the type of instrument he would like to run. After an option is selected, additional items can be added to it from the library (see Figure 25.10).

The instruments interface itself consists of several sections that will vary depending on the exact instrument you are running.

On the top toolbar of the Instruments window, various controls are present, such as those to pause, record, and restart the execution of the current target. Additionally, new targets can be selected from all running processes. The user also has control of setting an inspection range of any instrument that will filter items which do not occur between the left and right markers.

The instruments app will also save each run of the app so that changes to performance can quickly be compared to each other. The user can also add new instruments from the library in order to combine multiple tests. The left view, which can be toggled from the view menu, contains settings specific to the selected instrument. The bottom view will contain detailed information about the test being run, such as the Call Tree or Statistics; these also vary depending on the instrument selected. The last view is the right extended information view; this view will often contain the backtrace for the selected item in the center view.

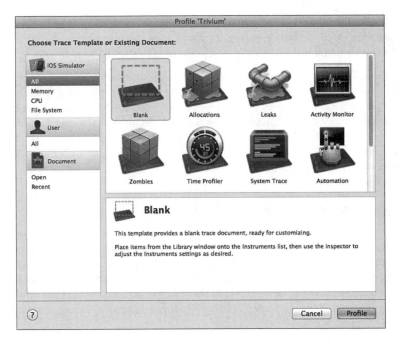

Figure 25.9   Selecting instruments to run after running an app in profile mode.

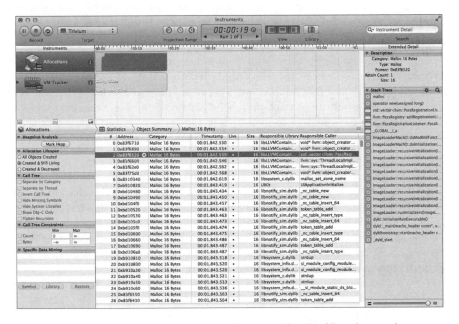

Figure 25.10   The basic instruments interface, shown running the Allocations tool.

Most base-level objects found in the center or right view can be double-clicked to provide additional information, such as the referencing section of code. Additional information about the instruments can be found if you click the "i" button next to the instrument name.

In the following sections, two of the most common instruments are examined. The first, Time Profiler, is used by developers to determine which code within an app is taking the most time to execute. By analyzing the time each line of code takes to run, the developer is able to provide optimizations and enhancements to that code to increase the overall speed and performance of the app. The second instrument set that is examined consists of the Leaks and Allocation toolsets. These enable the developer to analyze how memory is being used in her app, as well as easily find memory leaks and over-releases.

Exploring Instruments: The Time Profiler

The Time Profiler provides line-level information about the speed at which code is being executed. There are many bottlenecks that can cause an app to perform slowly, from waiting for a network call to finish to reading and writing from storage too often. However, a very common cause of performance issues and one of the easiest to address is the overuse of the CPU. Time Profile provides the developer with information about the CPU time resulting from various calls, which in turn enables the developer to focus on problem areas of the app and provide performance improvements.

Time Profiler can be selected from the list of instrument templates and can be run on either the simulator or the device. When you are profiling CPU usage, it is important to remember that the device is typically much slower than the simulator, and users will not be running software on the simulator.

Time Profiler being run on an app with high CPU usage is shown in Figure 25.11. The top section in purple represents percentage of CPU used; dragging the cursor over the time bar will reveal the exact CPU usage percentage. The call tree reports that 99.6% of the process time is spent in Main Thread, and if that information is expanded/dropped, 99.1% of the time is spent in `main()` itself. This information is not entirely helpful on the surface, because an Objective-C app should be spending a considerable amount of its time in `main()`, but it does let the developer know that there is very high CPU usage, at some points at 100%.

To retrieve more useful information from the Time Profiler, the first thing that should be done is inverting the call tree, which is a check box in the Time Profiler settings. Instead of grouping time spent from the top down, it will group from the base functions up. In addition to inverting the call tree, it can be helpful to check off the box for Hide System Libraries. Although system library calls might be taking up a considerable amount of processing time, they can often be traced back to the developers code itself. Viewing system calls can also be helpful for troubleshooting more difficult issues. Depending on whether the code base is using Objective-C only, it might also be helpful to use the Show Obj-C Only option.

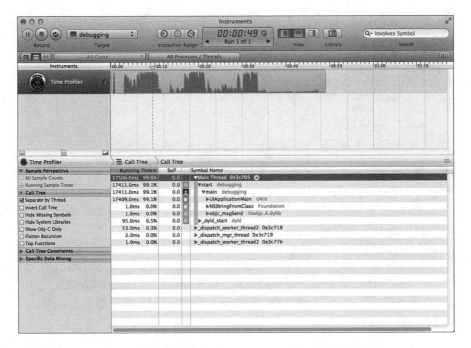

Figure 25.11   Running the Time Profiler instrument on an app with high CPU usage.

After the proper configurations have been made, what is left is a list of calls that the developer has specifically made and the amount of CPU time they are taking up. The best-practice approach is to optimize from the largest usage to the least, because often fixing a larger issue will cascade and fix a number of the smaller issues as well. To get more information on the code in question, double-click on the item that will be investigated in the call tree. This will reveal a code inspector that is broken down by line with annotations indicating the amount of processor time used relative to the method, as shown in Figure 25.12.

> **Note**
>
> The code cannot be edited using the instruments code inspector; however, clicking on the Xcode icon (shown in Figure 25.12) will open the code in Xcode.

Although Time Profiler is not smart enough to make recommendations on how to optimize the code that is running slowly, it will point the developer in the right direction. Not every piece of code can be optimized, but equipped with the line numbers and the exact overhead required to run them, the challenge is greatly reduced.

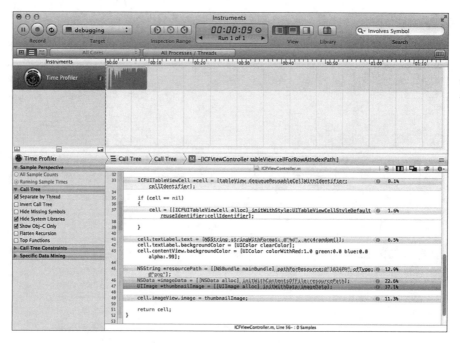

Figure 25.12   Inspecting Time Profiler information at a line-by-line level.

> **Tip**
>
> Using the inspection range settings in instruments is useful for pinpointing exact spikes or sections of time to be investigated. The controls are used to mark the beginning and end of the inspect range on a timeline.

Exploring Instruments: Leaks

The Leaks instrument, and by association the Allocations instrument, gives the developer a tremendous amount of insight into finding and resolving memory-related issues. It can assist in finding overuse of memory, leaks, retain cycles, and other memory-related issues. With the popularization of Automatic Reference Counting (ARC), the Leaks and Allocation tools are slowly falling from their previous grace; however, they can still offer tremendous benefits to the developer.

The Leaks instrument can be launched from the Instrument Selector window in the same fashion as the Time Profiler. When Leaks is launched, it will automatically also include the Allocations instrument, both of which can be run on the device and the simulator. In Figure 25.13 a poorly performing app is profiled, resulting in an increasing memory footprint, as indicated by the growing graph under the Allocations section. Additionally, several leaks have been detected, as indicated by the red bars in the Leaks section. Given enough time, these issues will likely result in the app running out of memory and crashing.

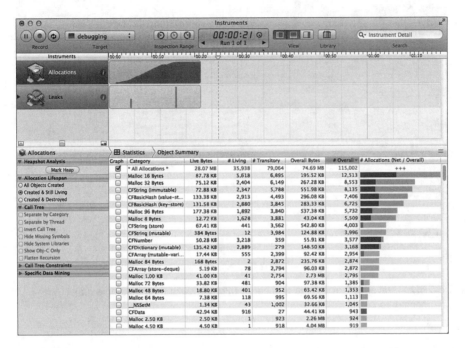

Figure 25.13   Running the Leaks and Allocation instruments against a project with memory leaks.

Although memory issues can also be debugged using the call tree grouping as shown in the Time Profiler section, it is sometimes more useful to look at the Statistics or Leaks presentation of information. To see the leaks, which are often the cause of increasing memory usage, select the Leaks instruments from the upper left. In this sample project shown in Figure 25.14, there are numerous leaks of a UIImage object.

Instruments will attempt to group leaks into identical backtraces; however, the system is not perfect and leaks being caused by the same problem might appear more than once in the list. Best practice calls for resolving the highest number of leaks first and then running the profiler again. To trace the leak back to a section of code, the left view needs to be exposed. This is done with the view controller in the title bar of the Instruments window. Selecting a leak will reveal the backtrace to that event. Double-clicking on the nonsystem-responsible call (typically shown in black text) will reveal the code in which the leak has occurred.

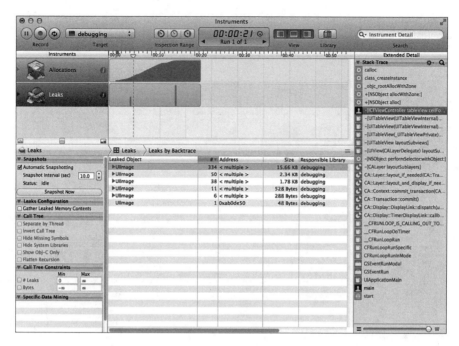

Figure 25.14   Investigating a large number of UIImage leaks from a sample project with a growing memory footprint.

> **Tip**
>
> Clicking the "i" button to the right of the Allocations instrument allows for additional configuration such as turning on Zombies. The use of Zombies enables the developer to troubleshoot and fix memory that is being over-released. Over-released memory is caused by trying to access memory that has been fully released and now has a retain count of zero. This will usually result in a crash of EXC_BAD_ACCESS.

There might be times when the memory footprint of an app grows to unacceptable levels but there are no leaks present. This is caused by the app using more memory than is available. To troubleshoot this information, select the Allocations instrument and view the call tree. The same approach to inverting the call tree, hiding system libraries, and showing only Obj-C from the Time Profiler section might be helpful here. In Figure 25.15, 27.12MB of memory is being allocated in cellForRowAtIndexPath:, which is causing the app to run poorly. Double-clicking on this object will reveal a code inspector that will pinpoint which lines are using the most memory, which will provide guidance in the areas to troubleshoot.

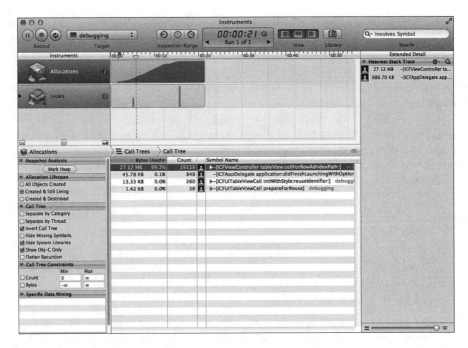

Figure 25.15   Investigating an Allocations call tree that shows a very large amount of memory being used in `cellForRowAtIndexPath:`.

Going Further with Instruments

Instruments is a highly explorable tool. After a developer has an understanding of the basic functionality and controls, the majority of instruments become very easy to deduce. Apple continues to aggressively improve on and push for developers to leverage instruments. At this point there are tools to troubleshoot just about everything an app does from Core Data to battery statistics, and there are even tools to help optimize animations in both Core Animation and OpenGL ES. To learn more about a particular instrument, visit Apple's online documentation at http://developer.apple.com/library/mac/#documentation/DeveloperTools/Conceptual/InstrumentsUserGuide/Introduction/Introduction.html.

Summary

This chapter, unlike most of the other chapters in this book, did not cover a sample project or demonstrate the proper usage of a new framework. Instead, it provided something more valuable, an introduction to debugging and code optimization. Debugging, in and of itself, is a huge topic that is worthy of not just one book but several books. We hope that this chapter has provided a jumping-off point for a lifelong passion of squeezing the most out of code and hunting down those tricky bugs. A developer who can troubleshoot, optimize, and debug quickly and effectually is a developer who never has to worry about finding work or being of value to a team.

Instruments and the Xcode IDE are Apple's gift to developers. Not too long ago, IDEs cost thousands of dollars and were hard to work with, and tools like Instruments were nonexistent. When Apple provided Xcode to everyone free, it was groundbreaking. Over the years they have continued to improve the tools that developers use to create software on their platforms. They do this because they care about the quality of software that third-party developers are writing. It has become the obligation of all iOS developers to ensure that they are using the tools and providing the best possible software they can.

Exercises

1. Spend some time exploring various instruments either with a personal project or with any of the sample code contained in this book. It cannot be stressed enough how important it is to understand what each instrument can analyze; otherwise, it is impossible to know when to use one.

2. Create an exception such as an out-of-bounds array error and see how it behaves when a global exception breakpoint is set compared to having global exceptions turned off.

Index

H

I

J

K

Kyle Richter
Joe Keeley

Covers
iOS 7
and
Xcode 5

iOS Components and Frameworks

Understanding the Advanced Features
of the iOS SDK

FREE
Online Edition

Safari
Books Online

Your purchase of *iOS Components and Frameworks* includes access to a free online edition for 45 days through the **Safari Books Online** subscription service. Nearly every Addison-Wesley Professional book is available online through **Safari Books Online**, along with over thousands of books and videos from publishers such as Cisco Press, Exam Cram, IBM Press, O'Reilly Media, Prentice Hall, Que, Sams, and VMware Press.

Safari Books Online is a digital library providing searchable, on-demand access to thousands of technology, digital media, and professional development books and videos from leading publishers. With one monthly or yearly subscription price, you get unlimited access to learning tools and information on topics including mobile app and software development, tips and tricks on using your favorite gadgets, networking, project management, graphic design, and much more.

Activate your FREE Online Edition at
informit.com/safarifree

STEP 1:   Enter the coupon code: JRBMPEH.

STEP 2:   New Safari users, complete the brief registration form.
Safari subscribers, just log in.

If you have difficulty registering on Safari or accessing the online edition,
please e-mail customer-service@safaribooksonline.com